To Don, [illegible]
with best [illegible]
— P David Moon

IN ONE ACCORD: RECONCILING FAITH AND SCIENCE

P. David Moon

In One Accord: Reconciling Faith and Science

CONTENTS

ACKNOWLEDGMENTS

My wife Pat and my daughters Jessica and Jaclyn
were immensely patient during the
research, writing, and editing of this book,
as well as contributing helpful critiques.
Their tolerance of my monologues on the subject of this book
has been monumental.

Without the support and encouragement of dear friends
Leslie and Wayne Howard
the book may have never seen publication.

I am grateful to Alex Doverspike for his
help with exploring avenues for the publication of this work,
and for his support and helpful criticisms.

Introduction

This is a book that was forty years in the writing.

At the age of just twelve or thirteen, I was confronted with a statement, made by a lay youth leader of the fundamentalist evangelical church in which I was raised, that one could not be a Christian and subscribe to the modern ideas of science, because scientific theories, particularly the theory of evolution, contradicted the Bible. The leader responded to my question as to why the two accounts could not be reconciled – and the underlying question of why faith cannot be compatible with physical reality – by publicly challenging me to a debate.

When the day of the debate came, I arrived prepared with an expectedly childlike but basically valid set of arguments, with points about translation derived from library dictionaries of Hebrew, Latin, and Greek, and points of agreement between scripture and science that were discovered by the simple expedient of looking for accord instead of discord. The youth leader made her presentation, which consisted solely of stating her beliefs in the inerrancy of the Bible, and I joined my classmates in listening politely. When she was finished, I went to the podium and, knees shaking and voice quavering, began my presentation by pointing out the oft-noted concordance between evolutionary theory and the order of creation of living things in the first chapter of Genesis. It would hardly have been decisive even if completed, I fear, but it hardly mattered what I said, because the youth leader began shouting me down before I finished the second sentence, and I finished few other sentences between interruptions.

I left the podium after the allotted time feeling both cheated and discouraged that I had not been able to present what I thought was a reasonable point of view. Much to my surprise, my classmates, including older, much cooler teens, came to me after the meeting to say that they felt I had been treated rudely, and that they were interested in hearing more about what I had to say on the subject of reconciling faith and science. It seemed that I was not alone in searching for a means of reconciling the concrete observations of the scientific community and the exploration of my faith.

All through high school, matriculation at a major university, and doctoral training in my chosen field of veterinary medicine, I was endlessly confronted with the validity and workability of the theory of evolution, and I became more and more convinced that a reconciliation between faith and science was the only chance for the survival of faith. Studying the biological sciences from the perspective of a believer, I marveled at the complexity and the enormity of scientific knowledge and its implications regarding the wisdom and intelligence of the Creator. At the same time, I saw that there was in science neither confirmation nor denial of my faith. But the more I studied the complex words, history, and interpretations of scripture, the more convinced I became that there was room within Christian belief for the acceptance of modern scientific theories.

When I became the lay leader for the teen group in another church of the same denomination, I felt that I could be of use and comfort to the teenagers in my charge by helping them to understand how their science classes could be reconciled with their budding faith. Most of the young people were interested in the subject and interested in my views – and they were presented as my personal views, not as the official position of that or any other church – and some expressed relief at the opportunity to reconcile their faith with what they saw as convincing evidence for scientific theories presented in their high school classes. But parents and the clergyman of the local church soon muzzled me on the subject - without hearing my arguments or my reasons for discussing the subject with the young minds in the group, they essentially decided that the reconciliation of faith with science was heretical.

Church leadership changed, and so did the leadership of the teen group. The reconciliation between faith and science became for me a life-long study. I repeatedly offered to teach a course on the subject to teenagers and to any adults that cared to attend, but I was always rebuffed. I was later to learn that when my own daughters were teenagers they were taught by that church, as countless others in conservative churches and evangelical organizations are taught, that science and faith are irreconcilable. Creationism is preached and defended from pulpits, in classes for both children and adults, in church-affiliated schools, and at overseas missions. (I personally heard a missionary in a church on a Caribbean island proclaim his belief that the dinosaurs coexisted with early mankind until being wiped out by Noah's flood.) Organizations exist for the sole purpose of preaching creationism through speeches, publications, and web sites. The tactics of denial and obstreperousness that I encountered in my early teens continue - more refined but no more convincing to those who understand modern science.

Few who preach creationism seem to consider an important question: If I demand a choice between faith and evidence, which should I expect my listeners to choose? The reconciliation of faith and science is more essential to faith than to science. The theories of science, including the theory of evolution, are much more than mere speculation – they are supported by volume upon volume of observations of the world around us, and that evidence is available to anyone in the modern world who chooses to examine it. Some choose to ignore that evidence so that they may not be troubled by it, but ignoring evidence does not make it false – it leads to false conclusions that themselves demand supporting falsehood. By reconciling their faith with the evidence of the material world, however, Christians can strengthen their faith instead of isolating it.

The belief that God created the universe by using the mechanisms of nature that science explores and discerns is most often called theistic evolution. Theistic evolution is an ancient concept, but a significant number of churches and evangelical organizations fail to teach it, creating conflict in the minds of young people and skeptics where none need exist. This volume attempts to summarize the theories of twenty-first century science, to show how they are reconcilable with monotheistic faith in general and the Judeo-Christian scriptures in particular, and to argue for the necessity of that reconciliation to the minds of believers and the continuation of the faith.

It is the hope and prayer of the author that, by presenting the case for theistic evolution in a single volume, some few may be persuaded that their faith is relevant to contemporary times and knowledge. Some readers will find evidence and kinship of thought to confirm their unexplored feeling that faith and science can be reconciled. Others who have been taught that reconciliation is impossible and find their faith weakening in the face of cogent evidence for science may find comfort and a renewal of their faith in the knowledge that reconciliation is, in fact, possible. Perhaps the greatest good can be done by convincing those who make creationism an article of Christian faith that other views can be tolerated and embraced without abandoning the message of forgiveness that is found in the person of Christ. The credibility of Christianity can be restored, to believers and non-believers alike, by consideration of theistic evolution.

Christianity is, more than anything else, a religion of reconciliation – by the suffering and death of Jesus, mankind may be reconciled to God, and by being reconciled with God we can be reconciled with our fellow man. So, too, the evidence of the universe around us – the observations and theories of science – can and must be reconciled with the testimony of scripture, because both are works of God. As has been said many times, truth cannot contradict truth. By the principle of reconciliation that is central to the faith, Christianity must, in the minds of many, reconcile the truths of God contained in His works and His words to remain viable. That reconciliation, like the journey of reconciliation that is our life on this earth and our test for the world to come, is a journey that challenges, excites, and satisfies the mind and the spirit.

For many men and women of faith, the explorations of science make their concept of God more awe-inspiring with each new discovery and every fresh understanding. I invite you to join them – us - in a faith that encompasses and embraces the knowledge, wisdom, and power of a truly omnipotent God. This volume invites you to consider, whether for the first time or to confirm your long-held beliefs, the position of theistic evolution.

Chapter 1

Truth and Belief

What you believe does not matter.

It is fashionable in neither political nor in many religious circles to say so, but absolute truth exists, and our individual beliefs do not affect truth. Our personal beliefs affect our perception of truth, our receptivity to truth, and our response to truth, as individuals and in groups defined as congregations, denominations, and political parties, but they do not affect absolute truth. The manner in which we assimilate known facts into our beliefs, ethics, and thoughts affects our values, our witness, and our credibility, but truth by its nature remains inviolate.

Scientists seek truth in observed facts and in the theories that mankind promulgates to explain relationships between facts. Men and women of religious faith seek truth in the knowledge of God, and, with or without referring to them as such, promulgate theories about the nature of God. Unfortunately, seekers in the disciplines of faith and science have often tried to exclude the thinking of the other. Some people immersed in the world of science are convinced that God does not exist, and regard expressions of faith as ignorant superstitions. Christians, on the other hand, sometimes see in modern scientific theories a contradiction with their understanding of scripture. Both need to understand that they are reacting to each other based on their chosen systems of belief, and that neither a belief in God nor atheism can be objectively confirmed.

Some groups of evangelical Christians feel their faith threatened by mankind's increasing understanding of the mechanisms by which our world came into being, and deny the theories and, in extreme cases, the underlying observations of science. These Christians typically stake their faith in the inerrancy of scripture literally interpreted. Any theory, then, that appears to contradict a narrow fundamentalist interpretation of holy writ threatens the foundation of their faith, and their confidence in salvation. Any fact that supports such a theory becomes suspect, and subject to denial and attack. The root of their objection to modern scientific theory is that they consider the Bible to be a unified document without error, provided by God to guide every aspect of their lives. Any contradiction or modification of the Bible's words renders it, in their own view, flawed and false.

Since neither falsehood nor error can come from a God who is both good and omniscient, any flaw or falsehood must arise from the human beings who contradict scripture. Since they see apparent contradictions between commonly discussed scientific theories and their interpretation of scriptures, many fundamentalist Christians regard all science as atheistic in nature. These conservative Christians hold that any and all who believe, teach, and research fields of study regarding the origins of the universe, the earth, and life, are unfailingly and inherently atheists. Some even see a worldwide conspiracy of scientists intent on discrediting the Bible and, with it, their entire system of religious beliefs. They believe that evidence supporting a literal interpretation of the creation story of Genesis is being suppressed and deliberately misinterpreted by all of science in order to suppress religious thought and discredit their faith.

Those men and women of science who pronounce their work to be proof that God does not exist, of course, do nothing to enhance their own credibility with conservative Christians, and therefore prevent themselves from effectively arguing the case of scientific theories. Some, rather, appear to take a perverse delight in antagonizing the faith community with their strong statements of atheism. It must be admitted that modern scientific thought is based on physical processes, mathematical probabilities, and algorithmic processes that can proceed without guidance from a higher intellect. It must be admitted just as readily, however, that to prove that something is not necessary is not the same as proving that it does not exist. As the late Carl Sagan put it, "Absence of evidence is not evidence of absence." Music, art, architecture, and literature are certainly not necessary to the survival of mankind as a species, but they enrich the lives of men and women to a degree that no rational person would deny. Religion, in a similar but sometimes less tangible way, enriches the lives of believers.

Scientists who claim to prove atheism are engaging in a basic error of logic in believing that because they have not found the object they seek, it does not exist. It is a basic theorem of logic that the non-existence of anything cannot be proven. Those who argue that science proves atheism make the same essential error in their arguments for which they condemn people of faith: they let their unproven beliefs affect their thinking, and in doing so they seek confirmation of personal belief instead of seeking truth. Those scientists who regard any belief in God as primitive superstition need to recognize that they are espousing opinion with no greater foundation than those they attack and denigrate. Science is incapable of evaluating the spiritual. It can no better explain the human reaction to a mountain vista, Van Gogh's *Starry Night*, or Beethoven's *Ninth Symphony* than it can the quiet peace of prayer; none are the less real for the lack of explanation.

The fact that spiritual matters cannot be measured or examined means, just as surely, that science and reason cannot prove the existence of God, though philosophers and theologians have tried for millennia. Among the wide-ranging philosophical arguments in his *Summa Theologica*, Thomas Aquinas (c.1225-1274) claimed five means of proving the existence of God by pure reason. The first argument was that the universe is in motion, and that some outside force, hence God, must put any object into motion. The second argues that everything has a cause, but to show causes infinitely far back necessitates arriving at an ultimate cause, God. The third and fourth argue, respectively "from possibility and necessity", and "from the gradation to be found in things." "The fifth way is taken from the governance of the world. We see that things which lack intelligence, such as natural bodies, act for an end, and this is evident from their acting always, in the same way, so as to obtain the best result. Hence it is plain that not fortuitously, but designedly, do they achieve their end. Now whatever lacks intelligence cannot move towards an end, unless it be directed by some being endowed with knowledge and intelligence; as the arrow is shot to its mark by the archer. Therefore some intelligent being exists by whom all natural things are directed to their end; and this being we call God."[1]

Such exercises are impressive and eloquent, but an honest reading reveals that, in the same way that some scientists argue from a premise of atheism to show that their findings exclude God, these and similar arguments presuppose the existence of God, and therefore fail as strict proofs from reason. Those Christians who argue that scientific theory should be somehow forced to accommodate their concept of God - and there are many – frequently and enthusiastically ignore the important point that the theories of science are based on the rational consideration of an enormous body of empirical evidence that can be confirmed by anyone with the will to do so, while their concept of God is a personal belief that, regardless of the sincerity with which it is held, cannot be indisputably confirmed by an outside observer. Science deals with objective truth which can be verified by repeated observations, while religion deals with faith and requires trust in that which cannot be verified.

Christian theologians regard God as a spirit being, existing outside the realms of space and time, and therefore immeasurable and unexplorable by any method of science. This is entirely appropriate in that it keeps faith within the realm of choice. Christianity teaches that God wants to commune with those of His creation who are willing to

---

[1] Aquina, Thomas. *Summa Theologica* (Benziger Bros. edition, 1947. Translated by Fathers of the English Dominican Province.) <www.ccel.org/ccel/aquinas/summa.pdf>.

enter into a loving and thankful relationship with Him. With a logic attributed to nineteenth-century philosopher Søren Kierkegaard, modern Christianity argues that if the existence of God were proven by scientific observation, no place would remain for faith, for no choice would exist. Precisely because God wants us to choose Him, He remains forever beyond proof. Faith is properly seen as a choice of belief, or, in the language of the Apostle Paul, "the conviction of things *not seen*."[1] If one's sense of awe leads one to belief in God, and thankfulness to Him, that remains the choice of that soul. If that same sense of awe leads another to belief only in randomness and probabilities, that choice remains a logically valid belief.

Lost and steadfastly ignored between the extremes of argument by the atheists who claim validation of their belief by science and the conservative Christians who reject legitimate findings and theories of modern science are large numbers of people who see value in both science and faith. Men and women of faith can be found among the practitioners, researchers, and teachers in every scientific field. They have found not only reconciliation between their faith and the findings of science, but reinforcement and confirmation of their faith as science advances its understanding of God's creation. Scientists and reflective Christians of all walks of life can choose to see the forces that shape our world and our universe – the laws of physics, chemistry, and biology, and the resulting processes of astronomical, geological, and biological evolution – as the inventions and tools of a creator God, whom they view with awe as they explore both the results and the means of His creation.

There is a truth regarding God, but it cannot be known by humans in the same way that material things are known. The evidence cited by believers – the sense of peace, forgiveness, and fulfillment that they embrace – is not measurable or verifiable, and is in fact testified to by adherents to faiths as diverse as Christianity, Islam, Judaism, Buddhism, and Hinduism. We may believe fervently and sincerely, so much so that we believe we have found truth, but our beliefs remain our choice. We as humans cannot know the truth of God in the same way that we know, by observation and confirmation, the truth of the world in which we live.

It is popular in some circles to teach that any belief is valid as long as it is sincerely and fervently held. Such teachings promote worthy goals of respect, tolerance, and peace. While it is essential to respect the rights of others to believe as they chose, truth does not change to accommodate the beliefs of the holder. Those who, through inebriation or psychosis, disbelieve the law of gravity are no less subject to it, no matter how sincere; some have died as a result of their sincerity. You may, if you choose, join the Flat Earth Society, and reject a millennium of global exploration, deny mankind's ventures into space (along with the photographs that have been taken from orbiting

[1] Hebrews 11.1. New Revised Standard Version. Emphasis added.

craft, the contributions of satellites to weather forecasting and storm tracking, etcetera), and ignore the Society's inability to produce a world map with consistently accurate distances and directions between various geographic points. Your beliefs do not affect truth.

Each of us remains forever free to choose our own beliefs. If persecuted, we still have the choice of sincerely renouncing our beliefs, publicly renouncing them and holding them private, or publicly proclaiming our belief and accepting whatever punishment the persecutor delivers. Each is a choice of belief.

Belief is a choice. Truth is eternal. Your belief does not affect truth. You may choose to let truth influence your belief, but Truth endures regardless of the flawed choices of humanity.

Gotthold Lessing, an eighteenth century German playwright, wrote: "If God were to hold all Truth concealed in his right hand, and in his left hand only the steady and diligent drive for Truth, albeit with the proviso that I would always and forever err in the process, and to offer me the choice, I would with all humility take the left hand, and say, Father, I will take this – the pure Truth is for You alone."

Pro deo et veritae.

Chapter 2

Fundamentalism and the Documentary Hypothesis

Reconciliation requires understanding. Science and scripture cannot be reconciled without comprehending the positions of each.

The current theories of science, although sometimes difficult to understand, are at least easy to discern. Scientists quibble about details, but the overwhelming majority is in agreement about the major processes which shaped the universe, the earth, and the living things that inhabit it.

Examining the teachings of scripture is much more difficult because of the diversity of interpretations of the Bible. The most conservative interpretation of the Bible is typically offered by fundamentalists. Christian fundamentalism developed in the late nineteenth and early twentieth centuries as a reaction to the development of what has become known as "Higher Criticism" of the Bible. Higher Criticism developed, in turn, because of difficulties in the literal interpretation of the Bible.

The Origin of the Documentary Hypothesis

If one opens any legitimate translation of the Bible and opens to the first page of text to begin reading, one first reads an account of God creating the earth in six days. That account fills the first chapter of Genesis and begins the second, but at Genesis 2:4 the narrative ends with the words "This is the account of the heavens and the earth when they were created." Then a new and different narrative abruptly begins: "When the LORD God made the earth and the heavens – and no shrub of the field had yet appeared on the earth and no plant of the field had yet sprung up, for the LORD God had not sent rain on the earth and there was no man to work the ground, but streams came up from the earth and watered the whole surface of the ground – the LORD God formed the man from the dust of the ground and breathed into his nostrils the breath of life, and the man became a living being." (The translation here quoted is one favored by evangelical Christians, the New International Version [Zondervan, 1973.] The capitalization of the word "LORD" is a standardized indication of the use of the name *YHWH* for God, the significance of which will be discussed shortly.) The second narrative differs not only in the apparent time frame of one day versus the six of the previous narrative, but also in the origin of waters and plant life.

Those first two chapters set a precedent: as the reader continues, a startling number of stories are told and then retold a second time from a differing perspective, sometimes with strikingly different chronologies and narratives. The two creation narratives differ from each other substantially. Noah receives two different sets of instructions to save first two of every kind of animal, and then seven of some and two of others, in apparent anticipation of two distinct endings, one with and the other without the ritual sacrifice of the additional animal passengers of the ark. The books of Kings and Chronicles relate many of the same events over a similar time period from differing perspectives. The Ten Commandments, or Decalogue, differ slightly when they are given a second time (Exodus chapters 20 and 34), and yet another version is offered when the story is retold in the fifth chapter of Deuteronomy. Other laws are issued, reissued, and sometimes contradicted in the first five books of the Bible.

The confusing mosaic led scholars, beginning in the middle of the eighteenth century, to examine the scriptures from the standpoint of a literary critic. The oldest available texts were sought and critiqued. Ongoing research and archeological efforts have made available even older texts than those available to the pioneers of biblical criticism, most notably those of the Dead Sea Scrolls, discovered between 1947 and 1956 in caves in Wadi Qumran, and dating from the third century BCE to the first century. Scholars studied vocabulary, syntax, writing style, and themes of passages (differences that make Hebrew and Greek of different eras as distinct as the English of Shakespeare or the King James version of the Bible are from modern English), along with references to known historical events and political leanings, in an attempt to understand by whom, when, and in what historical and cultural context the passages were written.

A primary result of that consideration was the Documentary Hypothesis, which holds that the first five books of the Bible, referred to as the Torah by Judaism or as the Pentateuch by Christian scholars, are compilations from four major sources, written between the ninth and fourth centuries BCE.[1]

---

[1] Davies, G. I. "Introduction to the Pentateuch." *The Oxford Bible Commentary*. Oxford: Oxford University Press, 2001. Pg 12-18.

The Elohist source, or E, takes its name from the fact that God is referred to as Elohim, a curiously plural name that connotes the power of God. The author of this source is believed to have been a resident of the northern Jewish kingdom of Israel (as opposed to the southern state of Judah or Judea) based on its consistent bias towards Israel in tales of conflict or competition between the two Jewish kingdoms. The priesthood of the Levites is favored, while the priestly class descended from Aaron is frequently portrayed as inept, unfaithful, or corrupt.

The Jehovist source, or J, is thought to have been written by a resident of the southern Jewish kingdom of Judah, since bias towards the southern kingdom is a characteristic of J passages. The priestly class descended from Aaron is portrayed positively. The modern translator Robert Alter describes the God of J thusly: "In this more vividly anthropomorphic account [the second account of creation], God, now called *YHWH 'Elohim* instead of *'Elohim* as in the first version, does not summon things into being from a lofty distance through the mere agency of divine speech, but works as a craftsman, fashioning (*yatsar* instead of *bar'a*, "create"), blowing life breath into nostrils, building a woman from a rib."[1] The source is referred to as Jehovist or Yahwist because the tetragrammaton YHWH, considered unpronounceable by ancient Jews, was given the pronunciation Yahweh by later Christians. The earliest and most prominent researchers carrying on criticism of the scriptures were German, and in the German language the letter "J" carries the sound associated with "Y" in English. (The name Jehovah was a further corruption of the YHWH tetragrammaton, the first recorded use of which was by William Tyndale in the early sixteenth century.)

The Priestly source, or P, uses Elohim in reference to God like E, but the style and themes of the writing differ, with P more devoted to priestly functions, rituals, and observances. Long genealogies and the first creation account are attributed to P. The writing style is considered by critics to be less erudite and polished than that of E and J.

The Deuteronistic source, or D, is named for the book of Deuteronomy, a book devoted almost entirely to the establishment of detailed rules and regulations governing the lives of its adherents. The legal pronouncements of Deuteronomy and similar shorter segments imbedded in other books are attributed to D.

The final contribution towards the Pentateuch was made by one or more individuals referred to as the Redactor. The Redactor served as a sort of editor, combining material from the four major sources and, when needed, contributing small amounts of text to tie the material together. The representation of a book as the work and words of a single author is a relatively modern concept. In ancient times, contributions in the form of embellishments and commentary by those reproducing and transmitting a

---

[1] Alter, Robert. *Genesis: Translation and Commentary.* New York: W. W. Norton, 1996. Pg 7.

work were considered appropriate and welcome. Accordingly, it was not the purpose of the Redactor to establish himself or any other person as a sole author, or to seek an original text by any single author; nor was it his purpose to create a unified narrative without contradiction or repetition; rather, the goal of the Redactor was to preserve the several oral traditions and writings that were available to him and valued by him and his culture. Although the Pentateuch was later attributed entirely to Moses, the purpose of the Redactor was to acknowledge that his several sources were, taken together, recollections and writings based on the words and wisdom of Moses.

The Documentary Hypothesis, although not universally accepted, has been a useful theory in explaining the repetitions and inconsistencies found in the Pentateuch and some other portions of the Old Testament. Today, many Biblical scholars debate details of the Documentary Hypothesis, but the overall concept of the Pentateuch being a compilation of writings and oral traditions from a variety of sources is not seriously challenged by experts in the fields of ancient languages and literature. As the Documentary Hypothesis was developed and published, however, so did a backlash against its methods and conclusions, and those of other aspects of Higher Criticism.

Christian Fundamentalism

Conservative interpreters of scripture objected to virtually all aspects of the Documentary Hypothesis, beginning with its perception of the contradictions and irregularities in the text, and often including the notion that any part of the scripture was anything less than the directly dictated words of God Himself. The term fundamentalism, as applied to Christians, stems from the outcry from American and British conservatives in the late nineteenth and very early twentieth century to reject the Documentary Hypothesis and all other aspects of Higher Criticism, along with the challenges to the traditional view of creation from the recently published work by Charles Darwin, *The Origin of Species*, in favor of a return to the "fundamentals" of the Christian faith. The fundamentals were defined by the General Assembly of the Presbyterian Church (USA) in 1910 as "1. The inerrancy of the Bible; 2. The virgin birth of Christ; 3. Christ's substitutionary atonement; 4. Christ's bodily resurrection; 5. The authenticity of Christ's miracles."[1] Other statements of fundamentalism were similar, but sometimes referred to the diety of Christ rather than His virgin birth.

Most fundamentalists consider "Biblical inerrancy" to mean that the Bible is completely true when literally interpreted, but literal interpretation of the Bible as a whole is a difficult position to maintain.

The Biblical literalist must first explain the multitude of repetitions and contradictions

[1] Pultz, David. "The Fundamentalist / Modernist Conflict." 1996. First Presbyterian Church in New York. 4 Nov 2007. <http://www.fpcnyc.org/fundamentalism.html>.

without relying on a theory of multiple authors. Such explanations generally appear to be contrived and convoluted, and are as a group more difficult to understand and believe than the relatively simple explanation of a compilation from several authors.

Literalists usually claim that the Pentateuch was dictated by God to Moses. If that is so, some explanation must be made for the differing vocabulary and writing styles from different eras of history of the Hebrew language. We must also wonder why the entire Pentateuch is written in the third person, and why Deuteronomy begins by saying that it is a record of the words of Moses spoken to his people on the other side of the Jordan River. Moses died on the east side of the Jordan River, never having entered the land of Canaan that was subsequently infiltrated and conquered by Israel, so the book of Deuteronomy at least was authored by someone living in Israeli Canaan, necessarily after the death of Moses. Further, one who maintains that the book of Deuteronomy was authored entirely by Moses must answer how he was able to describe his own death, in the past tense, in the thirty-fourth and last chapter of Deuteronomy, give his own memorial, describe the grieving of Israel and the ascension of his successor, and write his own glowing and immodest epitaph in verses ten through twelve.

Rabbi Abraham ibn Ezra argued simply and convincingly against the tradition of Mosaic authorship of Genesis in the twelfth century CE, by noting that the scripture speaks in the past tense during the life of Abraham, "at that time the Canaanites were in the land."[1] The rabbi reasoned that, since the Canaanites were still present during the life of Moses and the scripture clearly spoke in the past tense, the author had to be someone who lived after Moses.[2]

More generally, a reader has to ask why the narrative stops and starts again so frequently in such disjointed fashion. Why would Moses, or God Himself, refer to God as *Elohim* for long periods of his writing, then as *YHWH Elohim* in other blocks of text? Why do the characteristics of God vary with his name? Is there a reason that God, in trying to communicate with His people, would hide Himself in such a confusing mosaic of narratives, themes, vocabulary, and language? Why would He hide history and His message in redundant accounts with different and occasionally contradictory details and perspectives?

Other difficulties arise in the literal interpretation of Genesis. If the accounts of Genesis are complete, who did Cain marry? If only Adam, Eve, Cain, Cain's wife, and Cain's son Enoch were alive, why did Cain need to build a city in Genesis 4:17? Chapter six begins with a report of celestial misogyny: "The sons of God saw that the

---

[1] Genesis 12.6. New Revised Standard Version.

[2] Coogan, Michael, editor. "Introduction to the Pentateuch". *Oxford Annotated Bible.* 3rd ed. Oxford: Oxford University Press, 2001. Hebrew Bible pg 4.

daughters of men were beautiful, and they married any of them they chose. . . The Nephilim were on the earth in those days – and also afterward – when the sons of God went to the daughters of men and had children by them. They were the heroes of old, men of renown."[1] Who were the "sons of God"? Were there, then, others besides Christ born of God and man? The world nephilim means "fallen ones" in Hebrew. How could these half-gods be both fallen and heroic men of renown? Where did the obvious parallels arise between Hebrew scripture and Greco-Roman mythology if this account is the direct revelation of a monotheistic God?

Many passages in both the Old and New Testament were obviously not intended to be literally interpreted. The book of Job refers to rain as coming from "waterskins of the heavens."[2] In the nineteenth Psalms 19:4-5 we read "In the heavens he has set a tent for the sun, which comes out like a bridegroom from his wedding canopy, and like a strong man runs its course with joy."[3] In his second letter to the Corinthian church, Paul writes "For we know that if the earthly tent we live in is destroyed, we have a building from God, a house not made with hands, eternal in the heavens."[4]

Literalists do not claim, of course, that rain comes from a hidden collection of waterskins in the sky, nor that the sun lives in a tent when it is not seen and runs across the sky in a tuxedo during the day, nor that a human body can be stitched together from canvas. What they mean, but do not say, is that they reserve the right to decide which passages of scripture will be interpreted literally and which they will assign to literary device - an arbitrary, theologically dangerous, and vain proposal.

The non-literal interpretation of scripture has a long tradition in Christianity as well as in Judaism. Centuries before the development of the Documentary Hypothesis, the third century scholar Origen and his contemporaries in Alexandria developed theories of multiple layers of meanings within the scriptures, theories and traditions that continued through Augustine and permeated Christian scholarship unchallenged until the nineteenth century advent of fundamentalism.[5]

Jesus himself was famous for teaching in parables. Jesus regularly enriched his teaching with metaphors such as patching old clothes with new cloth, pouring new wine into old wineskins, the pernicious "yeast" of false teachings, and hiding a light under a basket. When He warned against hypocrisy by describing a man who strained at a gnat and swallowed a camel, or one who sought to pluck a speck from the eye of another while

[1] Genesis 6.4. New International Version.

[2] Job 38.37. New Revised Standard Version.

[3] Psalm 19.4-5. New Revised Standard Version, New International Version.

[4] 2nd Corinthians 5.1. New Revised Standard Version.

[5] Donahue, John R. "Guidelines for Reading and Interpretation." *New Interpreter's Study Bible.* Nashville: Abingdon Press, 2003. Pg 2261-2262.

carrying a plank in his own eye, none of his listeners took him literally enough to go looking for a man with an abdomen the size of a live camel or one with a board protruding from his face.

There is no reason to demand that His parables be literally true; He is not less for using the extended metaphor of parables in His teaching. One of His most famous parables, that of the Good Samaritan (Luke 10:25-37), was spun as an answer to the simple question, "Who is my neighbor?" Some literalists make the tortured claim that each of the parables of Jesus was an actual event known and witnessed by Jesus and subsequently used by Him for teaching purposes, but there is no scriptural reason to assert that Jesus had encountered or participated in a series of events such as He described. Similarly, a widow searching for a lost coin, trees and vines being pruned for productivity, and a shepherd seeking for lost sheep, were all situations familiar, or at least imaginable, to his listeners. He did not need to name an unfortunate widow who had lost a coin, identify a shepherd who had sought diligently for a lost member of his flock, or point out the results of pruning on individual trees or vines in order for the power of His teaching to be understood.

When He used a parable of a farmer sowing seeds on a variety of soils of varying receptivity and productivity, Jesus was speaking to members of an agrarian society. All were familiar with the fact that a skilled farmer carefully considered how much of his grain harvest to hold back from food use for planting the following season. Since seed was unavailable for food or for sale or trading to acquire other needed goods, wasting seed by sowing in untilled rocky ground or among thistles that would choke out the crop was wasting the produce of the farmer's previous crop and denying his family the food or other goods that were the result of his toil. Neither the speaker nor any of his audience needed to actually know such a foolish and unskilled farmer for the lesson of the parable to take hold – the mere consideration of the consequences of such foolish actions was enough to cause the listener to draw the desired parallels to the produce of their spiritual lives. To insist that such a farmer actually existed in Jesus' experience is to miss the point of his teaching. The illustrative nature of parables has long been recognized; Augustine of Hippo wrote in the early years of the fifth century that "the narration told by our Lord was a parable, and in this kind of narrative one is never expected to demonstrate that events told in the story literally happened."[1]

There are also clear instances of humorous hyperbole used in scripture. When Jesus said, "It is easier for a camel to go through the eye of a needle than for a rich man to enter the kingdom of God," He, if interpreted literally, condemned without consideration most of the modern western world, due to the wealth of developed

[1] Saint Augustine. *The Literal Meaning of Genesis.* Translated by John Hammond Taylor. New York: Newman Press, 1982. Vol 2 of 2, pg 39 (8.4.8).

nations relative to the majority residents of Africa, Asia, and South America. The morality and ethics of the current system of the distribution of wealth is beyond the scope of this work, but it is easy to imagine Jesus reacting to heavy-handed interpretation of this remark with, "Can't you guys take a joke?" The imagery is obviously intended to be humorous and sarcastic, not literal in either visualization or interpretation.

Jesus spoke forcefully in teachings recorded in the fifth chapter of Matthew and the ninth chapter of Mark, urging his followers to amputate a hand or pluck out an eye rather than to allow their hand or eye to cause them to do wrong. Particularly since being paired as it was in Matthew with the declaration that any man who views a woman with lust has effectively committed adultery, there should be a great number of blind males in any Christian church. Yet none who teach that the entire Bible should be interpreted literally either teach or practice that these, the very words of Jesus, should be followed in a literal sense; indeed, any who advocate or carry out such a practice is considered mentally ill, and is, quite reasonably and without objection, confined for the safety of himself and others.

Christian literalists who consider the words of Jesus himself, then, are faced with the difficult task of supporting the contention that the Old Testament must be interpreted literally while the words of the central figure of their religion, a member of the same culture that produced the earlier scriptures, freely used hyperbole, metaphor, and the extended metaphor of parables to make His points.

Further difficulties arise for literalism by considering the interpretation of scripture by the Apostle Paul himself. In the book of Acts, Luke quotes Paul speaking of himself, "I am a Jew, born in Tarsus in Cilicia, and brought up in this city [Jerusalem] at the feet of Gamaliel, educated strictly according to our ancestral law, being zealous for God, just as all of you are today."[1] Gamaliel the Elder was a well known scholar of scriptural law, the grandson and heir of the equally renowned teacher Hillel the Elder, himself the author of seven rules for the interpretation of scripture that became a standard for debate among Jewish scholars.[2] The Talmud uses the title "Rabban" in referring to Gamaliel, an honorific given to the chief judge of the Sanhedrin, a council of judges that served as the supreme interpreter of law. Both Gamaliel and his grandfather Hillel the Elder are quoted extensively in the Talmud, and continue to be revered in Judaism as a great teachers and scholars.

It can be certain, then, that Paul's rabbinical education was of the highest quality, and reflected the thinking of the best scriptural scholars of his time. Paul clearly identifies

---

[1] Acts 22.3. New Revised Standard Version.

[2] Donahue, John R. "Guidelines for Reading and Interpretation." *New Interpreter's Study Bible.* Nashville: Abingdon Press, 2003. Pg 2261.

himself as the writer of the Epistle to the Galatians and then writes, in Galatians 4:21-31, of an allegorical interpretation of the story of Hagar and Sarah. Paul briefly recapitulates the story, found in the sixteenth chapter of Genesis, of how Sarah, despairing of having a child of her own, gave her slave girl Hagar to her husband Abraham, resulting in a child named Ishmael. Sarah then bore Isaac, the heir of Abraham and forefather of the Jewish people, by a conception deemed miraculous because of Sarah's advanced age. Paul then declares the story to be an "allegory" (New Revised Standard Version), or an "illustration" (New Living Bible), with the characters intended to be viewed "figuratively" (New International Version). Paul then expounds upon his allegorical interpretation of the scripture, with Hagar and her son Ishmael corresponding to those enslaved by the law of the Jews and those Jewish Christians still dominating the faith in Jerusalem, and Sarah and her son Isaac representing those who have been freed by Christ. Paul ends his exhortation with "So then, friends, we are children, not of the slave but of the free woman. For freedom Christ has set us free. Stand firm, therefore, and do not submit again to a yoke of slavery."[1]

Regardless of whether one chooses a translation that uses the word "allegory," "illustration," or "figuratively," the literalist must confront a troubling paradox: a literal reading of the writings of Paul, the most prolific author of canonical Christian literature, not only endorses a non-literal interpretation of writings of the Pentateuch or Torah, but makes it clear that such interpretations have been a scholarly practice since at least the earliest moments of Christianity. The non-literal interpretation of scripture was, apparently, well established at the time of Jesus, is scripturally documented in the person of Paul, and continues into the present day. A strictly literal interpretation of scripture is seldom found advocated until the reactionary birth of Christian fundamentalism in the nineteenth century.

Christian fundamentalism is not without admirable qualities. Many would applaud its continued recognition of the deity of Jesus and the value of His death as a redemptive act. Reliance upon the supremacy of holy writ in deciding doctrinal matters is also admired in many quarters. Unfortunately, fundamentalism has also attracted elements of bigotry, intolerance, and regressive social policies that are difficult to justify by the example of Jesus' life. Most important for our discussion, a careful and rational consideration of literalism in interpretation of scripture, as practiced by modern-day Christian fundamentalists, finds it to be inherently inconsistent, insupportable, and contradictory to the very scriptures that conservative Christians purport to revere. Literalism may be the most insidious and dangerous false teaching in Christianity.

---

[1] Galatians 4.31-5.1. New Revised Standard Version.

Chapter 3

A History of the Scriptures

An understanding of the history of the scriptures – their origin, reproduction, and translations – is instrumental to their interpretation.

The Christian scriptures are composed of Old and New Testaments, and for some denominations, the writings referred to as the Apocrypha, or the Deuterocanon. The Old Testament and the Apocrypha relate events in the history of the Jews before the birth of Jesus, and the books of the New Testament are writings relating to Christ and the early Christians. The books of the Old Testament are regarded as holy writ by both Jews and Christians. The books of the Apocrypha are accepted as scripture, with some variability, by the Catholic Church and the various Orthodox churches, but are not included in most Protestant Bibles.

All Christian denominations accord these documents extraordinary respect, with most considering them to be inspired by God, and often referring to them as "the Word of God." To consider them, as some would have us believe, to be documents directly dictated by God to humans is not consistent with the scriptures themselves, however. The direct appearance of God to humans is comparatively rare in the Christian scriptures, and when it occurs it is noted with wonder. For God to have directly dictated thirty-nine books of the Old Testament, twenty-seven books of the New Testament, and perhaps more writings placed in the Apocrypha, each as a unified and completed document, would surely have been a series of events recorded with awe by the chosen transcribers, and just as surely the stenographer would feel a duty to mankind to make known the miraculous circumstances of his revelation. Yet only in five circumstances do the scriptures themselves claim to be directly related by God: the

Decalogue and Deuteronomy were delivered to Moses on Mount Sinai; Moses and Job had direct conversations with God; several of the prophets record warnings and foretellings spoken to them by God; Saul heard God challenge him from a blinding light to become Paul the disciple of Christ in Acts; and the Book of Revelation is a vision in which heavenly beings specifically instruct the writer to record what he sees and hears. Such claims are notably absent from the books of history, including those of the Pentateuch, the books of poetry and wisdom of the Old Testament and the Deuterocanon, and the gospels and epistles of the New Testament. Only Deuteronomy, the books of prophecy attributed to Hosea, Joel, Micah, Zechariah, and Malachi, and the book of Revelation, claim to be received from God in their entirety.

We may view the Bible, then, as a set of documents produced by man, with or without the inspiration of God as each chooses to believe, but nevertheless ancient and revered by multiple civilizations over the course of at least the last two millennia, and up to, for the oldest of the writings, five millennia.

The first five books of the Bible – Genesis, Exodus, Leviticus, Numbers, and Deuteronomy – are the oldest and are commonly referred to as the Pentateuch. The history of the Pentateuch, like that of the other books of the Old Testament and to a large extent the deuterocanonical books, is inextricably linked to the history of the Jewish people.

The book of Genesis begins with the creation of the earth, a subject that will be discussed in significant depth in future chapters. It progresses through a story of a catastrophic flood and how Noah built and sailed a large vessel to preserve the animal life of the planet, to the story of the Semitic patriarch Abraham, and how the semi-nomadic early Jews came to reside in Egypt and eventually to be enslaved there. The books of Exodus and Numbers describe their dramatic departure from Egypt under the leadership of Moses, a period of nomadic wandering, and the conquest and settlement of the land of Canaan, referred to variously in modern times as Palestine and Israel. The books of Leviticus and Deuteronomy established rites and religious laws that governed both civil and spiritual affairs.

The Origins of the Pentateuch

The Pentateuch undoubtedly began its existence as an oral tradition that took shape and was passed from generation to generation before being preserved in writing. The exodus from Egypt is believed to have occurred no later than 1200 BCE. The earliest written record contributing to the Pentateuch is thought to be that of the Jehovist source, with grammar and vocabulary dating it to around the ninth century BCE. It is, therefore, highly likely that most or all of these stories were passed down for at least two hundred years as oral tradition, and it is equally likely that some parts were embellished and others lost in the telling and retelling.

The Elohist source, for similar reasons, is thought to date to approximately the eighth century, and the Deuteronistic source to the seventh century BCE.[1]

When the Jews settled in Canaan after the exodus, each tribe was assigned their own territory, except the tribe of Levi which was dedicated to priestly duties and derived its income from tributes paid by the other tribes. The tribes formed a loose confederation, governed by religious judges, and over time became increasingly embroiled in intertribal warfare. The need to end the internecine conflict and unite against outside aggressors was, in Israel as in other parts of the world, the primary reason for the transition to a kingdom. The last of the judges was the prophet Samuel; Samuel acceded to the wishes of the citizenry and anointed Saul as the first king of Israel in approximately 1025 BCE. Saul's reign was unsuccessful in fully uniting the tribes, due in part to his reluctance to fully embrace theocracy, and Samuel anointed David as Saul's successor. David and his son Solomon were successful in both military and civil administration, unifying the Jewish people, repelling several would-be conquerors, establishing Jerusalem as the capital of the Jewish state, and undertaking building projects that included an extensive temple complex as the center of Jewish religious life.

David extended and secured the boundaries of Israel, but during the reign of Solomon, old tribal rivalries and the difficulties of administering and protecting a rather large empire led to instability even while the wealth and influence of the kingdom increased spectacularly. Upon the death of Solomon in 928 BCE[2], his son Rehoboam was challenged by a coalition of Jewish tribes from the northern part of the kingdom led by Jeroboam, the son of one of his father's high officials, and the kingdom teetered on the brink of civil war. Rehoboam mustered an army with the intent of subjugating the northern territories to his rule by force, but reconsidered just before launching the invasion and consented to the division of the kingdom. The southern kingdom was comprised of the tribes of Judah (from which it took its name), Benjamin (whose tribal territory included Jerusalem), and a portion of the unlanded Levite tribe, with Jerusalem still its capital and the temple the center of its religious life. The northern kingdom of Israel encompassed the remaining nine tribes and that portion of the Levite tribe that remained in the northern territories. (Ten tribes are often referenced in regard to the northern kingdom, because the original tribe of Joseph was later considered two, named after his sons Ephraim and Manasseh.)

---

[1] Davies, G. I. "Introduction to the Pentateuch". *Oxford Bible Commentary*. Oxford: Oxford University Press, 2001. Pg 19.

[2] Coogan, Michael D., Editor. *New Oxford Annotated Bible*. 3rd ed. Oxford: Oxford University Press, 2001, Essays page 527.

The Jehovist and Elohist sources are thought to have been written, then, in the period of the unified kingdom; most scholars believe the Jehovist source to have been written around a century before the Elohist source. Even though the kingdom was united at the time, the Jehovist bias towards the tribe of Judah and the priestly descendants of Aaron (the cohanim, as opposed to the Levites) betray the regional differences that would eventually split the kingdom. The Elohist source is believed to have been written by a scribe or group of scribes of the northern kingdom, and carries bias towards the northern tribes and the Levites as priests. The Deuteronistic source, residing in Judah, made its contribution to the body of writings sometime in the seventh century BCE, when separate northern and southern kingdoms were relatively well established and stable.

The Assyrian Conquest of Israel

The northern kingdom of the ten tribes of Israel would go on to become a regional military power until invaded by the Assyrians. The Assyrian king Shalmaneser V captured the last king of Israel, Hoshea, in 722 BCE (2 Kings 17.1-6).[1] The Assyrians pursued their usual strategy of minimizing the opportunity for nationalistic resistance by dispersing the local population into other territories of their empire and resettling the conquered territory with a diverse population drawn in turn from other conquests. The ten tribes of the northern kingdom would be lost to Judaism and to history, never to return. Only the tribes of Judah and Benjamin, who made their home on the southern high plains, along with those fragments of the other tribes who chose during the division of the kingdom to remain close to the worship center in Jerusalem, would be left to carry on the faith and culture of the Jewish people.

The southern kingdom of Judah became, by geographic necessity, the protector of the temple, and along with it, the scriptures and other traditions of the Jews. But Judah was not always a dedicated custodian.

Chapters 22 and 23 of Second Kings and chapters 34 and 35 of Second Chronicles relate that the temple had fallen into disrepair when King Josiah began his reign in 639 BCE.[2] In the twelfth year of his reign, Josiah began a systematic and ruthless purge of the priests, altars, and temples of competing religions, and in the eighteenth year, he undertook the restoration of the temple. During renovations, the High Priest Hilkiah found "the book of the law" in the temple. Most scholars believe this to be some version of Deuteronomy, but the wording of the story in Second Chronicles has led

---

[1] Coogan, Michael D., Editor. *New Oxford Annotated Bible.* 3rd ed. Oxford: Oxford University Press, 2001, Hebrew Bible page 560.

[2] Dietrich, Walter. "1 and 2 Kings". *Oxford Bible Commentary.* Oxford: Oxford University Press, 2001, page 262.

some to argue that it was the entire Pentateuch.[1] In any event, the authority of the found literature was validated by the prophetess Huldah, an event regarded by some as the first canonization of scripture.[2] When the lost book was read to Josiah, his anguish at the shortcomings of his predecessors caused him to tear his clothing in a ritualized display of grief. He restored the rites of ancestral Judaism, including reinstituting the celebration of Passover for the first time since the judges.

The scriptures had, then, apparently been ignored for a period of over 300 years; a significant part of them, and possibly the entire Pentateuch, had been misplaced in the neglected temple for such a long time that their reappearance was a surprise and their content, at least with regards to the rites and laws of Judaism, had been forgotten. Although the revival led by Josiah is much admired by the writers of the books of Kings and Chronicles, they hold that the neglect of his predecessors was enough to justify retribution by God, and the last remnant of Judaism would be enslaved by Babylon.

The Babylonian Conquest of Judah

The period of Israeli captivity by Babylon, in the sixth century BCE, appears to be crucial in the formation of the Torah. Combining references in the books of Jeremiah, Daniel, Second Chronicles, and Second Kings, it may be surmised that the Babylonians launched a series of invasions in an attempt to subjugate the southern Jewish kingdom of Judah. The apparent object of the first, during the reign of Jehoiakim, in 605 BCE[3], was to capture a limited number of high-profile individuals, including the king and part of the royal family, to serve concurrently as hostages and subjects of indoctrination. The tactic was apparently ineffective, however, for the reign of Jehoiakim's son Jehoiakin lasted less than four months before he, too, was taken captive to Babylon. Resistance continued under Jehoiakin's successor, Zedekiah, until the Babylonians launched one last brutal siege of Jerusalem in 586 BCE.[4] Zedekiah was captured and blinded, and the rest of the royal family was executed along with a substantial number of officers and priests. A sizeable portion of the populace was taken captive, excepting only impoverished rural peasantry, and the temple and the city of Jerusalem were razed. The Jews remained captive in Babylon until Babylon was overthrown by the Persian

---

[1] Mathys, H. P. "1 and 2 Chronicles". *Oxford Bible Commentary.* Oxford: Oxford University Press, 2001. Pg 395-396.

[2] Trible, Phyllis. "Authority of the Bible." *New Interpreter's Study Bible.* Nashville: Abingdon Press, 2003. Pg 2250.

[3] Coogan, Michael D., Editor. *New Oxford Annotated Bible.* 3rd ed. Oxford: Oxford University Press, 2001, Hebrew Bible page 1254.

[4] Coogan, Michael D., Editor. *New Oxford Annotated Bible.* 3rd ed. Oxford: Oxford University Press, 2001, Hebrew Bible page 669.

Empire in 538 BCE[1], when the Jews were allowed to return to their homeland by Cyrus the Great. Some chose to remain in Babylon, but substantial numbers chose to repatriate in several waves. Although the rebuilding of the temple began almost immediately, it took almost twenty years to complete. The Jewish religion was without its temple and its sacrificial altar, then, for nearly a century.

The exile in Babylon was significant to the development of the scriptures in three ways:

Firstly, in the absence of the temple and its rites, the traditional writings increased in importance to the Jews as symbols of their identity and their worship. This provided impetus for refining and editing the writings. The last of the major sources of the Documentary Hypothesis, the Priestly source, is believed by many scholars to have worked in Babylon during the captivity in an effort to preserve the heritage and faith of his people.

Secondly, the captivity provided opportunities for the two cultures to exchange stories and theories, particularly regarding pre-history. The story of Noah and the flood, for example, are strikingly similar to the Babylonian flood story in which the hero rescues the animal kingdom with an ark that comes to rest on a mountain after sending out a raven to test the receding waters. Less commonly recognized is the fact that elements of a Babylonian creation story are alluded to by reference to a sea creature, or "leviathan," in chapter 41 of Job and the 74th Psalm of the Old Testament and in Second Esdras 6.49-52 of the Apocrypha. In Babylonian mythology, the creator god slays a sea monster and eviscerates him to create the world, and the references to a leviathan are allusions to that creation story.[2] Hammurabi is said to have received a set of laws (the Code of Hammurabi, one of the first set of laws published and binding to both the populace and the leadership, in the early eighteenth century BCE) engraved in stone, on a mountaintop, from a Babylonian deity, in a story similar to that of Moses receiving the Ten Commandments around five hundred years later.

Thirdly, the Babylonian captivity produced heroes such as Daniel, whose heroic acts were composed of resistance to the advances of the Babylonian culture on the Jewish people. By maintaining his Jewish identity and faith even under the threat of torture and death, Daniel and his contemporaries provided heroic examples for later periods of Jewish persecution by Romans, the Inquisition, and German fascists.

The Second Temple

When the Second Temple was built after the return from Babylon, it became the

---

[1] Coogan, Michael D., Editor. *New Oxford Annotated Bible.* 3rd ed. Oxford: Oxford University Press, 2001, Hebrew Bible page 669.

[2] Barton, John. "Introduction to the Old Testament". *Oxford Bible Commentary.* Oxford: Oxford University Press, 2001. Pg 9.

primary repository of the Jewish scriptures. The Jews enjoyed the protection and encouragement of successive Persian administrations in re-establishing their traditions, autonomy, and religious practices. When Ezra led one of the later groups of repatriated Jews in 458, he made the Torah the governing authority for the Jews of Judah, with the apparent consent of the Persian king Artaxerxes I.[1]

More than one version of the Torah clearly existed during the Second Temple period. The Talmud relates that three differing Torah scrolls were kept for ready reference at the temple. All three were consulted on matters of law, so that if two disagreed, the third could serve to break the tie.

Although the Persians allowed the Jews to govern themselves according to their own traditions and writings, they and their successors in the occupation of Palestine did not allow the repatriated Jews to reestablish their monarchy. The lack of superseding local authority made the priests as a group, and the High Priest individually, the most influential members of Jewish society. The importance of the temple cult, its rituals, and its writings was greatly increased in Jewish culture.[2]

By the founding and early years of the Second Temple, the works of the prophets had been collected and committed to writing, and were added to the library of the Temple. Other works, probably including both the other now-canonical books of the Hebrew Bible (or Christian Old Testament), and other writings not now considered canonical, were added as they became available.[3] The book of Daniel is thought to have been written as late as the first century BCE and therefore could not have been added to the collection earlier.

The Jews who returned from Babylon were also surprised to learn that their religion had not been entirely abandoned in their homeland. The few Jews who had remained in the land after the mass deportations of Israel by Assyria and Judah by Babylon, probably in concert with individuals of other local tribes who had adopted their monotheistic beliefs and with whom they likely intermarried in the absence of their kinsmen, had continued to practice a version of Judaism based solely on the Torah of the First Temple. The returning Jews, rather than welcoming the local survivors into their fellowship, ostracized them and forbade them from participating in Temple activities. Those who did not suffer exile became the Samaritans, and the contempt felt for them by the Jews lent power to Jesus' inclusion of the Samaritan woman at the well

---

[1] Coogan, Michael D., editor "Ezra". *NewOxford Annotated Bible.* 3rd ed. Oxford: Oxford University Press, 2001. Hebrew Bible pg 671.

[2] VanderKam, James. "Culture and Religion Among the Ancient Israelites." *New Interpreter's Study Bible.* Nashville: Abingdon Press, 2003. Pg 2274-2279.

[3] Barton, John. "Introduction to the Old Testament". *Oxford Bible Commentary.* Oxford: Oxford University Press, 2001. Pg 6.

(John 4.1-42) and to the story of the Good Samaritan (Luke 10.25-37). The Samaritans founded their own temple on Mount Gerizim and preserved their own version of the Pentateuch, rejecting any and all additions to the literature of their faith made by mainstream Judaism. The history of the preservation of the Samaritan Pentateuch is less clear than that of other texts, but manuscripts dated as early as the eleventh century CE are in existence.

Early translations

In the late pre-Christian era, the use of the Hebrew language began to die out. Those Jews still living in the area of the eastern Mediterranean spoke Aramaic, the common language of the Middle East, and those who had been dispersed to other areas spoke Greek as the most common language of the wider world. The translation of the scriptures from Hebrew to the languages of the day became a necessity.

A Greek translation referred to as the Septuagint is the oldest complete version of the Pentateuch known. After the death of Alexander the Great in 323 BCE, his Grecian empire broke up. One of the components was the Ptolemaic kingdom in Egypt, based in Alexandria and led by a succession of kings of Greek heritage. The Septuagint was commissioned by Ptolemy II, motivated according to various authors by a desire to have a record of the Hebrew scriptures in the great library at Alexandria, an aspiration to better understand his Jewish subjects, or the wish to fill the need of the Jewish citizenry for a version of their own literature that they could understand.

Legend has it that the Septuagint was produced by a committee of seventy-two scholars, six from each of the tribes of Israel; hence the name arising from the Greek word for "seventy," and the abbreviation LXX, but the truth of that lore is suspect. Even less plausible is a tale that identical versions were produced by each of seventy-two scholars, each in seventy-two days, working independently in cells each isolated from the other. Modern critics believe that it was produced by various scholars working over a period of time during the first through third centuries BCE. Relatively complete copies of the Septuagint are in existence that date to the fourth and fifth century CE, and fragments have been found from as early as the first and second century BCE.

Any attempt to translate a literary work from its original language, whether as simple as a song or as complex as the interwoven narratives of the Pentateuch, is fraught with difficulty. One of the co-directors in the production of the New English Bible, Sir Godfrey Driver, notes "Hebrew writers are fond of playing on words, both common nouns and proper names; but no attempt has been made to reproduce such puns, if only because the result is generally something unnatural and bizarre."[1] Of the Septuagint in particular, Driver writes, "[It] is clearly the work of different translators of varying skill; for example, the Pentateuch is reasonably well translated, but the rest of the books, especially the poetical books, are often very poorly done and even contain sheer absurdities. Errors apart, this translation is now literal, now paraphrastic and now interpretive."[2] No matter how skilled or well intentioned the translator, any translation is necessarily based on the personal understanding of the base material by the translator, and bias is inherently introduced. Subtle nuances of language seldom survive translation.

Those who spoke Aramaic in this period, which was almost everyone in Palestine and its surrounding areas, developed the custom of interpreting the dying language of ancient Hebrew into the common tongue during synagogue worship services. The practice, and the widespread use of Aramaic, is thought by some to date to the Babylonian captivity, due to a reference in Nehemiah 8.8 to the Levites interpreting the book of the law brought by Ezra from captivity as they read it to the people.[3] The translations from Hebrew to Aramaic, referred to as Targums (from the Aramaic word for "translation"), often fell into common usage and were then inevitably transcribed into written form. The quality of these Targums vary widely, as may be expected, and range from those attacked as heretical by their contemporaries to others that are still in use by Torah and Old Testament scholars.[4]

At around the same time that the Septuagint and Targums were being created, a remarkable copy of the scriptures was being made and preserved in Hebrew. A small community of Jews founded a settlement near Wadi Qumran near the northwest shore of the Dead Sea around the middle of the second century BCE. They appear to have withdrawn from the mainstream of Jewish life, but they revered and studied the Hebrew scriptures. Most researchers believe them to have been affiliated with or an offshoot of the Essenes, a monastic sect of Judaism, which, along with the Sadducees and the Pharisees, were the three major parties or schools of thought among the Jews of that era. The Qumran community did not practice celibacy as did the Essenes, as evidenced by instructions for marriage and child rearing in one of their scrolls referred to as the "Damascus Document," and by the presence of women and children in their graveyard. The well-known Jewish historian Josephus professed first hand knowledge

---

[1] Driver, Godfrey. "Introduction to the Old Testament of the New English Bible". *New English Bible.* Oxford: Oxford University Press, 1970.
[2] Driver, Godfrey. "Introduction to the Old Testament of the New English Bible". *New English Bible.* Oxford: Oxford University Press, 1970.
[3] Harrelson, Walter J. "Reliability of Scripture." *New Interpreter's Study Bible.* Nashville: Abingdon Press, 2003. Pg 2244.
[4] Driver, Godfrey. "Introduction to the Old Testament of the New English Bible." *New English Bible.* Oxford: Oxford University Press, 1970.

of the Essenes, however, and wrote that certain of their number were permitted to marry and have families, so it may still be that the Qumran community was related to the Essenes.[1, 2]

The very existence of the Essenes, Pharisees, and Sadduccees betrays the fact that the meaning of scriptures was uncertain and debated in the era encompassing the life of Jesus. When considered along with the presence of multiple versions of the Torah in the Second Temple to accommodate deliberation of its meaning, and the writings of Josephus and contemporaries who report vigorous dispute about scriptures, it is clear that the interpretation of holy writ was already a field of study encompassing a diversity of opinions.

In any event, the Qumran community made the study of Jewish scripture their highest priority, and like many Jewish sects of the time, aspired by their preparations to welcome a Messiah who would restore Israel to greatness and return her to spiritual purity.[3] When the Romans threatened to overrun the settlement, community members had the foresight to hide their precious scrolls in nearby caves, where they would remain undiscovered for slightly more than two thousand years.

Sometime during the winter months of late 1946 or early 1947, a Bedouin herder idly tossing rocks heard the sound of breaking pottery after one of his throws. He found in a small cave the shards of a broken pot around a scroll. Exploration of that cave and other caves in the immediate vicinity in the ensuing months and years produced a find that has excited and enthralled scholars and the general public since.

The Dead Sea Scrolls include portions of every Old Testament book except Esther, two scrolls of Isaiah (one complete and one comprised of about half of the text), and a scroll containing the text and commentary on the first two chapters of Habakkuk,[4] along with other scrolls that contain material from deuterocanonical books, documents relating to the practices of the Qumran community, and other non-biblical religious writings.

The preservation of the Dead Sea Scrolls by the Qumran community was made even more remarkable and valuable by the fall of Jerusalem to Rome and the subsequent destruction of the temple in 70 CE. The governance of the Jews had been a difficult

---

[1] Priestly, William. "The Dead Sea Scrolls." Undated. BiblicalStudies.org.uk. 6 Nov 2007. <www.biblicalstudies.org.uk/article_dss.html>.

[2] VanderKam, James. "Culture and Religion Among the Ancient Israelites." *New Interpreter's Study Bible.* Nashville: Abingdon Press, 2003. Pg 2274-2779.

[3] Priestly, William. "The Dead Sea Scrolls." Undated. BiblicalStudies.org.uk. 6 Nov 2007. <www.biblicalstudies.org.uk/article_dss.html>.

[4] Driver, Godfrey. "Introduction to the Old Testament of the New English Bible". *New English Bible.* Oxford: Oxford University Press, 1970.

proposition for the Romans. The Hasmonean dynasty, founded by Judas Maccabeus in 165 BCE and chronicled in the first two books of Maccabees in the deuterocanon, had combined vigorous defense against other military powers of the region with equally determined rejection of Helenistic influences on Jewish life; both reflected a strong sense of cultural and religious identity within the Judean nation. The success of the Maccabean revolt against the collapsing Seleucid Empire, itself another vestige of the breakup of the empire of Alexander the Great, made the Judean kingdom fully independent for the first time since before the Babylonian exile.

The Diaspora

The relationship of Hasmonean Judah to Rome progressed from an alliance to a protectorate as the power of Rome increased and the Hasmonean dynasty waned. In 37 BCE, the Hasmonean dynasty ended with the installation of Herod the Great as king of the Roman client state. The Romans continued to have difficulty governing the proud people of the province, however; prospective revolutionaries were regularly apprehended and executed by the Romans, and the trumped-up charges against yet another accused insurgent named Jesus was hardly noticed by Roman authorities.

More aggressive Roman policy towards the conquered nations of their empire in general and diminishing patience with the Jews in particular led Rome in 70 CE to destroy the temple, sack and raze Jerusalem, and exile the population. The Jews would never again perform the rites of their religion in the temple as prescribed by their law, and the survivors of the Roman onslaught would disperse to all parts of the world. For the Jews, the Diaspora would mean not just the loss of their ancestral lands, but the beginning of an ongoing struggle to survive as a people. Authorities and inhabitants of various nations would, at their whim, welcome, tolerate, and persecute the Jews. Some Jews would assimilate into the populations of their host countries, but many would strive to remain at least somewhat apart, and to maintain their own culture and religion.

The word diaspora itself comes from a Greek word referring to the scattering of seeds; along with the dispersion of a people comes a connotation of survival, growth, and flowering. The Jews were faced with the dilemma of replacing the geographic focus of their culture and religion, the temple, with a unifying factor that could be present with each portion of their population, now far-flung in groups large and small. Like other cultures before and since, they found spiritual and emotional sustenance in their literature, a significant portion of which was composed of the stories that defined the Jews as a people. The Torah, the works of the prophets, and the other poems, hymns, and stories of their people became the focus of both their faith and their ethnicity.

Few manuscripts had survived the destruction of Jerusalem and the Temple, however. Jewish scholars and rabbis began reconstructing the Jewish scriptures from the few remaining manuscripts, often incomplete and damaged, and from the memories of themselves and their people. In the fourteenth chapter of Second Esdras, Ezra lamented that "the world lies in darkness, and its inhabitants are without light, for your law has been burned, and so no one knows the things which have been done or will be done by you[, God],"[1] before praying for the inspiration and stamina to restore the lost works. Jewish communities remaining in lands formerly ruled by Babylon and those dispersed elsewhere in Europe and the Middle East preserved copies of the Torah and other writings that were consulted and resourced. The restorative process culminated in the Masoretic text, which took its final and now-traditional form between the seventh and eleventh century CE as a result of the work of the masoretes, groups of scholars working in Jerusalem, Tiberias, and Babylonia to compile and edit the scriptures and add vowel marks to denote then-current pronunciations. The Masoretic text, then, is an amalgam of the work of countless contributors, and includes a considerable number of notations of alternate readings, suspected omissions and additions to the text, and possible corrections.[2]

The same process of study for reconstruction and preservation of the texts also led to a general consensus among the rabbis and scholars regarding what works were to be included in the canon of the Jews, similarly completed and standardized by the work of the masoretes.

By the middle ages, then, four sets of manuscripts existed for the Jewish scriptures that would become the Christian Old Testament: the Septuagint in Greek with its uneven quality and approach to translation, the Targums in Aramaic with similarly inconsistent translation skill, the reconstructed Masoretic text with its own notations of variations, and the Dead Sea Scrolls, remarkably similar to the Masoretic text and awaiting discovery in the caves of Wadi Qumran. A fifth text, the Samaritan Pentateuch, although incomplete in relation to the full body of works canonical to Judaism and Christianity, provided confirmation of the contents of the Pentateuch and Torah.

The various texts are, for all the faults noted by scholars, extraordinarily similar to each other in overall content. The books of Daniel and Esther are notable for displaying substantial differences between the Masoretic text and the Septuagint. The Greek translation of Daniel includes a considerable amount of text not included by the masoretes, which is presented in the Apocrypha as the books The Prayer of Azariah

---

[1] 2nd Esdras 14.20-21. New Revised Standard Version.

[2] Driver, Godfrey. "Introduction to the Old Testament of the New English Bible". *New English Bible.* Oxford: Oxford University Press, 1970.

and the Song of the Three Jews, Susanna, and Bel and the Dragon,[1,2] by those modern printings of the Bible that choose to acknowledge and treat with the disputed material. The Septuagint version of Esther includes material, apparently and sometimes awkwardly added by the Alexandrian translator, to "transform the comparatively subtle and enigmatic Hebrew story of Esther into a more conventional tale of divine intervention and exemplary Jewish piety."[3] The Samaritan Pentateuch differs from the Masoretic text in around six thousand places, most of them minor in importance. Around a third of the textual differences agree with the Septuagint.[4]

The Birth of Christianity

At about the same time that the Jews were dealing with the initial phases of the Diaspora, the destruction of the Temple, and with it the loss of a large body of their literature, a new religion was being born with its roots in Judaism. The new faith based on the life and teachings of Jesus spread rapidly, first among Jews, then explosively among Gentiles thanks in part to the relentless effort of the converted Jew Saul, who took the name Paul after his spectacular reversal from persecutor to proselytizer of Christianity.

The Christian faith spread at least as far as Rome within sixteen years of the crucifixion of Jesus. The historian Suetonius recorded that Emperor Claudius expelled from Rome in 49 CE "the Jews who under the influence of Chrestus (sic) were constantly causing disturbances."[5] Acts 18.2, in reporting the effect of the edict on two associates of Paul, describes the expulsion order as addressing all Jews, suggesting along with the phrasing of Suetonius that Christianity was first considered by the Romans to be a sect of Judaism. According to Tacitus, Nero attempted to blame Christians for the devastating fire of Rome in 64 CE that he himself is widely thought to have started, and used it as a pretense to brutally persecute Christians:

> Their founder, Christus, had been executed in the reign of Tiberius by Pontius Pilate, governor of Judaea. But despite this temporary setback the pernicious superstition had broken out anew, not only in Judaea, where the trouble had started, but even in Rome where all things horrible or shameful in the world

---

[1] Coogan, Michael, editor. "Esther (The Greek Version Containing the Additional Chapaters". *Oxford Annotated Bible.* 3rd ed. Oxford: Oxford University Press, 2001. Hebrew Bible page 1253.

[2] Davies, P. R. "Daniel". *Oxford Bible Commentary.* Oxford: Oxford University Press, 2001. Pg 563.

[3] Coogan, Michael, editor. "Esther (The Greek Version Containing the Additional Chapaters". *Oxford Annotated Bible.* 3rd ed. Oxford: Oxford University Press, 2001. . Apocrypha page 53.

[4] Driver, Godfrey. "Introduction to the Old Testament of the New English Bible". *New English Bible.* Oxford: Oxford University Press, 1970.

[5] Burge, Ted. *Science and the Bible: Evidence-Based Christian Belief.* Conshohocken, PA: Templeton Press, 2005. Pg 59-60.

> collect and find a vogue. First, Nero had Christians who confessed their faith arrested. Then, on their information, large numbers of others were condemned. . . They were torn to pieces by dogs, or crucified, or made into torches to be lit after dark as substitutes for daylight.[1]

The perception of Christianity as a Jewish sect and its known origin in Judea, along with the Romans' alarm at the zeal of its evangelists and the resulting threat to Rome's polytheism, may have contributed to the Romans' decision to deal harshly with the Jews by destroying Jerusalem and the Temple and initiating the Diaspora.

The increasing literacy of the western world combined with a degree of zealotry common among adherents to the new religion to produce a large body of Christian literature. Over thirty extra-canonical gospels are believed to have existed, with evidence ranging from entire surviving manuscripts to cryptic references in other documents. Most of the original twelve apostles were the subjects of books of their later acts, some more than one. Letters of instruction, exhortation, and correction proliferated as the Christian religion spread, new believers required instruction in their faith, and the central beliefs of the new religion coalesced. Over time, some books and letters came to be viewed as being more valuable to developing Christian thought. A certain degree of circular logic was displayed, in that documents that were consistent with orthodox thought became most widely accepted, and their acceptance as canon reinforced orthodox opinions. Although various lists were composed, and several meetings were held, it is probably more realistic to view these as ratifications of a growing consensus rather than as watershed decisions in the canonization process. Different writers consider as crucial events as disparate in time as the Festal Letter by Saint Athanasius, Bishop of Alexandria, in 367, the Synod of Hippo in 393, and the Council of Trent in 1546. In reality, the canon was at least somewhat disputed until the invention of the printing press, when the sheer volume of available copies of the scripture led to acceptance of the canon as a fait accompli. The Book of Revelation and the Epistle to the Hebrews appear to have been the most heavily debated. Martin Luther rejected Esther, James, and Revelation.[2] It is notable to modern Protestants that virtually all proposed and published Christian canons before the nineteenth century included the books of the Apocrypha.

The writings of the New Testament that were eventually canonized encompass four of the several Gospels (accounts of the life and words of Christ), an historical document recording the earliest days of the church referred to as the Acts of the Apostles, or simply Acts, a series of letters addressed to local churches or individuals in leadership

---

[1] Burge, Ted. *Science and the Bible: Evidence-Based Christian Belief.* Conshohocken, PA: Templeton Press, 2005. Pg 59.

[2] Trible, Phyllis. "Authority of the Bible." *New Interpreter's Study Bible.* Nashville: Abingdon Press, 2003. Pg 2248.

by other church leaders of greater authority than the addressees, and the apocalyptic vision of Revelation. Of these, only a few of the letters of the New Testament appear to have been produced in written form at a time contemporaneous with the events to which they refer. The Gospels appear to have been committed to writing sometime in the later years of the first century CE. This means that they were almost certainly not committed to writing by the authors whose name they bear; rather, the Gospel of Matthew should, for example, be thought of as the gospel as related by Matthew, committed to writing by a follower or close associate, perhaps a generation or two removed, who treasured the memories of Matthew's teaching and wished it to be preserved for posterity. Most Biblical scholars consider that the writers of the gospels of Matthew, Mark, and Luke had some knowledge of each other's work, although the exact relationship is debated, and that John was the only one of the currently accepted gospels that was produced with a significant independence of the others.

The epistles contained in the New Testament were produced, like the Gospels, at a time when preservation of written records was increasingly valued by Greco-Roman society. Some of them may have been preserved for some time in the originally written form, but none of the originals have survived to the current time, and no originals are directly referred to in any known writings contemporary to their production. Some have been judged by biblical critics to have survived relatively intact, and others are considered, for reasons of structure, writing style, and vocabulary, to be compilations of two or more independent writings edited together before preservation.

Since the possession and knowledge of Christian writings was considered evidence of Christian sympathy, and often carried a penalty of death during times of persecution, the various works of the New Testament, Apocrypha, and other documents that would eventually be regarded as extra-canonical were painstakingly copied and preserved at great personal risk until Emperor Constantine in 313 gave Christianity officially protected status with the Edict of Milan. Only then could the Christian writings, along with those of the Old Testament, be safely and openly copied, studied, and discussed. Constantine did more than legalize Christianity, however; he assumed the role of enforcer of church doctrine under which the Roman Church and civil authority would be increasingly entangled.

As Greek literacy declined in the early church, the need for Latin translations of the scriptures became evident. A patchwork of older less skillful Latin translations was largely replaced when Pope Damasus commissioned a new translation from Jerome around 383. The resulting translation is referred to as the Latin Vulgate. (The word vulgate, with the same roots as the English word vulgar, simply means common, ordinary, or in this instance colloquial, without the negative connotation of impropriety now associated.) The Vulgate translation was the most widely used Christian scripture for several centuries, and was revised for continued use as recently as 1979, at the behest of Pope John Paul II.

As the Roman Empire declined, governmental authority was assumed by those with the military ability to take and hold land. Fiefdoms were united under dukes, and duchies were united under kings; kingdoms became the precursors of the modern European states. Virtually every significant court hosted a representative of the Church.

The Protestant Reformation

The universal presence and overarching influence of the Church caused it to grow in authority, wealth, and bureaucracy. As the might of the Church increased, it inevitably attracted certain men who hungered more for power than for spirituality, and the opportunity for corruption was realized. The Church and its officials became entangled in base political intrigue, became party to land and border disputes, maintained armies, and even sanctioned assassinations. Simony, the purchase of offices and opinions of the Church, named for the Simon of Acts 8.18-24 who tried to purchase from Peter and Paul the ability to bestow the Holy Spirit by the laying on of hands, was the common and expected means of Church function. The Church persecuted, often brutally, any that it perceived as religious, economic, or political enemies, to protect its enterprise and power.

The sale of indulgences flourished, based on the proposition that the church held a "Treasure House of Merit" because of the good deeds of her Saints; the Church held that this goodwill was an asset that could be bought and sold. The sale of indulgences by the Church may have originated legitimately as a sort of civil fine levied in penance for minor infractions, but it was soon debased to become a means for the wealthy to purchase an escape from punishment for all manner of ruthlessness and depravity, while the Church profited from wrongdoing.

Just as inevitably as she attracted men greedy for wealth and power, the Church also drew and produced men of genuine faith and character who sought to reform her. The earliest Protestants were churchmen who believed that their Church had lost direction, and no longer reflected the humility and tenderness of Jesus or the universally available redemption preached by Paul. They sought to return the Church to the values and faith that they found in the New Testament. Because education in Latin was available only to the wealthy, which in this age constituted the church and the aristocracy with which the church was complicit, critics of the Church often translated scriptures into the vernacular languages to further their aims.

John Wycliffe was the first reformer to gain widespread popular support, in fourteenth-century England. First teaching and debating from a chair at Oxford, and later addressing his concerns both to Parliament and to the public by way of lay preachers who carried his endorsement, he held that the wealth and land holdings of the Church should be divested, and that the Pope should be a spiritual leader elevated above issues of politics and secular government. He personally translated the gospels, and perhaps the entire New Testament, into English, and students and associates completed the translation of the rest of the Bible for general use; early copies were produced around 1382. Since the printing press had yet to be invented, his Bibles were reproduced by hand copying and by block printing, both laborious undertakings. Although he initially found support among the Franciscan order, who took vows of poverty and service consistent in spirit with the opinions of Wycliffe, the Church hierarchy opposed him more and more vigorously as his views were more widely discussed and considered, and concurrently attempted to suppress his and other Bible translations excepting only the Latin Vulgate. Such was the fury of the Church towards Wycliffe that the Pope ordered his body exhumed and his bones crushed some forty-four years after his death.

The credibility of the Church in these years was not enhanced by the Western Schism, a period of forty years during which two papacies, based in Rome and in Avignon, competed and at times warred. Criticism of Church practices continued and grew.

John Hus, of Charles University in Prague, was excommunicated in 1411 and burned at the stake in 1415 for his development of Wycliffe's ideas. Like Wycliffe, he addressed first the Church hierarchy, but after failing to find support there, he took his message to lesser priests, scholars, and congregants. He taught and wrote that no pope or bishop should presume to make war in the name of the church, on the grounds of Jesus' teachings to pray for one's enemies and bless those who curse one. He vigorously condemned the sale of indulgences, teaching that forgiveness comes only through sincere repentance and faith. On trial for his life, he is said to have repeatedly offered to recant his teachings if his accusers could show him to be in error using the scriptures. He was nevertheless convicted of heresy and burned at the stake. The Moravian Church, perhaps the oldest viable Protestant denomination, traces its origins to the followers of Hus who organized immediately after his death.[1]

The German Martin Luther is popularly considered to have started the Protestant movement by posting his Ninety-Five Theses on the door of Castle Church in Wittenberg on October 31, 1517. Luther was a monk and an ordained priest, held a doctorate in theology, and was a professor at the University of Wittenberg. Stimulated by a new push for indulgences by Rome to pay for renovations to the Basilica of Saint Peter, he published his thoughts under the title "Disputation of Martin Luther on the Power and Efficacy of Indulgences." Whether he actually posted his document on the doors of the church is in doubt, but it was mailed to the pope, archbishop, and teachers at other universities at that time. The theses challenged the power of the pope to

---

[1] "Our History." Moravian Church in North America. 2007. Moravian Church. 20 Nov 2007. <http://www.moravian.org/history>.

forgive sins – "The pope cannot remit any guilt, except by declaring that it has been remitted by God" - and with it, the practice and sale of indulgences and the morality of the church's wealth.[1]

Like Wycliffe in England some 140 years earlier, Luther supported his contentions in part by translating the scriptures into the local language. His German translation of the New Testament was published in 1522, and a complete Bible translated by a committee of colleagues was published under his name in 1534. Luther's Bible was much more readily available due to the invention of the printing press in the intervening years.

The Printing Press

It is commonly said that the first document printed with movable type by its inventor, Johann Gutenberg, was a Bible. This does not appear to be literally true, since the oldest known copies of Gutenberg's Bible (which incidentally was the Latin Vulgate version) were bound and sold in 1455, and a 1448 calendar printed by Gutenberg is still in existence. Other documents believed to be printed by Gutenberg prior to the Bible include a papal letter and a textbook on Latin grammar. The printing of the Bible was, however, Gutenberg's largest project to that date.

As the Protestant movement took hold, the demand for translations of the scriptures into vernacular languages increased. The translations themselves came to be closely associated with Protestantism, fueling criticism of the Church and furthering the desire of Catholicism to suppress their circulation. The thriving Protestant movement and the ability to mass produce Bibles by means of the printing press combined to produce a rapid proliferation of Bible translations, including several English versions, while making their suppression increasingly difficult.

William Tyndale is credited with being the first to have an English translation of the New Testament produced by the printing press, in 1525. Before his translation was completed, pressure from English clerical hierarchy forced him to flee England, and after the publication of his work, he was condemned of heresy by Thomas Cardinal Wolsey. He lived in hiding for several years, but when his *Practyse of the Prelates* condemned the divorce of Henry VIII in 1530, the combined influences of the crown and the church led to his betrayal and subsequent execution. One of Tyndale's devotees, Myles Coverdale, is credited with the completion of the translation of the Old Testament, and the resulting complete English Bible, the first to be printed in 1535, is known as the Coverdale Bible. Another of Tyndale's supporters, John Rogers, published an English language Bible at about the same time under the pseudonym Thomas Matthew. The Geneva Bible followed in 1560, translated and published by

[1] "The 95 Theses of Martin Luther in English". Project Wittenberg. 18 Jul 1998. Concordia Theological Seminary. 20 Nov 2007. <www.ctsfw.edu/etext/luther/theses/theses_e.asc>.

refugees who had fled to Geneva under the protection of John Calvin from the effort of Queen Mary I to return England to Roman Catholicism. (Mary earned the sobriquet "Bloody Mary" by having over three hundred people burned at the stake during her five year reign.) The Bishop's Bible of 1568 was produced by the Anglican Church to counter the Calvinistic interpretations of the Geneva Bible, but the Geneva Bible remained more popular with laymen because it was easier to understand and had an extensive system of cross references. It is said that the Geneva Bible was the Bible of William Shakespeare, John Donne, John Bunyan, and the Pilgrims of the Mayflower. Soon after, the Roman Catholic Church abandoned as hopeless its efforts to suppress vernacular Bibles, and authorized the Rheims New Testament in English.

Modern Translations

In 1604, the clergy of the Anglican Church approached King James I of England to request a new translation of the Bible to supplant the Geneva Bible with its cross references and notes related to Protestantism in general and Calvinism in particular. The resulting translation, drawing heavily on the Tyndale New Testament, the Coverdale Bible, the Matthews Bible, the Geneva Bible, and the Rheims New Testament, was published in 1611 and has been known since as the King James Version or the Authorized Version of the Bible.

The King James Version took some time to supplant the Geneva Bible in popularity, but it had staying power. The first major new translation after its 1611 publication was the English Revised Version (of which the New Testament was published in 1881 and the complete Bible in 1885) and its Americanized edition, the American Standard Bible (1901). Many are surprised to learn that the English Revised and American Standard Bibles were the first major translations published without the books of the Apocrypha. The Revised Standard Version of the Bible, a scholarly 20th-century translation from Greek and Hebrew, restored the apocryphal writings to print.

The affection, esteem, and loyalty towards the King James Version of the Bible by many American evangelicals can be seen, in light of history, as being highly ironic. The King James Version was not the first English rendition of holy writ, nor was it quickly adopted by either Protestant leadership or the populace. Irony is further enhanced by the fact that it is not a Protestant version of the Bible at all, but produced as a reaction of Anglican clergy to the growing Protestant movement, in hopes of supplanting the Protestant-supported Geneva Bible. It nevertheless continues to possess considerable authority among some segments of the American evangelical community as the most traditional of scriptural sources.

The increasing influence of evangelicalism spurred the production of more recent translations with a conservative bent to the scriptural translation and the accompanying notes, such as the New International Version of 1973 and the New Living Translation of 1996, and of paraphrases such as the Living Bible of 1971 and The Message of 2002.

The scriptures as possessed by modern man have a long and complex history. All view them as important works of literature, critical to the development of western civilization. The force of their moral and ethical authority in shaping our body of law is immutable and ongoing. As holy writ they are both treasured and reviled. Few works are so well known, yet so incompletely understood; few have such a convoluted history, giving rise to such a wide span of interpretations. Yet for the faithful, the Bible remains the literary medium through which God inspires mankind to repentance, knowledge, and service. Its authority to inspire lies in the faith of the believer, in the same way that governments derive their just power from the consent of the governed.

To view the scriptures realistically, as a compilation of works from a variety of sources that has been handed down by various means, compiled, edited, and translated, is not to deny their authority; rather, only by understanding their true nature can their complexity be appreciated and their value as words guarded and treasured over millennia be fully valued and respected.

Chapter 4

Informed Interpretation

Careful consideration of the history of the scriptures leads the serious student of the Bible to conclude that adamancy is an unwise position.

The oldest portions of the scriptures, the Pentateuch, were passed from generation to generation as an oral tradition for at least two hundred years before being recorded in written form. The historical portions, the books of Genesis, Exodus, and Numbers, consist of the stories of a nomadic tribe that were undoubtedly enhanced in the telling and retelling. It is inevitable that, over time, protagonists are made more heroic and enemies more villainous with each repetition.

It is obvious from the differences in plot, detail, vocabulary, writing style, allegiances, and viewpoints that different hands played parts in the composition when the works were eventually committed to writing. Whether or not the exact assertions of the Documentary Hypothesis are embraced, it is clear that various accounts were at some point edited together to produce the Old Testament scriptures as they existed by the second century BCE. This is nowhere more obvious, and nowhere more pertinent to the attempts to resolve science and faith that are the subject of this book, than the first two chapters of Genesis, which give two different accounts of the creation. The accounts will be examined in more detail later in this volume, but it is sufficient for this argument to note that the first tells of creation occurring in six days, with the creation of the earth and heavens followed in order by plants, animals, and mankind, male and female; the second tells of creation being performed in a day (singular), and states clearly that no plants were created until after a male human was formed from soil, followed in order by plants and the rivers to nourish them, the animal kingdom, which was presented to the man to be named one by one, and finally, because no suitable companion had been found for man among the animals, a human female was formed from the rib of the first male. Christian fundamentalists attempt to resolve the two accounts by regarding the second count as an elaboration of the creation of man in the first account. These attempts fail by consideration of the widely differing chronologies apparent by a simple literal reading of the accounts, of the differing methods of creation by which God "summon[s] things into being from a lofty distance through the mere agency of divine speech" in the first account, "but works as a craftsman, fashioning (*yatsar* instead of *bar'a*, "create")"[1] in the second, and, once again, of the difference in vocabulary and writing style that is apparent to those literate in the ancient languages of the texts.

Accuracy of the Text

During the First Temple period, the scriptural texts then in existence were so lightly regarded that they were, according to the accounts later recorded in the books of Kings and Chronicles, lost for a period of at least several generations. Once the Pentateuch was committed to writing and compiled into a recognizable form, it was reproduced by hand copying for at least seventeen hundred years, measuring from the completion of the Septuagint, when the Pentateuch is known to have been treated as a unified document, or two thousand years if one makes the more dicey presumption that it was complete by the time the Jewish exile in Babylon ended and the Second Temple founded. The process of hand copying provided abundant opportunity for simple human error, a reality so basic that the Jews of the Second Temple period, as has been previously mentioned as being recorded in the Talmud, traditionally kept at least three copies of the scriptures available for the resolution of disputes between the texts then in existence.

The debates of the temple were the foundation for ongoing discussion and interpretation of the scriptures that was well established by the time of Christ. Hillel the Elder, the grandfather of Gamaliel the teacher of the Apostle Paul, codified the interpretation of scripture in rules that are still discussed among Hebrew scholars.[2] Rabbis of the Sanhedrin continued to debate and interpret the scriptures as they were used in the administration of law, and to pass their debates on as oral tradition.[3]

---

[1] Alter, Robert. *Genesis: Translation and Commentary.* New York: W. W. Norton, 1996. Pg 7.

[2] Donahue, John R. "Guidelines for Reading and Interpretation." *New Translator's Study Bible.* Nashville: Abingdon Press, 2003. Pg 2261.

[3] Spiro, Ken. "The History of the Talmud." *SimpleToRemember.com – Judaism Online.* Undated. Judaism Online. 3 Jan 2008. <http://www.simpletoremember.com/vitals/Talmud_History.htm>.

Even the multiple temple scrolls, with their inaccuracies and discrepancies recognized by the Jews of the time, were lost when the Romans destroyed the Second Temple, and the Hebrew manuscripts that are the precursors of all current texts were reconstructed by Jewish scholars and rabbis, leading up to the preservation efforts of the Masoretes.

The oral traditions of debate and interpretation by the Sanhedrin were preserved and expanded by continued scholarly debate into the Talmud, a complex, multi-layered commentary on Jewish law arising from centuries of rabbinical discussion. Contemporary Jewish author Rabbi Ken Spiro writes of the nature and purpose of the Talmud:

> This information was vital to the Jewish people because Jewish law was never applied by reading a sentence in the Torah and executing it to the letter. Take for example, "eye for an eye, tooth for a tooth." It was never Jewish law that if someone blinded you, that you should go and blind him. What is the good of having two blind people? It was always understood on two levels: 1) that justice must be proportional (it's not a life for an eye) and 2) that it means the value of an eye for the value of the eye, referring to monetary damages. Thus, the Talmud presented the written and oral tradition together.[1]

Translation

The process of translation from ancient Hebrew to Greek and Latin, and into the modern languages from all of the ancient sources, was again a source of difficulty, inaccuracies, and error. Anyone with even a rudimentary knowledge of a second language realizes that languages differ not only in vocabulary, but also in syntax. The art of translation, then, is much more difficult than simply finding a word to match the meaning of each word of the original text, for to do so would produce unintelligibly scrambled sentences in the new language. It is necessary, rather, for the translator to reach his or her own understanding of each phrase and sentence in order to render it fluently, with appropriate sentence structure, in the new language. The translator, no matter how well intentioned, cannot therefore produce a translation completely free of the translator's own inherent understanding and interpretation.

It is also well known among translators that puns, double entendre, and other word play is notoriously difficult to reproduce in a second language. The rhythm of poetry and of skillfully written prose that is produced with so much effort by talented authors is always difficult and often impossible to achieve in translation.

Robert Alter, in the introductory remarks to his recently published translation of

---

[1] Spiro, Ken. "The History of the Talmud." *SimpleToRemember.com – Judaism Online.* Undated. Judaism Online. 3 Jan 2008. <http://www.simpletoremember.com/vitals/Talmud_History.htm>.

Genesis, acknowledges the difficulty of a translator, not only in reproducing literary devices, but also in reconciling an intent for clarity with what may be intentional ambiguity by the original authors:

> Although many in the Christian evangelical community claim to understand the Bible as being literally true in every word, strictly literal interpretation of scripture is insupportable. Original Hebrew scriptures incorporate rich imagery, metaphor, hyperbole, and deliberate ambiguity (double entendre) as literary devices. Translators have as their goal clarity and accessibility, so they necessarily seek to remove ambiguity, and in doing so they are forced to impose their own interpretation.[1]

Walter J. Harrelson, Distinguished Professor Emeritus at Vanderbilt University Divinity School and General Editor of *The New Interpreter's Study Bible*, similarly recognized that translators "necessarily have to guess at the precise meaning of terms and idioms and allusions as they seek the contemporary equivalent of these, which will almost surely lead to over-translation – translation that makes the text clearer than the Hebrew, Aramaic, and Greek actually are."[2]

Lest the reader assume that such challenges are unique to modern languages, consider that the translator of the apocryphal book of Sirach (sometimes referred to as Ecclesiasticus), after identifying himself as the grandson of the original author, asks in the prologue for his readers to "be indulgent in cases where, despite our diligent labor in translating, we may seem to have rendered some phrases imperfectly. For what was originally expressed in Hebrew does not have exactly the same sense when translated into another language. Not only this book, but even the Law itself, the Prophecies, and the rest of the books differ not a little when read in the original."[3] The grandson made these observations on the task of translating the book from Hebrew to ancient Greek in the second century BCE.

In reading the works of modern scholars of ancient Hebrew, it is striking how frequently the meaning of individual words is not known. Modern translators frequently are left to discern the meaning of words from contextual and etymological clues because the precise meaning has been lost to antiquity, and apparently idiomatic phrases are common. It is difficult to understand how it can be held that translations into English or another modern language can be considered inerrant when the vocabulary of the original document is uncertain and at times unknown; only a fresh

---

[1] Alter, Robert. *Genesis: Translation and Commentary.* New York: W. W. Norton, 1996, xii of "To The Reader".

[2] Harrelson, Walter J. "Reliability of Scripture." *New Interpreter's Study Bible.* Nashville: Abingdon Press, 2003. Pg 2247.

[3] Sirach. Prologue. New Revised Standard Version.

divine revelation could seemingly result in the certainty of translation that is claimed by modern fundamentalists, and that sort of revelation is neither supported by scripture nor claimed by adherents.

The very real difficulties in translation are well illustrated by the figure of Moses in medieval paintings. Modern-day viewers of such paintings often confuse Moses with Satan, because Moses is routinely portrayed with horns. Jerome, an expert theologian and scholarly translator who was later sainted by the Church for his efforts, mistranslated the passage in which Moses descended from Mount Sinai after his audience with God, during which he received the Ten Commandments. Ancient Hebrew in its written form contained no vowels; readers were assumed to be literate enough to discern the proper vowels when a word was considered in context. When one set of vowels was inserted into a key word in this passage, the result was a word that described a radiance or glow; another set of vowels resulted in a word that translated as being horned. Jerome wrote, in his Latin translation that would be in common use until the Renaissance, that Moses' face upon descending from Mount Sinai was horned, instead of glowing from the reflected glory of God. Generations of painters portrayed Moses with horns on the authority of erroneously translated scripture.

One may, in reflecting on the myriad of opportunities for inaccuracies inherent in the long process of oral and hand-written transmission and subsequent translation, consider it remarkable that the scriptures, particularly the Pentateuch, are available in versions that are coherent and agree as fully as they do. Yet the most pressing question for the reader who insists on the inerrancy of scripture is to decide which version is inerrant, since even the primeval versions in the original language were known by their ancient custodians to have differed significantly, and subsequent copying, reconstruction, and translating could only have added to the difficulty in discerning the original meaning of any given passage. One glaring example of this difficulty is the fact that the age of Saul, the first king of Israel, at his ascendancy, and the length of his reign have both been lost. First Samuel 13.1 contains the text, but the number associated with his age is missing from all existing manuscripts, and only the "–two" (as in twenty-two, thirty-two, etc.) remains of the length of his reign. Some modern translations insert a "forty" as the first part of the number in the time of his reign, so that his reign is said to be forty-two years, but such a supposition does not arise directly from any known text of Samuel; rather, it is to put the passage in accordance with that of Acts 13.21, in which Paul, in reviewing the history of the Jewish people, states that Saul held the throne for a period of forty years, a statement that is presumed to result from Paul rounding the figure of forty-two years. That explanation attempts to reinforce inerrancy by creating consistency between the two passages, but fails in that even the adjusted figure of forty-two years does not exactly equate with the tradition apparently known to Paul of a forty year reign by Saul; rounding is inconsistent with literalism.

Difficulties with Historical Inerrancy

The doctrine of inerrancy, as defined by fundamentalists, states that the Bible "is free from error in what it says about geography, history and science as well as in what is says about God."[1] It follows that any demonstrable inconsistency of historical fact within the scriptures or between scripture and events verifiable through secular records render invalid the doctrine of inerrancy.

Discrepancies between different passages of scripture are myriad – their plethora, in fact, provided the very impetus for reexamination of the scriptures that led to the Documentary Hypothesis. The contradictions continue unabated after the creation stories.

An objective reading of the flood story makes it clear that two differing accounts were interwoven: Noah's family and the animals enter the ark twice and depart twice, two different sets of instructions are given for collecting animals, and one story ends with a ritual sacrifice by Noah (Genesis 8.20-22) while the other does not (Genesis 9.1-17, which markedly differs stylistically).

Other stories are blended in similar fashion at many places throughout the Pentateuch, and when the time of the Jewish Kings is discussed, two entire books, Kings and Chronicles, tell the history of the same time period, with differing details and perspectives. (The Christian canon divides each of the Jewish books into two halves.) One of the most familiar Bible stories, that of David slaying Goliath, itself the subject of countless tired analogies by sportscasters, is directly contradicted by 2 Samuel 21.19, which in a brief account gives credit to "Elhanan son of Jaare-oregim, the Bethlehemite" for the slaying of the menacing giant.

The Pentateuch contains two different versions of the revelation of YHWH (translated as the LORD in capitals in English versions) as God's name. Genesis 4.26 relates that God was known as YHWH since a time when Adam was still alive and procreating, but Exodus 6.3 explicitly states that God revealed His name to Moses for the first time, and that Abraham, Isaac, and Jacob did not know him by the name of YHWH.

Enoch is explicitly stated to be the grandson of Adam by way of Cain in the fourth chapter of Genesis. Yet in the following chapter, a genealogy relates Enoch to be six generations removed from Adam and descended from Seth, the son that was born to Adam and Eve to replace the slain Abel. And the New Testament letter of Jude says

---

[1] "Inspiration and Inerrancy of the Bible." *Moody: From the Word to Life.* Undated. Moody Bible Institute. 22 Nov 2007. < //www.moodyministries.net/crp_MainPage.aspx?id=600>.

that Enoch was seven generations after Adam.

One particularly egregious discrepancy in the scripture occurs in dating the reign of Jehoiachin, one of the last kings of Judah. Second Kings states that "Jehoiachin was eighteen years old when he began to reign."[1] Second Chronicles says "Jehoiachin was eight years old when he began to reign."[2] Some English versions such as the New International Version and the New Living Translation actually change the translation of Second Chronicles to maintain consistency with Second Kings, relegating to a footnote the fact that "most Hebrew manuscripts" say that Jehoiachin was eight years old when he took the throne, in a transparent attempt to achieve the consistency necessary to maintain a claim of inerrancy.

The New Testament is not lacking its own inconsistencies of historical record. Jesus' calling of His first disciples as they fished is tersely related in virtually identical language in the gospels of Matthew[3] and Mark,[4] but the account of Luke[5] places the event later in Jesus' ministry and differs noticeably in details, and that of John[6] differs quite substantially from the other three: Andrew is a disciple of John the Baptist, who advises Andrew to leave his own entourage and follow Jesus, Simon Peter is recruited by Andrew, and the next two disciples are identified as Philip and Nathanael rather than James and John. The event that Luke relates as the occasion in which Simon Peter, James, and John were discipled to Jesus – unsuccessful fishing followed by a miraculously large catch at Jesus' command – occurs in John after Jesus' resurrection.[7,8] In the incident in which Jesus healed the gravely ill member of the household of a Roman centurion, the centurion sought out Jesus personally in Matthew and John but communicated through two waves of envoys in Luke; Matthew relates that the ill person was a servant, and Luke similarly that he was a valued slave, but in John he is the official's son.[9] Notably and strangely absent from John's account of the passion is the agonized prayer of Jesus in the Garden of Gethsemane and His appearance before the Sanhedrin.[10] Such inconsistencies within scripture can be overlooked in considering the spiritual and theological message of the gospels and the larger Bible,

---

[1] 2nd Kings 24.8. New Revised Standard Version.
[2] 2nd Chronicles 36.9. New Revised Standard Version.
[3] Matthew 4.18-22.
[4] Mark 1.16-20.
[5] Luke 5.1-11.
[6] John 1.35-51.
[7] John 21.1-8.
[8] Wansbrough, Henry. "The Four Gospels in Synopsis." *Oxford Bible Commentary*. John Barton and John Muddiman, ed. Oxford: Oxford University Press, 2001. Pg. 1015-1016.
[9] Wansbrough, Henry. "The Four Gospels in Synopsis." *Oxford Bible Commentary*. John Barton and John Muddiman, ed. Oxford: Oxford University Press, 2001. Pg. 1018-1020.
[10] Wansbrough, Henry. "The Four Gospels in Synopsis." *Oxford Bible Commentary*. John Barton and John Muddiman, ed. Oxford: Oxford University Press, 2001. Pg. 1024-1027.

but cannot be reconciled with the modern concept of historical accuracy that is inherent in the doctrine of inerrancy.

Instances of stark discrepancies between scripture and contemporary secular records can also be identified.

The seventh chapter of Deuteronomy identifies the Hittites as one of the tribes residing in the land of Canaan prior to its possession by the Jews, but the Hittites lived in modern-day Turkey. Archeological digs give evidence that Jericho was a small village in the thirteenth century BCE, rather than the imposing walled city described in the book of Joshua. Its outer defenses, if any were present at all, were a wooden stockade or fence rather than a wall; it is, of course, common to enhance a hero's reputation by exaggerating the strength of his enemies.

Daniel 4.31-37 relates that Babylonian Emperor Nebuchadnezzar suffered an illness, perhaps a mental illness, that caused him to impose upon himself a period of exile, after which he returned to the throne of Babylon. The fifth chapter follows with a reference to King Belshazzar, a son of Nebuchadnezzar, in the story that gave birth to the phrase "The handwriting is on the wall." Contemporary references, however, do not mention any such episode afflicting Nebuchadnezzar. Other documents, including the Dead Sea Scrolls, record that a later Babylonian king named Nabonidus left his kingdom abruptly and was ill in exile for seven years before retaking the throne. Belshazzar was the son of Nabonidus, and served as a regent in his father's absence.[1] In its apparent confusion between the Nebuchadnezzar and Nabonidus, the brief biblical account is in error in four ways: by mistakenly stating that Nebuchadnezzar left the throne, by omitting Nabonidus' reign, by identifying Belshazzar as the son of Nebuchadnezzar rather than Nabonidus, and by identifying the office of Belshazzar as King rather than as steward or regent. These errors are established by contemporary documentation, including the Dead Sea Scrolls, documents that themselves lend credibility to the accuracy of subsequent reproduction and renderings of the Old Testament scriptures.

The census that, according to Luke 2.1-7, prompted Joseph to take Mary with him to Behlehem and there to give birth to Jesus, is recorded only in the New Testament. Records exist of similar Roman censuses in 28 BCE, 8 BCE, and 14 CE, but none during the reign of Caesar Augustus.[2]

The doctrine of inerrancy fails the test of historical consistency with contemporary documentation.

---

[1] Coogan, Michael D., editor. *New Oxford Annotated Bible.* 3rd ed. Oxford: Oxford University Press, 2001. Hebrew Bible page 1263.

[2] Coogan, Michael D., editor. *New Oxford Annotated Bible.* 3rd ed. Oxford: Oxford University Press, 2001. NewTestament pag 98.

Difficulties with Scientific Inerrancy

Since historical inerrancy fails on both of the two possible tests, is it possible to salvage a claim of scientific inerrancy? Even though it would still fail the definition of inerrancy proposed by fundamentalists themselves by excluding history, and setting aside the disputed theories of creation themselves, is it possible to maintain that the Bible is otherwise consistent with known scientific facts? If so, it would lend credence to the use of the Bible as a scientific text and the doctrine of inerrancy could be modified to include only science, and disregard the many messy and discouraging inaccuracies in its historical record.

In Genesis 30.25-43, Jacob hatches a plan to double-cross his maternal uncle and father-in-law Laban. Laban offers Jacob compensation for Jacob's profitable work in animal husbandry, and Jacob suggests that Laban compensate him with all the "speckled and spotted" sheep and goats. Laban consents, then deceives Jacob by having his herdsmen remove all the designated animals from his flocks and send them to the care of his sons, three days' travel away. Jacob responds by peeling strips of bark from wooden rods and setting them up in front of the feed troughs, under the belief that females who breed in front of the striped sticks would bear "young that were striped, speckled, and spotted."[1] "Whenever the stronger of the flock were breeding, Jacob laid the rods in the troughs before the eyes of the flock, that they might breed among the rods, but for the feebler of the flock he did not lay them there; so the feebler were Laban's [being solid colored], and the stronger [being multicolored] Jacob's."[2]

Jacob's plan was based on the mistaken notion of the time that the color and pattern of the coats of domestic animals was determined by what the female saw during the act of breeding. We now understand that coat color and pattern is genetically determined. The color and pattern of any individual animal's coat can be determined by several different genes acting from multiple locations on the chromosomes – the genetics of color and pattern in horses is particularly complex – but the probabilities of various patterns and colors in the coat of offspring can be predicted by knowing the coat color and pattern and the genetic makeup of the parents. It is indisputable that the visual field of the dam at the time of breeding has no influence on the color or pattern of the coat of her offspring.

The significance of this passage is not that the scientific principle is incorrect, for it has already been demonstrated that the Bible is incorrect in describing rain coming from waterskins in the sky and the sun hiding in a tent at night and running across the sky by day, and other misconceptions will come to light in later chapters. The doctrine of

---

[1] Genesis 30.39. New Revised Standard Version.

[2] Genesis 30.41-43. New Revised Standard Version.

inerrancy, after all, can only be upheld if the Bible contains no historical or scientific inaccuracies at all, so a single instance of error condemns the doctrine to failure. The importance of this passage is that it clearly demonstrates that at least this portion of Genesis was written by the hand of a human with a limited understanding of genetics in particular and biological science in general.

It is a point worth reiterating that this passage, free as it is from any attempt at poetic or symbolic language, and independent of any disputed interpretation of creation or cosmology, clearly demonstrates a limited knowledge on the part of its human author. There would be no reason for God the creator, with complete knowledge of the workings of genetics and inheritance, to write or dictate a passage containing a scientific theory that is, by the standard of later knowledge, comical in its inaccuracy and based on an overtly false premise. One may still regard the scripture as inspired by God, but this passage leads to the inescapable conclusion that it was produced by a person limited in his knowledge of science.

Anyone who has written a report, term paper, article, or book understands that one cannot speak of what one does not understand; nor can one write about that which one cannot comprehend as a result of experience, learning, or research. The remainder of the Bible consists of material that is within the realm of knowledge, either first hand or by the transmission of oral tradition, of the authors; only the first portion of Genesis contains material that is outside the knowledge or experience of any human being. The writers of Genesis could not have known or comprehended the truths of science regarding times before the dawn of mankind, and therefore could not have written them even if inspired. Indeed, if the human authors of Genesis had written of the nuclear fusion that powers stars, of light that takes years and millions of years to reach us from the visible stars, of mountains living and dying with the collision of tectonic plates, of islands forming from volcanic activity, or of a great tree of life that includes millions of extinct species and has its roots in simple microscopic organisms over three billion years ago, the writing would have lacked the very credibility and value that caused it to be preserved relatively intact for several thousand years. One must conclude that this passage and, unless one is willing to discard the story as being the result of a process somehow different from that which produced the rest of the Bible, the words of Genesis and the Bible are limited by the knowledge of those who composed it, transmitted it through the years of oral tradition, and committed it to writing.

Even more telling on this point is the parable of the mustard seed, told by Jesus in each of the three synoptic gospels. In the accounts of both Mark and Matthew, the mustard seed is referred to as the smallest of seeds. Mustards seeds are one to two millimeters in diameter; the seeds of petunias and begonias are much smaller, being grains too small to handle individually; orchid seeds, too, are extremely small, as small as eighty-five microns (or 0.085 millimeter); although not true seeds, fern spores are around fifty microns in size. The point of Jesus' parable is not lost by knowing that mustard seeds are not the smallest seeds in existence, for they are indeed quite small, and were very probably the smallest seed encountered by the human Jesus and known by His audience, but as a scientific statement the parable is in error. If the accounts of Jesus' words are accurate, Jesus Himself made the error; perhaps He did not intend His words to be examined from a scientific standpoint by succeeding generations, but intended instead to teach a spiritual truth. Perhaps a similar principle was in play in the writing of the creation accounts in Genesis.

Inerrancy versus Infallibility

The doctrine of inerrancy, as defined by fundamentalists, then, fails on every count. The doctrine of infallibility, taken to mean that the Bible has ultimate authority in matters theological and spiritual, may be assumed by men and women of faith, but the doctrine of inerrancy with regard to history and science is an insupportable position created by man, not claimed by the scriptures themselves, and demonstrably false.

The Bible must be read and studied for what it is: a collection of documents written by the hand of man, with all of the human capacity for literary expression, error, and bias. Its subject is God and His relationship with mankind, and some will see in its words the inspiration of God Himself.

The twin doctrines of literalism and inerrancy are not herein disputed in order to disparage those who hold such beliefs. The overwhelming majority of those who believe in inerrancy and the literal translation of scripture are people of sincerity and good will, who have themselves unquestioningly accepted the doctrines from others with ecclesiastical authority in teaching and dogma. At issue, however, is the true meaning of the collected writings of the Bible, particularly the stories and comments of the Bible regarding creation. The scriptures can be accepted as a collection of spiritual and theological truths without claiming scientific and historic inerrancy. The several inconsistencies and inaccuracies of the scripture, only a select few of which are documented herein, are unimportant to a spiritual interpretation of holy writ. If they are regarded as mere examples and illustrations used in relating a concept of God, they become unimportant details within a more important and defensible argument, whereas if inerrancy is maintained, its demonstrable failure necessarily causes insurmountable problems concerning the credibility of the entire body of work.

A passage often quoted by fundamentalists to justify their faith in the doctrine of inerrancy, reads in full in the New Revised Standard Version: "All scripture is inspired by God and is useful for teaching, for reproof, for correction, and for training in righteousness, so that everyone who belongs to God may be proficient, equipped for every good work."[1] The conservatively oriented New International Version differs only slightly in wording and not at all in content: "All scripture is God-breathed and is useful for teaching, rebuking, correcting, and training in righteousness, so that the man of God may be thoroughly equipped for every good work."[2]

The clear message of this verse in both translations is that the scriptures known to the writer, which in the first century were composed of the Old Testament in the Hebrew language, in form and content very similar to that familiar to modern scholars and readers, is authoritative in teaching matters of faith to those seeking knowledge of and service to God. Notably absent is any claim to veracity in historical or scientific facts. The passage supports the view that the scriptures are inspired by God, but does not support the doctrine of historical or scientific inerrancy; that doctrine is an invention of mankind.

The purpose of the biblical histories was not historical accuracy, but to relate stories that unified the Israelites as a people and in their devotion to their God. The editors of the Oxford Annotated Bible have this to say about historical writing in the Biblical era:

> The idea that historical writing should capture the events "as they really were," that historians should attempt to write an objective account of the events of the past, is a relatively recent notion that developed in the European universities several centuries ago. Before that, history was often didactic in nature, teaching the readers how to be good citizens or how to lead proper religious lives. . . Thus, it should not be surprising that the biblical writers are not primarily interested in the accurate recording of real events; rather, they use narratives about the past to illustrate various issues of significance to their earliest audient, the ancient Israelite community.[3]
>
> [B]iblical historians each wrote accounts, sometimes using sources, to illustrate particular perspectives concerning the relationship between God and Israel. It is these religious and religio-political perspectives that we must try to appreciate as we study these books; if we read them as we read modern historical accounts, we will misunderstand these texts in the most fundamental way.[4]

As an historical reference the Bible omits any mention of the civilizations of China, dating twenty-one centuries before the time of Christ, that of India beginning three millennia before the Common Era, and any of the ancient civilizations of the Americas.

---

[1] 2nd Timothy 3.16-17. New Revised Standard Version.

[2] 2nd Timothy 3.16-17. New International Version.

[3] Coogan, Michael D., editor. "Introduction to the Historical Books". *Oxford Annotated Bible.* 3rd ed. Oxford: Oxford University Press, 2001. Hebrew Bible pg 309.

[4] Coogan, Michael D., editor. "Introduction to the Historical Books". *Oxford Annotated Bible.* 3rd ed. Oxford: Oxford University Press, 2001. Hebrew Bible pg 313.

If the purpose of the Bible is not as an historical text in the contemporary sense, neither is it intended as reference for science, a subject about which it has far less to say than history. None of the Judeo-Christian scriptures mention nuclear fusion, the process that powers the sun and stars and produces all of the elements heavier than hydrogen, nor do they mention geological oil deposits, electricity, DNA, radioactivity, nor even the spherical shape of the earth.

The Bible makes no mention of a theory of gravity, either Newtonian or relativistic as per Einstein. The scriptures refer in several places (Job 38.8-11, Jeremiah 5.22, and Proverbs 8.27-29, in addition to the most familiar Genesis 9.1, for examples) to God gathering the seas together or setting boundaries for the sea. We now understand that gravity holds the seas in place, but in the absence of any understanding more than the intuitive acceptance of its everyday effects, the writers could not attribute the boundaries of the sea to the effect of gravity on its fluid mass; it was enough for them to recognize God as the creator who causes things to be as they were.

Rainbows are caused by a combination of refraction and reflection of sunlight by airborne water droplets. The author of Genesis 9.8-17 saw the rainbow as the sort of bow that hurls arrows, a weapon of God pointing away from the earth as a gesture of peace, and in his ignorance of the refraction of light, he was content to see beauty and be thankful to God for His covenant of peace with mankind.

Because the Bible is a document centering on the nature of God, the central statement of the Bible regarding creation is that all was created by God. The sun and the moon, deities to peoples contemporary to the ancient Israelites, are presented by Genesis as creations of God. Leviathan, that great sea monster that played a role in the creation fables of other Middle Eastern cultures, was not a creator at all, but created by God. Plants and animals and the earth itself – everything that mankind needs and uses and everything in which we find beauty – was created by God.

The writers of Genesis and the rest of the Old Testament could not have understood scientific theories that boggle the mind of many even today, and therefore could not have written them. They did not try to understand the means of God in undertaking His creation, for that was not their purpose; it was enough to know that God was the creator. Mankind would take several more millennia to even begin to understand how God created the cosmos and life and mankind.

Chapter 5

The Big Bang Wasn't

After examining what scripture says about the creation, the second aspect of the controversy between scripture and science that must be understood is, of course, the version of creation that is the result of scientific inquiry. That explanation begins with the Big Bang. But the Big Bang was not a big bang – it was silent, in fact, because there was no matter capable of transmitting sound, and no space in which sound could be transmitted.

A Russian mathematician named Alexander Friedmann, working with the equations of general relativity published by Einstein in 1916, proposed in 1922 that the universe was inexorably expanding, and expanding uniformly on a large scale. The idea was highly controversial for several years; Einstein himself initially rejected the idea, solely because it offended his sense of order, but later reversed himself. It follows, however, that if the expansion is reversed going backward in time, matter would converge to a single point. Friedmann used that logic to suggest that the universe began with an explosive event radiating matter, energy, and space itself from an unimaginably small node. Neither Friedmann nor Einstein termed the idea the Big Bang; the Big Bang is a name that was coined in derision by astrophysicist Sir Fred Hoyle. The name stuck, but its original sense of ridicule has been replaced by acclaim. Acceptance of the theory has grown with increasing supporting evidence, and the overall recognition of the theory among experts in the fields of astronomy and physics is almost universal.

The theory of the Big Bang was largely confirmed when it was observed that other galaxies are moving away from us, and the further they are from us, the faster they are moving away.

Astronomers noticed that the characteristic spectral bands of hydrogen, helium, and other elements making up the matter of stars were present in their telescopic images, but were of slightly lower frequency than those of the sun or of the spectral bands of the same elements in laboratory analysis here on earth. Spectral bands are patterns of different frequencies of light emitted when chemical elements are heated, and are unique to each element due to the configuration of their electron shells. These spectral bands are measured by spectrophotometers and used to determine the chemical composition of unknown substances. The shift in frequency towards the red, or lower frequency, end of the spectrum, of the light from distant stars is due to the Doppler effect. When any wave form, including light or sound, is generated by a moving object, the waves will appear to be accelerated towards an observer towards which the object is moving and therefore arrive more rapidly and produce a higher observed frequency; if the origin of the waves is moving away from an observer, the waves arrive more slowly, spread farther apart, and the observed frequency is lower. The Doppler effect is what causes the noise of engines and sirens to sound higher pitched when they are approaching and lower in pitch when they are moving away.

Astronomers and physicists realized that the Doppler effect was causing a red shift in the spectral lines from distant stars and galaxies, and that the degree of shift varied between sources. When they combined the data from spectral analyses with the distances to various light sources calculated by triangulation, they realized that the farther away light sources were, the greater was the degree of red shift; galaxies furthest away are moving away the most rapidly. Although other astronomers had made similar observations previously, Edwin Hubble is credited with generalizing the observation to more distant stars and galaxies; a 1929 paper by Hubble and colleague Milton Humason led to widespread acceptance of the principle known as Hubble's Law. The red shift of light from distant stars and galaxies provided profound confirmation of Friedmann's theory. (Hubble's groundbreaking observation that there were other galaxies besides our own, made at a time when the Milky Way was assumed to encompass the entire universe, combined with his important observations concerning the red shift of light from distant sources and other contributions to astronomy, caused admirers to name NASA's Hubble Space Telescope after him.)

Singularity

A point from which all the matter of the universe would arise would resemble an enormously massive black hole, a phenomenon which is itself quite outside the realm of normal human experience. When a star becomes so massive that the force of its gravity overpowers the expanding force of its nuclear fusion, it begins to collapse in upon itself. The matter of the star becomes increasingly dense, further increasing the power of its gravitational field, and a vicious cycle results in the astoundingly dense mass of matter at the core of a black hole. At such a point the rules of physics and chemistry break down, because the matter is so dense and the resulting force of gravity is so strong that the forces holding atoms together on the one hand and defining the space occupied by any given atom on the other are both overcome. Matter becomes an amalgam not recognized by conventional chemistry, and not even light escapes the gravitational field of the extremely high mass of the black hole. The breakdown of the normal laws of physics and chemistry that occurs inside a black hole is referred to as a singularity.

The existence of black holes was hypothesized well before one was ever found. Pierre Simon, marquis de Laplace, in the waning years of the eighteenth century, first conceived of a star so massive that even light could not escape its gravity, but an astronomer named Karl Schwarzschild produced the modern concept of black holes. Schwarzschild studied Einstein's theory of general relativity soon after its publication, in his spare time while on assignment as an artillery officer during World War I, and his solution to Einstein's equations described black holes. (Schwarzschild tragically did not survive the war, becoming one of the many victims of disease during the conflict.) It is, of course, of enormous credit to a theory that its predictions are eventually confirmed as fact, especially when its predictions include something as utterly bizarre as the black holes predicted by Einstein and Schwarzschild. The first likely candidate for a black hole to be discovered was Cygnus X-1, a star system in our own galaxy in which a visible star appears to be orbiting around nothing. Because of its otherwise-inexplicable motion, it is thought to be half of a binary star system with two stars orbiting around each other, a fairly common arrangement among stars. Since its partner is invisible, and only a black hole could be invisible and still be massive enough to have such a profound gravitational effect on a body as massive as a star, the visible star is thought to be paired with a black hole. The National Aeronautics and Space Administration (NASA) reports that at least ten binary systems are now known or suspected to be composed of visible stars paired with black holes,[1] and black holes are present at the center of most or all spiral galaxies, including our own Milky Way. The black hole at the center of the Milky Way is estimated to be two and a half million times as massive as the sun, and the black holes at the center of quasars are thought to contain the mass of more than a billion suns.[2]

The primordial singularity, the origin of the Big Bang, was a black hole that included not just the matter of a star or even a galaxy, but the matter and mass of an entire universe. It was not an enormous mass of matter hanging in a vacuum, but an

---

[1] "Black Holes." *NASA's Imagine the Universe.* 6 Sep 2006. Goddard Space Flight Center Laboratory for High Energy Physics. 27 Nov 2007. <http://imagine.gsfc.nasa.gov>.
[2] Greene, Brian. *The Elegant Universe,* 2nd ed. New York: Random House, 2003.

infinitesimally small structure with an unimaginably huge mass, approaching the infinite, and there was nothing – not even empty space – outside of its boundaries. Its density, expressed in units of mass per volume, such as grams per milliliter or kilograms per liter, also approached the infinite. Because of its incredible density it had such an enormous gravitational field that not only did light find it impossible to escape, but space itself was bent and wrapped around it.

According to Albert Einstein's Theory of General Relativity, which though bizarre and difficult to understand has proven reliable in observation after otherwise-fantastic observation, gravity is actually a curve in the fabric of a four-dimensional space/time continuum. The curvature of space around ordinary stars is measurable, as demonstrated by the fact that, during solar eclipses, stars near the edge of the solar disc appear to change their position ever so slightly as the sun grazes the path taken by their light to the earth. Similar measurements involving observed black holes demonstrate that their effect on the curvature of space, as predicted by Einstein's calculations, and the calculations of others based on his theories, and evidenced by their gravitational effect on light, are considerably larger than that of ordinary stars. The reason that black holes are black is because light itself cannot escape their gravitational field if it comes inside a boundary called the event horizon, and its path is bent if it passes outside the event horizon. The event horizon is so called because any events that occur inside its boundaries cannot be observed; space is bent so severely that even light bends endlessly around the singularity at the core of the black hole, and neither light nor any other evidence of what goes on inside a black hole can leave it to be observed or measured.

The black hole at the heart of the Big Bang was so enormously massive and dense that the entire fabric of space/time wrapped itself completely around the singularity. Light did not escape or pass by, not only because there was no external source of light, but also because there was no space in which light could travel. Space itself did not exist outside the singularity, and it was infinitesimally small.

This Big Bang singularity was, then, the most massive possible black hole, containing not only all of the matter of the universe, but also all of the energy and all of the space in the universe compressed into an impossibly small blob. Such a mass was, of course, unstable – it is meaningless to say how long it existed, because time did not exist, either – but its inherent instability caused it to explode, between eleven and sixteen billion years ago,[1] with inconceivable force, force sufficient to disperse all of the matter to all parts of the universe, unfold space from a point into the three dimensions, and start the mysterious process of time. (Time actually depends on the expansion of the universe.

---

[1] Wright, Edward L. "Age of the Universe." *Ned Wright's Cosmology Tutorial.* 2005. UCLA. 27 Dec 2007. <www.astro.ucla.edu/~wright/age.html>.

Calculations by those well-versed in astrophysics and general relativity suggest that, should the universe ever reach a peak expansion and start contracting again under the force of gravity, time would actually run backwards. There is ongoing debate about whether the combined mass and speed of the various components of the universe give it sufficient momentum to forever overcome the effects of gravity and prevent its eventual contraction, but the majority opinion currently is that the universe will not contract and that time will not run backward. Belief does not affect truth, however.)

Expansion

Temperature is a measure of the energy and motion of particles. The mercury column in an old-fashioned thermometer rises with increasing temperature because the mercury atoms become more active, colliding with each other and taking up more space within the glass tube. Because the mass of the Big Bang singularity approached the infinite and its volume was infinitesimal, the number of collisions between particles also approached the infinite, the temperature was high beyond measurement or comprehension, and the energy of the particles caused them to separate into the most basic units of matter.

The explosive force of the Big Bang dispersed matter in the form of quarks and leptons. Quarks are building blocks of matter smaller than atoms, smaller and more basic even than protons and neutrons. Physicists describe quarks as having six different "flavors" (up, down, charm, strange, top, and bottom – one wonders who thinks up these names) distinguished by having electrical charge of positive 2/3 (up, charm, and top quarks) or negative 1/3 (down, strange, and bottom quarks), spin of positive ½ or negative ½ (the spin seems to be an inherent property of the quark rather than a movement that can be changed by an outside force, or perhaps no one has yet built a brake caliper small enough for the job), and the colors red, green, and blue (which have nothing to do with color as we know it, describing the perception of different wave lengths of light, and the explanations of which leave this author floundering so that he appreciates even more the impossibility of the writers of Genesis trying to write down the wonders of modern physics and biological evolution without comprehending them). Quarks like to clump together in groups of three, one of each color, for reasons equally unclear to all but nuclear physicists. Neutrons are composed of two "down" quarks and one "up" quark, giving them neutral charge, and protons are composed of two "up" quarks and one "down" quark, giving them a charge of positive one. The other four types of quarks are very unstable, and known only because they are detected for tiny fractions of seconds in particle accelerators. Since they have never been recognized in nature, they are presumed to have survived for only a short period of time after the Big Bang. Leptons are easier than quarks: Electrons are one of three types of lepton, and the other two kinds are understood by no one outside of university physics departments.

The explosion of the Big Bang was also, of course, an event that released a tremendous amount of energy as it dispersed primordial matter. When the theory of the Big Bang was first presented and was being hotly debated among astronomers and physicists, two physicists at Princeton University, Bob Dicke and Jim Peebles, presented convincing arguments to the scientific community that the explosion, if it occurred, should have left traces of radiation, and that the radiation from the farthest reaches of the universe should be detectable, due to the Doppler effect, as microwaves. At the same time, two researchers named Arno Penzias and Robert Wilson were working on a sensitive microwave detector being brought online by Bell Telephone Laboratories, also in New Jersey. Penzias and Wilson were frustrated by low but consistent readings given by the instrument in every direction in which it was pointed. In one of the marvelous serendipities of science, Penzias and Wilson heard of the plans of Dicke and Peebles to look for the residual microwave radiation from the Big Bang and realized that the readings that they thought were erroneous were actually the very radiation for which Dicke and Peebles were searching, red shifted by the Doppler effect out of the visible spectrum and into the range of microwaves just as Dicke and Peebles predicted. Penzias and Wilson were awarded the Nobel Prize in 1978 for their discovery and its powerful confirmation of the Big Bang theory, while Dicke and Peebles received fame but no cash.

Within about two minutes of the Big Bang, the dispersion of matter allowed the temperature to cool to a level around that of the center of the hottest stars, but still cool enough for protons and neutrons to form from quarks and to combine together to form small nuclei, chiefly hydrogen with one proton with or without a neutron, but also, due to the randomness of collisions, some amount of helium (two protons), and decreasing amounts of lithium (three), and beryllium (four).

As matter dispersed after the Big Bang, there were fewer collisions between particles and the temperature decreased. A few hours after the event, the particles had spread out so much that collisions were few and weak, and the nuclei of atoms ceased to be formed. The temperature dropped further, and the activity and speed of the negatively charged electrons decreased enough that they were captured by the nuclei carrying positive charges, and recognizable atoms formed.

Gravity

For the next million years or so, all that happened was continued expansion and cooling. As a matter of fact, nothing except expansion and cooling would have ever happened if the distribution of matter had been perfectly uniform, but it was not.

The uncertainty principle and the laws of quantum mechanics are a means for mathematicians to handle the fact that not everything is mathematically predictable.

The uncertainty principle states that neither the position nor the velocity of a particle can be measured with absolute precision, because the very act of measurement alters one or the other. Furthermore, the more precisely one attempts to measure the position, the more one alters the velocity, and vice versa. The outgrowth of this realization led to a branch of mathematics and physics called quantum mechanics, in which outcomes of observations are not expressed in absolute values, but in probability curves for a spectrum of outcomes. In the world of quantum mechanics, particles are not distinguished from waves – bodies large and small have a duality of properties explainable by characteristics of both waves and particles.

The laws of quantum mechanics also meant that the distribution of matter after the explosion was not completely uniform. It appears to be uniform on a large scale, but on the smaller scale of quantum mechanics, there were regions of greater and lesser density. As an analogy, think of dropping a blob of paint on a floor. The splatter would appear to be symmetrical at first glance, denser at the center and decreasing in density as the paint radiated out from the center. But if the messy painter gets down on his knees and looks closely, particularly at the perimeter of the splatter, he will notice that the droplets are not exactly the same distance from each other or precisely the same size – the paint distributed itself with a certain degree of randomness.

The same randomness in the early universe meant that the dispersing matter was ever so slightly irregular in density. Where density is increased, the force of gravity is increased, and more matter is attracted towards the center of the increased density. Increased mass leads to a further increase in gravitational force, and the process feeds on itself to ever increase the differences in density that resulted from the inherent randomness of the initial explosion.

After around five billion years, gravity acted to condense regions of matter into the first galaxies and stars. The majority of galaxies are spiral galaxies, rotating majestically around a central bulge. (Other types of galaxies are thought to have been distorted by close encounters with other galaxies, or to result from collisions between galaxies, or to be galaxies in the process of gravitational collapse.) It may seem odd that the majority of galaxies take the form of a rotating disc shape, until one considers that a state of no rotation is only one of an infinite number of possible states (the others being states of rotation at every possible speed). If any rotation at all is present, it is enhanced by gravitational contraction in the same manner that a figure skater speeds up a spin by tucking in his or her arms. (The rotational momentum of a body is the product of its radius and the linear velocity of its outer rim; therefore, when the radius decreases, the velocity of its outer rim must increase proportionally for the momentum to remain the same, which it must do unless acted upon by an outside force.) With rotation established, discs tend to form in the plane of rotation.

Irregularities within the matter of galaxies were gravitational centers in their own turn, and rotated for the same reasons. Eventually the centers of these gravity-powered accumulations of matter became quite massive, and, although the average temperature of the overall universe continued to decrease, in these regions the number of collisions between atoms began to increase and they began to heat up. As their mass increased, so did their temperature and their density, and the number and energy of collisions between particles. Electrons disassociated from their nuclei, and a plasma of hot, active nuclei formed at the center of each gravitational node. The temperature and pressure continued to build as matter accumulated, until nuclei began to crash into each other so hard that they fused. Heavier elements were formed with a tremendous release of energy. The energy released in nuclear fusion balanced the compressive force of gravity, and the stable, glowing mass of a star took shape.

The process was repeated countless times throughout the universe. Astronomers estimate that there are around a hundred billion galaxies within view of modern telescopes, each of them containing an average of around a hundred billion stars. Each star burns with a brilliance that is determined by its temperature, and its temperature is determined in turn by how much matter and mass it accumulates by its gravity.

The mass of a star determines its ultimate fate, as well. Stars are fueled primarily by hydrogen, the simplest and therefore most plentiful of the elements created by the Big Bang. The supply of hydrogen available to the gravity of any one star is enormous, but finite. At the end of the millions of years that it takes a star to run out of hydrogen, nuclear fusion slows dramatically and the balance between the expansive force of the fusion reaction and the contractile force of gravity is lost. As the star contracts, it again heats up and the heavier elements in its outer layers expand once again to form a star type called a Red Giant.

If the star is less massive than about 1.44 times the mass of the Sun (a value called the Chandrasekhar limit, after a student physicist who conceived of the concept and calculated its value in his leisure time aboard a ship traveling from his native India to Cambridge, England to work on his doctorate), the increased heat and pressure at the core of the Red Giant causes helium atoms to fuse into carbon atoms with six protons. The carbon nuclei are too stable for further fusion, so this fusion process, too, is rapidly exhausted and all fusion ceases. The star spins off its outer layers into a nebula and the core continues to shrink and cool, a dying ember with the only radiance coming from the dissipation of previously generated heat. Such a star is referred to as a White

Dwarf, and its dead ember is referred to as a Black Dwarf.[1]

If a star is larger than the Chandrasekhar limit, the pressure causes nuclear fusion to progress even further, fusing even otherwise-stable atoms such as carbon and oxygen to form heavier elements like magnesium, silicon, and iron nuclei with twenty-six protons each. Iron nuclei are too stable for nuclear fusion to progress further even with the gravity and heat of the largest stars. Without the expansive power of nuclear fusion, the star collapses very abruptly, in less than a second, under the enormous force of its gravity, producing a temperature of over a hundred billion degrees. At that point the repulsive force between the positively charged nuclei becomes so strong that the core rebounds with explosive force, sending shock waves through the outer layers of the star, fusing new and even heavier elements, like zinc, gold, platinum, and uranium, and exploding the star into a supernova. The conventional elements in the outer layers are dispersed by the supernova explosion, leaving only a bizarre core of material – neutrons formed by the fusion of electrons and protons. The smaller cores are neutron stars - rapidly spinning, incredibly dense spheres of nuclear material with a halo of electrons moving so rapidly that they approach the speed of light and emit large amounts of x-ray and gamma-ray radiation. The radiation from some of these stars pulse, and the stars are called pulsars. If the parent star was even more massive, though, larger than around two and a half times the mass of the Sun, even neutrons do not survive the collapse and a black hole is born.[2]

Relative Densities of Selected Materials	
Material	Density (g/ml)
Hydrogen	8.99×10^{-5} 0.0000899
Water	1.00
Iron	7.87
Gold	19.28
Uranium	19.05
Sun	1.40
White dwarf	1.91×10^{6} 1,910,000
Neutron star	6.50×10^{16} 65,000,000,000,000,000

The material dispersed by the explosions of Red Giants, nebulae, and supernovae, joins the primordial atoms from the Big Bang in becoming available for new generations of stars, formed by the same progression of irregular density, gravitational attraction, accumulation of mass, and nuclear fusion. At least some stars, and perhaps most, are joined by orbiting bits of matter that remain from the stellar disc which, along with other matter that is captured by the star's gravity or spun out by the star's rotation as it forms, coalesces into spheres because of their own

---

[1] "The Life Cycles of Stars." *NASA's Imagine the Universe.* 21 Nov 2002. Goddard Space Flight Center Laboratory for High Energy Physics. 29 Nov 2007. <http://imagine.gsfc.nasa.gov/docs/teachers/lifecycles/LC_main3.html>.

[2] "The Life Cycles of Stars." *NASA's Imagine the Universe.* 21 Nov 2002. Goddard Space Flight Center Laboratory for High Energy Physics. 29 Nov 2007. <http://imagine.gsfc.nasa.gov/docs/teachers/lifecycles/LC_main3.html>.

gravitational centers, and become planets. These planets can contain elements heavier than helium, including the carbon and oxygen necessary to the organic compounds essential to all known forms of life, only because these elements were formed by previous generations of stars and redistributed by their supernovae.

Among the one hundred billion known galaxies is one called the Milky Way, and among the at least two hundred billion of its stars is a modestly sized one, located on the inner edge of one of its spiraling arms, called the Sun.

The third planet from that nondescript star has some unusual properties – no one is sure how unusual, because the planets of other star systems are too far away to observe in detail with any telescope yet developed, and are detected primarily because of the effects of their gravity. This particular planet contains a rather large amount of iron – over 30% of its total mass and almost 90% of its core – and significant amounts of other heavy elements, suggesting that its material came in large part from a previous star larger than the Chandrasekhar limit and its resulting supernova. It is of just the right mass so that its gravity causes matter to be firmly attracted without being crushed. Its rotational axis is not exactly at right angles to its orbit, being off by a little over 23 degrees, giving it discernible seasons in much of its globe. Perhaps most important of all to its history, it is the right distance from its star and has cooled just enough so that water can form and condense on its surface in large quantities.

The planet, of course, is called Earth, and its properties make it the only place in the universe where life is known to exist.

Author's note: Much of the author's understanding of the Big Bang and immediately subsequent events was either gleaned from or stimulated by Stephen Hawking's books, A Brief History of Time *(New York: Random House, 1988) and* A Briefer History of Time *(with Leonard Mlodinow. New York: Random House, 2005). For those who desire an explanation of modern astrophysical theories offered by a man of the highest level of expertise, yet readable and understandable (with study) by laymen, Hawking's work is certainly unexcelled, and in the author's reading experience unmatched.*

Chapter 6

The Planet of Life

The history of the earth is the history of life. There is no way to say whether planets of other star systems have the conditions necessary for life, because they are too far away to discern their properties by any means yet invented, but no other planet in the solar system has been shown to support life on even a microscopic level (although explorations continue), and, much to the disappointment of science fiction buffs, no verifiable evidence exists for life outside the solar system. On earth, however, the oldest known rocks date back 3.8 billion years; chemical traces of microorganisms are present in rocks of that age, and fossils of primitive bacteria-like organisms have been dated to 3.5 billion years.[1]

The fossil record is a wordless documentation of the ever-increasing complexity and diversification of life on earth. It includes bursts of speciation like the Cambrian explosion, during which the seas were filled with new and sometimes bizarre adaptations, and periods of mass extinctions like that caused by a large meteor which wiped out most species of dinosaurs by striking earth near the Yucatan peninsula. The testimony of paleontology is that the life of earth is in a constant state of flux.

For an unimaginably long time, however, life progressed little in complexity. After the first billion years, the only existent organisms were composed of single cells without nuclei, similar to bacteria. Divisions within cells eventually developed which were dedicated to specific biological functions, and nucleated, or eukaryotic, single-celled organisms, similar to modern algae, began to flourish. Once these single cells grouped

---

[1] Taylor, T. N., and E. L. Taylor. "Cyanobacteria." University of California Museum of Paleontology. 1993. U C Berkeley. 30 Nov 2007. <http://www.ucmp.berkeley.edu/bacteria>.

into colonies, individual cells within the colony could take on special functions such as light detection, and the next small step was a simple multicellular organism, differing from a colony in being composed wholly of cells descended from a single progenitor cell rather than an amalgam of cells arising independently from different sources.

As of the beginning of the Vendian Period around six hundred and thirty million years ago, animal life was still quite simple in form - organisms with just two or three tissue layers and only the most basic abilities to sense and respond to their environment. During the subsequent Cambrian Period, though, rapid diversification was promoted by a combination of favorable ecological factors and the development of a series of genes that organize animal bodies into the axial and segmented body plans that we take for granted in observing the animal kingdom. Animals with exoskeletons developed and filled the seas; crabs, spiders, and insects would eventually descend from these primitive forebears. Other animals would begin to develop characteristics that would lead to vertebrates.

Early precursors of vertebrates did not much resemble fish, amphibians, reptiles, or mammals; they remind an observer more of corrals, being colonies of filter feeders, but they had an internal structure that gave their bodies a bit of rigidity. That early structure, called a stomochord, elongated into a notochord that supported the shape and motion of a free-swimming animal with a recognizable tail and a band of nerve tissue running along its length. True vertebrates were the next step, with a vertebral column of cartilage or bone and a recognizable swelling, a primitive brain, at the front end of the associated nerve tissue.

While the taxonomic classes into which vertebrates are sorted are useful for most modern animals, many of the most interesting fossils defy neat categorization as fish or amphibians, or as reptiles or mammals.

Primitive fish that lived in the shallows developed fleshy fins adapted to pushing themselves along the bottom, and as those fish pursued prey from the edges of the water onto the edges of the shore, those fins became more powerful and developed a structure of bones that are still present in terrestrial animals. The use of the swim bladder in oxygen exchange was advantageous in times of drought and in more prolonged pursuit of prey out of the water, and lungs developed concurrently with limbs. These animals, neither fully fish nor fully adapted to land, are referred to by paleontologists as stem tetrapods – animals with four (tetra) feet (pod) that occupy a stem position from which the major classes of land vertebrates branch.

Alas, legs and lungs, however advanced – and neither were so in stem tetrapods – do not solve every problem in colonizing land. The eggs and newly hatched young of fish and amphibians can only survive in water. Reptiles, birds, and mammals have the ability to reproduce on dry land. In the case of reptiles, birds, and the unusual species of mammals that lay or incubate eggs, a structure of the egg itself called an amnion resists desiccation and promotes the exchange of oxygen and carbon dioxide without the egg being bathed in water. In mammals, the amnion becomes a component of the placenta, through which the mother provides fluids, gas exchange, and nutrients to the developing embryo. Reptiles, birds, and mammals are therefore together termed amniotes after the development of the amnion. Even without observing their reproductive behavior, taxonomists can classify animals as amphibians or reptiles based on other anatomic features that, in living species, are highly correlated with the type of egg (amniotic or anamniotic) they produce. The fossil record offers abundant evidence of animals with anatomic characteristics intermediate between amphibians and reptiles. Fragile eggs are seldom preserved as fossils, but those animals that display transitional anatomy are assumed to be transitional in their mode of reproduction, as well, and are thus termed stem amniotes.

From stem amniotes, two groups of terrestrial tetrapods - sauropsids and synapsids - arose that are differentiated by features of their skull. Gaps in the outer walls of the skull, called fenestrae, lighten the skull of most modern tetrapods and provide the space and attachments for jaw muscles to arrange themselves in ways that generate more power. Sauropsids include animals with no fenestrae, the anapsids, and a descendant group with two fenestrae on each side of the skull, the diapsids. Anapsids include stem amniotes, the earliest reptiles, and a line leading to and including modern turtles and tortoises, while most other living and extinct reptiles are diapsids.

Members of the other group, the synapsids, have a single large fenestra in the region of the temple on each side of the skull. All mammals are synapsids, and all surviving synapsids are mammals, but fossil synapsids are unlike any surviving creature, neither reptile nor mammal. The large sail-backed lizard-like creature called *Dimetrodon*, often included in sets of model dinosaurs, is not a dinosaur at all, but one of a large variety of non-mammal synapsids that proliferated and filled a variety of ecological niches, including herbivores and predators of all sizes. Although not part of popular conceptions about prehistory (and therefore not having a commonly used colloquial name), the synapsids dominated terra firma for a period of sixty or seventy million years.

Two hundred and fifty-one million years ago, the most severe extinction event evidenced by the fossil record ended the dominance of the synapsids. This extinction event opened the land to the diversification of reptiles, and the age of the dinosaurs, which has captured the imagination of so many, dawned around two hundred million years ago.

Dinosaurs were the dominant vertebrates for perhaps a hundred and forty million years, ending with another worldwide extinction event, with strong evidence indicating its cause to be a catastrophic meteor impact between sixty-five and sixty-six million years ago. Although dinosaurs were never again to dominate life on land, it is not entirely true to think dinosaurs to be completely extinct. Birds retain the anatomic features that define dinosaurs and differentiate them from other reptiles, and are in fact descended rather directly from predator dinosaurs with body plans similar to *Tyrannosaurus rex*. Several dinosaur species have been shown to have downy feathers, almost certain to have initially functioned to retain body heat. One of the most famous fossil discoveries of all time, *Archaeopteryx*, is a creature with many of the features of dinosaurs, but with long feathered forelimbs developed as wings. The flight capability of *Archaeopteryx* and other transitional species since discovered is often debated; although early flight was neither graceful nor sustained, the ancestors of modern birds gained ever increasing abilities that began with primitive wings making them more able to lunge at prey, either from the ground or from branches to which they had climbed, and progressed as anatomical changes gradually made them more able. *Archaeopteryx* fossils are around a hundred and fifty million years in age, so the development of birds from dinosaurs predates the extinction event that ended the reign of earth-bound dinosaurs; survivors continued developing and diversifying into the widely varied avian species of modern times.

The near-extinction of dinosaurs opened a wealth of ecological niches to exploitation and removed the most important predators from the land in one stroke. In a comeback worthy of John Elway, the animals that benefitted the most from the extinction of the dinosaur were the once-vanquished synapsids.

In the millions of years that the dinosaurs developed the traits and diversity that made them enormously successful, the surviving remnants of the synpasids also progressed. They developed means of maintaining a stable body temperature, including both physiologic mechanisms and haired skin, which enabled them to survive in a wide variety of climates, alongside both anatomical and behavioral characteristics that better provided for their young and thus enhanced their survival. These more developed synapsids, of course, were mammals, and although they were at the dawn of the new age neither numerous nor diverse, and were not themselves untouched by the extinction event that decimated the dinosaurs, they were poised to become the next dominant group of land animals.

The mammals that coexisted with the dinosaurs and survived the dinosaurs' extinction were almost exclusively small animals resembling rodents. From that rather modest base, they diversified into the myriad of roles currently observed – grazers and browsers large and small, predators equally disparate in size, scavengers, and even branches of the family that took to the air and returned to the seas. The fossil record of mammalian development is extensive, as might be intuitively expected due to their status as the most recently developed class; large mammals have left more sturdy remnants than their smaller cousins, whose tinier and more fragile bones are more easily chewed, crushed, and otherwise rendered unrecognizable. Thus, the developmental history of bats is somewhat irregularly known, while the progression from wading animals to fully aquatic whales and dolphins is more thoroughly recorded in the fossil record. The family trees of some animals, such as elephants, are extensively known. The fossil record regarding the development of horses is complete enough in its continuity that some individual specimens with intermediate characteristics are difficult to classify to species and genus.

The descent of humans from ape-like ancestors over the past six million years has left a similarly continuous record of increasing brain size, skull and facial development, and progression towards an upright posture, with, again, such a high degree of continuity that the exact classifications of some intermediate specimens are problematic. Indeed, the increase in brain size and the movement of the brain case from behind the face to above it, producing a taller and more prominent forehead - the most recognizable feature differentiating human skulls from those of apes – has continued to become more pronounced since the emergence of the first recognizable specimens of *Homo sapiens* around a hundred and thirty thousand years ago.

It is a misconception to think of a linear progression by which mammals proceeded from reptiles, which proceeded from amphibians, which proceeded from fish. It is far more accurate to conceive of the tree of life as a branching structure: modern fish and land animals having common ancestors, and fish developing more refined features adapted to their aquatic existence while tetrapods colonized the land; reptiles and amphibians sharing common ancestors, from which amphibians and reptiles developed to most effectively fill their niches; reptiles and mammals diverging, each in their own direction, from common ancestors with intermediate features. In the same way, the derivation of species whose ancestry is well documented, such as horses, elephants, and humans, are themselves not simple linear progressions, but complex family trees with far more extinctions and developmental dead-ends than surviving species.

What remains of this chapter is a more detailed account – though still but a summary of the vast quantity of information available – of the development of life on earth, with examples of species and genera that demonstrate the development of important anatomic characteristics. Readers not versed in the biological sciences may find it difficult. The intention is to provide strong evidence for the contention that the history of life is a history of slow but relentless change and adaptation, and that a wealth of intermediate functional forms are known for all or most of the major anatomic developments. The reader who can stipulate to that contention may choose to go on to the next chapter and refer back as necessary to the material presented, but the reader who remains skeptical should take the pains to carefully examine and consider the overwhelming evidence of gradual progression of features that is present in the fossil record.

The beginning of life

The earth, like most heavenly bodies, started out extremely hot, and as it cooled an outer crust gradually formed - a crust that is yet incompletely formed and mobile as is evidenced by continued lava flows, volcanic eruptions, and earthquakes in various parts of the world. The crust is composed of several plates of various sizes that float somewhat freely on a viscous fluid core. The drift of these plates is very slow but measurable (the Mid-Atlantic Ridge moves the North American plate away from the Eurasian plate by about 2.5 cm per year, for example[1]), and the overwhelming majority of the planet's volcanic and seismic activity occurs at places where the plates are either separating or crashing into each other.

The temperature of the earth in its early history made any accumulation of liquid water impossible. The planet was in a chaotic portion of the galaxy with a star and its planets accruing matter from at least one previous supernova, and probably from a variety of such sources, and so it was bombarded with space debris of various sizes, some substantial. Large impacts struck with explosive force, raising temperatures, projecting debris, and disrupting the formative elements of the atmosphere.

The atmosphere of the primordial earth was vastly different from that of today. Hydrogen sulfide gas, methane, ammonia, carbon dioxide and other gasses leached from the cooling rocks to form most of the atmosphere. Oxygen was present only in minute amounts – the nearly twenty percent oxygen composition of the atmosphere of modern earth would be produced primarily by photosynthesis.

In this seemingly inhospitable environment of a hot, chaotic young planet with a poisonous atmosphere, life began. Its origins are obscure, but probably are rooted in a self-replicating macromolecule, possibly composed largely of amino acids like modern proteins. Experiments at the University of Chicago in 1953 by Stanley Miller and Harold Urey established that complex organic molecules including amino acids would be produced in conditions common to the primitive earth. In 1969, the Murchison meteorite impacted earth, and was found to contain amino acids in similar proportions to those of the Miller-Urey experiment, as well as components of DNA and RNA, all of non-biological origin.[2] In the years since Miller and Urey published their work,

---

[1] Kious, W. Jacquelyne, and Robert L. Tilling. *This Dynamic Earth: The Story of Plate Tectonics.* "Understanding Plate Motions." 1993. United States Geological Survey. 29 Nov 2007. <http://pubs.usgs.gov/gip/dynamic/understanding.html#anchor6715825>.

[2] "Organics in Murchison Meteor." Brigham Young University. 18 Dec 2007. <http://www.physics.byu.edu/faculty/allred/343R/Organics%20in%20Murchison%20Meteor.htm>.

astronomers have found spectrographic evidence for over a hundred and thirty organic molecules in space, with perhaps the largest such discovery being that of a cloud of methyl alcohol 463 billion kilometers (288 billion miles) long, by Lisa Harvey-Smith and colleagues at the Jodrell Bank Observatory in Great Britain. The interstellar alcohol cloud is located in a portion of the Milky Way that is actively forming stars, and alcohols have also been detected in the developing planetary discs of nascent stars.[1] Since organic molecules are far more common than thought in the 1950s, it is probable that Miller and Urey significantly underestimated the availability of organic molecules in the primordial earth, and the formation of macromolecules is even more probable.

In an environment rich in the basic building blocks of life, it is justifiable to consider that an amalgam of the components of a living cell may have been rare, but what is rare is not necessarily impossible. As those complex molecules came together in the rich mélange of the primordial earth, their associations into simple systems that assimilated nutrients and divided into daughter cells began the first competition for resources, and initiated the process of survival and reproduction of the most able that defines life itself. Among the billions of billions of interactions between molecules, those components, relatively few in the most basic cells, need only have encountered each other a few times, or perhaps only once, as long as that most basic unit could reproduce.

The origin or origins of life – that first combination of macromolecules capable of replication – has left no fossil record as yet discovered, and the discovery of so small a relic in all the matter of the earth is unlikely. The oldest known fossils are of very simple photosynthetic bacteria, the cyanobacteria. The cyanobacteria that became fossilized three and a half billion years ago were primitive, with the simplest of membranes and a scant few functioning enzymatic proteins inside, but they worked, because they could grow and reproduce themselves, and they had no competition.[2]

The archaeans developed at the same time or somewhat previously to the cyanobacteria; chemical traces unique to archaeans have been found in rocks dating to 3.8 billion years, indicating that they probably existed as soon as the earliest crust formed. Archaeans were previously considered to be bacteria but are now assigned to a different domain, a division of taxonomy larger than the kingdom. Although they appear similar to bacteria, with a simple structure lacking organelles or other divisions, their cell membranes use isoprenes where other cells have lipids, they possess unique biochemical systems, and they differ substantially in their DNA sequences from other

---

[1] "Alcohol cloud spotted in deep space." ABC News Online. 4 Apr 2006. Accessed 29 Jan 2008 at <http://www.abc.net.au/news/newsitems/200604/s1607840.htm>.

[2] Taylor, T. N., and E. L. Taylor. "Cyanobacteria." University of California Museum of Paleontology. 1993. U C Berkeley. 30 Nov 2007. <http://www.ucmp.berkeley.edu/bacteria>.

microbes. Archaeans thrive in otherwise hostile environments of high heat, acidity, salinity, and destructive chemicals like ammonia and methane. They survive today in unfriendly settings like geysers and undersea vents and in hypersaline waters, as well as in the open sea.[1] Being so suited to hostile environments, they were probably more plentiful in the early history of the earth, before being supplanted by other forms as the planet became more hospitable to the forms of life that we today consider more conventional.

The first nucleated cells

The archaeans and cyanobacteria were the only inhabitants of the earth for over a billion years, during the Archean Eon which ended two and a half billion years ago.[2] During the subsequent Proterozoic Eon, which lasted nearly two billion years more, the metabolic activity of plentiful cyanobacteria enriched the oxygen content of the atmosphere and eukaryotic cells (nucleated cells with internal structures) developed.[3] The first steps toward complex cell structures were probably simple invaginations of the cell membrane that ingested and stored available nutrients. The membrane surfaces then became available as hosts for more complex functions. Genetic material was segregated into nuclei and separated by its own membrane. Cyanobacteria were ingested and became chloroplasts in a symbiotic relationship that would be key to establishing the plant kingdom.[4] Engulfed proteobacterial cells entered into a similarly symbiotic relationship and specialized in the use of oxygen to produce energy, using the Kreb's cycle painfully memorized by generations of biochemistry students. They became mitochondria, and like chloroplasts they have their own DNA and reproduce independently of the host cells.

The first eukaryotes were simple algae, existing first in single cells and then in colonies. Similar algae still exist as some of the most prolific kinds of seaweed and kelp. Some algae developed flagellae (simple whip-like cell appendages used for locomotion). While many species of flagellated algae live as single cells, species of the modern genera *Eudorina* form spherical clumps of up to thirty-two cells, and those of the *Gonium* genus form disc-shaped colonies of similar size. Members of the genus *Pandorina* form spherical colonies with hollow centers and, with each cell of the colony having

---

[1] Waggoner, Ben. "Archaea." University of California Museum of Paleontology, 11-25-1994. U C Berkeley. 18 Dec 2007. <http://www.ucmp.berkeley.edu/archaea/archaea.html>.

[2] This and all names and dates related to the ages of the earth are consistent with guidelines published by the International Commission on Stratigraphy. 1 Dec 2007. <http://www.stratigraphy.org>.

[3] Taylor, T. N., and E. L. Taylor. "Cyanobacteria." University of California Museum of Paleontology. 1993. U C Berkeley. 30 Nov 2007. <http://www.ucmp.berkeley.edu/bacteria>.

[4] Taylor, T. N., and E. L. Taylor. "Cyanobacteria." University of California Museum of Paleontology. 1993. U C Berkeley. 18 Dec 2007. <http://www.ucmp.berkeley.edu/bacteria>.

individual means of detecting light, move toward light in a somewhat coordinated manner, such motion having its obvious benefits to the photosynthetic colony.

Volvox colonies are larger algae colonies and, like *Pandorina*, form a hollow sphere, but *Volvox* is remarkable in several ways. Some individual cells are specifically light sensitive, and clump together into primitive eye spots that coordinate the movement of the colony towards light. Asexual reproduction is accomplished through daughter colonies that bud off into the interior of the sphere of the mother colony before being extruded to independent life. Other cells within the colony form primitive reproductive cells that recombine their own genetic material with that from other colonies to provide the advantages of sexual reproduction.[1] These traits constitute distinct specialization of individuals within the algae colony in an obvious transition towards multicellular organisms with discrete tissues.

The first animal life

By the last phase of the Proterozoic Eon (the Edicarian Period, 630 to 542 million years ago, sometimes called the Vendian Period), simple animals with two and three layers of tissue developed. The most primitive animals known today are placozoans (phylum *Placozoa*, with just one species, *Trichoplax adhaerens*, as its sole surviving representative), little-known animals that are composed of just four cell types[2] and live like multi-cellular amoebas, moving by cellular streaming and digesting the cellular contents of algae while leaving behind the cellulose shell.[3] The organism reproduces by fissure and budding, and although it is quite fragile and easily broken up by handling, the fragments frequently regenerate into complete animals.[4] Although their simple soft bodies understandably have left no fossils yet found, the simplicity of the placozoans argue for their status as one of the earliest animal forms.

---

[1] Van Egmond, Wim. "Volvox, One of the Seven Wonders of the Micro World." 2003. Microscopy U K. 18 Dec 2007. <http://www.microscopy-uk.org.uk/mag/indexmag.html?http://www.microscopy-uk.org.uk/mag/artdec03/volvox.html>.

[2] Collins, Allen G. "Introduction of Placazoa." University of California Museum of Paleontology. June 2000. U C Berkeley. 29 Dec 2007. <http://www.ucmp.berkeley.edu/phyla/placozoa/placozoa.html>.

[3] Howey, Richard L. "A Weird Wee Beastie: *Trichoplax adhaerens.*" 1998. Microscopy-UK. 28 Dec 2007. < http://www.microscopy-uk.org.uk/mag/indexmag.html?http://www.microscopy-uk.org.uk/mag/artoct98/tricho.html>.

[4] Howey, Richard L. "A Weird Wee Beastie: *Trichoplax adhaerens.*" 1998. Microscopy-UK. 28 Dec 2007. < http://www.microscopy-uk.org.uk/mag/indexmag.html?http://www.microscopy-uk.org.uk/mag/artoct98/tricho.html>.

Other Vendian fauna were for the most part small soft-bodied animals, and left scant but intriguing fossil records. Simple worm-like creatures left tracks in mud that became sedimentary rock. Some fossils are similar to sponges (phylum *Porifera*). Others resemble anemones, jellyfish, and corals (*Cnidaria*), the last of which secrete shells that make up reefs of various sizes and are easily fossilized. Many pre-Cambrian fossils are believed to be representatives of extinct phyla.[1] Although animals in the sense that they consume and digest nutrients as opposed to performing photosynthesis, all were simple structures with minimal sensory apparatus and no real cognitive abilities.

Reference Chart

Eons, Eras, Periods, and Epochs

of Earth History

Eon	Era	Period	Epoch	Starting date (millions of years ago)
Phanerozoic	Cenozoic	Quarternary	Holocene	0.0118
			Pleistocene	1.806
		Neogene	Pliocene	5.332
			Miocene	23.03
		Paleogene	Oligocene	33.9
			Eocene	55.8
			Paleocene	66.5
	Mesozoic	Cretaceous		145.4
		Jurassic		199.6
		Triassic		251.0
	Paleozoic	Permian		299.0
		Carboniferous		359.2
		Devonian		416.0
		Silurian		443.7
		Ordovician		488.3
		Cambrian		542.0
Proterozoic				2500
Archean				3800

[1] Collins, Allen G. "Life of the Vendian." University of California Museum of Paleontology. 9 June 1994. U C Berkeley. 29 Dec 2007. <http://www.ucmp.berkeley.edu/vendian/vendianlife.html>.

The Cambrian explosion

The Paleozoic Era opened with the Cambrian Period, 542 million to 488 million years ago, well known for its rapid diversification of life. Over eighty-five percent of the history of life was pre-Cambrian, but during the Cambrian Period speciation occurred so rapidly that the period is often referred to as the Cambrian explosion. (The period of diversification took place over a period of thirty to forty million years, however, a rather leisurely pace for an "explosion.") The causes of the relatively rapid period of diversification were multiple. The atmospheric oxygen content continued to rise due to the metabolism of a large biomass of cyanobacteria. A mass extinction at the end of the Proterozoic Eon opened up a multitude of ecological niches to be exploited. The homeobox genes, a gene sequence governing embryonic development common to animals higher than *Cnidaria*, developed early in the Cambrian Period. The combined result of these developments was that animal life was free to develop in a profusion of unprecedented ways, and almost all surviving animal phyla, and several more extinct ones, made their first appearance before the end of the Cambrian Period.[1]

Brachiopods are filter-feeding animals similar to clams, but with even simpler anatomy, that developed in the Cambrian Period. The earliest had unhinged shells, but forms that developed in the Ordovician Period (488-444 million years past) developed hinged shells and are easy to mistake for mollusks.

The first deuterostomes developed during the Cambrian Period. Deuterostomes are the superphylum that includes chordates and, within the chordates, vertebrates. The first deuterostomes, however, did not resemble vertebrates – they were the echinoderms, a group that in the present day includes starfish, brittle stars, sea urchins, sand dollars, and sea cucumbers. Fossil echinoderms include groups with no discernable symmetry, some sessile and others mobile by simple contraction and elongation of their bodies. The phylum is composed of mostly bottom-dwelling sea animals (it is the largest phylum, in fact, not to include fresh-water or terrestrial species) and characterized by calcium carbonate plates in the skin that together make up a primitive exoskeleton. The exoskeleton ranges from independent plates resulting in complete flexibility in sea cucumbers, through those that touch but move independently, maintaining shape but allowing the movement of starfish, to interlocking plates making up the rigid shell of sand dollars.[2]

---

[1] "Burgess Shale Fossil Specimens." Smithsonian National Museum of Natural History. 2007. SNMNH. 15 Mar 2008. <http://paleobiology.si.edu/burgess/burgessSpecimens.html>.

[2] Waggoner, Ben. "Introduction to the Echinodermata." University of California Museum of Paleontology. 16 Jan 1995. U C Berkeley. 30 Dec 2007. <http://www.ucmp.berkeley.edu/echinodermata/echinodermata.html>.

The Cambrian Period also saw the development of the first arthropods, the most immediately successful of which were the trilobites. Nine orders of trilobites have been recognized with over fifteen thousand species, making them the most diverse group of extinct animals known. Trilobites were oval shaped animals, shaped much like horseshoe crabs, but with jointed bodies and crescent-shaped heads with or without compound eyes. With time, the exoskeleton became sufficiently flexible that fossils of later species have been found rolled into a ball in an apparent defensive posture. Although trilobites became extinct around 245 million years ago, they were so plentiful during their heyday, and their exoskeleton fossilized so readily, that fossil trilobites are sold as trinkets in souvenir stores and on e-Bay. There is evidence, in the Burgess shale (of the British Columbia Rocky Mountains) and elsewhere, that trilobites were preceded by soft-bodied ancestors, which for obvious reasons left fewer and less distinct fossils.[1, 2]

A fossil trilobite, *Phacops rana*, from the Wannakah Shale in Hamburg, New York, dating from the middle Devonian, approximately 400 million years ago. Trilobites were common marine animals for 300 million years, from the early Cambrian until the late Permian. Trilobites left characteristic paired tracks which were sometimes preserved, as shown below in a specimen from the middle Silurian Rochester Shale, Middleport, New York.

The Ordovician Period followed the Cambrian, still encompassed by the Paleozoic Era, from 488 to 444 million years ago. Trilobites became plentiful and the early echinoderms developed into forms more similar to those of the current era. Graptolites, the common fossil resembling a branching or coiled saw blade, developed, as did

[1] Gon, Sam III. "A Guide to the Orders of Trilobites." 22 Dec 2007. Sam Gon III. 30 Dec 2007. <http://www.trilobites>.

[2] Waggoner, Ben. "Introduction to the Trilobita." University of California Museum of Paleontology. 28 Feb 1995. U C Berkeley. 30 Dec 2007. <http://www.ucmp.berkeley.edu/arthropoda/trilobita/trilobita.html>.

cephalochordates similar to amphioxus (or lancelets), and the agnathostomes, or jawless fish; each has features important to the further development of animal life. The Ordovician also saw the development of the first true plants; earlier photosynthetic organisms, although sometimes impressive in size, were colonial algae, lacking the more complex structures of true plants.

The closest surviving relatives of graptolites are acorn worms; both are grouped together as hemichordates. Hemichordates have from one to several pairs of branchial openings, or primordial gill slits, as well as a dorsal nerve chord and a short supporting structure called a stomochord.[1] Branchial slits, a dorsal nerve chord, and a supporting structure for the nerve chord are all characteristics of vertebrates.

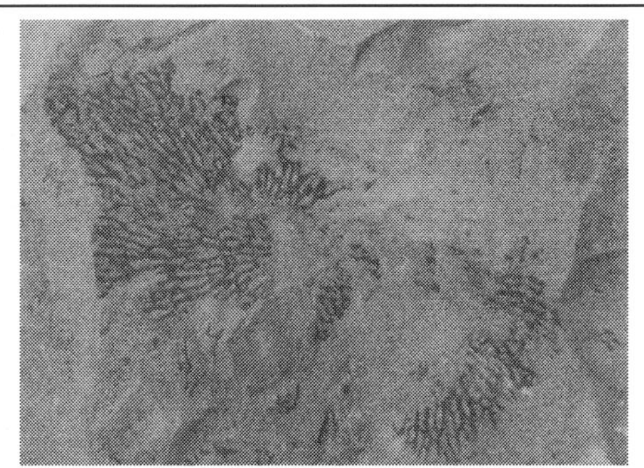

A fossil graptolite, *Desmograptus micronematodes*, from the Silurian Period, recovered from the Rochester Shale, Middleport New York. Graptolites were branched colonies of sessile filter feeders which had many of the important features of later vertebrates.

In the cephalochordates the abbreviated stomochord is replaced by a notochord that runs the entire length of the animal and supports the hollow dorsal nerve chord with the segmentally branching nerves of a chordate. A postanal tail, another feature of vertebrates, is present, but the sense organs are poorly developed and the brain is minimal.[2] Cephalochordates are sometimes referred to as Acraniata.[3] Both words describe the same trait in similar ways: Acraniata means no cranium, or brain; cephalochordata means that the brain is indistinguishable from the spinal chord. Recent studies have demonstrated that, although the brain of amphioxus is extremely simple anatomically, the expression of developmental genes correspond to the three primary regions of vertebrate brains.[4] Although modern cephalochordate lancelets are

---

[1] Waggoner, Ben. "Introduction to the Hemichordata." University of California Museum of Paleontology. 12 Jan 1997. U C Berkeley. 8 Mar 2007. <http://www.ucmp.berkeley.edu/people/bmw/bmw.html>.

[2] Waggoner, Ben. "Introduction to the Cephalochordata." University of California Museum of Paleontology. 7 Feb 1996. U C Berkeley. 8 Mar 2007. <http://www.ucmp.berkeley.edu/chordata/cephalo.html>.

[3] Benton, Michael J. *Vertebrate Palaeontology,* 3rd edition. Malden, MA: Blackwell, 2005. Pg 4.

[4] Benton, Michael J. *Vertebrate Palaeontology,* 3rd edition. Malden, MA: Blackwell, 2005. Pg 13-14.

sessile, fossil forms are believed to have been free-swimming like modern juveniles.[1]

The first vertebrates

Jawless fish, like the modern hagfish, are more advanced than cephalochordates by a small step. Hagfish have a cartilaginous spine and skull, containing a small brain. A nostril with a sensory organ to detect scents, leading into the pharynx, is also present in hagfish.[2] Respiration occurrs by passing water in through the nostril, through the pharynx, and out through the gill slits, now reinforced with cartilage. With the development of a spine continuing to a tail, a dorsal nerve chord with a brain at its front end, and bronchial pouches and slits, the basic body plan from which vertebrates could diversify was in place.

Jawless fish (or agnatha) from the Chengjiang site in southwest China are the earliest and most primitive known chordate. The most abundant of these fish, known collectively as Mylookunmingiida, is *Haikouichthys*, represented by over five hundred specimens. The species is only around twenty-five millimeters in length, streamlined and slender, with a poorly defined head and a small cartilaginous brain case. Gill arches extend for about one-third of its body length, and muscle segmentation is clear. The notochord is clearly present, and some specimens show a series of widely spaced rectangular elements along the notochord, believed to be cartilaginous vertebrae.[3]

Jawless fish survive in the present day as lampreys and hagfish. Lampreys live as parasites on bony fish, while hagfish, closer to basal vertebrates, feed on invertebrates and dead organic matter in mud. Both have simple relatively straight digestive tracts, paired pharyngeal gill slits, and a small brain enclosed by a cartilaginous skull. The braincase of lampreys is more complete than that of hagfish, and they have cartilaginous vertebrae that hagfish lack. (It is the lack of vertebrae, along with other primitive features, that cause paleontologists to place hagfish closer to the basal chordates.)[4, 5, 6] Hagfish have changed little from their earliest appearance in the fossils

---

[1] "*Pikaia gracilens* (a primitive chordate)." Smithsonian National Museum of Natural History. 2007. SNMNH. 15 Mar 2008. <http://paleobiology.si.edu/burgess/pikaia.html>.

[2] Speer, Brian R. "Introduction to the Myxini." University of California Museum of Paleontology. . 12 Jun 1997. U C Berkeley. 9 Mar 2007. <http://www.ucmp.berkeley.edu/verte brates>.

[3] Benton, Michael J. *Vertebrate Palaeontology.* 3rd edition. Malden, MA: Blackwell, 2005. Pg 39.

[4] Speer, Brian R. "Introduction to the Myxini." University of California Museum of Paleontology. 12 Jun 2007. U C Berkeley. 5 Apr 2008. <http://www.ucmp.berkeley.edu/vertebrates>.

[5] Waggoner, Ben. "Introduction to the Petromyzontiformes." University of California Museum of Paleontology. 13 May 1997. U C Berkeley. 5 Apr 2008. <http://www.ucmp.berkeley.edu/vertebrates>.

[6] Benton, Michael J. *Vertebrate Palaeontology,* 3rd edition. Malden, MA: Blackwell, 2005. Pg 44-45.

record some 300 million years ago.[1]

The teeth of another group of agnatha, the conodonts, were known since 1856, but only associated with a complete fossil fish in 1983. The conodonts have features more advanced than hagfish and lampreys[2], but their place in the developmental processes of fish is not clear; they could be a group very successful in their day but without surviving descendants. A variety of other jawless fish, many armored and some not, some with gill coverings and most with multiple gill openings, many with more developed spines, brains, and skulls than the earlier agnatha, appear to be just such developmental dead ends.

Jaws and roots (not the movies)

The Ordovician Period ended with a mass extinction, probably related to a massive increase in glaciers and a resulting drop in sea levels.[3] The Silurian Period, at only 28 million years rather brief as geologic ages go, followed; fossil evidence from the Silurian demonstrates the earliest clear colonization of land by both plants and animals, and the first well documented jawed fish.

The jaws of fish, retained by subsequent vertebrates, have long been thought to be modified gill arches, based on embryology. The knowledge that one of the earliest and most primitive sharks that is fully described, *Cladoselache*, has incomplete and weak joints between mandible and skull lends further credence to the development of jaws from gill arches. Recent studies have demonstrated the development of jaws to be more complex than simple migration of the structures, but the tissues of the anterior gill arches contain segments that become elements of the upper and lower jaws.[4] Shigeru Kuratani and his colleagues at the Center for Developmental Biology in Kobe, Japan, have in recent years made impressive strides towards understanding the biochemical basis, rooted in modified expression of Hox genes, for the transformation of the tissues of the first pharyngeal arches to jaws.[5]

The development of jaws was a profound step in the development of vertebrates. Fish

---

[1] Speer, Brian R. "Introduction to the Myxini." University of California Museum of Paleontology. 12 Jun 2007. U C Berkeley. 5 Apr 2008. <http://www.ucmp.berkeley.edu/vertebrates>.

[2] Benton, Michael J. *Vertebrate Palaeontology.* 3rd edition. Malden, MA: Blackwell, 2005. Pg 45-47.

[3] Speer, Brian R. "The Ordovician." University of California Museum of Paleontology. 11 May 1998. U C Berkeley. 10 Mar 2007. <http://www.ucmp.berkeley.edu/ordovician/ordovician.html>.

[4] Benton, Michael J. *Vertebrate Palaeontology.* 3rd ed. Malden, MA: Blackwell, 2005. Pg 51-53.

[5] Shigeru Kuratani. "Evolution of the vertebrate jaw: comparative embryology and molecular developmental biology reveal the factors behind evolutionary novelty." Journal of Anatomy (2004) 205, pg 335-347.

without jaws could only feed by sucking up and digesting small bits of organic matter. Fish with jaws became predators. With predation came increased mobility, increased sensory abilities in order to locate prey, and increased brain function needed for learning where to find prey and tactics of predation such as ambush, interception, and pursuit.

Fossils of terrestrial centipedes and arachnids have been found in sediments of the Silurian period.[1] Arachnids, with their jointed exoskeletons, are close cousins of the trilobites that were still plentiful in aquatic environments. Sea scorpions were plentiful and well equipped to colonize tidal flats and beaches. Fresh water arthropods in swamps and along the shores of ponds and lakes were tested by changing water levels and pursued prey into the air. At about the same time, primitive plants gained a foothold on dry land. It is easy to imagine a similar process: aquatic arthropods, living in shallow water, made excursions onto the shore of increasing duration, just as crabs are commonly seen to do, and marine plants, living in shallow water, became adapted first to minimal exposure by receding tides and water tables, and by adapting became progressively more capable of terrestrial life.

The most primitive land plant of which the fossil record bears complete witness is *Cooksonia*. *Cooksonia* was a small and simple plant - most specimens are no larger than two or three centimeters in size, and consist of a scant few branches tipped with spore-bearing sporangia – but it had a vascular structure and the characteristics necessary to support its own weight without the buoyancy of water. The contemporaneous lives of sea scorpions and *Cooksonia* are dramatized by the existence of at least one fossil of *Cooksonia* growing entwined with a molted exoskeleton of a sea scorpion.[2] Other experiments in terrestrial growth by plants were less successful, and died out: *Nematothallus* consisted of a mat of fine filaments, *Parka* is known only as a patch of sporangia, and *Pachytheca* were small globes of photosynthetic cells.

The Devonian Period, from 416 to 359 million years ago, is often referred to as "the age of fishes." The hugely successful trilobites were still abundant, alongside other arthropods, brachiopods, corals, and ammonites, but fish diversified and began to dominate the seas due to the advantages of vertebrate anatomy. A brain and spinal chord meant that fish could sense, evaluate, and respond to their environment like no other animal then in existence. A spine, with its segmental muscles and nerves, and its extension into the new invention of a tail, made them mobile to an unprecedented degree. Gill arches and an efficient circulatory system allowed many species of fish to

---

[1] Speer, Brian R., et al. "Life of the Silurian." University of California Museum of Paleontology. 5-11-1998. U C Berkeley. 3-10-2007. <http://www.ucmp.berkeley.edu/silurian/silulife.html>.

[2] Virtual Fossil Museum. "Primitive Silurian Plant Cooksonia Growing on Eurypterus Exoskeleton." Accessed 3-11-2008. <www.fossilmuseum.net/plantfossils/Buthotrephus/PS2996_Buthotrephus.htm>.

reach sizes that exceeded the limits of the exoskeleton and the more primitive respiration and circulation of arthropods.

Although the species of fish familiar to our aquariums and our dinner plates took some time to develop, the advantages of the vertebrate body plan were immediately apparent in the success of fish. Among the earliest jawed fish were the placoderms – fish with plates of bony armor covering their heads and necks. The earliest specimens date from the Silurian, but they became plentiful and diverse during the Devonian, and died out rather abruptly near the end of the Devonian for reasons not apparent.[1] Placoderms were the first vertebrates with paired pelvic fins, and some species appear from the fossil record to have developed swim bladders or lungs. Their appearance varied from those looking like ugly but ordinary fish with helmets, to others with thick blunt bodies, shapes like skates and rays, and strange shapes with pointed snouts or wing-like extensions of their head shields.[2]

Chondrichthyes – fish with skeletons made completely of cartilage, like sharks and rays – became numerous during the Devonian; the first complete specimens date from the middle Devonian. Teeth and scales have been found dating as far back as 450 million years, near the end of the Ordovician Period. The chondrichthyes of the Devonian, such as the *Cladoselache* discussed above in relation to the development of jaw structures, developed into sharks and rays with modern features in the Jurassic Period, at the time when dinosaurs dominated terra firma.[3]

The ray-finned fish, actinopterygians, also made their first appearance in the Devonian, and by the Cenozoic were the dominant group among aquatic organisms; about half of surviving vertebrate species are actinopterygians.[4] Within the actinopterygians are the teleosts, the most familiar fish with gill covers, scales, and symmetrical tails. A crucial feature common to actinopterygians and their cousins the lobe-finned fish, but lacking in chondrichthyes, is the swim bladder. The swim bladder is an air-filled sac that develops embryologically as an out pouching of the upper digestive tract, and in fish helps control buoyancy. In some actinopterygians the opening closes off during the development of the embryo, and a system for secreting and absorbing gas into the

---

[1] Waggoner, Ben. "Introduction to the Placodermi." University of California Museum of Paleontology. 7-22-2000. U C Berkeley. 3-15-2008. <http://www.ucmp.berkeley.edu/vertebrates>.

[2] Benton, Michael J. *Vertebrate Palaeontology*. Malden MA: Blackwell, 2005. Pg 55-58.

[3] Wagonner, Ben. "Introduction to the Chondrichthyes." University of California Museum of Paleontology. 7-23-95. U C Berkeley. 3-15-2009. <http://www.ucmp.berkeley.edu/vertebrates>.

[4] Waggoner, Ben. "Introduction to the Actinopterygii." University of California Museum of Paleontology. 7-17-1995. U C Berkeley. 3-15-2008. <http://www.ucmp.berkeley.edu/vertebrates>.

swim bladder develops; in others, the opening to the pharyngeal region remains patent.[1]

Land, ho!

Ironically, the group of fish that is least familiar and has the fewest surviving representatives is also the most important to the further development of animal life. The sarcopterygians, or lobe-finned fish, are represented by two known species of coelacanths and three genera of lungfish. Although the exact relationships are still a subject of active discussion among paleontologists, the thick fleshy fins of the sarcopterygian fish are demonstrated by the fossil record to have developed into the limbs of terrestrial tetrapods.

The coelacanths were known from the fossil record, but believed extinct until one was caught off the coast of Africa in 1938. A population of coelacanths was subsequently discovered in the area of the Comoran islands between the east coast of Africa and the northern end of Madagascar, and more recently in the waters of Indonesia.[2, 3] The coelacanths retain a primitive notochord that is clearly visible in the tail of intact fish. The tail itself consists of a central extension of the spine with thin fin-like fans above and below, thought to be a predecessor to the asymmetrically forked tail of chondrichthyes and the symmetrical tail of most actinopterygians.[4] The fleshy fins attach to the pectoral girdle by a single bone, the humerus, and to the pelvic girdle by a single femur, and move in an alternating fashion like tetrapods.[5, 6, 7]

As intriguing as are the features of coelacanths, they are currently thought to be "a side branch in the basal portion of the vertebrate lineage, closely related to but distinct from

---

[1] Waggoner, Ben. "Actinopterygii: More on Morphology." University of California Museum of Paleontology. 7-17-1995. U C Berkeley. 3-15-2008. <http://www.ucmp.berkeley.edu/vertebrates>.

[2] "Sulawesi Coelacanth." University of California Museum of Paleontology. 11-12-1999. U C Berkeley. 3-15-2008. <http://www.ucmp.berkeley.edu/vertebrates>.

[3] Jewitt, Susan L. "The Coelacanth: More Than Living Fossil." Smithsonian National Museum of Natural History. May 2003. SNMNH. 15 Mar 2008. <http://www.mnh.si.edu/highlight/coelacanth/>.

[4] Jewitt, Susan L. "The Coelacanth: More Than Living Fossil." Smithsonian National Museum of Natural History. May 2003. SNMNH. 15 Mar 2008. <http://www.mnh.si.edu/highlight/coelacanth/>.

[5] Murphy, Dennis C. "More About Lobe-Fins: Sarcopterygii." Devonian Times. 9 July 2005. Dennis C. Murphy. 15 Mar 2008. <http://www.devoniantimes.org/who/pages/lobe-fins.html>.

[6] Jewitt, Susan L. "The Coelacanth: More Than Living Fossil." Smithsonian National Museum of Natural History. May 2003. SNMNH. 15 Mar 2008. <http://www.mnh.si.edu/highlight/coelacanth/>.

[7] Benton, Michael J. *Vertebrate Palaeontology.* 3rd ed. Malden, MA: Blackwell, 2005. Pg 70.

the ancestor of tetrapods."[1] They are best understood, in other words, as a fish that evolved from an ancestor held in common with tetrapods, and because of their close relationship to that common ancestor, they give insight into the probable characteristics of the ancestral species.

The lungfish, or dipnoi, are thought to be even more closely related to the lineage of the vertebrates leading to tetrapods. Like the coelacanths, they have paired fleshy fins with discernible humeri and femurs.[2] Their swim bladders absorb oxygen and remove wastes such as carbon dioxide. Not only are they able to live out of water for long periods of time by breathing with their lung/swim bladders, but the oxygen exchange of those organs have become so essential that they will drown if submerged for too long.[3] Lungfish were a plentiful and diverse group by the end of the Devonian. Fossils of lungfish and the burrows that they make during dry periods, when they rely exclusively on air breathing, are abundant.[4]

Surviving species of lungfish, like by all indications their ancestors, thrive in waters that are both shallow and seasonal. Teleosts have features that are more advanced relative to their existence in a stable aquatic environment, but cannot survive where waters periodically dry up. The features of lungfish, described by many writers as primitive or primordial, allow their survival in their particular ecological niche, a niche that allows and encourages further adaptation to terrestrial life. The lesson of the lungfish is that the presence of rudimentary lungs, and of fleshy fins capable of bearing some amount of weight and propelling the fish through shallow waters by pushing against the bottom, both facilitated their own survival in their particular environment and set the stage for the development of land-based vertebrates.

Although lungfish shed further light on the progression from lobe-finned fish to tetrapods, they, too, are currently thought to be a side branch of the process, albeit a closer side branch than the coelacanths. An extinct third group of sarcopterygians called the rhipidistians, and more specifically within the rhipidistian group the

---

[1] Jewitt, Susan L. "The Coelacanth: More Than Living Fossil." Smithsonian National Museum of Natural History. May 2003. SNMNH. 15 Mar 2008. <http://www.mnh.si.edu/highlight/coelacanth/>.

[2] Murphy, Dennis C. "More About Lobe-Fins: Sarcopterygii." Devonian Times. 9 July 2005. Dennis C. Murphy. 15 Mar 2008. <http://www.devoniantimes.org/who/pages/lobe-fins.html>.

[3] Speer, Brian R. "Introduction to the Dipnoi." University of California Museum of Paleontology. 29 May 2000. U C Berkeley. 15 Mar 2008. <http://www.ucmp.berkeley.edu/vertebrates>.

[4] Murphy, Dennis C. "Unidentified Lungfish (Dipnoi)." Devonian Times. 9 Jul 2005. Dennis C. Murphy. 15 Mar 2008 <http://www.devoniantimes.org/who/pages/lungfish>.

osteolepiforms, are currently believed to be the most likely ancestor of tetrapods.[1]

The prototypical early osteolepiform rhipidistian is *Eusthenopteron*. *Eusthenopteron* is one of the most famous, thoroughly studied, and important fossils ever found. A Swedish paleontologist named Erik Jarvik invested his career in the study of a remarkably complete specimen found in Quebec in 1925. He found that its skull was very similar to early amphibians, flattened with conventionally placed nostrils. Paired bony choanae, the posterior terminus of nasal passages, are present only among sarcopterygian fish and tetrapods, and testify to the existence of nasal passages. The teeth have complex folds of dentine and enamel, a structural condition referred to as labyrnthodontia, also present in some early tetrapods. Most dramatically, the fins contained not just the single bone of the upper limb of tetrapods, but the paired bones of lower limbs, as well. Each pectoral fin, in other words, had a humerus connecting to a more distal radius and ulna, and each pelvic fin contained a femur connecting to a fibula and a tibia. Of *Eusthenopteron* it has been said: "Its interior skeleton clearly anticipates that of a terrestrial tetrapod, but in scale, fin, and tail, it is undeniably a fish."[2]

Panderichthys is another osteolepiform genus, representative of a group bearing its name, with features suggestive of further progression towards tetrapods. The skull was flattened and the eyes were positioned on top of the skull, indicating that it fed on sources at or above the water's surface. It had no dorsal fins or anal fins, but had heavily fleshed lobed fins in pectoral and pelvic pairs.[3]

A more recently discovered osteolepiform, *Tiktaalik roseae*, is notable not only for its anatomy, but for the means of its discovery. *Tiktaalik* had scales, fins, gills, and the lower jaw and palate of sarcopterygian fish, but it also had lungs, a flexible neck, and a well developed rib cage. Its skull was flattened like that of *Panderichthys*, with the eyes on top of the head, more like a crocodile than a fish, and, also unlike fish, it could move its head independently of its spine and shoulders. The skeleton supporting its front fins had a recognizable scapula, humerus, paired radius and ulna, a carpus (or a set of wrist bones), and a splay of metacarpal and digital bones (bones of the hands and fingers). The bones are true endochondral bone, as opposed to calcified cartilage, and the joints are true synovial joints (with a joint capsule and joint fluid) as found in tetrapods. Although tipped with webbed fins, the front limb/fin was capable of a full range of movements. (The rear fins have not been found as of this writing.) *Tiktaalik*

---

[1] Ahlberg, Per E., and Zerina Johanson. "Osteodepiforms and the ancestry of tetrapods." *Nature*, vol 395, pg 792-794, 22 October 1998.

[2] Ludvigsen, Rolf, and Brian Chatterton. "Eusthenopteron – the Prince of Miguasha." *Past lives: Chronicles of Canadian Paleontology*. 7 Feb 2008. Geological Survey of Canada. 15 Mar 2008. <http://gsc.nrcan.gc.ca/paleochron/22_e.php>.

[3] Benton, Michael J. *Vertebrate Palaeontology*. 3rd ed. Malden, MA: Blackwell, 2005. Pg 72.

could, at the very least, prop himself up in the water and propel himself along the bottom of shallows with his powerful front limbs. It is possible that he could move himself along the water's edge, in a clumsy gait like a seal, for short periods.[1, 2, 3]

Of nearly equal importance to the anatomic features of *Triktaalik* is the fact that its discovery was not serendipitous. Any good scientific theory is tested by its predictions. The team of paleontologists that found and documented *Triktaalik*, led by Neil Shubin from the University of Chicago, Farish Jenkens, Jr., of Harvard University, and Ted Daeschler, the vertebrate zoology chair of Philadelphia's Academy of Natural Sciences, predicted, due to their knowledge of the fossils of other osteolepiform fish and early amphibian tetrapods, that intermediate forms would be discovered in a relatively narrow window of seventeen million years in the middle Devonian. They sought out exposed rock deposits of the target age, and, with a diligent effort over a period of four summer seasons (excavation was impossible during much of the year, because the target location was in arctic Canada), they located several specimens of the remarkable fish, dubbed *Triktaalik* at the behest of local Inuit elders.[4]

One of the early tetrapods that allowed the *Tiktaalik* searchers to set the late limit on their search window was a creature called *Acanthostega gunnari*. (Earlier tetrapods such as *Elginerpeton* and *Obruchevichthys* are known by incomplete skeletons, and features are not sufficiently different from *Acanthostega* to justify a full discussion in a work of this purpose.) Taken as a whole, its skeleton looks like an amphibian. Its limbs, although containing all of the component bones, were neither strong nor fully flexible, however, and ended in eight digits on each limb. The spine was based on a flexible notochord, with vertebrae that were insufficient for the prolonged support of the body on land. These features, taken together with such characteristics as an incomplete rib cage and the presence of extensive fin structures on its tail lead paleontologists to think that it was primarily or entirely aquatic, using its limbs to assist its swimming by pushing along the bottom of shallow waters of swamps.[5]

Ichthyostega species appear to be somewhat better adapted to terrestrial excursions. The rib cage is substantial; in fact, ribs overlap to form a rigid barrel-shaped protective cavity, well capable of supporting the weight of the body organs. Forelimbs are well

---

1 "Tiktaalik roseae." 2007. University of Chicago. 16 Mar 2008. <http://tiktaalik.uchicago.edu/>.
2 Daeschler, Edward B., Neil H. Shubin, and Farish A. Jenkins, Jr. "A Devonian tetrapod-like fish and the evolution of the tetrapod body plan." *Nature*, vol 440, pg 757-763 (April 6, 2006).
3 Daeschler, Edward B., Neil H. Shubin, and Farish A. Jenkins, Jr. "The pectoral fin of *Tiktaalik roseae* and the origin of the tetrapod limb." *Nature*, vol 440, pg 764-771 (April 6, 2006).
4 "Tiktaalik roseae." 2007. University of Chicago. 16 Mar 2008. <http://tiktaalik.uchicago.edu/>.
5 Clack, Jennifer A. "*Acanthostega. Acanthostega gunnari.*" 13 Jun 2006. The Tree of Life Web Project, http://tolweb.org/. 16 Mar 2008. <http://tolweb.org/Acanthostega>.

developed and powerful, sufficient to bear weight, but the hind limbs less so. The disproportionate development of the limbs has led to speculation that the animal may have pulled itself onto beaches in a manner similar to seals.[1]

Tetrapod fossils from the Carboniferous Period (359.2 to 299 million years ago) include *Whatcheeria* and *Pederpes*, closely related species with limbs for the first time better adapted to walking than to swimming.[2]

Acanthostega, *Ichthyostega*, and their cousins are considered by some to be the first amphibians, but most paleontologists refer to them as "stem tetrapods." Stem tetrapods are outwardly similar to salamanders, and even the more fully terrestrial species returned to the water to breed and lay eggs, as do modern amphibians, but modern amphibians like frogs, toads, newts, and true salamanders did not develop until the Jurassic Period (199.6 to 145.5 million years ago) of the Mesozoic Era (251 to 65.5 million years ago),[3] well known due to a popular film as the period dominated by the dinosaurs. Still, as awkward and difficult as their terrestrial locomotion may have been, tetrapods had, before the end of the Devonian, emerged from the waters to make vertebrates' first tentative steps on land.

The plant kingdom was not idle while Devonian animals were developing spines, lungs, and legs, and taking the first beach vacations. Club mosses and horsetails made their appearance, and in the following Carboniferous Period would grow to the size of trees and form some of the earliest forests. By the end of the Devonian, ferns developed the first leaves with branched veins in the plant kingdom, and the first seed plants produced seeds along their branches, without specialized organs like cones or flowers.[4] The first true trees, *Archaeopteris*, grew to diameters of up to a meter and heights of thirty meters, had extensive root systems and wood trunks, and were prolific enough to form the basis of extensive forests.[5] With neither competition nor any consequential number of herbivorous animals on land, plants spread and diversified rapidly, leading to the vast biomass of the Carboniferous Period that became earth's coal deposits.

---

[1] Clack, Jennifer A. "*Ichthyostega*." 9 Feb 2006. The Tree of Life Web Project, http://tolweb.org/. 16 Mar 2008. <http://www.tolweb.org/Ichthyostega>.

[2] Benton, Michael J. *Vertebrate Palaeontology*. 3rd ed. Malden, MA: Blackwell, 2005. Pg 87-88.

[3] Speer, Brian R., and Ben Waggoner. "Amphibia: Fossil Record." University of California Museum of Paleontology. 19 Jul 1995. U C Berkeley. 17 Mar 2008. <http://www.ucmp.berkeley.edu/vertebrates>.

[4] Speer, Brian R., et al. "Life of the Devonian." University of California Museum of Paleontology. 1 Feb 1998. U C Berkeley. 17 Mar 2008. <http://www.ucmp.berkeley.edu/devonian/devlife.html>.

[5] Murphy, Dennis C. "*Archaeopteris* spp. (progymnosperm tree)." *Devonian Times*. 9 Jul 2005. Dennis C. Murphy. 17 Mar 2008. <http://www.devoniantimes.org/who/pages/archaeopteris.html>.

Arthropods, too, diversified and multiplied in the novel environment of the land. Spiders, mites, and early wingless insects made their first terrestrial appearance during the Devonian and continued to proliferate, both in numbers and in forms, during the Carboniferous Period.[1] By the end of the Carboniferous, insects like cockroaches and mayflies are present in the fossil record.[2]

The first land animals

The next important milestone in the development of terrestrial vertebrates was the amniotic egg. The non-amniotic eggs of fish and amphibians are composed of an embryo and a yolk sac, with an outer membrane whose only significant function is to contain and bind the other two components. Metabolic wastes leave the embryo by simple diffusion, and oxygen is similarly acquired. Without an aquatic environment to surround the egg, however, two other membranes become necessary: an amnionic sac provides a cushioning and stabilizing aquatic environment for the embryo, and the allantois is a receptacle for waste. The outer chorionic membrane fuses with the allantois in at least a portion of their adjacent surfaces and becomes a respiratory surface. The result is a self-sufficient capsule that is both independent of the aquatic environment and provides for the hatching or birth of a fetus more fully developed than the offspring of non-amniotic eggs.[3]

Not all amniotic eggs are hard surfaced; many are leathery. The developmental path of amniotic eggs is not known. Neither non-amniotic nor most amniotic eggs fossilize well, and it is reasonable to suspect that the transition states may have been soft and fragile, and similarly not amenable to fossilization. This suspicion would seem to be confirmed by the fact that the earliest fossil animals with characteristics of amniotes date to the late Carboniferous Period, approximately 310 million years ago, while the oldest known amniotic egg dates to about 220 million years ago, in the early Triassic Period of the Mesozoic Era, 90 million years later.[4]

The transition to a fully terrestrial existence required adaptations in other systems besides reproduction. The integument had to become thicker and more resistant to

---

[1] Speer, Brian R., et al. "Life of the Devonian." University of California Museum of Paleontology. 1 Feb 1998. U C Berkeley. 17 Mar 2008. <http://www.ucmp.berkeley.edu/devonian/devlife.html>.

[2] Waggoner, Ben. "Fossil Record of the Uniramia." University of California Museum of Paleontology. 2 Mar 1995. U C Berkeley. 19 Mar 2008. <http://www.ucmp.berkeley.edu/arthropoda/uniramia/uniramiafr.html>.

[3] Laurin, Michel, and Jacques A. Gauthier. "Amniota. Mammals, reptiles (turtles, lizards, Sphenodon, crocodiles, birds) and their extinct relatives." 1 Jan 1996. The Tree of Life Web Project, http://tolweb.org. 19 Mar 2008. <http://www.tolweb.org/Amniota>.

[4] Laurin, Michel, and Jacques A. Gauthier. "Amniota. Mammals, reptiles (turtles, lizards, Sphenodon, crocodiles, birds) and their extinct relatives." 1 Jan 1996. The Tree of Life Web Project, http://tolweb.org. 19 Mar 2008. <http://www.tolweb.org/Amniota>.

desiccation. The kidneys became more adept at concentrating urine, thereby conserving water. Similarly, the colon, whose primary function it is to absorb fluid from fecal material, became larger relative to the small intestine. Tear glands developed to keep the eye moist, and nasal passages increased in surface area and in their capacity to produce mucus, to moisten the inhaled air of more arid environments. Ear mechanisms developed and advanced rapidly in their ability to amplify the sound waves transmitted through air and convert them to neuroelectrical signals for processing by the brain. Components of the musculoskeletal system became more robust to support the body weight without the buoyancy of water.[1] As the limbs of tetrapods became more adapted to land, their gait changed, as well; the limbs of amphibians are advanced primarily by undulating movements of the spine similar to a swimming motion, while the limbs of reptiles are more capable of movement independent of the trunk, and lateral flexion of the vertebral column is reduced or eliminated.

Many intermediate forms are difficult to categorize as either amphibians or reptiles, and are often referred to as "stem amniotes" for their intermediate characteristics, in the same way that the term "stem tetrapods" is applied to those genera that defy firm classification as either fish or amphibians. Several groups have the sort of intermediate characteristics that cause paleontologists to refer to them as stem amniotes.

The temnospondyls were prominent tetrapods of the Carboniferous Period and remained common through the Permian (the last period of the Paleozoic Era, 299 to 251 million years ago) and Triassic Periods (the first period of the Mesozoic Era, 251 to 199.6 million years ago) before becoming less common and diverse during the Jurassic and dying out in the early Cretaceous Period (145.5 to 65.5 million years ago). During their 150 million year existence they encompassed 170 genera in 40 families. The limbs of *Balanerpeton* and *Dendrerpeton*, two genera of the early and late Carboniferous respectively, are relatively long and well-formed for terrestrial use, with strong shoulder and pelvic girdles.[2] Temnosondyls have patterns of ridges on their skulls that indicate that their skin was both thick and tightly adhered. The palate was incomplete, and the teeth were pedicellate, meaning that they had a crown and a root. The tooth roots only rested on the bone – it did not have a socket within the bone – but the pedicellate tooth was an advance over earlier teeth that were attached only to the soft tissues of the mouth.[3]

The fossil records of the temnospondyls tell a tale of the adaptation of the ear to

---

[1] Laurin, Michel, and Jacques A. Gauthier. "Amniota. Mammals, reptiles (turtles, lizards, Sphenodon, crocodiles, birds) and their extinct relatives." 1 Jan 1996. The Tree of Life Web Project, http://tolweb.org. 20 Mar 2008. <http://www.tolweb.org/Amniota>.

[2] Benton, Michael J. *Vertebrate Palaeontology*. 3rd ed. Malden, MA: Blackwell, 2005. Pg 88-91.

[3] Steyer, Jean-Sébastien and Michel Laurin. "Temnospondyli." 11 Dec 2000. The Tree of Life Web Project, http://tolweb.org. 24 Mar 2008. <http://tolweb.org/Temnospondyli/15009>.

terrestrial life. Baphetids are a group of tetrapods from the early Carboniferous, preceding the temnospondyls, that are known almost exclusively from skull fossils, but which may include the more complete skeleton *Eucritta melanolimnetes*.[1] Baphetids had deeply recessed otic notches (the notch in the skull where the ear drum will develop in later animals), but the stapes (the last of the three bones in the middle ear that transmits vibrations from the ear drum to the inner ear) is too large to have been functional in conjunction with an ear drum.[2] The otic notch of temnospondyls was similarly associated, in early species, with a stapes too large to operate with a tympanum. These larger stapes were attached to the skin and ligaments near the shoulder, and were functional in detecting low frequency sound waves such as those of footsteps. Vibrations were transmitted up the forelimb to the skin and/or the ligaments, transmitted by the stapes, and sensed by nerves very close to the brain. Over the history of the temnospondyl group, the otic notch became deeper and, in the youngest species, enclosed, consistent with the presence of a tympanic membrane, while the stapes reduced in size and remained associated with the otic notch as it developed.[3, 4] The hearing apparatus of modern reptiles typically consists of a tympanum and stapes connecting directly to the detection apparatus.

Lepospondyls were a sister group of the temnospondyls during the Carboniferous. The lepospondyls include lizard-like animals highly adapted to terrestrial life, aquatic species with reduced limbs, and even a group of limbless snake-like animals, the aistopods. The aistopods and nectrideans, a group of aquatic lepospondyl tetrapods with bizarre, large wing-like processes on their skulls, were the first animals with one-piece vertebrae.[5]

Anthracosaurs were also contemporary to the Carboniferous temnospondyls. Terrestrial species like *Proterogyrinus* were characterized by deep skulls with distinct surfaces for the roof and cheek areas of the skull. The limbs were less sprawling and therefore more agile than those of many other terrestrial tetrapods.[6, 7]

---

[1] Clack, Jennifer A. "*Eucritta melanolimnetes.*" 9 Feb 2006. The Tree of Life Web Project, http://tolweb.org. 24 Mar 2008. <http://tolweb.org/Eucritta_melanolimnetes/58012>.
[2] Clack, Jennifer A. "Baphetidae." 9 Feb 2006. The Tree of Life Web Project, http://tolweb.org. 24 Mar 2008. <http://tolweb.org/Baphetidae/15011>.
[3] Steyer, Jean-Sébastien and Michel Laurin. "Temnospondyli." 11 Dec 2000. The Tree of Life Web Project, http://tolweb.org. 245 Mar 2008. <http://tolweb.org/Temnospondyli/15009>.
[4] Huttenlocker, Adam. "Dissorophoidea, Bolt 1969." 12 Mar 2007. The Tree of Life Web Project, http://tolweb.org. 12 Mar 2007. <http://tolweb.org/Dissorophoidea/17607>.
[5] Benton, Michael J. *Vertebrate Palaeontology.* 3rd ed. Malden, MA: Blackwell, 2005. Pg 88-94.
[6] Waggoner, Ben, and Brian R. Speer. "Life of the Carboniferous." University of California Museum of Paleontology. 11 May 1998. U C Berkeley. 28 Mar 2008. <http://www.ucmp.berkeley.edu/carboniferous/carblife.html>.
[7] Benton, Michael J. *Vertebrate Palaeontology.* 3rd ed. Malden, MA: Blackwell, 2005. Pg 95.

The temnospondyls, as mentioned above, thrived through the Permian, during which they were joined by the reptiliomorph groups Seymoriamorpha and Diadectomorpha. The temnospondyls of the Permian included the two-meter-long *Eryops*, whose size, heavy limbs, and upright agile build made it one of the top predators of its day. Another Permian genus, *Doleserpeton*, and its related dissorophid group of temnospondyls, was characterized by short skulls with large eye sockets and large ear drums, adaptations suited to a terrestrial lifestyle.[1]

The seymouriamorph group, like the temnospondyls, exhibit dermal molding of the skull, indicating again a thick, tight skin. Scales or their impressions have been preserved in many species. They also have a well-defined otic canal and a small, delicate stapes. The palate was complete, separating the nasal passages from the oral cavity and thereby allowing breathing to continue during ingestion, without which chewing is impractical. A sacrum is uniformly present, consisting of one and sometimes two vertebrae.[2, 3, 4, 5] The sacrum firmly links the spine to the hind limbs, increasing their capacity to bear weight. It may seem odd for those familiar with the anatomy of modern animals to realize that early tetrapods had a pelvic girdle with only soft tissue attachments to the spine, until they realize that the forelimbs of modern animals have, to date, no bony attachment to the spine; rather, the forelimbs support their share of the body's weight (usually an amount slightly exceeding that of the hind limbs) via the sling-like muscular attachments of the scapula to the ribs and sternum. The genus *Seymouria* itself was around sixty centimeters (2 feet) long with powerful limbs and, due at least in part to its well-developed girdle structures, held its body higher off the ground in the most upright position of any animal to date.[6]

Diadectomorphs were reptile-like animals of the late Carboniferous and early Permian, similar in many ways to seymouriomorphs, but with teeth adapted to an herbivorous diet. *Diadectes* was more stocky that *Seymouria*, and probably slower, but such features are not deleterious to herbivores, and *Diadectes* is the first clear and well-documented herbivorous tetrapod in the fossil record.[7]

Amphibians – non-amniotic tetrapods that must lay their eggs in water - developed into

---

[1] Benton, Michael J. *Vertebrate Palaeontology*. 3rd ed. Malden, MA: Blackwell, 2005. Pg 97-100.
[2]Laurin, Michel. "Seymouriamorpha." 15 Jan 1998. The Tree of Life Web Project, http://tolweb.org. 24 Mar 2008. <http://tolweb.org/Seymouriamorpha/15005>.
[3] Laurin, Michel. "*Utegenia shpinari*." 1 Jan 1996. The Tree of Life Web Project, http://tolweb.org. 24 Mar 2008. <http://tolweb.org/Utegenia_shpinari/17542>.
[4] Klembara, Jozef. "*Discosauriscus*." 1 Jan 1996. The Tree of Life Web Project, http://tolweb.org. 24 Mar 2008. <http://tolweb.org/Discosauriscus/17544>.
[5] Laurin, Michel. "*Seymouria*." 1 Jan 1996. The Tree of Life Web Project, http://tolweb.org. 24 Mar 2008. <http://tolweb.org/Seymouria/17546>.
[6] Benton, Michael J. *Vertebrate Palaeontology*. 3rd ed. Malden, MA: Blackwell, 2005. Pg 97-101.
[7] Benton, Michael J. *Vertebrate Palaeontology*. 3rd ed. Malden, MA: Blackwell, 2005. Pg 101.

modern forms during the Jurassic Period. Salamanders of the genus *Karaurus* from the middle of the Jurassic have heavier skulls and skeletons, but are recognizable as essentially modern amphibians. Frogs and toads, of course, have distinctive short spines and large powerful hind legs, consistent with their jumping abilities. The earliest known frog, *Triadobatrachus*, from the early Triassic, looks like a somewhat short salamander with hind legs a bit more long and powerful than the front. By the early Jurassic, genera such as *Vieraella* and *Prosalirus* had the disproportionate hind legs and markedly shortened trunk of modern frogs.[1]

Reptiles and more

Once equipped for terrestrial life, and with the entire land mass of a planet to colonize, the amniotes diversified rapidly. Amniotes are differentiated by paleontologists based on the distinctive characteristics of their skull. Openings called fenestrae (fenestra in the singular) provide anchor points for the attachment of jaw muscles in more powerful configurations and allow the muscles to bulge out, while at the same time lightening the skull. The stem amniotes and the earliest reptiles were anapsids, with no fenestrae, and the anapsid condition continues in the turtles as it did in their extinct relatives. Diapsids have two fenestrae on each side of the skull; the diapsids encompass lizards, crocodilians, birds, and extinct relatives including the dinosaurs. (The skull structures of anapsids and diapsids together – living and extinct reptiles - are referred to as sauropsids.) Synapsids have single temporal fenestrae on each side, and include a large group of extinct creatures with reptilian features, as well as the mammals and their extinct relatives.[2] (Non-mammalian synapsids are sometimes erroneously referred to as synapsid reptiles or as mammal-like reptiles, erroneously in both cases because they are not, in fact, reptiles, in spite of many reptile-like characteristics, but are more properly seen as stem species.)

There are no surviving non-mammal synapsids, but they were once the dominant tetrapods on earth. The earliest group of basal synapsids, the pelycosaurs, appear in the fossil record near the middle of the Carboniferous Period (320 million years ago), and by the early Permian had become the most numerous and diverse land vertebrates.[3] In the early Permian Period, seventy percent of known genera of amniotes were pelycosaurs; they far exceeded the true reptiles (diapsids and anapsids) in both numbers

---

[1] Benton, Michael J. *Vertebrate Palaeontology.* 3rd ed. Malden, MA: Blackwell, 2005. Pg 102-103.
[2] Laurin, Michel and Jacques A. Gauthier. "Amniota. Mammals, reptiles (turtles, lizards, Sphenodon, crocodiles, birds) and their extinct relatives." 1 Jan 1996. The Tree of Life Web Project, http://tolweb.org. 30 Mar 2008. <http://tolweb.org/Amniota/14990>.
[3] Laurin, Michel and Robert Reisz. "Synapsida. Mammals and their extinct relatives." 6 Apr 2007. The Tree of Life Web Project, http://tolweb.org. 30 Mar 2008. <http://tolweb.org/Synapsida/14845>.

and diversity.[1, 2]

Early pelycosaurs include the ophiacodonts, eothyrids, varnopids, and caseids. Ophiacondonts were carnivores of the mid-Carboniferous to early Permian, with large heads and thick limbs, and ranged up to three meters in length. Eothyrids were early Permian carnivores considerably smaller than ophiacodonts, with a shorter skull somewhat resembling that of a cat. Varanopids, too, were small carnivores of the Permian era, with long triangular snouts and long, light, agile limbs. Caseids were herbivores of the mid-Permian with unusually large nostrils in a disproportionately small skull. All had small but distinct temporal fenestrae.[3]

The most widely known pelycosaur dates to the early Permian: *Dimetrodon*, a lizard-like beast with a large sail on its back, the image of which is widely known. Many people think it was a dinosaur, but the dinosaurs were diapsids and *Dimetrodon* was a synpasid. And *Dimetrodon* had other features that separated it from dinosaurs and other true reptiles.

Dimetrodon means, literally, "two measurements [of] teeth." Fossil *Dimetrodon* skulls display incisor-like shearing teeth in front, impressive canines for seizing prey, and shorter cutting teeth not unlike the premolars of modern carnivores further back in the cheeks. Having different kinds of teeth is termed heterodonty, and heterodonty is present among surviving species only in mammals. Heterodonty, combined with the development of a palate to separate the breathing passages from the oral cavity, allowed chewing, which in turn allowed more efficient digestion and a higher metabolic rate.

The sail on the back of *Dimetrodon* was composed of skin stretched between the tremendously elongated dorsal spinous processes of the vertebrae, structures that persist as sites for muscle attachment in mammals. The fossil vertebrae of *Dimetrodon* demonstrate that a large blood supply was present in the sail. It was almost certainly used as a solar collector to warm the body of the large animal (specimens often reach or exceed three meters, or ten feet, in length), to facilitate more vigorous predatory activity earlier in the day.[4, 1, 2] A higher metabolic rate is again facilitated.

---

[1] Speer, Brian R., et al. "Introduction to the Pelycosaurs." University of California Museum of Paleontology. 1 May 2000. U C Berkeley. 30 Mar 2008. <http://www.ucmp.berkeley.edu/synapsids>.

[2] Laurin, Michel and Robert Reisz. "Synapsida. Mammals and their extinct relatives." 6 Apr 2007. The Tree of Life Web Project, http://tolweb.org. 30 Mar 2008. <http://tolweb.org/Synapsida/14845>.

[3] Benton, Michael J. *Vertebrate Palaeontology*. 3rd ed. Malden, MA: Blackwell, 2005. Pg 120-123.

[4] Speer, Brian R., et al. "Introduction to the Pelycosaurs." University of California Museum of Paleontology. 1 May 2000. U C Berkeley. 30 Mar 2008. <http://www.ucmp.berkeley.edu/synapsids>.

Not all pelycosaurs were predators; at least two major groups were herbivorous, including a large herbivorous sail-back similar in overall appearance to *Dimetrodon*, called *Edaphosaurus*. And, the popularity of images of *Dimetrodon* and *Edaphosaurus* notwithstanding, not all pelycosaurs had dorsal sails. The general trend towards smaller sails among later species of pelycosaurs is taken by some as an indication that they moved towards endothermy, or being "warm-blooded."[3] Other paleontologists point out that most pelycosaurs lacked sails and still competed well enough to leave extensive fossil records over several million years.[4] The pelycosaurs also exhibited a trend in later species to move the limbs from a sprawling, mostly horizontal position, to a more vertical position with an upright stance, resulting in a stride called a parasagittal gait.[5, 6]

All synapsids subsequent to the pelycosaurs, including mammals, are referred to as therapsids. Therapsids are distinguished from pelycosaurs by enlarged temporal fenestrae, loss of a particular skull component (the supratemporal bone), changes to the lower jaw and the jaw joint, and more modern structures in the shoulders, pelvises, and hind limbs.[7]

The oldest known therapsid is the early Permian *Tetraceratops*, a large carnivore with four skull protrusions giving him his name. Like other transitional therapsids such as *Biarmosuchus*, they resembled pelycosaurs in many respects, but had subtle changes – somewhat enlarged fenestrae, fewer palatal teeth, loss of the supratemporal bone, and subtle changes to other parts of the skull – that nudge them towards the therapsid group. The late Permian saw the development of more distinct therapsids such as the dinocephalia, with forty known genera, and dicynodonts, a group of over seventy genera "with barrel-shaped bodies and unsatisfactory tails," that invites comparison to pigs.[8]

---

[1] Laurin, Michel and Robert Reisz. "Synapsida. Mammals and their extinct relatives." 6 Apr 2007. The Tree of Life Web Project, http://tolweb.org. 30 Mar 2008. <http://tolweb.org/Synapsida/14845>.

[2] "Synpasida: Sphenacodontia." *Palaeos: the Vertebrates.* Undated. Palaeos.org. 1 Apr 2008. <http://www.palaeos.com/Vertebrates/Units/Unit390/400.html#Dimetrodon>.

[3] Speer, Brian R., et al. "Introduction to the Pelycosaurs." University of California Museum of Paleontology. 1 May 2000. U C Berkeley. 30 Mar 2008. <http://www.ucmp.berkeley.edu/synapsids>.

[4] Benton, Michael J. *Vertebrate Palaeontology.* 3rd ed. Malden, MA: Blackwell, 2005. Pg 124.

[5] Laurin, Michel and Robert Reisz. "Synapsida. Mammals and their extinct relatives." 6 Apr 2007. The Tree of Life Web Project, http://tolweb.org. 30 Mar 2008. <http://tolweb.org/Synapsida/14845>.

[6] Speer, Brian R., et al. "Introduction to the Pelycosaurs." University of California Museum of Paleontology. 1 May 2000. U C Berkeley. 30 Mar 2008. <http://www.ucmp.berkeley.edu/synapsids>.

[7] Benton, Michael J. *Vertebrate Palaeontology.* 3rd ed. Malden, MA: Blackwell, 2005. Pg 125.

[8] Benton, Michael J. *Vertebrate Palaeontology.* 3rd ed. Malden, MA: Blackwell, 2005. Pg 125-129.

The gorgonopsians were therapsid predators of the late Permian. One particularly well-studied genus, *Lycaenops*, is named for its similarity to wolves in its long skull, prominent canine teeth, size, and its long-limbed, light, and agile build. Its general body form lead paleontologists to strongly suspect that it was endothermic (warm blooded), due to the muscle metabolism necessitated by the parasagittal gait and long legs.[1,2] *Lycaenops* and other gorgonopsian genera like *Arctognathus* and *Leontocephalus* had imposing canine teeth that presage those of the saber-tooth tiger; they must have been fearsome weapons at the disposal of these successful and dominating predators.

The late non-mammal therapsids include the therocephalians of the late Permian and Triassic. Therocephalians had many mammal-like skull features, including a mammal-like bony palate without teeth, and enlargement of the temporal fenestrae to the extent that the bone separating it from the eye socket is lost, leaving only the strip of the zygomatic arch, or cheekbone, that is characteristic of mammals.[3,4]

Cynodonts date from near the end of the Permian and diversified in the Triassic Era. The cynodonts, which include mammals, have widely flaring zygomatic arches that gave room for enlarging jaw muscles, along with other modifications of the skull that are familiar to mammalian anatomists.[5] The cheek teeth had multiple cusps, giving rise to the name cynodonts, translated as "dog teeth." The features of the cynodonts were overall so mammal-like that most paleontologists think it likely that they were endothermic (warm-blooded) and had hair.[6] (The oldest hair recovered by paleontologists to date is associated with a mid-Jurassic mammaliaform docodontan.[7])

The age of the reptiles

The Permian period ended with the most severe extinction event known to paleontology. Over the relatively short period of a half million years, seventy-five percent of tetrapod families and fifty percent of marine invertebrate families died out, totaling by various estimates eighty to ninety-six percent of existent species. The cause

[1] Speer, Brian R. "Introduction to the Gorgonopsia." University of California Museum of Paleontology. 17 May 2000. U C Berkeley. 2 Apr 2008. <http://www.ucmp.berkeley.edu/synapsids>.
[2] "Gorgonopsia: *Lycaenops.*" *Palaeos: The Vertebrates.* Undated. Palaeos.org. 2 April 2008. <http://www.palaeos.com/Vertebrates/Units/400Therapsida/400.800.html#Gorgonopsia>.
[3] Benton, Michael J. *Vertebrate Palaeontology.* 3rd ed. Malden, MA: Blackwell, 2005. Pg 130.
[4] "Therapsid: Theriodontia." *Palaeos: The Vertebrates.* Undated. Palaeos.org. 18 Apr 2008. <http://www.palaeos.com/Vertebrates/Units/400Therapsida/400.800.html#Therocephalia>.
[5] Benton, Michael J. *Vertebrate Palaeontology.* 3rd ed. Malden, MA: Blackwell, 2005. Pg 130-133.
[6] "Cynodontia: Overview." *Palaeos: The Vertebrates.* Undated. Palaeos.org. 18 Apr 2008. <http://www.palaeos.com/Vertebrates/Units/410Cynodontia/410.000.html>.
[7] Laurin, Michel and Robert Reisz. "Synapsida. Mammals and their extinct relatives." 6 April 2007. Tree of Life Web Project, http://tolweb.org. 19 Apr 2008. <http://tolweb.org/Synapsida>.

of the extinction is believed by some to be an asteroid impact, like the one that ended the age of the dinosaurs, but the evidence is less compelling. Evidence does exist, however, for massive and prolonged volcanic eruptions in Siberia near the end of the Permian, which would have resulted in the release of vast quantities of carbon dioxide and sulfur dioxide, with resulting oxygen depletion and relatively rapid global warming,[1] which may have been the proximate cause of the Permian extinction event.

Whatever the cause, the results were catastrophic to plant and animal life. Complex ecosystems were reduced to traces, and myriad ecological niches were opened. The dominance of the synapsids had ended, albeit temporarily; the reptiles were poised to dominate the planet of life.

In the late Carboniferous Period, contemporary to the early pelycosaurs and predating *Dimetrodon*, protorothyridids represented the anapsids and araeoscelids the diapsids. Protorothyridids include the first certain amniotes, *Hylonomus* and *Paleothyris*. Both were lizard-like animals with light agile builds. Permian reptilians, often termed "parareptiles," include aquatic species (mesosaurs), the first bipedal tetrapods (bolosaurids), and some with early experiments in fenestrae (millerettids). None were plentiful or diverse.[2, 3]

More successful anapsids made their appearance in the late Permian. Procolophonids were herbivores with lizard-like but stocky bodies and broad skulls. Their skulls have features similar to the later turtles, leading some to think that they are ancestral to turtles. Parieasaurs and captorhinids had more upright postures with the legs extending beneath them. Parieasaurs were large, up to three meters in length with thick legs and massive ribcages. Their build and the presence of closely spaced plates of dermal armor lead some to the conclusion that they, rather than procolophonids, were the ancestors of turtles. Captorhinids were smaller and lighter, averaging around forty centimeters in length, but with a rather large skull which, lacking fenestrae, was also rather heavy.[4, 5, 6] (Thankfully, no one seems to think captorhinids were the ancestors of turtles.)

---

[1] Benton, Michael J. *Vertebrate Palaeontology.* 3rd ed. Malden, MA: Blackwell, 2005. Pg 133-134.
[2] Benton, Michael J. *Vertebrate Palaeontology.* 3rd ed. Malden, MA: Blackwell, 2005. Pg 113-117.
[3] "Basal Anapsids." *Palaeos: The Vertebrates.* Undated. Palaeos.org. 19 Apr 2008. <http://www.palaeos.com/Vertebrates/Units/Unit200/100.html>
[4] Benton, Michael J. *Vertebrate Palaeontology.* 3rd ed. Malden, MA: Blackwell, 2005. Pg 117-118.
[5] Laurin, Michel. "Introduction to Procolophonoidea." University of California Museum of Paleontology. 11 July 1996. U C Berkeley. 19 Apr 2008. <http://www.ucmp.berkeley.edu/anapsids/procolophonoidea.html>.
[6] Laurin, Michel. "Introduction to Pareiasauria." University of California Museum of Paleontology. 11 July 1996. U C Berkeley. 19 Apr 2008. < http://www.ucmp.berkeley.edu/anapsids/pareiasauria.html>.

Among the diapsids, the araeoscelid *Petrolacosaurus* was a contemporary to *Hylonomus* (late Carboniferous) and shared the body plan of a slender lizard-like creature. It has upper and lower temporal fenestrae as well as a fenestra in the palate common to later diapsid reptiles. Diapsids remained relatively rare and of low diversity throughout the Permian, but late Permian forms include the first archosaurs *Protorosaurus*, with long legs and a long flexible neck, and the lizard-like *Youngina*.[1] The archosaurs are sometimes referred to as thecodonts, since they were the first animals to develop thecodont dentition, or teeth set in sockets within the bones of the upper and lower jaws.[2]

With the extinction of so many of the dominant synapsids at the end of the Permian, competition for various ecological niches was weak or nonexistent, and reptiles diversified to fill the many vacancies that existed in the early Triassic Period of the Mesozoic Era. Archosaurs of the early Triassic took the predatory roles of the gorgonopsids. With lizard-like bodies, short powerful skulls lightened by fenestrae in front of the eyes and in the lower jaw, and relatively long agile legs, they were efficient hunters. The early Triassic *Proterosuchus* was about one and a half meters long and likely fed on small species of the pig-like dicynodonts. *Vjushkovia* reached sizes up to five meters and was capable of preying on the larger species. *Euparkeria* reached sizes of only a half meter in the mid-Triassic, and had hind legs with a length and shape sufficient to enable a bipedal gait part of the time.[3, 4]

In the late Triassic Period, reptiles diverged again into the crurotarsi, a group with characteristic limb features, that would lead to crocodiles and alligators, and the ornithodira, with their own contrasting limb structures, that would lead to dinosaurs and, eventually, to birds.[5]

Crurotarsi, crocodile-like animals from the late Triassic, include a lightly-built, long-legged and probably bipedal insectivore called *Saltosuchus*, along with a genus more crocodile-like in appearance, *Sphenosuchus*.[6] *Protosuchus* and *Orthosuchus* of the early Jurassic Period show most of the characteristics of modern crocodilians, including hind legs that betray their bipedal origins by being longer than the front legs. Crocodilians became quite diverse and plentiful, ranging from one-meter-long terrestrial carnivore *Argentinosuchus* to an early Cretaceous species, *Sarcosuchus*, with a skull 1.8 meters long

---

[1] Benton, Michael J. *Vertebrate Palaeontology.* 3rd ed. Malden, MA: Blackwell, 2005. Pg 119.
[2] "Archosauromorpha: Overview." *Palaeos: The Vertebrates.* Undated. Palaeos.org. 19 Apr 2008. <http://www.palaeos.com/Vertebrates/Units/270Archosauromorpha/270.000.html>.
[3] Benton, Michael J. *Vertebrate Palaeontology.* 3rd ed. Malden, MA: Blackwell, 2005. Pg 138-141.
[4] Speer, Brian R., et al. "Introduction to Euparkeria." University of California Museum of Paleontology. 24 Oct 1997. U C Berkeley. 4 May 2008. < http://www.ucmp.berkeley.edu/diapsids>.
[5] Benton, Michael J. *Vertebrate Palaeontology.* 3rd ed. Malden, MA: Blackwell, 2005. Pg 141, 153.
[6] Benton, Michael J. *Vertebrate Palaeontology.* 3rd ed. Malden, MA: Blackwell, 2005. Pg 145-146.

and an estimated length of twelve meters (or forty feet).[1,2] Another Cretaceous species, *Chimaerasuchus*, is believed to have been herbivorous.[3] By the late Cretaceous, crocodilians had attained essentially modern characteristics, and were much more plentiful and widespread during the Paleogene (65.5 to 23.03 million years ago) and Neogene Periods (23.03 to 5.332 million years ago) of the Cenozoic Era (65.5 million years ago until the present) than in the present day.[4]

The line leading to dinosaurs, the ornithodira, has tibias (the largest bone in the shin) longer than the femurs (the bone of the upper leg), simplified hinge-like ankle joints, and feet with the three central toes elongated to be notably longer than the first and fifth digits. The animals used a digitigrade stance, standing and walking on the upright toes in the same manner as birds, which, combined with the fully upright position of their hind legs, made them much more agile than other reptiles.[5] The middle Triassic dinosaur-like *Marasuchus* and *Scleromochlus* shared similar body plans with the earliest true dinosaurs in the late Triassic, *Eoraptor* and *Herrerasaurus*. All were bipeds with long upright rear legs and shorter front limbs, horizontal spines with long heavy tails to balance the body, and heavily fenestrated skulls.[6]

Such a body plan, most familiar in the form of *Tyrannosaurus rex* of the late Cretaceous Period, served to place the dinosaurs in a variety of ecological niches. Predators and herbivores shared the mobility of the bipedal digitigrade stance. Front limbs ranged from reasonably dextrous grasping limbs such as those of *Struthiomimus* to reductions that left them as little more than pincers in the maniraptoran *Mononykus*. The relatively few dinosaurs that were quadrupeds betrayed their bipedal ancestry, like the crocodiles, by the presence of longer more powerful hind legs, as represented by the facultative biped/quadrapeds *Plateosaurus* of the late Triassic and *Iguanadon* of the early Cretaceous, and the obligate quadrapeds like *Stegosaurus* and the sauropods of the Jurrasic. (Sauropods were the massive animals with long necks such as *Cetiosaurus*. More derived sauropods visibly progress through the fossil record to the point that the front limbs are more elongated than the rear in *Brachiosaurus*.)[7]

Debate continues as to whether the dinosaurs were endothermic (warm-blooded, controlling their own core temperatures like birds and mammals), exothermic (cold-blooded, modifying their body temperature from ambient temperature only by their

---

[1] Benton, Michael J. *Vertebrate Palaeontology*. 3rd ed. Malden, MA: Blackwell, 2005. Pg 232-238.
[2] "SuperCroc." National Geographic Society. Undated. 4 May 2008. <http://www.nationalgeographic.com/supercroc>.
[3] Benton, Michael J. *Vertebrate Palaeontology*. 3rd ed. Malden, MA: Blackwell, 2005. Pg 237.
[4] Benton, Michael J. *Vertebrate Palaeontology*. 3rd ed. Malden, MA: Blackwell, 2005. Pg 237.
[5] Benton, Michael J. *Vertebrate Palaeontology*. 3rd ed. Malden, MA: Blackwell, 2005. Pg 190-191.
[6] Benton, Michael J. *Vertebrate Palaeontology*. 3rd ed. Malden, MA: Blackwell, 2005. Pg 153-155.
[7] Benton, Michael J. *Vertebrate Palaeontology*. 3rd ed. Malden, MA: Blackwell, 2005. Pg 187-219.

activities and behaviors such as warming in the sun), or inertial homeotherms (so massive that their body temperature changed only slightly and slowly). Obviously, many dinosaurs were so large that inertial homeothermy was a significant factor in the maintenance of core temperature. Just as obviously, smaller dinosaur species that ranged down in size to less than a meter lost body heat much more readily than their massive cousins.

The arguments in favor of endothermy in dinosaurs include their close relationship to the fully endothermic birds, their upright body posture and presumed high activity levels, a high growth rate that can be demonstrated in several species in which juveniles are known, microscopic bone structures typical of modern-day endotherms, and the reduced predator/prey ratios of dinosaurs that are more typical of endothermic than exothermic ecologies. Those who believe that dinosaurs were exotherms point out that none of the above factors can fully exclude exothermy, and that the Mesozoic Era was generally warm enough over much of the globe to support exothermic animals with a high metabolic rate.[1, 2] Birds, as we will see soon, are direct descendants of the dinosaurs (actually the only surviving dinosaurs) and are true endotherms. It remains that endothermy developed at some uncertain time in the lineage from the extinct dinosaurs to surviving birds. It is possible that the larger dinosaurs were largely inertial homeotherms, but that their smaller relatives developed the mechanisms to maintain a constant body temperature.

The debate about endothermy is related to the knowledge that a significant number of dinosaurs developed feathers. Since being discovered in 1996 in highly preserved specimens of the early Cretaceous dinosaur *Sinosauropteryx*, feathers have been found in at least six other species dating back as far as the middle Jurassic. The feathers of the earliest species appear to be simple down-like feathers, but later species such as *Protoarchaeopteryx* had contour feathers as well. These animals were certainly not capable of flight, so the feathers were virtually assured to play a role in maintaining at least a relatively constant body temperature, possibly with the addition of some display function for the contour feathers of later species. The current thought of paleontologists is that all coelurosaurs, a large group that includes *Tyrannosaurus rex*, were feathered.[3] (The picture of *Tyrannosaurus rex* in a fluffy coat of feathers is a little hard on his fearsome image, but sometimes the truth is painful to bear. At least the debate about whether he was a predator or a scavenger seems to have been settled by the discovery of healing bite wounds on the bones of a hydrosaur; only live prey could

---

[1] Benton, Michael J. *Vertebrate Palaeontology*. 3rd ed. Malden, MA: Blackwell, 2005. Pg 219-223.
[2] Hutchinson, John R. "Hot Blooded or Cold Blooded?" University of California Museum of Paleontology. 28 Nov 1995. U C Berkeley. 5 May 2008. < http://www.ucmp.berkeley.edu/diapsids/metabolism.html>.
[3] Benton, Michael J. *Vertebrate Palaeontology*. 3rd ed. Malden, MA: Blackwell, 2005. Pg 199-201.

show healing of the wound, so the big fluff ball was at least partly predatory in his habits.[1])

The Mesozoic Era and the reign of the dinosaurs ended 65.5 million years ago at the K-T boundary. K is for the German spelling of Cretaceous. T is for the Tertiary Period, an older term for the early to middle Cenozoic Era that, although not used in the current standards of the International Commission on Stratigraphy, is commonly referred to in paleontology. The Tertiary (third) Period encompassed what is now referred to as the Paleogene and Neogene Periods of the Cenozoic Era. The Paleogene spans the time from 65.5 to 23.03 million years ago (and the Paleocene, Eocene, and Oligocene Epochs), and the Neogene 23.03 to 1.806 million years ago (the Miocene and Pliocene Epochs). The Quarternary (fourth) Period then completes the Cenozoic Era, extending from 1.806 million years ago to the present day. The Pleistocene Epoch spans the early Quarternary from its beginning to 11,800 years ago; the Holocene Epoch extends until the present day.

It was long known that a major extinction event involving all large dinosaurs (and many other species) occurred worldwide at the same time, and was followed by a major increase in the fern population. Ferns are commonly the earliest plants to colonize land after volcanic ash falls, severe fires, and similar catastrophic events. Luis Alvarez and his colleagues recognized that there existed worldwide, in rocks at the K-T boundary, a thin band of iridium, an element rare on earth but common in certain types of meteors, and in 1980 proposed that the impact of a large meteor and the resulting climate irregularities caused the major extinction event. After ten years of debate and research, the Chicxulub Crater was discovered on the Yucatan Peninsula of Mexico.

The Chicxulub Crater is 195 kilometers (120 miles) in diameter. The walls and floors of the crater have abundant amounts of shocked quartz (quartz with the grain disrupted by extremely high pressures) and glass spherules (small round globules of melted rock and sand material) that chemically match the underlying bedrock. The amounts of shocked quartz and spherules decrease with distance from the crater, but are still a centimeter thick 2000 kilometers away in Colorado, and are detectable all over the world. At least twenty-five archeological sites in surrounding areas are known to show evidence of tsunamis at the K-T boundary. One such site, at Beloc in Haiti, on the island of Hispaniola off the east end of Cuba, shows a remarkable sequence of a layer of glassy spherules, thrown hundreds of miles by the immediate impact of the meteor, with a layer of limestone marls and clays deposited by the tsunamis on top, crowned by a layer of iridium and shocked quartz particles that later settled from the dust

---

[1] Holtz, Thomas R., Jr. "Tyrannosauridae." 29 Aug 2000. Tree of Life Web Project, http://tolweb.org. 5 May 2008. <http://tolweb.org/Tyrannosauridae/15896>.

suspended by the explosive impact.[1, 2]

The impact from the approximately ten kilometer diameter meteor suspended so much dust and debris in the atmosphere that the entire earth was plunged into darkness, and photosynthesis was impossible for a period estimated to be from two to twelve months long. Because of the loss of sunlight, temperatures plummeted to below freezing over much of the earth. Massive forest fires, ignited by debris heated by both the impact itself and by atmospheric re-entry of meteor fragments and impact debris, left layers of charcoal and soot around the world. Carbon dioxide and sulfur oxides released by the impact then caused greenhouse warming that lasted for several centuries.[3]

The effect of the meteor impact on the animal population was irregular. The dinosaurs were famously wiped out along with their cousins the pterosaurs (winged flying reptiles) and plesiosaurs (aquatic predatory reptiles), and birds and marsupial mammals suffered the extinction of seventy-five percent of extant families, but fish, amphibians, lizards, and non-marsupial mammals were only mildly affected. There is some evidence that species of limited geographical distribution, and therefore already somewhat fragile in their survival, were at greater risk of extinction, while those with broader distribution apparently had a greater chance of finding niches in which to survive.[4, 5]

Birds had begun to develop prior to the K-T event. *Archaeopteryx*, justly one of the most famous fossils of history, was discovered in 1860 in late Jurassic deposits of approximately 150 million years of age, in Germany. Five complete and undisputed specimens are now known, along with a separate feather specimen. A sixth complete specimen is considered by many to be *Archaeopteryx*, but is argued to be a different species by some because of its larger size, differences in the bones of its limbs, and shorter tail.[6, 7]

Archaeopteryx bears a striking resemblance to the maniraptor dinosaurs from which it is

---

1 Benton, Michael J. *Vertebrate Palaeontology*. 3rd ed. Malden, MA: Blackwell, 2005. Pg 248-255.
2 Kring, David A. "Chicxlub Impact Event." Undated. *NASA/UA Space Imagery Center's Impact Cratering Series*. 6 May 2008.
<http://www.lpl.arizona.edu/SIC/impact_cratering/Chicxulub/Chicx_title.html>.
3 Kring, David A. "Chicxlub Impact Event." Undated. *NASA/UA Space Imagery Center's Impact Cratering Series*. 6 May 2008.
<http://www.lpl.arizona.edu/SIC/impact_cratering/Chicxulub/Chicx_title.html>.
4 Benton, Michael J. *Vertebrate Palaeontology*. 3rd ed. Malden, MA: Blackwell, 2005. Pg 248-255.
5 Hutchinson, John R. "What Killed the Dinosaurs: the Great Mystery." University of California Museum of Paleontology. 28 Nov 1995. U C Berkeley. 6 May 2008.
<http://www.ucmp.berkeley.edu/diapsids/extinction.html>.
6 Benton, Michael J. *Vertebrate Palaeontology*. 3rd ed. Malden, MA: Blackwell, 2005. Pg 257-258.
7 J, R. P. , et al. "*Archaeopteryx*." University of California Museum of Paleontology. 7 Jan 1996. U C Berkeley. 7 May 2008.
<http://www.ucmp.berkeley.edu/diapsids/birds/archaeopteryx.html>.

descended, retaining a long bony tail, teeth, similar features of the pelvis and hind limbs, a relatively flat sternum, gastralia (rib-like structures protecting the abdomen) and clawed fingers on the leading edge of each wing. Yet the specimens are so well preserved that they clearly show wings covered with layered feathers, making *Archaeopteryx* capable of flight. Paleontologists differ in their opinions as to whether flight originated from the animals' lunging pursuit of insects (remembering that many flying insects at the time were the size of small birds, themselves), or from their efforts to move from limb to limb or from limb to ground after climbing, but there is wide agreement that the structure of *Archaeopteryx* is essentially flight capable.[1, 2]

Birds developed and diversified considerably during the Cretaceous Period. Many retained teeth and long tails, but *Confuciusornis* had a beak and a shortened tail segment composed of fused vertebrae, called a pygostyle, more like modern birds, as well as a sternum with a somewhat larger keel, the area of attachment on the sternum for the most powerful flight muscles. Members of a later Cretaceous group, the enantiornithes, were mostly toothed, but they had characteristics at the bases of their wings that enhanced the wing function and are preserved in modern birds, and their tarsal and metatarsal bones are partially fused, in a development obviously intermediate to the fully fused tarsometatarsal of modern birds. Some late Cretaceous species were secondarily flightless swimming birds, while others had a deep keel, small short pygostyle, and other modern features, while retaining teeth.[3]

Modern birds encompass over nine thousand species in a hundred and fifty-three families, most of which developed after the K-T event. Fossils are scarce and often incomplete, due to the fragility of the small, light, thin-walled avian bones. With so many ecological niches open after the mass extinction of the dinosaurs, however, some of the known species are quite impressive. *Argentavis* was a bird of prey with a wingspan of six meters, about twice that of its cousin the condor. Fossil penguins are as large as a man. In the absence of terrestrial carnivores, the phorusrhacids of Europe and South America and the dromornithids of Australia reached heights of three meters and weights of up to five hundred kilograms (almost ten feet tall and well over a thousand pounds). The Australian dromornithids survived up to about twenty-six thousand years ago. Moas, ostrich-like birds of New Zealand that also ranged in size up three meters, survived until hunted to extinction by prehistoric Polynesian immigrants around 1250 CE.[4, 1]

---

[1] Benton, Michael J. *Vertebrate Palaeontology.* 3rd ed. Malden, MA: Blackwell, 2005. Pg 259-260.
[2] J, R. P. , et al. "*Archaeopteryx*." University of California Museum of Paleontology. 7 Jan 1996. U C Berkeley. 7 May 2008. <http://www.ucmp.berkeley.edu/diapsids/birds/archaeopteryx.html>.
[3] Benton, Michael J. *Vertebrate Palaeontology.* 3rd ed. Malden, MA: Blackwell, 2005. Pg 265-275.
[4] Benton, Michael J. *Vertebrate Palaeontology.* 3rd ed. Malden, MA: Blackwell, 2005. Pg 275-286.

The Cenozoic Era – the age of mammals

This narrative left the synapsid line (animals with one temporal fenestra on each side, which would lead to mammals) with the cynodonts prior to the Permian extinction event. Cynodonts were animals with lizard-like bodies and tails and upright limbs, skulls, and teeth with mammalian features not terribly unlike stocky breeds of dogs. Cynodonts and relatives survived the mass extinction at the end of the Permian in small numbers and in limited diversity, and their mammalian descendants survived the dominance of the dinosaurs during the Mesozoic Era, to diversify and become the dominant but not unchallenged order of vertebrate land animals in the Cenozoic Era.

The early cynodonts *Procynosuchus* and *Dvinia* of the late Permian and *Thrinaxodon* of the early Triassic had a number of skull characteristics that remain characteristic of mammals: a distinct sagittal crest ran over the middle of the top of the skull, the zygomatic arch (cheekbone) was well defined, and the coronoid process of the lower jaw passes inside it, all to provide for the attachment of strong jaw muscles; the hard palate is nearly complete, and the teeth take more mammalian form with reduced numbers of incisors and well-defined cheek teeth. *Thrinaxodon* added a more refined joint between the skull and the first vertebra (two occipital condyles, or articular surfaces, instead of the single condyle of reptiles and more primitive synapsids), a more distinct division between thoracic and lumbar vertebrae, and a limb posture still more upright than earlier forms.[2]

Major changes occurred in the jaw joint and the ear mechanism of later cynodonts. The jaw joint of reptiles, basal synpapsids, and early cynodonts was between the quadrate bone of the skull and the articular bone of the lower jaw. The fossil record shows the development of a second jaw joint, between the squamosal bone of the skull and the dentary bone of the jaw, in front of the older joint, and many cynodont genera as well as the morganucodontids (discussed below) have both sets of joints. The newer jaw joint was more mobile than the old hinge-like joint, and allowed the front-to-back motions that are necessary for gnawing by incisors and the sideways motion necessary for more efficient grinding of foodstuffs by molars. Tritheledontids, dated to the late Triassic and early Jurassic, depended almost entirely on the new squamosal-dentary joint, and the bones involved in the old jaw joint were reduced to rod-shaped elements that transmitted sound to the ear. Fossils of later forms show these bones, after being freed from their role in the primitive older style jaw joint, becoming more closely associated with the ear and migrating into the positions where they are now referred to

---

[1] Wroe, Stephen. "The Bird from Hell?" *Nature Australia* 26.7 (2001) Pg 56-63. Australian Museum Online. <http://www.austmus.gov.au/mammals/fossil/bird_from_hell.htm>.
[2] Benton, Michael J. *Vertebrate Palaeontology.* 3rd ed. Malden, MA: Blackwell, 2005. Pg 289-292.

as the malleus and incus of the mammalian middle ear.[1, 2, 3, 4]

A partial skull of *Adelobasileus* from the late Triassic shows features identifying it as a mammal, as does the skull of *Sinoconodon* from the early Jurassic Period, but the earliest mammals that are known by complete skeletons were the morganucodontids of the early Jurassic. They were small insect eaters similar to shrews, rather rodent-like except for their diet. Their jaws had both the old and the new jaw joints, but the new joint appears to be more functional, with the elements of the old joint reduced and rod-shaped, appearing to function more in sound conduction than in jaw articulation. The teeth met in interlocking patterns referred to as occlusion, and were replaced in only two sets, the milk teeth and permanent teeth typical of mammals. The pelvis had a well-formed acetabulum, or hip socket, and the ball on the femur was equally well developed, allowing for a fully upright posture. Lumbar ribs were no longer present; the presence of a distinct separate thoracic rib cage is a strong indicator for the presence of a diaphragm.[5, 6]

At least twenty families of mammals made their appearance during the Mesozoic era, but the largest group by far was the multituberculates. Multituberculates were rodent-like animals, with forms resembling mice, prairie dogs, and squirrels, but were not true rodents. Rodents have just one incisor in each side of their upper jaws, with enamel on the front only, so that the tooth wears unevenly and stays sharp with use. Multituberculates have the same sort of incisors in their lower jaws, as well as a premolar adapted for shearing that rodents lack. Although quite successful in their day, the multituberculates died out in the late Eocene.[7, 8, 9]

Monotremes – mammals that lay eggs

The most primitive of surviving mammals are the monotremes. The only modern

---

[1] Benton, Michael J. *Vertebrate Palaeontology.* 3rd ed. Malden, MA: Blackwell, 2005. Pg 294-298.
[2] "Mammaliformes: Overview." *Palaeos: The Vertebrates.* Undated. Palaeos.org. 19 May 2008. <http://www.palaeos.com/Vertebrates/Units/Unit420/420.000.html>.
[3] "Mammaliformes: Docondonta." *Palaeos: The Vertebrates.* Undated. Palaeos.org. 19 May 2008. <http://www.palaeos.com/Vertebrates/Units/Unit420/420.200.html>.
[4] "Mammaliformes: Symmetrodonta.." *Palaeos: The Vertebrates.* Undated. Palaeos.org. 19 May 2008. <http://www.palaeos.com/Vertebrates/Units/Unit420/420.300.html>.
[5] Benton, Michael J. *Vertebrate Palaeontology.* 3rd ed. Malden, MA: Blackwell, 2005. Pg 298-303.
[6] "Mammaliformes: Docondonta." *Palaeos: The Vertebrates.* Undated. Palaeos.org. 19 May 2008. <http://www.palaeos.com/Vertebrates/Units/Unit420/420.200.html>.
7 Benton, Michael J. *Vertebrate Palaeontology.* 3rd ed. Malden, MA: Blackwell, 2005. Pg 305-306.
8 "Mammaliformes. Allotheria" *Palaeos: The Vertebrates.* Undated. Palaeos.org. 19 May 2008. <http://www.palaeos.com/Vertebrates/Units/Unit420/420.100.html#Multituberculata>.
9 Weil, Anne. "Introduction to Multituberculates." University of California Museum of Paleontology. 6 July 1997. U C Berkeley. 19 May 2008. < http://www.ucmp.berkeley.edu/mammal/multis/multis.html>.

monotremes are the platypus and four species of echidnas of Australia and New Guinea, but fossils are known as early as the Cretaceous Period.[1] Monotremes lay eggs, then tend the nest and nurse the hatchlings with mammary glands lacking nipples.[2] Although primitive in some traits, the monotremes are possessed of a more developed brain typical of mammals. Echidnas are notoriously difficult to keep captive; aware that their subjects were capable of tunneling through earth and digging holes in wood and plastic, researchers at the University of Melbourne built a pen of corrugated metal only to find that the echidnas had cleverly stacked their water bowls into a staircase in one corner of the pen and used them to climb out and escape.[3] The term monotreme refers to the presence of a single opening that serves the terminal digestive tract, the urinary tract, and the reproductive tract, a condition shared with reptiles including birds, amphibians, and some primitive placental mammals such as golden moles.[4]

The division between the reproductive systems of monotremes, marsupials, and placental mammals is not as stark as many people believe. Monotremes retain their eggs in the uterus for some time, and some limited but active exchange of nutrients and waste products occurs before the egg is laid and the hatchling nursed.[5] Marsupials, or metatherians, retain an egg in the uterus until it hatches, nourishing the developing embryo by means of both the yolk sac contents and nutrients that cross into the enhanced vascular beds of the yolk sac. The newborn marsupial is extremely immature, with internal organs poorly developed, usually without eyes or ears, and often with hind limbs little more than buds. Litters weigh less than one percent of the dam's body weight. The larva-like young metatherian crawls to the mammary gland, mainly by grasping the mother's hair with its more-developed forelimbs, and latches on firmly where it stays for a prolonged period, often but not invariably protected by a pouch.[6, 7] Placental mammals, or eutherians, form a placenta that is more vascular with more intimate contact between fetus and dam, enabling a longer gestation period and a more

---

1 Speer, Brian R. "Monotremata: Fossil Record." University of California Museum of Paleontology. 29 Nov 1997. U C Berkeley. 19 May 2008. <http://www.ucmp.berkeley.edu/mammal>.
2 "Mammalia." *Palaeos: The Vertebrates.* Undated. Palaeos.org. 19 May 2008. <http://www.palaeos.com/Vertebrates/Units/430Mammalia/430.100.html#Monotremata>.
3 Stewart, Doug. "The Enigma of the Echidna." *National Wildlife* 41.3. Apr/May 2003. National Wildlife Federation. 19 May 2008. http://www.nwf.org/nationalwildlife/article.cfm?articleId=763&issueId=61.
4 Benton, Michael J. *Vertebrate Palaeontology.* 3rd ed. Malden, MA: Blackwell, 2005. Pg 325.
5 "Mammalia." *Palaeos: The Vertebrates.* Undated. Palaeos.org. 19 May 2008. <http://www.palaeos.com/Vertebrates/Units/430Mammalia/430.100.html#Monotremata>.
6 Freyer, Claudia, et al. "The marsupial placenta: A phylogenetic analysis." *Journal of Experimental Zoology* vol 229A issue 1 pg 59-77. 25 Aug 2003. Wiley-Liss. 19 May 2008. <www3.interscience.wiley.com/journal/104555452/abstract>.
7 Wund, Matthew, and Phil Myers. "Infraclass Metatheria: marsupial mammals." *Animal Diversity Web.* 2006. University of Michigan Museum of Zoology. 19 May 2008. <http://animaldiversity.ummz.umich.edu/site/accounts/information/Metatheria.html>.

mature newborn. Carnivores such as dogs and cats give birth to young with unopened eyes and ears, but still further developed than marsupials, while the young of grazing animals such as horses, cattle, deer, and antelope are able to stand, walk, and run within minutes of birth.

Early marsupials and placental mammals

Some mammalian fossils from the early Cretaceous are too incomplete to identify confidently as either marsupials or placental mammals;[1, 2] other Cretaceous mammals such as *Sindelphys* and *Deltatheridium* are more completely known but have skeletal characteristics intermediate between known metatherians and known eutherians, and are therefore considered to be basal therians (therian being a term that encompasses both metatherians and eutherians).[3]

Skeletal remains of metatherians and eutherians are distinguishable by a number of characteristics. The presence of epipubic bones, projecting forward from the pelvis in the abdominal wall, is typical of metatherians and monotremes. The braincase of metatherians is generally long and narrow as opposed to a rounder shape in eutherians, and the hard palate of metatherians is heavily fenestrated. The teeth differ in that, excepting wombats, the number of incisors is different in the upper and lower jaws of metatherians, with up to five in the upper jaw and four in the lower, while eutherians typically have equal numbers in the upper and lower jaws with a maximum of three on each side.[4] Metatherians have three premolars and four molars, while eutherians have four or five premolars and three molars.[5, 6]

Marsupials date to the early Cretaceous in North America (*Kokopellia*), and by the end of the Cretaceous the fossil record registers thirty species in three families in North America, South America, and Asia.[7] Placental mammals, too, date to the early Cretaceous (*Eomaia* from China, a remarkably well preserved specimen dating to a hundred and twenty-five million years ago[8]) with ten families known from North

---

1 Benton, Michael J. *Vertebrate Palaeontology.* 3rd ed. Malden, MA: Blackwell, 2005. Pg 308-309.
2 Speer, Brian R., "Eutheria: Fossil Record." University of California Museum of Paleontology. 29 Nov 1997. U C Berkeley. 30 May 2008. <http://www.ucmp.berkeley.edu/mammal/eutheria/eutheriafr.html>.
3 Benton, Michael J. *Vertebrate Palaeontology.* 3rd ed. Malden, MA: Blackwell, 2005. Pg 308-309.
4 Wund, Matthew, and Phil Myers. "Metatheria." *Animal Diversity Web.* 2006 University of Michigan Museum of Zoology. 1 June 2008. <http://animaldiversity.ummz.umich.edu/site/accounts/information/Metatheria.html>.
5 Wund, Matthew, and Phil Myers. "Metatheria." *Animal Diversity Web.* 2006 University of Michigan Museum of Zoology. 1 June 2008. <http://animaldiversity.ummz.umich.edu/site/accounts/information/Metatheria.html>.
6 Benton, Michael J. *Vertebrate Palaeontology.* 3rd ed. Malden, MA: Blackwell, 2005. Pg 309.
7 Benton, Michael J. *Vertebrate Palaeontology.* 3rd ed. Malden, MA: Blackwell, 2005. Pg 309.
8 Benton, Michael J. *Vertebrate Palaeontology.* 3rd ed. Malden, MA: Blackwell, 2005. Pg 310-311.

America and Asia.[1] The K-T extinction event that spelled the end of the non-avian dinosaurs also decimated the mammals, but in the absence of competition for many ecological niches, the mammals radiated extensively in the Cenozoic Era.

Marsupials

Metatherians spread across South America, Antarctica, and Australia when those continents were a part of a land mass called Gondwana. In the isolation of Australia, marsupials had no serious competition and diversified enormously beginning in the middle Paleogene Era. By the Pleistocene Epoch, the Australian marsupials included such spectacular genera as *Procoptodon*, a giant kangaroo that reached heights of three meters (ten feet),[2, 3] herds of a hippopotamus-sized leaf-eating animal, *Diprotodon*, that resembled wombats but were two meters tall at the shoulder and three meters long (and were hunted and butchered by the early Aborigines),[4, 5] and the marsupial lion *Thylacoleo*. Koalas were well-established, having originated in the middle Miocene,[6] and *Thylacinus cynocephalus* (variously referred to as the thylacine, the Tasmanian wolf because of its head and skull, or the Tasmanian tiger because of its striped coat) ranged over much of Australia.[7] Thylacines, like Tasmanian devils, became extinct on the Australian mainland in prehistoric times, apparently due to competition from the dingoes that accompanied humans in colonizing the remote island continent. The last thylacine confirmed in the wild was shot on Tasmania in 1930, and the last known survivor of the species died in a Hobart, Australia zoo in 1936,[8] but unconfirmed sightings of varying quality persist both in Tasmania and on the Australian mainland.[9] The marsupials of Australia developed and diversified because all available ecological niches – browsers, grazers, carnivores – were open without competition from placental mammals. The only terrestrial eutharians that preceded European settlement of Australia were bats, native Aboriginal people and the dingo dogs that accompanied their prehistoric migration, and rodents (about sixty species of rats and mice - no squirrels, beavers, or any of the other twenty-four rodent families - diversified from

---

[1] Benton, Michael J. *Vertebrate Palaeontology*. 3rd ed. Malden, MA: Blackwell, 2005. Pg 310-312.
[2] Benton, Michael J. *Vertebrate Palaeontology*. 3rd ed. Malden, MA: Blackwell, 2005. Pg 313-314.
[3] "Giant Short-faced Kangaroo (*Procoptodon goliah*)." 2004. *Australia's Lost Kingdoms*. Australian Museum. 1 June 2008. < http://www.lostkingdoms.com/facts/factsheet51.htm>.
[4] Benton, Michael J. *Vertebrate Palaeontology*. 3rd ed. Malden, MA: Blackwell, 2005. Pg 313-314.
[5] "Diprotodon (*Diprotodon optatum*)." 2004. *Australia's Lost Kingdoms*. Australian Museum. 1 June 2008. <http://www.lostkingdoms.com/facts/factsheet48.htm>.
[6] Benton, Michael J. *Vertebrate Palaeontology*. 3rd ed. Malden, MA: Blackwell, 2005. Pg 314.
[7] "Tasmanian Thylacine." 2004. *Australia's Lost Kingdoms*. Australian Museum. 1 June 2008. <http://www.lostkingdoms.com/facts/factsheet57.htm>.
[8] Campbell, Cameron R. "Introducing the Thylacine." 2006. *Thylacine Museum*. Natural Worlds. 1 June 2008. <http://www.naturalworlds.org/thylacine>.
[9] Campbell, Cameron R. "The Natural History of *Thylacinus cynocephalus*: Alleged Mainland Thylacine Sightings." 2006. *Thylacine Museum*. Natural Worlds. 1 June 2008. <http://www.naturalworlds.org/thylacine/naturalhistory/alleged_mainland_sightings_1.htm>.

ancestors that arrived around fifteen million years ago).[1]

At the time of the K-T extinction and for much of the following Cenozoic Era, South America was isolated similarly to Australia, resulting in similar but independent development of marsupial mammals resembling dogs, saber-tooth tigers, and bears,[2] alongside placental rodents weighing up to a ton.[3] Opossums are known from very early Cenozoic fossils in South America; they became extinct in North America at the K-T boundary, and re-colonized the northern continent only after a land bridge (the Isthmus of Panama) opened about three million years ago.[4]

Placental mammals of South America

Unlike Australia, where metatherians were unchallenged by eutherians until the arrival of humans and their companion species, South America also was the home of a significant population of placental mammals, some of which survived the extinction event at the end of the Mesozoic Era and diversified during the Cenozoic Era into unusual forms. Xenarthrans, a super-order encompassing sloths and anteaters (order Pilosa), and armadillos (order Cingulata), have origins unique to South America.[5] Armadillo fossils can be found as far back as the early Paleogene, relatively soon after the K-T boundary, and fossil forms range in size up to the one thousand kilogram (twenty-two hundred pound) *Glyptodon*. Like opossums, armadillos colonized the North American land mass after the Panama land bridge opened. Fossil sloths are known from the late Paleogene. Some were small and adapted to life in the trees like modern sloths, but the ground sloths were large animals; *Megatherium* reached six meters (twenty feet) in length and weighed over three thousand kilograms (seven thousand pounds).[6,7] Giant ground sloths of several species migrated to North America with armadillos and opossums, and became extinct only around eleven thousand years ago.[8]

Both the age and the anatomic features of fossil South American rodents suggest that they were present at or soon after the continent separated from Africa and became isolated as an island. Unusual rodents like guinea pigs and chinchillas developed in the

---

[1] "Wildlife of Tasmania: Mammals of Tasmania: Rodents." 5 March 2008. Tasmania Parks and Wildlife Service. 28 May 2008. <http://www.parks.tas.gov.au/wildlife/mammals>.

[2] Benton, Michael J. *Vertebrate Palaeontology.* 3rd ed. Malden, MA: Blackwell, 2005. Pg 314-320, 358.

[3] Rinderknecht, Andrés, and R. Ernesto Blanco. "The largest fossil rodent." *Proceedings of the Royal Society B: Biology.* 275: 1637, pg 923-928, 22 Apr 2008.

[4] Benton, Michael J. *Vertebrate Palaeontology.* 3rd ed. Malden, MA: Blackwell, 2005. Pg 316-320.

[5] "Xenarthrans." Xenarthra.Org. April 2006. *SlothWerks.* 2 June 2008. <http://www.xenarthra.org/xenarthra/ >.

[6] Benton, Michael J. *Vertebrate Palaeontology.* 3rd ed. Malden, MA: Blackwell, 2005. Pg 317-319.

[7] "Ancient Sloths." Xenarthra.org. April 2006. *SlothWerks.* 3 June 2008. <http://www.xenarthra.org/sloth/ground/>.

[8] Benton, Michael J. *Vertebrate Palaeontology.* 3rd ed. Malden, MA: Blackwell, 2005. Pg 317-319.

isolated land mass, as did forms that dwarf the capybara, remarkable as the largest surviving rodent at fifty to seventy kilograms (a hundred ten to a hundred fifty-five pounds). *Telicomys*, from about four million years ago, has been compared in size to a small rhinoceros; *Phoberomys*, from eight million years ago, reached sizes of three meters and seven hundred kilograms (ten feet and fifteen hundred pounds)[1]; the largest rodent known to date is *Josephoartigasia*, discovered in early 2008 in deposits two to four million years old, which weighed in at a thousand kilograms (twenty-two hundred pounds).[2]

Rodents and rabbits

Although modern rodents are a fraction of the size of the South American behemoths of antiquity, the rodents are by any other measure one of the most successful of mammalian orders. Around two thousand of the five thousand living species of mammals are rodents, and they thrive on every major land mass except Antarctica.[3] Fossil rodents dating back sixty million years have been found in North America, Europe, and Asia, and biomolecular studies and geographical distribution suggest origins as early as a hundred to a hundred and twelve million years ago. Muridae, the rats and mice, originated in the Eocene Epoch (the middle epoch of the Paleogene Period) and left an extensive fossil record of their diversification on the way to their current representation by eleven hundred species.[4] Beavers date at least to the Oligocene Epoch, and some fossil forms from as recently as the Pleistocene Epoch were as large as bears.[5] Squirrels and their relatives in the sciuridae family - chipmunks, marmots, and prairie dogs - originated about thirty six million years ago, and now occupy a variety of habitats on every major land mass except Antarctica, Australia and New Zealand, and Madagascar.[6]

Lagamorphs – rabbits, hares, and pikas – diverged from rodents about fifty million years ago.[7] Although their body shape, skulls, diets, and lifestyles are similar to rodents,

---

[1] Benton, Michael J. *Vertebrate Palaeontology.* 3rd ed. Malden, MA: Blackwell, 2005. Pg 356-359.
[2] Rinderknecht, Andrés, and R. Ernesto Blanco. "The largest fossil rodent." *Proceedings of the Royal Society B: Biology.* 275: 1637, pg 923-928, 22 Apr 2008.
[3] Myers, Phil. "Rodentia." *Animal Diversity Web.* 2000. University of Michigan Museum of Zoology. 3 June 2008. <http://animaldiversity.ummz.umich.edu/site/accounts/information/Rodentia.html>.
[4] Benton, Michael J. *Vertebrate Palaeontology.* 3rd ed. Malden, MA: Blackwell, 2005. Pg 323, 354-359.
[5] Myers, Phil. "Castoridae." *Animal Diversity Web.* 2000. University of Michigan Museum of Zoology. 8 June 2008. <http://animaldiversity.ummz.umich.edu/site/accounts/information/Castoridae.html>.
[6] Steppan, Scott J., and Shawn M. Hamm. "Sciuridae. Squirrels." 13 May 2006. *Tree of Life Web Project*, http://tolweb.org/. 13 May 2006. < http://tolweb.org/Sciuridae/16456/2006.05.13>.
[7] "*Lepus.*" *The Hall of Florida Fossils.* Undated. Florida Museum of Natural History, U of Florida. 10 June 2008. <http://www.flmnh.ufl.edu/fossilhall/Library/Lepus/LeapingLepus.htm>.

their dentition differs in that the lagamorphs have a second set of small incisors in each side of the jaw.

Elephants and their relatives

The breakup of Gondwana left Africa relatively isolated, resulting in a group of mammals with uniquely African origins, some of which later migrated to other parts of the world via the land bridge that would form at the eastern end of the Mediterranean Sea. The Afrotherians include the aardvark, the insectivorous *Afrosoricida* which in turn includes twenty-four species of tenrecs (hedgehog-like animals) and eighteen species of golden moles, and the Paenungulata. The paenungulates diversified in the early Eocene into three lines. The hyraxes are six species of rabbit-sized herbivores, sometimes referred to as conies or dassies, which live in Africa and the Middle East. The manatees, or sea cows, are aquatic animals that inhabit warm coastal waters. Early forms such as *Pezosiren* had short legs for walking on land and in shallow waters, but by the Miocene, *Dusisiren* had paddles for front legs, vestigial rear limbs, and a large horizontal tail like modern forms.[1]

The third group of paenungulates is the Proboscidea – the elephants and their relatives, the fossil record for which is dramatic and extensive. *Phosphatherium* weighed about fifteen kilograms (thirty-three pounds) and is known from late Paleocene and early Eocene fossils in Morocco.[2, 3] Like its later and somewhat larger relation *Moeritherium*, it is thought to have lived like a small hippopotamus, grazing on aquatic plants in shallow waters. *Moeritherium* was seventy to a hundred centimeters (two to three feet) tall, and is well represented in north African fossils of the late Eocene and Oligocene.[4] Aside from prominent incisors developing towards tusks and a short flexible snout like a tapir, *Moeritherium* was similar in appearance and habits to its cousin and contemporary, the early sea cow *Pezosiren*. A series of fossils follows in north Africa, showing animals of increasing size and with ever enlarging tusks. Deinotheres branched away from elephantiforms in the late Eocene. Deinotheres that survived until the mid-Pleistocene were massive animals up to five meters (sixteen feet) tall with lower tusks protruding from the bottom of the lower jaw and curling under the chin. [5, 6]

Phiomia of the late Eocene and early Oligocene was up to 2.4 meters (seven to eight feet) tall and had a short trunk. Like its predecessors, it grazed in shallow waters, and

---

1 Benton, Michael J. *Vertebrate Palaeontology.* 3rd ed. Malden, MA: Blackwell, 2005. Pg 323-326.
2 Benton, Michael J. *Vertebrate Palaeontology.* 3rd ed. Malden, MA: Blackwell, 2005. Pg 326.
3 Koehl, Dan. "The genus *Phosphatherium.*" *Elephants Encyclopedia.* 2008. Absolut Elephant. 12 June 2008. <http://www.elephant.se/phosphatherium.php>.
4 Benton, Michael J. *Vertebrate Palaeontology.* 3rd ed. Malden, MA: Blackwell, 2005. Pg 326.
5 Benton, Michael J. *Vertebrate Palaeontology.* 3rd ed. Malden, MA: Blackwell, 2005. Pg 326.
6 Koehl, Dan. "The family *Deinotherium.*" *Elephants Encyclopedia.* 2008. Absolut Elephant. 12 June 2008. < http://www.elephant.se/deinotherium.php>.

its shovel-shaped lower tusks projected forward almost to the end of the trunk, apparently for scooping food.[1] A descendant genus with a similar skull and lower tusks, *Gomphotherium*, spread to Europe, southern Asia, and North America before dying out in the Pleistocene.[2] Mastodons, equal in size to modern elephants but with rounded cusps in the cheek teeth, originated in central Asia, and by the early Miocene had rapidly spread throughout Asia, Europe, Africa, and North America, where they survived until about ten thousand years ago.[3]

Mammoths and modern elephants have molars with alternating ridges of enamel, cement, and dentine, making them efficient at processing tough plant materials. Mammoths appear in the fossil record beginning about two million years ago, originating in Africa and spreading to Europe, Asia, and North America. They became extinct in Europe only about twelve thousand years ago, in North America ten thousand years ago, and from a remote island of arctic Russia only four thousand years ago. Our knowledge of mammoths is not limited to the fossil record, however; frozen carcasses have been excavated from Siberia and Alaska.[4] The two surviving species of elephants are the last remnants of a group that were important and even dominating elements of the fauna of all the continents except Australia and Antarctica for well over thirty million years, until a time barely preceding the historical record of mankind.

Extinct Paleocene mammals

The Paleocene Epoch saw rapid radiation of placental mammals in other parts of the world, as well, including the rodents and their cousins the lagamorphs, insectivores, carnivores, primates, perissodactyls (hoofed animals with an odd number of hooves, one or three), and about fifteen other groups that left no surviving descendants. Extinct lines include small shrew-like animals, a group superficially resembling otters but not closely related, and rooting and browsing animals of various sizes up to that of *Uintatherium*, an animal the size of a rhinoceros with multiple skull protuberances that made him famously ugly. Exctinct carnivores from the Paleocene include odd wolf-like creatures with hoofs and one species, *Andrewsarchus*, with a skull eight hundred thirty millimeters (thirty-two inches) long and five hundred sixty millimeters (twenty-two inches) wide, indicating a body length of five to six meters (sixteen to twenty feet).[5]

---

[1] Koehl, Dan. "*Phioma.*" *Elephants Encyclopedia.* 2008. Absolut Elephant. 12 June 2008. <http://www.elephant.se/phiomia.php?open=Extinct%20Proboscidea>.

[2] Koehl, Dan. "The genus *Gompotherium.*" *Elephants Encyclopedia.* 2008. Absolut Elephant. 12 June 2008. <http://www.elephant.se/gomphotherium.php>.

[3] Benton, Michael J. *Vertebrate Palaeontology.* 3rd ed. Malden, MA: Blackwell, 2005. Pg 326-328.

[4] Benton, Michael J. *Vertebrate Palaeontology.* 3rd ed. Malden, MA: Blackwell, 2005. Pg 326-329.

[5] Benton, Michael J. *Vertebrate Palaeontology.* 3rd ed. Malden, MA: Blackwell, 2005. Pg 329-334.

Bats

Bats (chiropterans) are nearly as diverse as rodents, with around a thousand species grouped in two clades, the fruit bats, or megachiropterans, and the smaller insectivorous microchiropterans. Because the bones of bats are small, light, and fragile in being adapted for flight, they do not fossilize readily, but bat fossils have been detected as early as fifty-six million years ago, in the late Paleocene Epoch, and the early Eocene *Icaronycteris* is both well preserved and well developed in its features.[1] The wings of bats, unlike birds and the flying reptiles of the Mesozoic Era, are supported by elongated elements of all four fingers. The first digit, or pollex, homologous to the human thumb, remains as a small clawed appendage used for climbing and walking on the ground. (Contrary to popular conception, some bats move about extensively on the ground in search of insect prey.)[2]

Insectivores

The closest relatives of bats are the animals of the insectivore order, or Lipotyphla. The term insectivore rightly applies to any animal that consumes insects, but zoologists and paleontologists also take the confusing course of referring to this order, composed of the moles, shrews, hedgehogs, and solenodons, as insectivores, as if animals of other orders do not eat insects. They radiated in the late Cretaceous, at least ninety million years ago, and are the basal members of a group that includes such diverse animals as cattle, pigs, horses, carnivores, and whales. True shrews (at last, not a "shrew-like" animal) date to the mid-Paleocene, and moles and hedgehogs each branched off in the Eocene.[3] Solenodons deserve mention because of their basal anatomy and their severely endangered status. Although they are now only represented by two species, one each on the islands of Cuba and Hispaniola, they inhabited a large portion of North America around thirty million years ago. They look like small opossums (or, dare it be said again, large shrews) and have largely succumbed to predation by dogs, cats, and mongooses that were imported for the control of rodents. They are notably primitive in their skeletal and dental features, and although they form true placentas, their young are born in an immature state and latch on to one of the two nipples (oddly located on the mother's caboose) in a manner reminiscent of marsupials. Unusual features include a grooved lower second incisor that can deliver toxic saliva to prey, and an extra jointed bone in the end of their impressive snout that allows it extraordinary

---

[1] Benton, Michael J. *Vertebrate Palaeontology*. 3rd ed. Malden, MA: Blackwell, 2005. Pg 335-336.

[2] Speer, Brian R. "Chiroptera." University of California Museum of Paleontology. 20 Aug 1995. U C Berkeley. 30 May 2008. <http://www.ucmp.berkeley.edu/mammal/eutheria/chiroptera.html>.

[3] Benton, Michael J. *Vertebrate Palaeontology*. 3rd ed. Malden, MA: Blackwell, 2005. Pg 335-336.

agility in the exploration of small nooks and crannies.[1]

Perissodactyls – horses and their relatives

Early in the Eocene Epoch, the perissodactyls diversified and began to replace the basal placental mammals in their role as browsing herbivores.[2] The perissodactyls are hoofed herbivores with an odd number of toes. The most fully derived perissodactyl limb structure is found in horses, asses, and zebras. The hoof of equines is the nail of the third finger or toe. The third phalanx, the last bone of the digit, is fully encased in the hoof, and the first and second phalanges and their knuckles are markedly reduced in relative length and incorporated into the lower segment of the leg that horsemen call the pastern. The fetlock or ankle of the horse is the metacarpophalangeal (in the front leg) or metatarsophalangeal (in the rear leg) joint, the joint between the long bones of the hand or foot and the first segment of the finger or toe, what would be referred to as the first knuckle of the human fist. The canon of a horse, the long portion of the lower limb, is composed primarily of the third metacarpal of the hand or the third metatarsal of the foot, with second and fourth metacarpals and metatarasals each reduced to a small nub at the upper end that contributes a small amount to the joint surface, attached to thin shafts that taper to nothing at a point half or two-thirds of the way down the canon. (These bones are called splint bones by horsemen.) No trace of the first or fifth digits, metacarpals, or metatarsals can be found in normal equines. The joint that is referred to as the knee of the horse is actually the carpus, or wrist, and the hock is the tarsus, or ankle. The partially fused radius and ulna in the front leg, and the fully fused tibia and fibula in the rear leg, are heavy and powerful, placing the elbow and the true knee, or stifle, slightly above the bottom edge of the trunk. The humerus and femur are relatively short, thick, and powerfully built.

The extraordinary length of the lower limb that we take for granted when we see a modern horse makes the animal very efficient in moving from one grazing site to the next and swift enough to outrun almost any predator. The fossil record shows that the unusual limb structure of the horse, as well as check teeth that allow it to live primarily on grasses high in silicate and therefore abrasive and wearing to teeth, developed over a period of fifty million years.

---

[1] Ciszek, Deborah. "Solenodontidae." *Animal Diversity Web.* 2000. University of Michigan Museum of zoology. 12 June 2008. <http://animaldiversity.ummz.umich.edu/site/accounts/information/Solenodontidae.html>.

[2] Benton, Michael J. *Vertebrate Palaeontology.* 3rd ed. Malden, MA: Blackwell, 2005. Pg 345-346.

The family tree of horses includes twenty-eight genera on its several branches,[1] the only surviving one being *Equus* with its one species each of horses, asses and donkeys, and desert onagers, and three species of zebras. (A seventh *Equus* species, the quagga, became extinct only in the late nineteenth century.) The earliest equine was *Hyracotherium*, often called eohippus; it was so primitive that it is regarded by some as the common ancestor of horses, rhinoceroses, and tapirs. Eohippus was a small browser of leaves and fruit, twenty five to fifty centimeters tall (ten to twenty inches), with each jaw containing three incisors, a canine, three well-differentiated premolars, and three molars. Its front feet had four toes and its rear three, with pads like dogs and cats and small hoof-shaped nails on each toe. The *Hyracotherium* species were quite successful and thrived from fifty-five to forty-five million years ago (early Eocene), and around fifty-two million years ago gradually transitioned to and coexisted with *Orohippus*. *Orohippus* was the same size, with the same padded feet with four toes in the front and three in the rear (although the vestigial toes disappeared entirely), but its last premolar became a grinding tooth, shaped like a molar. Around forty-seven million years ago, *Epihippus* added the second premolar to the grinding teeth of the cheek and joined its cousins in browsing the Eocene scrub and woodlands of North America. At thirty-seven to forty million years, species of the genus *Mesohippus* began to appear, with still another premolar converted to grinding molar functionality, giving a total of six in each jaw, a feature retained in all subsequent genera leading to modern horses. *Mesohippus* was also somewhat taller at sixty centimeters (twenty-four inches) and had longer legs, neck, and face.[2, 3] The forelimbs of *Mesohippus* had three toes, reduced from the four of its predecessors, and the third digit of all four limbs was notably thicker than the second and fourth, from the level of the metacarpals and metatarsals down through the phalanges of the fingers and toes.[4]

About thirty-six million years ago (late Eocene), *Miohippus* branched off from *Mesohippus*, and species of the two genera coexisted for around four million years. *Miohippus* was slightly larger than *Mesohippus*, had a longer face and a ridge along its upper cheek teeth, and developed from its parent genus in a series of known and documented intermediates. In the early Miocene, around twenty-four million years ago, a burst of rapid diversification gave birth to three distinct lines from *Miohippus*. The first branch, species of the genus *Archeohippus*, were slender and graceful of build, but smaller than *Miohippus*, about the size of a collie. They were a short-lived group,

---

[1] McFadden, Bruce J. "Fossil Horses – Evidence for Evolution." *Science,* vol 307, no 5716 (18 March 2005) , pg 1728-1730.

[2] Hunt, Kathleen. "Horse Evolution." 4 Jan 1995. *TalkOrigins Archive.* 16 June 2008. <http://www.talkorigins.org/faqs/horses/horse_evol.html>.

[3] "Fossil Horse Gallery." *Fossil Horse Cybermuseum.* 16 June 2008. Florida Museum of Natural History, U of Florida. 16 June 2008. < http://www.flmnh.ufl.edu/fhc/Stratmap1.htm>.

[4] Benton, Michael J. Vertebrate Palaeontology. 3rd ed. Malden, MA: Blackwell, 2005. Pg 346-347.

becoming extinct about thirteen million years ago and leaving no descendants. The second branch was the anchitheres, a succession of browsing three-toed horse-like animals beginning with the donkey-sized *Anchitherium*, progressing to *Hypohippus* of seventeen to eleven million years ago, *Megahippus*, weighing 265 kg (585 pounds) and living from fifteen to eleven million years ago, and *Sinohippus* of the east Asian Miocene.[1, 2]

The third branch arising from *Miohippus* were grazing animals, adapting to the then-developing grasslands of North America. Over the course of its existence, twenty-four to seventeen million years ago, *Parahippus* developed the higher crowns, continuous growth, and multiple layers of dentine and cement in the cheek teeth that were necessary for horses to feed on the abrasive high-silicate grasses. It also developed a system of elastic ligaments that suspended and stabilized the fetlock joint. (Modern horses have a springy joint referred to as the suspensory apparatus that contributes to the stride without muscular effort by the horse.) The direct successor to *Parahippus*, documented in a series of fossils so complete that some specimens are difficult to place in one genus or another, was *Merychippus*. *Merychippus* stood about a hundred centimeters tall (forty inches), and had high-crowned teeth with distinct ridges and crests and complex layers, a fully developed fetlock suspensory apparatus, fused radius and ulna and a reduced fibula that limited rotation in the lower limbs, and a larger and more complex brain that its forebears. The central third phalanx was enlarged, and the second and fourth phalanges reduced, to the point that they did not touch the ground in many species. From seventeen to eleven million years ago, *Merychippus* was the smarter, faster, more agile grazer that dominated the new expanses of grasslands.[3, 4]

Merychippus became the base for another major radiation. The protohippines were a group of small grazing horses in three genera. The hipparions were a group of four genera of large three-toed grazers and browsers that spread through much of North America, Europe, and Asia. The true equines began with *Dinohippus* of the middle to late Miocene, thirteen to five million years ago. Most previous species had deep fenestrae of unknown function in front of the eyes, as did the contemporary *Pliohippus*, but the fenestrae were markedly reduced in *Dinohippus* and are absent in modern species of *Equus*. *Dinohippus* had a large central toe on each foot, with second and fourth toes either absent or too small to reach the ground. It was the first horse to possess the

---

[1] Hunt, Kathleen. "Horse Evolution." 4 Jan 1995. *TalkOrigins Archive.* 16 June 2008. <http://www.talkorigins.org/faqs/horses/horse_evol.html>.
[2] "Fossil Horse Gallery." *Fossil Horse Cybermuseum.* 16 June 2008. Florida Museum of Natural History, U of Florida. 16 June 2008. < http://www.flmnh.ufl.edu/fhc/Stratmap1.htm>.
[3] Hunt, Kathleen. "Horse Evolution." 4 Jan 1995. *TalkOrigins Archive.* 16 June 2008. <http://www.talkorigins.org/faqs/horses/horse_evol.html>.
[4] "Fossil Horse Gallery." *Fossil Horse Cybermuseum.* 16 June 2008. Florida Museum of Natural History, U of Florida. 16 June 2008. < http://www.flmnh.ufl.edu/fhc/Stratmap1.htm>.

ability to lock its legs for rest, a characteristic retained in modern equines.[1, 2]

The genus *Equus* is about five million years old. The first members of the genus were stocky and thick-necked, but definitely modern equines with single central toes, a complete suspensory apparatus of the fetlock, fusion of the ulna with the radius and the fibula with the tibia, and a larger brain than *Dinohippus.* When the major glaciers formed about 2.6 million years ago in the late Pleiocene, equines migrated from North America to Europe, Asia, and from there to Africa, and with the opening of the Isthmus of Panama, to South America, where the Clydesdale-sized *Hippidion* developed only to die out about ten thousand years ago. Equines were the dominant grazing animals on all continents except Antarctica and Australia until about a million years ago, when most of the large mammals of the Americas, including saber-tooth tigers and mammoths along with horses, began a decline that led to their extinction.[3, 4]

Besides horses, the other surviving perissodactyls are the rhinoceroses and the tapirs, browsing animals with three hoofed toes on each limb. Rhinoceroses in their heyday were as widespread as horses and mammoths, ranging over North America, Europe, and Asia. Early forms of the Eocene and Oligocene, like *Hyracodon*, were, as expected, similar to horses and tapirs. Later rhinoceroses included the largest land mammal that ever lived, *Paraceratherium* (known also as *Indricotherium* and as *Baluchitherium*), five and a half meters (over seventeen and a half feet) tall at the shoulder and weighing thirteen thousand five hundred kilograms (thirty thousand pounds), and the wooly rhinoceros *Coelodonta* that was widely hunted - and depicted in cave paintings - by early humans in Europe and Russia before dying out around ten thousand years ago. Tapirs, too, originated in North America and migrated extensively before dying out to their present populations in Central and South America and southeast Asia. Extinct lines of perissodactyls include the brontotheres, heavily built animals resembling rhinoceroses that lived only during the Eocene, and the chalicotheres, strange browsing animals with long hooved forelimbs and short hind limbs giving them the stance of a gorilla with the head of a horse, that died out in the Pleistocene.[5]

---

[1] Hunt, Kathleen. "Horse Evolution." 4 Jan 1995. *TalkOrigins Archive.* 16 June 2008. <http://www.talkorigins.org/faqs/horses/horse_evol.html>.
[2] "Fossil Horse Gallery." *Fossil Horse Cybermuseum.* 16 June 2008. Florida Museum of Natural History, U of Florida. 16 June 2008. < http://www.flmnh.ufl.edu/fhc/Stratmap1.htm>.
[3] Hunt, Kathleen. "Horse Evolution." 4 Jan 1995. *TalkOrigins Archive.* 16 June 2008. <http://www.talkorigins.org/faqs/horses/horse_evol.html>.
[4] "Fossil Horse Gallery." *Fossil Horse Cybermuseum.* 16 June 2008. Florida Museum of Natural History, U of Florida. 16 June 2008. < http://www.flmnh.ufl.edu/fhc/Stratmap1.htm>.
[5] Benton, Michael J. *Vertebrate Palaeontology.* 3rd ed. Malden, MA: Blackwell, 2005. Pg 347-348.

Artiodactyls – animals with paired hooves

Although hunting by early humans and environmental changes played their roles, one of the primary reasons for the decline of the perissodactyls was competition from artiodactyls – pigs, cattle, deer, and related animals. Artiodactyls have even numbers of toes, two or four. The center two toes, the third and fourth digits, usually bear hooves and are always the primary weight bearing digits, most often the only digits bearing weight.

A defining feature of artiodactyls is a characteristic of the tarsus (or the hock, or ankle joint) called the double-pulley astragalus. The astragalus is a bone in the tarsus also known as the talus. In other terrestrial mammals, the tarsus is composed of three rows of bones. The top row, immediately below the tibia, has two bones, the talus and the calcaneous. The talus has a spool-shaped top surface, the condyle, that articulates with the bottom of the tibia, and the calcaneous (the heel) provides a lever for the attachment of the muscles that extend the tarsus. The second row is a single disk-shaped bone, the central tarsal. The third row, just above the metatarsals of the foot, is composed of four small roughly cubical bones that are most common referred to by number (first tarsal, second tarsal, etc.). Most of the motion of the hock joint is between the tibia and the talus, but the other layers of bone allow a small amount of rotation and lateral flexion. In artiodactyls the tarsus has spool-shaped condyles both on top, articulating with the tibia as in other animals, and on the bottom, articulating in a unique way with the central tarsal. The central tarsal has a corresponding hollow and, in most artiodactyls, is fused with one or more of the lower tarsals. The other lower tarsals are often reduced and fused as well. This modification transforms the hock joint into a hinge with virtually no lateral or rotational movement and, combined with the tendons and ligaments that cross the joint, gives the joint a degree of passive elasticity or "spring." The talus with a condyle on each end is what paleontologists refer to as the double-pulley astragalus, typical of artiodactyls with or without the other more derived modifications of tarsal fusion.

The oldest known artiodactyl, *Diacodexis*, descended in the very early Eocene from even more basal mammals called condylarths. *Diacodexis* had four toes on each limb, with the third and fourth digits notably enlarged and hoofed, to bear most of the weight of the rabbit-sized body. The double-pulley astragulus was already a feature of the tarsus of this basal artiodactyl. These and other basal artiodactyls survived into the Oligocene, to coexist with more derived descendant artiodactyls.[1]

Suiforms, the group that includes pigs and hippopotami, diversified and radiated in the late Eocene. By the end of the Oligocene, pigs and peccaries were present in North America and Europe, and a large relative called the entelodont, up to three meters (ten

---

[1] Benton, Michael J. *Vertebrate Palaeontology*. 3rd ed. Malden, MA: Blackwell, 2005. Pg 339.

feet) long was common in North America. Fossil hippopotami from Kenya date to the Miocene.[1] Living peccaries have several features that are transitional to more derived artiodactyls, in the fusion of metacarpals and metatarsals, the fusion of the ulna to the radius, and the development of a complex stomach.[2]

Ruminants – cattle, sheep, goats, antelope, bison, buffalo, and deer – are artiodactyls that digest plant material by means of a stomach with up to four chambers. The first and largest chamber, the rumen, serves as a fermentation vat for microbes to digest the ingested plant material. A ruminant may regurgitate and re-chew the material – chew its cud - to further break it down, remix it, and give the resident microbes further access to the plant material. The partially digested plant material and a large measure of the microbes in the slurry are eventually passed through the other chambers of the stomach and into the intestinal tract where the nutrients are extracted and absorbed for use by the host ruminant animal.

The digestive tract of ruminants makes more efficient use of plant material than the simple stomach of perissodactyls, and at least partly for that reason, ruminants became the dominant group of grazing animals in most parts of the world. *Hypertragulus*, a rabbit-sized animal with dental and skeletal characteristics of ruminants, appeared in the late Eocene and its descendent traguloids are common fossils through the Oligocene. In the Miocene, the modern groups radiated (and included some spectacular specimens like *Megaloceros*, the Irish Elk, which stood over two meters [seven feet] tall and carried antlers spanning over three and a half meters [twelve feet] during the Pleistocene) and the decline of perissodactyls began. Graphs of the numbers of genera of each group show perissodactyls declining in numbers and diversity while artiodactyls expand throughout the Oligocene, Miocene, Pliocene, and Pleistocene.[3, 4] In these more derived forms, the metacarpals and metatarsals, or canon bones, are shaped like an inverted Y, fused for much of their length but with separate articular surfaces for each of the remaining third and fourth digits, and fusion of bones in the last row of the tarsus is almost universal.[5] Again, living intermediates exist, in the form of mouse deer or tragulids of Africa and southeast Asia. The canon bones of tragulids are only

---

[1] Benton, Michael J. *Vertebrate Palaeontology*. 3rd ed. Malden, MA: Blackwell, 2005. Pg 339-340.
[2] "The Collared Peccary, or Javelina." *Big Bend National Park*. 27 Aug 2006. National Park Service, U. S. Dept. of Interior. 22 June 2008. <http://www.nps.gov/bibe/naturescience/javelina.htm>.
[3] Benton, Michael J. *Vertebrate Palaeontology*. 3rd ed. Malden, MA: Blackwell, 2005. Pg 340-343.
[4] Waggoner, Ben. "Artiodactyla: Fossil Record." *University of California Museum of Paleontology*. 26 Jan 1996. U C Berkeley. 22 June 2008. <http://www.ucmp.berkeley.edu/mammal>.
[5] Myers, Phil. "Order Artiodactyla: even-toed ungulates." *Animal Diversity Web*. 2001. U of Michigan Museum of Zoology. 22 June 2008. <http://animaldiversity.ummz.umich.edu/site/accounts/information/Artiodactyla.html.>

partially fused, the tarsal bones are unfused (although the ubiquitous artiodactyl double-pulley astragalus is present), and small remnants of the second and fifth digits remain.[1]

Mounting evidence of recent years, both biochemical studies and anatomic observations from fossils discovered since the beginning of the twenty-first century, strongly suggests that whales and dolphins descended from artiodactyls. The earliest known predecessor of modern whales lived about fifty-five million years ago, in the very early Eocene. Although the skeletons are incomplete, enough is known of *Pakicetus* and two similar genera to determine that they were land-dwelling wading carnivores with the double-pulley astragalus of artidactyls, and nostrils placed well down the snout, but with an ear structure and other features of later whales.[2, 3] The skeleton of *Ambulocetus* is nearly complete, and the similar *Rhodocetus* and *Artiocetus* less so, dating to around forty-seven million years ago. All had four fully developed limbs, with the double-pulley astralgus present in the tarsi, but with reduced sacrums (the portion of the pelvis that connects to the spine). The limbs were paddle-shaped but, at least in the case of *Rhodocetus*, the digits of the front limbs bore small hooves. The limbs were probably used like those of a modern seals on land, with an awkward lunging gait, with the hind limbs and tail used for propulsion in the water.[4, 5, 6] *Basilosaurus* had a long narrow trunk and small head that has led some to compare it to mythical sea serpents, while *Zygorhiza* and its relatives, the dorudontids, had proportions more like a modern dolphin. Both lived from thirty-five to forty million years ago, in the late Eocene, and were distributed in most or all of the warm seas of the time. The hind limbs are greatly reduced but still present with all their bony elements, and the pelvis does not attach to the spine.[7, 8] Oligocene fossils include a notable specimen,

---

[1] Myers, Phil. "Family Tragluidae: chevrotains and mouse deer." *Animal Diversity Web.* 2001. U of Michigan Museum of Zoology. 22 June 2008. <http://animaldiversity.ummz.umich.edu/site/accounts/information/Tragulidae.html>.

[2] Benton, Michael J. *Vertebrate Palaeontology.* 3rd ed. Malden, MA: Blackwell, 2005. Pg 342-345.

[3] Thewison, J. G. M. "Pakicetidae." *Whale Origins Research: The Thewison Lab.* Undated. Northeast Ohio Universities Colleges of Medicine and Pharmacy. 23 June 2008. <http://www.neoucom.edu/DEPTS/ANAT/Thewissen/whale_origins/index.html>.

[4] Benton, Michael J. *Vertebrate Palaeontology.* 3rd ed. Malden, MA: Blackwell, 2005. Pg 342-345.

[5] Gingerich, Philip D., et al. "Origin of Whales from Early Artiodactyls: Hands and Feet of Eocene Protocetidae from Pakistan." 21 Sept 2001. *Science,* vol 293, no 5538, pg 2239-2242.

[6] Milinkovitch, Michel C., and Olivier Lambert. "Cetacea: Whales, dolphins, and porpoises." 7 Aug 2006. *Tree of Life Web Project,* http://tolweb.org/. 23 June 2008. <http://www.tolweb.org/Cetacea/15977>.

[7] Benton, Michael J. *Vertebrate Palaeontology.* 3rd ed. Malden, MA: Blackwell, 2005. Pg 342-345.

[8] Thewison, J. G. M. "Basilosaurids and Dorudontids." *Whale Origins Research: The Thewison Lab.* Undated. Northeast Ohio Universities Colleges of Medicine and Pharmacy. 23 June 2008. <http://www.neoucom.edu/DEPTS/ANAT/Thewissen/whale_origins/index.html>.

Aetiocetus, with skull and jaw features typical of baleen whales but bearing a full set of teeth.[1] During the late Oligocene and Miocene, whales differentiated into the toothed whales, or odontocetes, including dolphins, orcas, belugas, and sperm whales, and the baleen whales, the great filter feeders like the humpback whale and the largest animal to ever live, the blue whale. Modern whales have vestiges of a pelvic girdle, while the forelimb is functional as the pectoral fin.[2]

Carnivores

To understand the origins of carnivores – dogs, cats, bears, seals, and their relatives – we return yet again to a time fifty-five million years ago, near the border between the Paleocene and Eocene Epochs, a time when many ecological niches were available after the extinction of the dinosaurs. Early primitive mammals had multiplied and were beginning to diversify and specialize, as we have seen time and again.

(The carnivores of this discussion, in the same manner as the insectivores previously discussed, are a taxonomic grouping, and the reader should note that not all members of the order carnivore are meat eaters, and that members of other orders may be primarily or exclusively carnivorous in their dietary habits.)

The distinctive characteristic of carnivores is the presence of pronounced canine teeth and carnassial teeth. Carnassials consist of the last premolar in the upper jaw and the first molar in the lower jaw, which in carnivores are blade shaped. Because the lower jaw is slightly narrower than the upper, and the jaw joint of carnivores is modified to minimize lateral (sideways) motion, the upper and lower cheek teeth close like scissors to shear flesh and small bones. Chewing, however, in the sense of the grinding function of flattened molars, is reduced or absent.[3, 4, 5]

The earliest known animals with carnivore dentition are the miacids of the late Paleocene and early Eocene, represented by *Vulvapus* and *Tapocyon*. They were small to

---

[1] Waggoner, Ben M. "Introduction to the Cetacea: Whales and Dolphins." University of California Museum of Paleontology. 2 Feb 2001. U C Berkeley. 23 June 2008. <http://www.ucmp.berkeley.edu/mammal/cetacea/cetacean.html>.

[2] Benton, Michael J. *Vertebrate Palaeontology*. 3rd ed. Malden, MA: Blackwell, 2005. Pg 342-345.

[3] Benton, Michael J. *Vertebrate Palaeontology*. 3rd ed. Malden, MA: Blackwell, 2005. Pg 348.

[4] Myers, Phil, and Allison Poor. "Order Carnivora: carnivores." *Animal Diversity Web*. 2007. U of Michigan Museum of Zoology. 25 June 2008. <http://animaldiversity.ummz.umich.edu/site/accounts/information/Carnivora.html>.

[5] Waggoner, Ben M. "Morphology of the Carnivora." *University of California Museum of Paleontology*. 14 Jan 1996. U C Berkeley. 25 June 2008. <http://www.ucmp.berkeley.edu/mammal>.

medium-sized terrestrial and arborial animals, many with retractable claws.[1,2]

In the late Eocene, carnivores diverged into feliforms and caniforms. Civets and their relatives, the viverrids, originated on Madagascar in the late Eocene and spread to mainland Africa and to southern Europe and Asia.[3,4] Among their descendants are the true felines, dating from the early Oligocene. Cats, ranging in size from the 1.4 kilogram (three pound) sand cat *Felis margarita* of desert areas of north Africa, the Arabian peninsula, and southwestern Asia,[5] to modern tigers *Panthera tigris* weighing over four hundred kilograms (nine hundred pounds),[6] and the *Smilodon* genus of saber-tooth tigers that lived from the late Pleistocene until about ten thousand years ago and weighed twice as much as modern tigers,[7] are and have been the most specialized and capable hunters among the terrestrial mammals, as well as the most fully dedicated carnivores. Other members of the Carnivora order are, to one extent or another, omnivores or scavengers, as can be attested by anyone who has ever muttered invectives against the neighborhood dogs while cleaning up from the yard the produce of a tipped garbage can. Among other feliforms, mongooses arose in the late Oligocene and hyenas in the Miocene.[8]

The caniforms, dogs and their closest relatives, are the other major branch of carnivores. Fossils recognizable as canines, such as *Hesperocyon*, can be found beginning in the late Eocene, and modern dogs, wolves, coyotes, and foxes can be traced from their origins. Bears arose from early dog-like ancestors from the late Eocene and spread through much of the northern hemisphere. Raccoons and their relatives diverged in the Oligocene, and the mustilids – weasels, badgers, ferrets, otters, and

---

[1] Benton, Michael J. *Vertebrate Palaeontology.* 3rd ed. Malden, MA: Blackwell, 2005. Pg 349-350.

[2] Dykens, Margaret, and Lynett Gillette. "*Tapocyon robustus.*" *Fossil Field Guide.* Undated. San Diego Natural History Museum. 25 June 2008. < http://www.sdnhm.org/exhibits/mystery/fg_tapocyon.html>.

[3] Benton, Michael J. *Vertebrate Palaeontology.* 3rd ed. Malden, MA: Blackwell, 2005. Pg 349-350.

[4] Myers, Phil. "Viverridae." *Animal Diversity Web.* 2000. U of Michigan Museum of Zoology. 25 June 2008. <http://animaldiversity.ummz.umich.edu/site/accounts/information/Viverridae.html>.

[5] Wheeler, Shanna, and Phil Myers. "*Felis margarita.*" *Animal Diversity Web.* 2004. U of Michigan Museum of Zoology. 25 June 2008. <http://animaldiversity.ummz.umich.edu/site/accounts/information/Felis_margarita.html>.

[6] Dacres, Kevin, and B. Lundrigan. "*Panthera tigris.*" *Animal Diversity Web.* 2007. U of Michigan Museum of Zoology. 25 June 2008. <http://animaldiversity.ummz.umich.edu/site/accounts/information/Panthera_tigris.html>.

[7] Waggoner, Ben M. "Saber-Tooth Cats." *University of California Museum of Paleontology.* 14 Jan 1996. U C Berkeley. 25 June 2008. <http://www.ucmp.berkeley.edu/mammal/carnivora/sabretooth.html>.

[8] Benton, Michael J. *Vertebrate Palaeontology.* 3rd ed. Malden, MA: Blackwell, 2005. Pg 349-350.

martens – in the early Miocene.[1,2] Seals, sea lions, and walruses are also caniforms, having developed from bear-like ancestors in a fossil series stretching back to the late Oligocene.[3]

Primates

Primates originated from tree shrews via the plesiadapiforms, squirrel-like animals of the late Paleocene and Eocene that transition to lemur-like adapiforms. Adapiforms of the Eocene, Oligocene, and Miocene had all the characteristic traits of primates – grasping hands and feet, a larger brain relative to other animals the same size, forward-looking eyes with stereoscopic vision, a narrow bar of bone separating the eye socket from the temporal fossa, and single births followed by extended maternal care. Omomyids, similar to tarsiers, and tarsiers themselves were contemporaries of adapiforms from the early Eocene. Fossils of true lemurs date to the Oligocene, and those of the related lorises and galagos, or bushbabies, to the Eocene.[4]

Monkeys and apes, often referred to as the higher primates or anthropoids, probably originated in Africa, although some paleontologists believe southern Asia is a more likely birthplace. *Algeripithecus* is an incompletely known anthropoid from the middle Eocene; *Catopithecus* is more complete and dates from the late Eocene of Egypt, and *Aegyptopithecus* is dated to the Oligocene. *Victoriapithecus* is a Miocene genus from Kenya ancestral to macaques and baboons. By the end of the Miocene, descendants had migrated to southern Europe and Asia, eventually reaching as far north as the British isles.[5]

The true apes, or hominoids, were abundant and diverse in the early Miocene of east Africa. One branch, the pongines, migrated to Asia and left an extensive fossil record as they developed into the orangutans and their relatives, including *Sivapithecus*, also known as *Ramapithecus*, from the late Miocene of southern Asia, thought until 1980 to be a human ancestor.[6] The pongine branch diverged from the other great apes ten to

---

[1] Benton, Michael J. *Vertebrate Palaeontology.* 3rd ed. Malden, MA: Blackwell, 2005. Pg 348-352.

[2] Myers, Phil, et al. "Suborder Caniformia." *Animal Diversity Web.* 2008. U of Michigan Museum of Zoology. 25 June 2008. <http://animaldiversity.ummz.umich.edu/site/accounts/classification/Caniformia.html>.

[3] Benton, Michael J. *Vertebrate Palaeontology.* 3rd ed. Malden, MA: Blackwell, 2005. Pg 352-353.

[4] Benton, Michael J. *Vertebrate Palaeontology.* 3rd ed. Malden, MA: Blackwell, 2005. Pg 366-368.

[5] Benton, Michael J. *Vertebrate Palaeontology.* 3rd ed. Malden, MA: Blackwell, 2005. Pg 368-371.

[6] Benton, Michael J. *Vertebrate Palaeontology.* 3rd ed. Malden, MA: Blackwell, 2005. Pg 371-375.

eleven million years ago.[1] The other branch, the hominins, continued to develop in Africa. *Proconsul* is a widespread genus of fossil apes in east Africa that lived from twenty-four to sixteen million years ago. It has a long horizontal trunk, no tail, grasping hands and feet, and some primitive skull features like large projecting canine teeth. Its brain averaged a hundred and fifty cubic centimeters (cc) in size. The kenyapithecines, too, were most common in eastern Africa during the period from twenty to fourteen million years ago, but are also known from fossils found in Turkey and Europe. Later apes such as *Dryopithecus* populated southern Europe until seven million years ago.[2]

The lineage from apes to man is controversial, but only in its details. There are numerous fossil species connecting modern man to Miocene apes – and, indeed, numerous fossils that are so transitional in nature that their species and even genus are debated. The debate among paleoanthropologists about the origin of humankind is not whether we descended from more primitive species, but exactly which species was the direct ancestor of the next, and which species became extinct without descendant species. As the species progress towards modern man, bipedalism (an upright stance on two legs) developed early and was a consistent feature, with the twin advantages of elevating the eyes above the brush and grass of the developing savannahs to spot both predators and prey, and freeing the hands for other tasks besides ambulation. The brain also increased steadily in size as the intermediate species progressed towards modern man.

Sahelanthropus tchadensis[3] and *Orrorin tugenensis* both lived about six million years ago, at about the time that molecular dating indicates that chimpanzees and the human lineage diverged. *Sahelanthropus* had a brain size of three hundred and fifty cc, within the three hundred twenty to four hundred eighty cc range of modern chimpanzees.[4] It had small canines like later hominids, but it is currently unknown whether it was bipedal or went on all fours. *Orrorin* is known only from fragmentary remains, but sufficient lower limb structure is known to determine that it was bipedal to a large degree.

Ardipithecus ramidus lived 4.4 million years ago. It had long curved fingers and thin tooth enamel like apes, with a lower skeleton similar to chimpanzees, but with changes

---

[1] Cronin, J. E., et al. "Molecular evolution and speciation in lesser apes. *The Lesser Apes: Evolutionary and Behavioral Biology*, H. Preuschoft, et al, ed. Pg 467-485. Edinburg, Edinburg University Press, 1984. Cited by Schwartz, Jeffrey H. *Orang-utan Biology*. Oxford: Oxford University Press, 1988. Pg 293.

[2] Benton, Michael J. *Vertebrate Palaeontology*. 3rd ed. Malden, MA: Blackwell, 2005. Pg 371-375.

[3] Brunet, Michel, et al. "A new hominid from the Upper Miocene of Chad, Central Africa." *Nature*, vol 418, pg 145-151 (11 July 2002).

[4] Mazzonetto, Paolo. "*Pan troglodytes* – Chimpanzee." 2008. *Tree of Life Web Project*, www.tolweb.org. 3 July 2008. <http://www.tolweb.org/treehouses/?treehouse_id=4718>.

consistent with increased bipedalism. The foramen magnum, the opening in the skull through which the spinal cord passes, is situated on the bottom of the skull, as it is in humans and their fully bipedal relatives, rather than on the back of the skull like apes with horizontal postures.[1, 2]

Australopithecus anamensis, the earliest of a genus that lived for two to three million years (depending on how it is defined – more on that subject later) is known from incomplete fossils 4.2 to 3.9 million years old. Although much of the skull is unknown, the parts that have been found are apelike, but its lower skeleton demonstrates that it was fully bipedal.[3, 4] *A. afarensis* (Page 126, Figure 1), represented in the fossil record by the remains of over three hundred individuals, lived from 3.9 to 3.0 million years ago. It had a prognathic face, with a projecting muzzle like a chimp, and curved finger and toe bones. *A. afarensis* skulls exhibit a marked postorbital constriction, the term paleontologists use for the deep depression that separates the face from the brain cases in apes and in early hominids, and makes the rims of the eye sockets appear more prominent. (The postorbital constriction disappears as the face becomes more fully integrated into the braincase to unify the skull.) The teeth of *A. afarensis* are arranged in a U shape, with the cheek teeth in parallel rows, also like apes, rather than in a parabolic shape like the human dental array. Yet is was clearly bipedal, and its brain size ranged from three hundred eighty to five hundred cc, averaging four hundred thirty cc, a slight increase from that of modern chimpanzees.[5, 6] *A. afarensis* is the likely source of a remarkable and much-discussed set of footprints, found by Mary Leakey at Laetoli, preserved when an early bipedal hominid walked across fresh volcanic ash after a

---

1 "The Human Family Tree." *Becoming Human: Paleoanthropology, Evolution and Human Origins.* 27 June 2008. Institute of Human Origins, Arizona State University. 30 June 2008. <becominghuman.org>.

2 "Resource Guide to Paleoanthropology." Undated. Smithsonian National Museum of Natural History. 30 June 2008. <http://anthropology.si.edu/humanorigins/faq/Encarta/encarta.htm>.

3 "The Human Family Tree." *Becoming Human: Paleoanthropology, Evolution and Human Origins.* 27 June 2008. Institute of Human Origins, Arizona State University. 30 June 2008. <becominghuman.org>.

4 "Resource Guide to Paleoanthropology." Undated. Smithsonian National Museum of Natural History. 30 June 2008. <http://anthropology.si.edu/humanorigins/faq/Encarta/encarta.htm>.

5 "The Human Family Tree." *Becoming Human: Paleoanthropology, Evolution and Human Origins.* 27 June 2008. Institute of Human Origins, Arizona State University. 30 June 2008. <becominghuman.org>.

6 "Hall of Human Ancestors." March 2006. Smithsonian National Museum of Natural History. 30 June 2008. <http://anthropology.si.edu/humanorigins/index2.htm>.

rainstorm.[1, 2]

At this point, there is a divergence of hominids into two distinct lines, a "robust" group adapted to heavy chewing, and a "gracile" group that became more human-like with time. The robust hominids are sometimes referred to as members of the *Australopithecus* genus, but it is becoming more common for them to be referred to as a separate genus, *Paranthropus*, a designation that will be adopted herein. *Paranthropus aethiopicus* (Page 126, Figure 2) is a probable descendant of *A. afarensis* and progenitor to the other common *Paranthropus* species, *robustus* and *boisei*.[3] *P. aethiopicus* appears in the fossil record from 2.7 to 2.5 million years ago. Their brain averaged four hundred ten cc. The skull featured a very prominent sagittal crest, the line of projecting bone running front to back along the top of the skull, to which is attached some of the jaw muscles for chewing, and its face was wide, prognathic, and had a marked postorbital constriction.[4] *Paranthropus boisei* (Page 126, Figure 3), formerly known as *Zinjanthropus boisei*[5], appears in the fossil record from 2.3 to 1.2 million years ago and has a brain from four hundred ten to five hundred thirty cc behind its wide, concave, prognathic face.[6] *P. robustus* lived from 2.0 to 1.0 million years ago and had a brain of five hundred thirty cc. Its skull exhibits a small sagital crest, a wide flat face with a heavy brow ridge, and a marked postorbital constriction.[7]

Australopithecus africanus (Page 126, Figure 4) appears in the fossil record about 3.3 million years ago and continues until 2.3 million years.[8] The face of *A. africanus* was

---

1 "The Human Family Tree." Becoming *Human: Paleoanthropology, Evolution and Human Origins.* 27 June 2008. Institute of Human Origins, Arizona State University. 30 June 2008. <becominghuman.org>.

2 "Resource Guide to Paleoanthropology." Undated. Smithsonian National Museum of Natural History. 30 June 2008. <http://anthropology.si.edu/humanorigins/faq/Encarta/encarta.htm>.

3 "Hall of Human Ancestors." March 2006. Smithsonian National Museum of Natural History. 30 June 2008. <http://anthropology.si.edu/humanorigins/index2.htm>.

4 "The Human Family Tree." *Becoming Human: Paleoanthropology, Evolution and Human Origins.* 27 June 2008. Institute of Human Origins, Arizona State University. 30 June 2008. <becominghuman.org>.

5 "Resource Guide to Paleoanthropology." Undated. Smithsonian National Museum of Natural History. 30 June 2008. <http://anthropology.si.edu/humanorigins/faq/Encarta/encarta.htm>.

6 "The Human Family Tree." *Becoming Human: Paleoanthropology, Evolution and Human Origins.* 27 June 2008. Institute of Human Origins, Arizona State University. 30 June 2008. <becominghuman.org>.

7 "The Human Family Tree." *Becoming Human: Paleoanthropology, Evolution and Human Origins.* 27 June 2008. Institute of Human Origins, Arizona State University. 30 June 2008. <becominghuman.org>.

8 "Resource Guide to Paleoanthropology." Undated. Smithsonian National Museum of Natural History. 30 June 2008. <http://anthropology.si.edu/humanorigins/faq/Encarta/encarta.htm>.

wide and prognathic, with a moderate postorbital constriction. The skull had a minimal sagittal crest.[1] It is more gracile in both skull and limb, and is considered by most to be the likely ancestor of the *Homo* genus.

The earliest fossil species assigned to the *Homo* genus, *H. habilis* (Page 127, Figure 5), appears 1.9 to 1.8 million years ago. The first specimen was found in 1964 at Olduvai Gorge in Tanzania, eastern Africa by the renowned paleoanthropology team of Louis Leakey, Philip Tobias, and John Napier. Its brain was six hundred eighty cc in volume[2] (specimens discovered later ranged from five hundred to eight hundred cc) and it had a mildly prognathic face, small brow ridges, and a small postorbital constriction.[3] A contemporary of *H. habilis*, H. *rudolfensis*, is known from a single skull dated to 1.9 million years.[4]

The species *H. ergaster* is composed of African specimens that were formerly considered to be early examples of *H. erectus*, into which *H. ergaster* smoothly blends. *H. erectus* fossils date from 1.8 million to 300 thousand years ago, and even later in isolated areas of Indonesia.[5] *H. erectus* diverged from *H. ergaster* and spread into Asia around 1.6 million years ago.[6] The skull has a low crown, midsized brow ridges, and a very small postorbital constriction. The brain of *H. erectus* (Page 127, Figure 6) ranges in size from seven hundred fifty to twelve hundred fifty cc, with a strong trend towards increasing brain size in more recent specimens.[7] The species includes finds previously referred to as Java man, *Pithecanthropus erectus*, and Peking man, *Sinanthropus pekinensis*.[8]

Small populations of *H. erectus* survived on the Indonesian island of Java until just fifty

---

[1] "The Human Family Tree." *Becoming Human: Paleoanthropology, Evolution and Human Origins.* 27 June 2008. Institute of Human Origins, Arizona State University. 30 June 2008. <becominghuman.org>.
[2] "Hall of Human Ancestors." March 2006. Smithsonian National Museum of Natural History. 30 June 2008. <http://anthropology.si.edu/humanorigins/index2.htm>.
[3] "Hall of Human Ancestors." March 2006. Smithsonian National Museum of Natural History. 30 June 2008. <http://anthropology.si.edu/humanorigins/index2.htm>.
[4] "Hall of Human Ancestors." March 2006. Smithsonian National Museum of Natural History. 30 June 2008. <http://anthropology.si.edu/humanorigins/index2.htm>.
[5] "The Human Family Tree." *Becoming Human: Paleoanthropology, Evolution and Human Origins.* 27 June 2008. Institute of Human Origins, Arizona State University. 30 June 2008. <becominghuman.org>.
[6] "Hall of Human Ancestors." March 2006. Smithsonian National Museum of Natural History. 30 June 2008. <http://anthropology.si.edu/humanorigins/index2.htm>.
[7] "The Human Family Tree." *Becoming Human: Paleoanthropology, Evolution and Human Origins.* 27 June 2008. Institute of Human Origins, Arizona State University. 30 June 2008. <becominghuman.org>.
[8] "Hall of Human Ancestors." March 2006. Smithsonian National Museum of Natural History. 30 June 2008. <http://anthropology.si.edu/humanorigins/index2.htm>.

thousand years ago.[1] Even more remarkably, a population of small hominids standing just one meter tall (three feet) has been found to have existed on the remote island of Flores from ninety-five thousand years ago until just thirteen thousand years ago. The fossils of this people, designated *H. floresiensis*, have low sloping foreheads, prominent arched brow ridges, and a significant postorbital constriction. Spear points and cut marks on associated dwarf stegodont fossils (an elephant relative that reached sizes similar to that of African elephants on the Asian mainland but were markedly smaller on Flores) demonstrate that *H. floresiensis* hunted and butchered the animal, an activity that would have required cooperative social effort. It is hypothesized that *H. floresiensis* is descended from a group of *H. erectus* that migrated from larger islands and, in the isolation of the remote island, decreased in stature.[2] It is intriguing to suppose that early *Homo sapiens* may have encountered surviving *H. erectus* populations as they spread into Indonesia, or possibly even the *H. floresiensis* population on Flores if their explorations took them that far before thirteen thousand years ago.

Homo erectus was long thought to be the direct ancestor of *Homo sapiens*, but discoveries in recent years have led many anthropologists to interpose another species, *H. heidelbergensis* (Page 127, Figure 7), as the descendant of *H. erectus* and most immediate progenitor of *H. sapiens*. (Another proposed species, *H. antecessor*, is not widely accepted as of this writing, chiefly because it is represented by a single immature individual that many experts think may actually be a juvenile of another species.) *H. heidelbergensis* lived from six hundred thousand to one hundred thousand years ago. Its brain was eleven hundred to fourteen hundred cc in size, and it had a large wide face with a weak chin, a higher skull than *H. erectus*, midsized brow ridges, and almost no postorbital constriction.[3]

H. heidelbergensis is believed to be the ancestor of both *H. neanderthalensis* (Page 127, Figure 8), or Neanderthal man, and modern humans of the species *H. sapiens* Page 127, Figure 9).

Neanderthals were not the knuckle-dragging brutes commonly depicted. Their build, shorter and stockier than *H. sapiens*, made them well adapted to the ice ages during which they flourished. They had a low forehead, projecting cheekbones, a prominent brow ridge, and no chin, but their brain was thirteen hundred to seventeen hundred

---

1 "Hall of Human Ancestors." March 2006. Smithsonian National Museum of Natural History. 30 June 2008. <http://anthropology.si.edu/humanorigins/index2.htm>.
2 Morwood, Mike, et al. "The People Time Forgot: Flores Find." *National Geographic*, Apr 2005. 30 June 2008. <zshttp://ngm.nationalgeographic.com/features/world/asia/georgia/flores-hominids-text/1>.
3 "The Human Family Tree." *Becoming Human: Paleoanthropology, Evolution and Human Origins.* 27 June 2008. Institute of Human Origins, Arizona State University. 30 June 2008. <becominghuman.org>.

fifty cc in size[1], comparable to *H. sapiens*, and the postorbital constriction was minimal. The skull of Neanderthals was long and low-crowned, with the face situated more in front of the brain case than below it like *H. sapiens*. Part of the reason that Neanderthals are so fully known is that they buried their dead, often with signs of ritual such as flowers, tools, and food items, indicating an awareness of life and death, ceremony, and possibly a belief in an afterlife.[2] Neanderthals are not thought to be ancestral to modern humans; after thriving for nearly two hundred thousand years over Europe and western Asia, they disappeared about thirty thousand years ago as *H. sapiens* became prominent. It is not clear whether their extinction occurred because of competition from modern humans, direct violent conflict between the two species, or dilution of the genome by interbreeding, although DNA studies from four Neanderthal skeletons show little or no contribution by Neanderthals to the modern human genome and make the latter theory highly unlikely.[3]

Homo sapiens fossils are found in Africa dating to a hundred and thirty thousand years ago, and in the Middle East to ninety thousand years ago.[4] From their origins in Africa, they have migrated to all parts of the world. Modern humans have brains ranging from one thousand to seventeen hundred cc[5] and averaging thirteen hundred fifty cc.[6] The location of the face below the braincase gives the modern human skull a high forehead, a feature that has increased from the earliest *H. sapiens* fossils until today's representatives of the species, and makes the widest part of the skull the braincase rather than the face. The face projects only slightly, brow ridges are very small, and the postorbital constriction is absent or barely detectable. The shape of the skull of *H. sapiens* has continued to change since the early appearance of the species, with the braincase continuing to enlarge, the forehead becoming taller, and the face even less prognathic.

---

[1] "The Human Family Tree." *Becoming Human: Paleoanthropology, Evolution and Human Origins.* 27 June 2008. Institute of Human Origins, Arizona State University. 30 June 2008. <becominghuman.org>.

[2] "Hall of Human Ancestors." March 2006. Smithsonian National Museum of Natural History. 30 June 2008. <http://anthropology.si.edu/humanorigins/index2.htm>.

[3] "The Human Family Tree." *Becoming Human: Paleoanthropology, Evolution and Human Origins.* 27 June 2008. Institute of Human Origins, Arizona State University. 30 June 2008. <becominghuman.org>.

[4] "The Human Family Tree." *Becoming Human: Paleoanthropology, Evolution and Human Origins.* 27 June 2008. Institute of Human Origins, Arizona State University. 30 June 2008. <becominghuman.org>.

[5] "The Human Family Tree." *Becoming Human: Paleoanthropology, Evolution and Human Origins.* 27 June 2008. Institute of Human Origins, Arizona State University. 30 June 2008. <becominghuman.org>.

[6] "Resource Guide to Paleoanthropology." Undated. Smithsonian National Museum of Natural History. 30 June 2008. <http://anthropology.si.edu/humanorigins/faq/Encarta/encarta.htm>.

Only *Homo sapiens*, in all the history of life on earth, has created art. Beginning with swirling and crisscrossing finger marks in the soft limestone walls of caves in southern Australia twenty-four thousand years ago,[1] and continuing through such masterpieces as Michelangelo's *David*, the work of Vincent Van Gogh, and the masterful compositions of Mozart, Beethoven, Stravinsky, and Barber, mankind has sought to enrich his life with beauty.

Even more telling, only *Homo sapiens* and his nearest relatives have entertained contemplative thoughts, seeking truths about the world around him, his own spirit, and a power greater than himself. Only *Homo sapiens* has wondered at his own existence and explored the mysteries of his past.

---

[1] "The Human Family Tree." *Becoming Human: Paleoanthropology, Evolution and Human Origins.* 27 June 2008. Institute of Human Origins, Arizona State University. 30 June 2008. <becominghuman.org>.

Fossil Hominid Skulls

Photographs by Smithsonian National Museum of Natural History

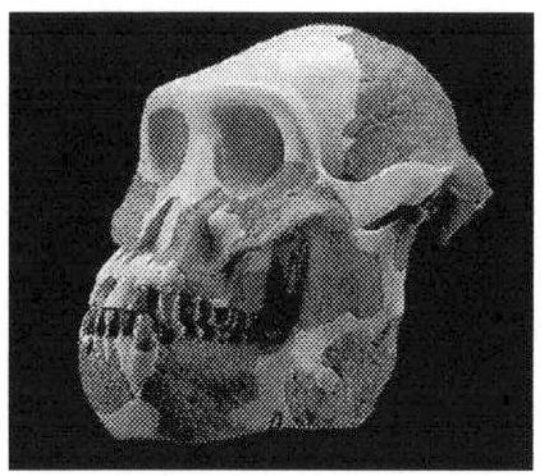

Figure 1
Australopithecus afarensis
3.9 to 3.0 million years ago
Brain size 380 to 500 cc,
average 430 cc

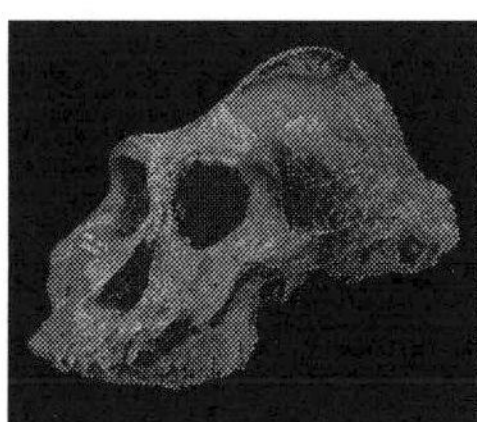

Figure 2
Paranthropus aethiopicus
2.7 to 2.5 million years ago
Average brain size 410 cc

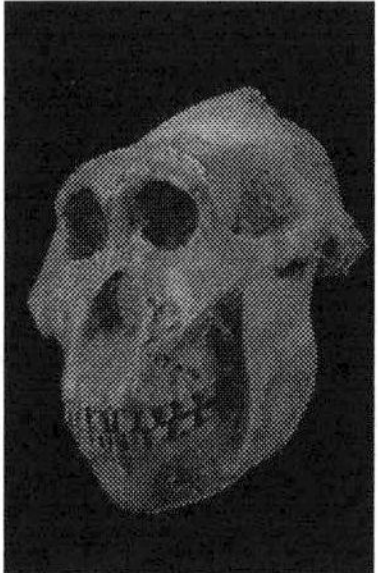

Figure 3
Paranthropus boisei
2.3 to 1.2 million years ago
Brain 410 to 530 cc

Figure 4
Australopithecus africanus
3.3 to 2.3 million years ago
Brain 420 to 500 cc

Fossil Hominid Skulls

Photographs by Smithsonian National Museum of Natural History

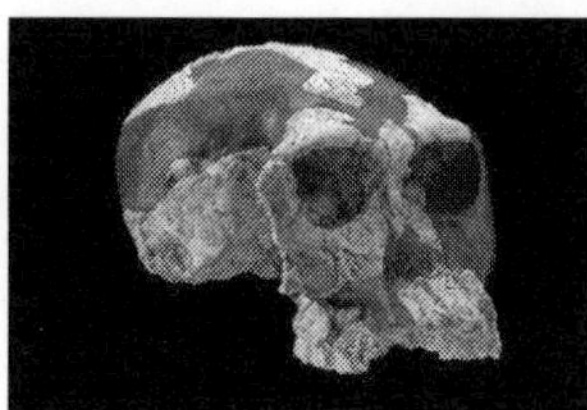

Figure 5
Homo habilis
1.9 to 1.8 million years ago
Brain 500 to 800 cc

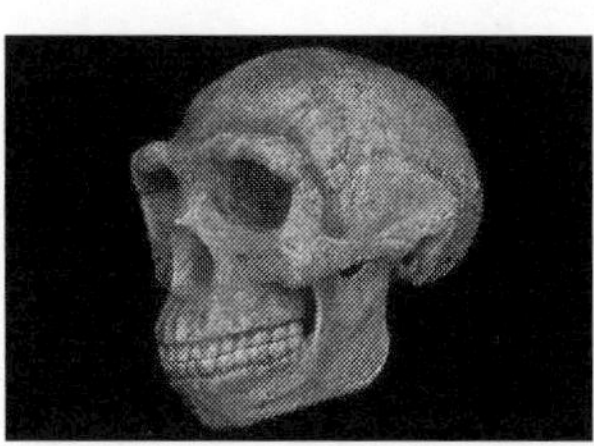

Figure 6
Homo erectus
1.8 million to 300,000 years ago
Brain 750 to 1250 cc

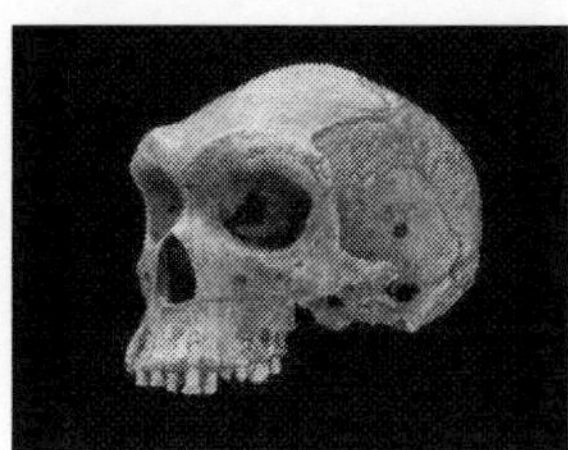

Figure 7
Homo heidelbergensis
600,000 to 100,000 years ago
Brain 1100 to 1400 cc

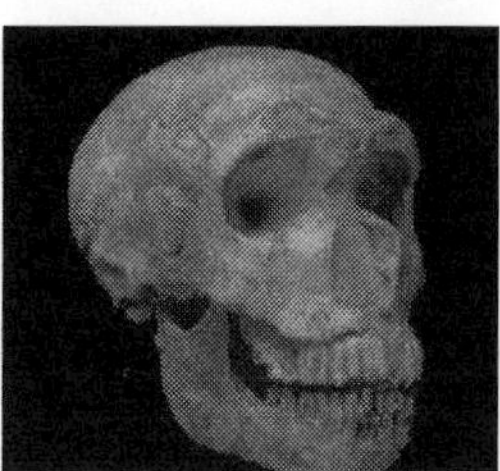

Figure 8
Homo neanderthalensis
200,000 to 30,000 years ago
Brain 1300 to 1750 cc

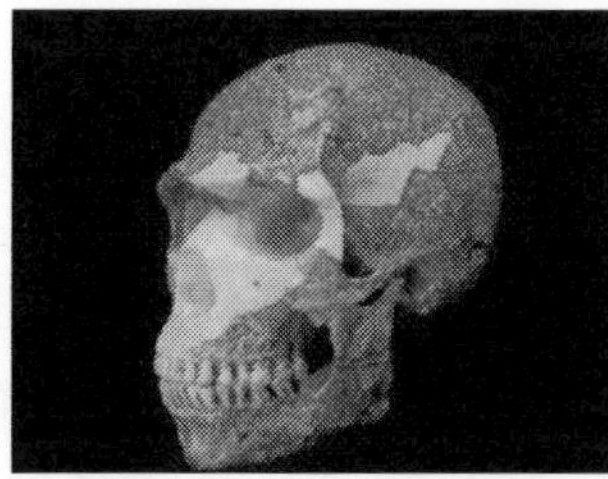

Figure 9
Early *Homo sapiens* from 90,000 years ago
130,000 years ago to present
Modern brain size 1000 to 1750 cc, averaging 1350 cc

Chapter 7

Darwin Defended

The foregoing chapter on the history of life mentions only a tiny fraction of the known living and fossil species of animals; it achieves whatever brevity it possesses by barely mentioning the plant kingdom, ignoring entire families of living animals, and touching only the most superficial knowledge possessed by paleontologists regarding only the most important and dramatic animals in the fossil record. Yet even such a cursory treatment of the enormous and expanding body of information from paleontology makes it clear that life in general, and animal life in particular, has gradually developed in a series of small steps to adapt itself to a variety of environments on earth. Such a gradual process is appropriately termed evolution, although the word was deliberately avoided in both the presentation of the fossil evidence in this manuscript and, until the last sentence - indeed, the last word - of *The Origin of Species.*

The word evolution, today and in the day of Charles Darwin, invites dispute and controversy in some quarters, yet to evolve simply means to progress and develop gradually, as opposed to either remaining static without change, or changing abruptly without intermediate steps. The fossil record clearly is one of gradual change – evolution. Neither a steady state nor abrupt spontaneous changes without precursor are supported by paleontological evidence. A variety of words in the previous chapter – developed, appeared, became, arose, descended, derived – could have been replaced by a form of the word evolve without substantially changing the meaning of the text, yet the word evolution is the one that invites dissent and, from some quarters, rancor.

Although few would disagree that the fossil records shows the gradual development of plants and animals, and few would disagree that living things possess an inherent ability to adapt to the demands of new and changing environments, the unification of these two simple premises in Charles Darwin's theory has fueled what is arguably the most vociferous and persistent dispute of the last century and a half.

Charles Darwin

There could hardly be a less likely candidate for demonization than Charles Darwin had he not written about his theory. He was born in 1809 into the considerable comforts of the English gentry. His parents dallied with both the Anglican and Unitarian churches, and young Charles attended an Anglican boarding school and later studied briefly towards a career as an Anglican clergyman at Cambridge's Christ College. Darwin's attention kept returning to the study of the natural world, however, and when one of his professors recommended him for an unpaid position as a naturalist for a journey to chart the coast of South America, he signed on over the objections of his father.

Darwin's famous journey aboard the H.M.S. Beagle lasted for five years. When he returned to England in 1836, his collection of geological, botanical, and zoological specimens brought him immediate fame. He published his journal (still in print under the title *The Voyage of the Beagle: Charles Darwin's Journal of Researches*) in 1837 and, with a reputation as an eminent naturalist secured, and with an income guaranteed by the prudent investments of his wealthy father, he spent the rest of his days in the thoughtful analysis of his collections and their relation to the further observations of nature by himself and others.

The first words of Darwin's own introduction to *The Origin of Species* remind the reader that he first recognized the implications of his observations on the origins of species while still aboard the Beagle, and that when he returned home he began "patiently accumulating and reflecting upon all sorts of facts."[1] He studied his observations for some eight years before he "enlarged [his notes] in 1844 into a sketch of the conclusions, which then seemed probable,"[2] and then worked for another fifteen years, reviewing his own observations, consulting other naturalists, and refining his thoughts. Prompted by knowledge that another noted naturalist and correspondent of Darwin, Alfred Russel Wallace, was about to publish his own similar treatise, Darwin finally published *On the Origin of Species by Means of Natural Selection, or the Preservation of Favoured Races in the Struggle for Life* in 1859, at age fifty. He provided a considerable body of the

---

[1] Darwin, Charles. *The Origin of Species.* New York: Random House, 1979. Pg 65. (Introduction.) Original publication by John Murray, London, 1859.

[2] Darwin, Charles. *The Origin of Species.* New York: Random House, 1979. Pg 65. (Introduction.)

details of his thought process "to show that I have not been hasty in coming to a decision."[1]

Darwin had clearly been anything but hasty, but was in fact careful, methodical, and patient in considering the manifold implications of his theory. Since the word "evolution" had already acquired connotations of atheism, Darwin avoided using it in his book. In letters responding to inquiries from other naturalists, including Wallace, he stated that he was intentionally avoiding the subject of human evolution, although he would later publish a separate book on the subject, *The Descent of Man, and Selection in Relation to Sex*, in 1871. Darwin monitored the reactions to *Origin* carefully, and although he largely left defense of his theory to his contemporaries, he was said by friends and relatives to be sensitive to criticism.

It says much about Charles Darwin that he presented his theory in such detail and with such thorough justification while his autobiography is slim and brief.

The beliefs of Darwin

The Autobiography of Charles Darwin gives insight into a modest man, devoted to family, fascinated by every aspect of the natural world, much given to contemplation, and deeply and carefully respectful of the faith of others while professing agnosticism for himself. His son, Sir Francis Darwin, appended his father's *Autobiography* with a section entitled "The Religion of Charles Darwin," in which he quotes a letter by his father, "What my own views may be is a question of no consequence to any one but myself. But, as you ask, I may state that my judgment often fluctuates. . . . In my most extreme fluctuations I have never been an Atheist in the sense of denying the existence of a God."[2] In another letter, an unidentified family member writes at the behest of Charles Darwin, "He [Darwin] considers that the theory of Evolution is quite compatible with the belief in a God; but that you must remember that different persons have different definitions of what they mean by God."[3]

A story persists that Darwin renounced his theory and accepted Christianity on his deathbed in 1882. The story originated with Lady Elizabeth Hope, an evangelist and temperance campaigner, who claimed to have been present and to have witnessed Darwin's renunciation. Darwin's children vigorously disputed her account, and stated unequivocally that she was not a visitor to Darwin when he was near death, or, to the best of their recollection, at any other time. Hope's claims are made more dubious by

---

[1] Darwin, Charles. *The Origin of Species.* New York: Random House, 1979. Pg 65. (Introduction.)

[2] Darwin, Francis. "Appendix II: The Religion of Charles Darwin." In *The Autobiography of Charles Darwin,* Third Edition. Cambridge: Icon Books, 2003. Pg 139.

[3] Darwin, Francis. "Appendix II: The Religion of Charles Darwin." In *The Autobiography of Charles Darwin,* Third Edition. Cambridge: Icon Books, 2003. Pg 142.

the fact that she waited thirty-three years, until 1915, to make her claims, in a speech to an evangelical group opposed to the teaching of evolution.[1]

Letters and other writings by Darwin make it clear that he was unconvinced by attempts at rational proofs of the existence of God, but that at various times in his life he found inspiration in his observations of nature. In any event, it is readily apparent that Darwin himself did not consider his theory to be atheistic in nature, as it is often portrayed by claimants at both the scientific and the religious poles of debate. The last sentence of *The Origin of Species* reflects both his wonder and his respect for religious tradition: "There is grandeur in this view of life, with its several powers, having been originally breathed by the Creator into a few forms or into one; and that, whilst this planet has gone cycling on according to the fixed law of gravity, from so simple a beginning endless forms most beautiful and most wonderful have been, and are being evolved."

The work of Darwin

In *The Origin of Species*, Charles Darwin described the reasoning by which he arrived as his conclusions, and defended them with a formidable body of knowledge of geology, botany, and zoology. The book is mind-numbing in both its detail and its florid language, typical of the time; it is certainly not to be recommended to any like the author who think that Hawthorne's *The Scarlet Letter* would have made a good short story. Darwin gave scores of examples to illustrate his theory, based on his extensive observations.

Darwin began his arguments by discoursing on the ability of mankind to make a profound impact on the form of domestic species by selective breeding. He cited examples of traits selected for by breeders in a variety of domestic species, but he was particularly taken by the many varieties of pigeons produced by fanciers, and the fact that their widely varying traits made them scarcely recognizable as the same species. Darwin related that many breeders of pigeons, rabbits, and cattle were so enamored of the traits of their animals that they believed their favorite breeds to be descended from separate species, but Darwin realized that the various breeds were produced from common aboriginal stock by selective breeding.

Darwin next asked if any conditions in nature could play a role similar to mankind in selecting animals or plants for breeding. He correctly recognized selective pressure in every aspect of the environment – climate, terrain, predation, the availability of food sources, and events such as droughts and floods. Darwin realized that such factors

---

[1] Cincinnati Skeptics: The Association for Rational Thought. "Darwin's Deathbed Recantation" http://www.cincinnatiskeptics.org/blurbs/darwin-deathbed.html. Accessed 12-2-2007.

allowed plants and animals with adaptive traits to survive and reproduce themselves, while individuals and populations without such traits would, at least in the locales and conditions that challenged their survival, die out. His extraordinary knowledge of zoology and botany allowed Darwin to recognize instances of continuous variation within single species, the extremes of which appeared unrelated. He realized that the extinction of the intermediate forms, through any of the myriad forces of nature, would cause taxonomists to recognize the two extremes as distinct species.

In the words Darwin used in the final chapter, "Recapitulation and Conclusion", of *The Origin of Species*: "If man can by patience select variations useful to him, why, under changing and complex conditions of life, should not variations useful to nature's living products often arise, and be preserved or selected? What limit can be put to this power, acting during long ages and rigidly scrutinising the whole constitution, structure, and habits of each creature,-favouring the good and rejecting the bad? I can see no limit to this power, in slowly and beautifully adapting each form to the most complex relations of life."[1]

His knowledge of living species and the then-available fossil record led him to propose, in the only illustration of his book, a branching structure in which species with new and modified traits were continually being produced by this process of natural selection, with the majority of species becoming extinct but with the relatively few surviving species becoming ever more diverse in order to survive in their differing environments.

From the fourth chapter of *Origin*, "Natural Selection": "The affinities of all the beings of the same class have sometimes been represented by a great tree. . . The limbs divided into great branches, and these into lesser and lesser branches, were themselves once, when the tree was small, budding twigs . . . Of the many twigs which flourished when the tree was a mere bush, only two or three, now grown into great branches, yet survive and bear all the other branches; so with the species which lived during long-past geological periods, very few now have living and modified descendants. From the first growth of the tree, many a limb and branch has decayed and dropped off; and these lost branches of various sizes may represent those whole orders, families, and genera which have now no living representatives, and which are known to us only from having been found in a fossil state. . . As buds give rise by growth to fresh buds, and these, if vigorous, branch out and overtop on all sides many a feebler branch, so by generation I believe it has been with the great Tree of Life, which fills with its dead and broken branches the crust of the earth, and covers the surface with its ever branching and

[1] Darwin, Charles. *The Origin of Species*. New York: Gramercy, 1979, Pg 459-460. (Chapter XIV: Recapitulation and Conclusion.) Original publication by John Murray, London, 1859.

beautiful ramifications."[1]

The process of variation and selection known as evolution, acting as we now know over the three and a half billion years of the known history of life on the planet, caused plants and animals to continuously diversify and become more complex, and to encompass both the currently surviving species and the countless species, known and unknown, that have become extinct. Evolution is strongly supported by the fossil record, which clearly demonstrates the development, diversity, and increasing familiarity and modernity of the species as time approaches the present day. Evidence from the fossil record is enhanced by observations from botany, zoology, embryology, and the modern disciplines of cellular biology, biochemistry, and DNA analysis.

The power of natural selection is evident, too, in everyday experiences. Consider for a moment the familiar task of weeding a flower bed. Some weeds are easily pulled up by the roots, but others too easily break off at the level of leaves or stems, leaving roots behind. The gardener has two choices in the latter case: either do a bit of digging to remove the separated roots, or see the weed re-grow. A gardener with any experience at all will dig out the roots, because he or she knows that the same plant will break off and re-grow time and time again, with every attempt at pulling it. The weeds are displaying an adaptation born of natural selection. The weeds that break off easily survive, re-grow from their roots, and propagate, thus passing on to the next generation the fragility of their leaves and stems, a fragility that helps them to survive not just diligent gardeners but herbivorous animals as well. The weed that is easily pulled up whole may have adapted in another way to ensure its propagation – early seed production, perhaps, or wide dispersion of large numbers of seeds – but that particular plant will neither be a further bother to our gardener nor have any further opportunities to propagate its kind.

The components of the theory of evolution are all present in our gardening effort: first, that observable variation in the traits of living things exist; second, that some such variations make a difference in the survivability of the individual or population holding the trait; and third, that traits that enhance survival also enhance the opportunity for reproduction of the desirable trait and of the individual or population possessing the trait. It is difficult to entertain any objection to the components of the theory, except that Darwin concludes that the accumulation of varying traits, selected for by differences in such factors as climate and food sources, results in differentiation between species.

Detractors insist that gradual change by an identifiable process is inherently atheistic.

---

[1] Darwin, Charles. *The Origin of Species*. New York: Gramercy, 1979. Pg 171-172. (Chapter IV: Natural Selection.)

Although it denies the independent creation of each species, the theory of evolution is atheistic only in the sense that it is an algorithmic process that, like other less controversial processes identified by modern science, can proceed with or without the guidance of a deity. Many workings of mammalian bodies – blood clotting, the activities of the immune system, and increasingly the working of the brain - have been removed from the miraculous and joined the realm of processes understood by science, with far less debate and rancor than that stimulated by Darwin's theory.

Darwin's defenders

Charles Darwin, after the publication of *The Origin of Species*, lived in fragile health and in relative seclusion. Although he wrote several more books on such subjects as human evolution (*The Descent of Man, The Expression of Emotions in Man and Animals*), and botany (*The Effects of Cross and Self Fertilisation in the Vegetable Kingdom, The Power of Movement in Plants*), and works addressing such specific subjects as insectivorous plants, the fertilization of orchids by insects, and living and extinct barnacles, and corresponded extensively with colleagues, Darwin remained notably absent from the lively debate provoked by *Origin*. In a day when public lectures provided both exposure and a significant source of income, Charles Darwin seldom spoke publicly in defense of his theory, and on the rare occasions when he did, his chosen audiences were scientific societies and his remarks were modest and circumspect.

The most visible English proponent of Darwinism in the years immediately following the publication of *Origin* was the largely self-educated naturalist, zoologist, and anatomist Thomas Huxley. Huxley proclaimed himself to be "Darwin's bulldog," a sobriquet that persisted to Huxley's probable glee. He shared Darwin's nebulous and uncertain religious beliefs, and in fact coined the term "agnostic" to apply to his own inability to proclaim with conviction a belief in either theism or atheism. Huxley vigorously defended Darwin's theory in writings, lectures, and public debates, most famously against the Lord Bishop of Oxford Samuel Wilberforce, but he held private reservations based on his own observations; he felt that the theory of evolution was sound, logical, and unrivaled, but while his anatomic studies provided him with evidence of the results of evolution, it could not address its mechanism with surety. Typical was an exchange between Huxley and Darwin in which Huxley first appealed to pure empiricism, along with a definition of speciation that is common but also has common exceptions: "Until selection and breeding can be seen to give rise to varieties which are infertile with each other, natural selection cannot be proved," to which Darwin responded, "The empirical evidence you call for is both impossible in practical terms, and in any event unnecessary. It's the same as asking to see every step in the transformation (or the splitting) of one species into another,"[1] and to pragmatically defend his ideas as the best explanation for the available data. In spite of his private protests to his friend, Darwin's bulldog never lost his ferocity or stamina for public defense of the theory of natural selection.

The man who is generally acknowledged as the leading American proponent of Darwin's then-new theory in the late nineteenth century was the noted botanist Asa Gray, and he remains one of Darwin's most eloquent apologists. Gray was the first holder of Harvard University's Fisher Professorship of Natural History, a member of the Board of Regents of the Smithsonian Institution, a president of the American Academy of Arts and Science, honorary member of scientific academies in London, Berlin, Munich, Paris, Saint Petersburg (Russia), and Stockholm, and a prolific author. His *Manual of the Botany of the Northern United States*, first published in 1847, remains a standard in the field of botany, with its eighth edition having been published in 1987. He authored books directed variously to school children, gardeners, and fellow botanists, and a recent search of the website of a major bookseller yielded no less than seventeen different titles authored by Asa Gray that are still in print. Gray was an important collaborator of Darwin and defender of his theory, but he was also a man with firmly held Christian beliefs, a lifelong member of protestant Congregational and Presbyterian churches, and a vocal evangelical. Gray and Darwin met in 1839 and corresponded extensively at least as early as 1855, four years before the publication of *The Origin of Species*, with a portion of the correspondence consisting of requests from Darwin and answers from Gray regarding Gray's observations and their applicability to Darwin's emerging theory; Gray is one of several naturalists mentioned with respect in *Origin* as an authority in his field and a contributor of factual information that played a role in the formulation of Darwin's theory. It is a measure of both his reputation and Darwin's esteem for him that Asa Gray was one of only three people, and the only American, to whom Darwin sent manuscripts of *Origin* for comment and critique before publication.[2] Gray rejected the assertion that acceptance of the theory of evolution was inherently irreligious. He came to believe that evolution by means of natural selection was a process guided by God as His select means of creation, and so to defend Darwinian evolution against charges of atheism with extensive writings and lectures. A collection of his essays in defense of the theory of evolution, titled *Darwiniana*, is one of the books by Asa Gray that is still in print.

Gray found no conflict between Darwin's theory and his own devout religious beliefs, as evidenced by a two-lecture series that he delivered at the invitation of the theological

---

[1] Darwin, Francis, and A. C. Seward. *More Letters of Charles Darwin.* London: John Murray, 1903.

[2] Farlow, W. G. "Memoir of Asa Gray." 17 Apr 1889. National Academies Press. <books.nap.edu/html/biomems/agray.pdf>

school of Yale College. The text of the lectures was originally published by Charles Scribner and sons in 1880, but is now available online and in reprinted volumes from several publishers. Early in his first lecture, Gray stated clearly his faith in scripture: "Its fundamental note is, the declaration of one god, maker of heaven and earth, and of all things, visible and invisible, a declaration which, if physical science is unable to establish, it is equally unable to overthrow."[1] Still, he clearly and forcefully stated his confidence in Darwin's theory near the end of the same lecture, "Natural selection is not an hypothesis, nor even a theory. It is a truth – a catena of facts and direct inferences from facts. . . There is no doubt that natural selection operates; the open question is, what do its operations amount to. . . The differences between one species and another now existing, and between these and their predecessors, has come to pass in the course of nature; that is, without miracle."[2] In the second lecture he reiterated his acceptance of the processes of natural selection and continued, "I have no particular dread of any of the consequences which legitimately flow from them beyond the general awe and sense of total insufficiency with which a mortal man contemplates the mysteries which shut him in on every side. I claim, moreover, not merely allowance, but the right to hold these opinions along with the doctrines of natural religion and the verities of the Christian faith. There are perplexities enough to bewilder our souls whenever and wherever we look for the causes and reasons of things; but I am unable to perceive that the idea of the evolution of one species from another, and of all from an initial form of life, adds any new perplexity to theism."[3] As a fervent Christian and one of the most knowledgeable and respected scientists of his time, Asa Gray set a precedent for generations to come by making the simple accommodation of retaining his deep faith in a creator God while simultaneously acknowledging the ability of the mind of man to discover and explore His methods of creation.

Although he could not be said to have adopted Asa Gray's view of evolution as a tool of theism, neither did Darwin discourage Gray in his beliefs. In one letter Darwin assured his friend and ardent defender, "With respect to the theological view of the question; this is always painful to me.--I am bewildered.--I had no intention to write atheistically."[4] Clearly, neither Gray nor Darwin himself considered the ideas of *The*

---

[1] Gray, Asa. "Natural Science and Religion: Two Lectures, Delivered to the Theological School of Yale College." New York: Charles Scribner's Sons, 1880. Accessed 25 Sept 2008 at <http://home.att.net/~a.caimi/Gray.html>.

[2] Gray, Asa. "Natural Science and Religion: Two Lectures, Delivered to the Theological School of Yale College." New York: Charles Scribner's Sons, 1880. Accessed 25 Sept 2008 at <http://home.att.net/~a.caimi/Gray.html>.

[3] Gray, Asa. "Natural Science and Religion: Two Lectures, Delivered to the Theological School of Yale College." New York: Charles Scribner's Sons, 1880. Accessed 25 Sept 2008 at <http://home.att.net/~a.caimi/Gray.html>.

[4] Darwin, Charles. *The Correspondence of Charles Darwin* 8, 1860 . Cambridge: Cambridge University Press, 1993. Pg 224.

Origin of Species to necessitate or even suggest a position of atheism.

It is ironic that vocal Christian critics, to a greater extent than scientists working in fields like paleontology, zoology, cellular biology, and medicine, are more commonly and more publicly insistent that a theory of evolution based on Darwin's observations and reasoning is atheistic. Many capable scientists, including some doing the most advanced work in fields governed by the principles of natural selection and evolution, are men and women of faith who find the produce of their work to be entirely consistent and compatible with their religious beliefs.

Francis Collins received a Ph.D. in physical chemistry from Yale University and, intrigued by the prospects for scientific advancements in the field of genetics and cellular chemistry, trained as a physician at the University of North Carolina and became a respected expert in genetic diseases. Collins headed the Human Genome Project, the massive undertaking coordinated through the National Institutes for Health that mapped all three billion base pairs of human DNA, and he was honored for his work with the Medal of Freedom, the highest honor given to civilians by the government of the United States. Much like Asa Gray, he combines impeccable and highly respected scientific credentials and an unsurpassed knowledge of his field with firmly held evangelical Christian beliefs. His 2006 book *The Language of God: A Scientist Presents Evidence for Belief* authoritatively defends the theory of evolution, describes his own journey from atheism to Christianity, and justifies the harmonization of the two central premises of his intellectual life in his acceptance of theistic evolution, for which he coined the term "BioLogos" (a label that has yet to find widespread acceptance). He finds that in theistic evolution "an entirely plausible, intellectually satisfying, and logically consistent synthesis emerges: God, who is not limited in space or time, created the universe and established natural laws that govern it. Seeking to populate this otherwise sterile universe with living creatures, God chose the elegant mechanism of evolution to create microbes, plants, and animals of all sorts. Most remarkably, God intentionally chose the same mechanism to give rise to special creatures who would have intelligence, a knowledge of right and wrong, free will, and a desire to seek fellowship with Him."[1]

Kenneth R. Miller is a professor of biology at Brown University, specializing in cellular biology, with a curriculum vitae that includes a doctorate from the University of Colorado, teaching and research positions at Colorado, Harvard University, and Brown University, and authorship or co-authorship of over fifty papers in journals such as the *Journal of Cell Biology*, *American Journal of Pathology*, and *Scientific American*, and of textbooks for both secondary school and collegiate biology courses. His 1999 book, *Finding*

---

[1] Collins, Francis S. *The Language of God: A Scientist Presents Evidence for Belief.* New York: Simon & Schuster, 2006. Pg 200-201.

Darwin's God: A Scientist's Search for Common Ground Between God and Evolution, presents with devastating clarity the evidence in favor of evolution, reconciles it with his own resolute Catholic faith, and argues effectively that creationists and intelligent design proponents are damaging the credibility and inclusiveness of their own religion. "There is neither logical nor theological basis for excluding God's use of natural processes to originate species, ourselves included. There is therefore no reason for believers to draw a line in the sand between God and Darwin."[1] His 2008 book *Only A Theory: Evolution and the Battle for America's Soul* is an exposé of the intelligent design movement's declared intent to change the very nature of permissible scientific thought, and the resulting danger to the advancement of human knowledge. Miller speaks and debates widely in defense of the theory of evolution, and in doing so clearly proclaims his belief in a creator God.

Theodosius Dobzhansky was one of the twentieth century's leading geneticists. He was born in Ukraine and became a professor at the University of Leningrad before moving to the United States and teaching at Columbia University, California Institute of Technology and Rockefeller University and retiring to emeritus status at University of California, Davis. He authored a 1973 essay for *The American Biology Teacher* with the revealing title "Nothing in Biology Makes Sense Except in Light of Evolution." In his now-famous treatise Dobzhansky wrote from the perspective of a man who had clearly reconciled life in the upper echelons of science with his lifelong affiliation with the Eastern Orthodox Church: "Does the evolutionary doctrine clash with religious faith? It does not. It is a blunder to mistake the Holy Scriptures for elementary textbooks of astronomy, geology, biology, and anthropology."[2] And more personally: "It is wrong to hold creation and evolution as mutually exclusive alternatives. I am a creationist and an evolutionist. Evolution is God's, or Nature's method of creation."[3] Dobzhansky was characteristically blunt in assessing the arguments of creationists:

> Disagreements and clashes of opinion are rife among biologists, as they should be in a living and growing science. Antievolutionists mistake, or pretend to mistake, these disagreements as indications of dubiousness of the entire doctrine of evolution. Their favorite sport is stringing together quotations, carefully and sometimes expertly taken out of context, to show that nothing is really established or agreed upon among evolutionists. . . . Let me try to make crystal clear what is established beyond reasonable doubt, and what needs

---

[1] Miller, Kenneth R. *Finding Darwin's God: A Scientist's Search for Common Ground Between God and Evolution.* New York: HarperCollins, 1999. Pg 267.

[2] Dobzhansky, Theodosius. "Nothing in Biology Makes Sense Except in the Light of Evolution." *American Biology Teacher*, vol 35 pg 125-129 (March 1973). Pg 129. Accessed 5 Sept 2008 at <http://people.delphiforums.com/lordorman/Dobzhansky>.

[3] Dobzhansky, Theodosius. "Nothing in Biology Makes Sense Except in the Light of Evolution." *American Biology Teacher*, vol 35 pg 125-129 (March 1973). Pg 127. Accessed 5 Sept 2008 at <http://people.delphiforums.com/lordorman/Dobzhansky>.

> further study, about evolution. Evolution as a process that has always gone on in the history of the earth can be doubted only by those who are ignorant of the evidence or are resistant to evidence, owing to emotional blocks or to plain bigotry. By contrast, the mechanisms that bring evolution about certainly need study and clarification. There are no alternatives to evolution as history that can withstand critical examination. Yet we are constantly learning new and important facts about evolutionary mechanisms.[1]

Father George Coyne is a Jesuit priest with degrees in mathematics and philosophy from Fordham University and a doctorate in astronomy from Georgetown University. He directed the Vatican Observatory, with major telescopic facilities at Castel Gondolfo, Italy, and at the Steward Observatory of the University of Arizona, from 1978 until 2006. In an address at Palm Beach Atlantic University, Father Coyne asserted that modern science, rather than inhibiting faith, "provides for those who believe in God a marvelous opportunity to reflect upon their beliefs."[2] He went on to expound on how his own knowledge of God was deepened by his scientific work: "For the religious believer modern science reveals a God who made a universe that has within it a certain dynamism and thus participates in the very creativity of God."[3]

It may be that no one has taken the integration of evolution and Christianity further than Pierre Teilhard de Chardin, the French Jesuit, philosopher, geologist, and paleontologist who was a principal investigator of Peking Man, a rich collection of *Homo erectus* fossils near Beijing, China. The writings and teachings of Pierre Teilhard de Chardin were considered by the Catholic Church to be so unorthodox that he was ordered to cease publication and teaching. Fully respecting his Jesuit vows of obedience, he refrained from publicizing his thoughts and spent most of the remainder of his life in China researching Peking Man. His friends, however, after pointing out that his vow of obedience would not survive his death, convinced him to write and leave his thoughts for posthumous publication. He did so, prolifically, and thanks to his and their dedication we have such thought-provoking works as *The Phenomenon of Man* and a remarkable collection of essays.

Teilhard not only accepted evolution as a biological reality, but saw it as a powerful force in the development of human spirituality and religion. He held that the progression of matter from quarks to atoms to molecules to macromolecules to cells to primitive organisms to advanced animals to mankind was an inherent characteristic of

---

[1] Dobzhansky, Theodosius. "Nothing in Biology Makes Sense Except in the Light of Evolution." *American Biology Teacher*, vol 35 pg 125-129 (March 1973). Pg 129. Accessed 5 Sept 2008 at <http://people.delphiforums.com/lordorman/Dobzhansky>.

[2] Coyne, George V. "A Catholic Scientist Looks at Evolution." *Catholic Online*, 1 Feb 2006. Accessed 5 Sept 2008 at <http://chem.tufts.edu/answersinscience/coyne-evolution.htm>.

[3] Coyne, George V. "A Catholic Scientist Looks at Evolution." *Catholic Online*, 1 Feb 2006. Accessed 5 Sept 2008 at <http://chem.tufts.edu/answersinscience/coyne-evolution.htm>.

creation, purposed for the continual advancement of cognizance, thought, self-awareness, and spirituality. "[O]nce it has emerged from the inorganic, life continues naturally . . . to become complexified externally and more conscious internally; and this extends up to the psychological emergence of reflection."[1] God acts in a continuous process of creation within His own laws, and reveals Himself in teleology: "Without any doubt, there lies hidden beneath the ascending movement of life, the continuous action of a being who raises up the universe from within. . . Considered objectively, material facts have in them something of the Divine."[2] Mankind, as a population of reflective beings aware of the universe, its origins, and their own place in it, is the inevitable product of creation by a divinity that draws all things to itself, and will continue to approach unity with God, referred to by Teilhard as "Omega Point," through expansion of its knowledge of both the physical and spiritual realms. "We now see beings as like threadless fibres, woven into a universal process. . . Through its history, every being is co-extensive with the whole of duration; and its ontogenesis is not more than the infinitesimal element of a cosmogenesis in which is ultimately expressed the individuality – the face, we might say – of the universe."[3] Tielhard's theology remains controversial, but his ability to reconcile his unconventional view of Christianity with scientific theory is clear, and his need to achieve that reconciliation is central to his thinking; it was essential to Tielhard's thinking that cosmic, geologic, and biological evolution is a fact that must be accommodated by any religious system.

Collins, Miller, Dobzhansky, Coyne, and Teilhard may be among the most prominent, but they are just a few of the multitude of practitioners, researchers, and teachers in various branches of science who reconcile traditional Christian faith with an understanding and a functional use of evolutionary theory. They recognize that the theory of evolution has not been threatened by the findings of the last 150 years, but has in fact been strengthened by the ever-increasing knowledge of paleontology and the workings of biological systems, and they accept evolution as the means of creation by a monotheistic creator God.

It is remarkable that Charles Darwin could so clearly conceive of his theory with knowledge of the fossil record that was scant by today's standards, and in the complete ignorance of his time in the fields of genetics, biochemistry, and cellular biology. Yet, as any valid theory should, the theory of evolution does not merely accommodate, but

---

[1] Tielhard de Chardin, Pierre. "A Sequel to the Problem of Human Origins: The Plurality of Inhabited Worlds." *Christianity and Evolution: Reflection on Science and Religion."* Orlando: Harcourt, 1971. Pg 230.
[2] Tielhard de Chardin, Pierre. "Note on the Modes of Divine Action in the Universe." *Christianity and Evolution: Reflection on Science and Religion."* Orlando: Harcourt, 1971. Pg 29.
[3] Tielhard de Chardin, Pierre. "How I Believe." *Christianity and Evolution: Reflection on Science and Religion."* Orlando: Harcourt, 1971. Pg 104.

indeed predicts, subsequent findings in paleontology and the various branches of the biological sciences.

Evidence for evolution in paleontology

Much has been written of the dramatic discovery of *Tiktaalik*, and not just because of its status as a transitional animal in the process of aquatic animals colonizing land, but because of the means of its unearthing – the team of paleontologists predicted a time period in which it would be found, sought an accessible deposit of sedimentary rocks of appropriate age, and successfully located and excavated fossils with the expected features in the expected time frame. In a very real sense, though, *Tiktaalik* is just one of millions of finds that confirm the evolutionary process, for each and every fossil species that is found and dated to a time appropriate to its characteristics fulfills an essential prediction of Darwinian thought, that life forms progressed gradually, by means of descent with modification, with each species arising from and, if successful, giving rise to, similar species, all in a gradual and predictable series.

The fossil record, viewed in its ever-expanding entirety, is highly consistent with a theory of gradual change and development that accumulates and, with the loss of intermediate forms, leads to the differentiation of species from species, genus from genus, family from family, and so on. Such a pattern of descent and development is the central prediction of Darwinian evolution, and has been confirmed time and time again by paleontological excavations. That the fossil record so clearly and consistently demonstrates a gradual development of organisms from simple to complex, from ancient and otherwise unknown towards modern and familiar, with a wealth of intermediate forms, some so manifestly transitional in nature that they defy classification, each appropriately placed in a geological time frame consistent with its characteristics, is itself an unanswerable argument in favor of the evolutionary development of life.

Evidence for evolution in geography

The geographic distribution of plants, animals, and their fossilized predecessors was central to the reasoning put forth by Darwin in *The Origin of Species* – so much so that he devoted two chapters to the subject.

An important part of Darwin's theory was the idea that, given a single species of plant or animal with a wide range, anything that divides that range separates the species into two populations that subsequently develop independently. Harking to his knowledge of geology, Darwin reflected that "geographical and climatal changes, which have certainly occurred within recent geological times, must have rendered discontinuous the formerly continuous range of many species."[1] Once again, subsequent advances in knowledge of geology, including the understanding of plate tectonics, repeated cycles of ice ages and tropical interims, highly variable sea levels, and the opening and closing of land bridges, all expand and confirm the predictions of Darwin's theory.

On every continent, unique animals are found in association with fossils with similar features. Darwin was fond of using as an example the fact that armadillos are native to South America, where are also found fossils of a variety of relatives found nowhere else on earth, ranging in size up to that of *Glyptodon*, weighing over a ton. Such evidence necessarily has accumulated in parallel to the other evidence uncovered for paleontology. Equines are known to have evolved on the grasslands of North America and migrated to other continents. Mammoths and mastodons are clearly demonstrated to have descended from African ancestors and migrated to most of the northern hemisphere before dying out with habitat changes, predation, and hunting by prehistoric man, leaving as surviving relatives only the recent precursors of modern elephants back home in Africa and southern Asia. Fossils of transitional cetaceans have been found almost exclusively in Pakistan, where an impressive and geographically unique succession of fossils leads from semiaquatic forms to animals that could take fully to the sea and spread throughout the world's oceans. The histories of the descent and migration of modern species in and to the locations where they are native in modern times is limited only by our knowledge of the fossil record, and every case known demonstrates branching descent of a species from forebears with similar features, modified or not by patterns of migration and extinction. Each of the ever-growing number of established patterns of descent and migration has a pattern consistent with the theory of evolution.

Conversely, Darwin noted that there are no mammals common to any combination of the continents of Europe, Australia, or South America, because no migratory routes were available since the earliest days of mammalian history. If animal species were independently created, there is no reason for their distribution to be either consistent with migratory routes or limited thereby; nothing would prevent a creator from placing a successful design in more than one location. The fact that migratory routes and patterns can be established in the case of so many groups of animals is consistent with a theory of descent with modification.

The island continent of Australia, first charted by Europeans in the early seventeenth century and not explored until colonization began in 1770, provides a living laboratory in the effects of isolation on the process of selection. As late as the Jurassic Period, all major land masses of the world were in contact with each other, having begun to

---

[1] Darwin, Charles. *The Origin of Species*. New York: Gramercy, 1979, Pg 350. (Chapter XI: Geographical Distribution.)

separate from the single mass now called Pangea. South America, Antartica, Australia, and part of southern Asia were contiguous within a supercontinent named Gondwana. Marsupials were the only mammals to reach Australia while it was still a part of Gondwana, migrating across then-temperate Antartica to reach the portion of Gondwana that would become Australia before eutherians were well established and distributed through the world. Australia and Antartica separated from the rest of Gondwana, then split to go their own ways, leaving a population of marsupials in Australia isolated without competition from placental mammals.

The animals discovered in Australia by its earliest European explorers were so bizarre that accounts elicited reactions ranging from polite skepticism to blunt accusations of falsehood. In the absence of successful carnivores like wolves and big cats, the role of the large predator was assumed by an animal, the thylacine, which had developed the skull, trunk, and limb structures necessary to a successful predator, but retained the strange reproductive methods of marsupials. Marsupials, in fact, filled every terrestrial mammalian habitat. Koalas browsed in the trees, and gliders resembling flying squirrels flitted from canopy to canopy. Tasmanian devils and quols filled the roles of small carnivores and foragers, preying sometimes on the wombats that root and burrow like pigs. Marsupial moles burrowed underground, feeding and living in the same manner as the placental moles familiar to Europeans. A furry egg-laying aquatic browser with a duck-like bill was thought to be a hoax, but the platypus is real. Even the kangaroo, although as unlike deer and antelope as can be imagined, fills the same ecological niche as the more familiar herd-oriented mobile grazing animals. All developed to fill a role that was filled elsewhere in the world by placental mammals; many developed features similar to their placental counterparts due to the convergence necessitated by natural selection. The species that were successful in other parts of the world were not transplanted to Australia, but the independent development of marsupials had filled every ecological niche, often with animals that possessed similar adaptations to similar needs. It would be a strange decision for a designer to separately create an entire ecosystem of marsupial animals instead of merely recreating or transplanting a successful design of a placental mammal from elsewhere in the world. A pattern of migration, isolation, and separate evolutionary development provides a more reasonable explanation for the adaptation of marsupials to so many diverse ecological niches and their prominence in the absence of placental mammals, and one consistent with our modern understanding of tectonic movement.

South America was isolated also, later in earth's history, and developed its own crop of unusual animals, including not just armadillos, but unusually large and diverse rodents, sloths, and a small number of its own marsupials. The isolation ended with the opening of a land bridge to North America at the Isthmus of Panama around three million years ago. Armadillos, ground sloths, opossums, and porcupines migrated north as horses, predatory cats, and bears colonized the southern continent.

In contrast to the species of more temperate climates, bounded as they are by barriers to migration such as oceans and mountain ranges, species adapted to arctic and alpine climates tend towards a more generalized distribution. During glacial periods, barriers to migration were bridged by ice sheets that became relatively stable vehicles for migration that spanned even large expanses of ocean.

The Galapagos Islands are indelibly linked to Charles Darwin; indeed, theirs would not be a recognized name to most people without Darwin's extensive observation and discussion of their flora and fauna. His most important point was that the relatively fewer number of native species present on islands of increasing isolation, the types of plants and animals found on islands, their similarity to plants and animals of nearby land masses, and the plausibility of various means of migration, all lead to the suggestion that they arrived by migration and descent with modification. Darwin needs little assistance in making his case, and in *Origin* he reinforced his points with examples that, to modern readers, grow tedious. The very fact of their repetitiveness, however it may compromise the enjoyment of a casual reader, evidences the consistency of the observations supporting Darwin's theory.

> Oceanic islands are sometimes deficient in animals of certain whole classes, and their places are occupied by other classes; thus in the Galapagos Islands reptiles, and in New Zealand gigantic wingless birds, take, or recently took, the place of mammals.[1]
>
> I have carefully searched the oldest voyages, and have not found a single instance, free from doubt, of a terrestrial mammal (excluding domesticated animals kept by the natives) inhabiting an island situated above 300 miles from a continent or great continental island; and many islands situated at a much less distance are equally barren.[2]

Terrestrial mammals have to traverse long ocean distances without assistance (with small rodents transported on flotsam being a possible exception), while flying insects, birds, and bats, consistent with their increased range both in flying and in being blown by winds while aloft, more readily colonize remote islands. Birds and bats can also be vehicles for small animals and plants that can travel, as adults, eggs, larvae, or seeds, in the grasp of such animals as potential prey, in the gastrointestinal tract, or on the feet, fur, or feathers of the winged animal. By a variety of circumstances, the animals and plants that most easily migrate are the ones that are present on the most remote islands.

---

[1] Darwin, Charles. *The Origin of Species*. New York: Gramercy, 1979, Pg 380-381. (Chapter XII: Geographical Distribution – continued.)

[2] Darwin, Charles. *The Origin of Species*. New York: Gramercy, 1979, Pg 385-386. (Chapter XII: Geographical Distribution - continued.)

The fact that the native flora and fauna of such islands are capable of migration combines with the equally striking fact that they invariably share a close resemblance to similar species on larger land masses upstream in wind and sea currents to lead to the inescapable conclusion that they arose by means of migration followed by descent with modification.

> The naturalist looking at the inhabitants of these volcanic islands in the Pacific, distant several hundred miles from the continent, feels that he is standing on American land. Why should this be so? Why should the species which are supposed to have been created in the Galapagos Archipelago, and nowhere else, bear so plainly the stamp of affinity to those created in America? There is nothing in the condition of life, in the geological nature of the islands, in their height or climate, or in the proportions in which the several classes are associated together, which closely resembles the conditions of the South American coast: in fact, there is a considerable dissimilarity in all these respects. On the other hand, there is a considerable degree of resemblance in the volcanic nature of the soil, in the climate, in the height, and size of the islands, between the Galapagos and Cape de Verde Archipelagoes: but what an entire and absolute difference in their inhabitants! The inhabitants of the Cape de Verde Islands are related to those of Africa, like those of the Galapagos to America. Facts such as these, admit of no sort of explanation on the ordinary view of creation: whereas on the view here maintained, it is obvious that the Galapagos Islands would be likely to receive colonists from America, whether by occasional means of transport or (though I do not believe in this doctrine) by formerly continuous land, and the Cape de Verde Islands from Africa; such colonists would be liable to modification,-- the principle of inheritance still betraying their original birthplace.[1]

The findings of the last century and a half, in geology and the geographic distribution of living things as in paleontology, are fully consistent with a theory of the evolution through descent, modification, and natural selection.

The mechanism of inheritance with variation

Darwin's theory, as important and well supported as it is, was however only half of what is now referred to as evolutionary synthesis or neo-Darwinism. Darwin deduced from his voluminous and meticulous observations that natural selection acted on heritable variations, but he had no real understanding of how those variations arose. His writings predict that such a mechanism exists, characterized by a degree of heritability high enough to transmit to each new generation the characteristics and survivability of the parents, alongside a certain inherent instability necessary to produce the variation upon which selection pressures could act. Darwin proposed the theory of

[1] Darwin, Charles. *The Origin of Species*. New York: Gramercy, 1979, Pg 354. (Chapter XI: Geographical Distribution.)

pangenesis, by which each cell of the body contributed hereditary information to offspring by means of gemmules that circulated in the blood. Darwin believed, similarly to Jean-Baptiste LaMarck, that the environment itself was the initiator of variations, and that such acquired characteristics would be inherited by pangenes via gemmules. The theory of pangenesis has been discarded, and the knowledge of the real mechanism of heredity with variation was not discovered during Darwin's lifetime, but the characteristics of heredity as currently understood are, absent the heritability of acquired characteristics, consistent with the requirements predicted by Darwin's theory of natural selection.

The first pioneer of modern genetics was the Austrian monk Gregor Mendel, who by careful observations of pea plants in the garden of his abbey deduced that simple traits were transmitted by means of dominant and recessive genes from each parent that combined to produce in their offspring traits that were, within the population, mathematically predictable. Mendel was a contemporary of Darwin, having presented and published his findings in 1865 and 1866. (Recall that Darwin published *The Origin of Species* in 1859 and *The Descent of Man*, which contained perhaps the most complete statement of his theory of pangenesis, in 1871, and died in 1882.) Mendel's work was seminal - he is now considered the father of modern genetics – but was largely ignored until around1900, and it was still debated for another two decades before being widely accepted.

Mendelian genetics arose from the monk's observation that certain simple traits of his pea plants arose in ratios approximating three to one, and from his experimentation investigating how that ratio occurred. To understand the basis of Mendelian genetics, consider as an example the genetics of human eye color. Ignoring for the moment the less common green and hazel eye colors, we can represent the gene for brown eyes with "B" and the one for blue eyes with "b." The gene for brown eyes, B, is dominant, and the one for blue eyes, b, is recessive. Each parent contributes one gene to his or her offspring. A person with blue eyes, since b is a recessive gene, must have two genes for blue eyes, or a genome of bb. A person with brown eyes may have received a dominant brown eye gene from each parent, in which case his or her genome would be BB, or a dominant brown gene from one parent and a recessive blue gene from the other, for a genome of Bb, in which case the B gene for brown eyes is dominant and expressed, and the b gene for blue eyes, because it is by nature recessive, is hidden. In the lingo of geneticists, the genetic makeup of an individual (BB, Bb, or bb in this example) is the genotype, the observable expression of genes (blue or brown eyes) is the phenotype, and the different varieties of each gene, (B or b) are alleles.

Obviously, two people with bb genotype will have children with blue eyes, and two people with BB genotype will have children with brown eyes. Perhaps less obviously, anyone with one parent with a BB genotype will have brown eyes, regardless of the genotype of the other parent, because he or she could only receive the dominant B gene from that BB parent, and therefore could not have a bb genotype with even one parent who was BB. More interesting results arise when two brown-eyed people with Bb genotypes, referred to as heterozygotes, have children. Children who receive a B from each parent will carry the genotype BB and have brown eyes. Children who receive a b gene from each parent will carry the genotype bb and have blue eyes even though both parents had brown eyes. The other two possibilities are that a child will receive a B gene from the father and a b gene from the mother, or that he or she will receive a b gene from the father and a B gene from the mother; in either case, the child will have brown eyes like his parents but, also like each of the parents, carry the unexpressed recessive gene for blue eyes. Since the distribution of the B and b genes from the parents are random, each of the means of achieving the Bb phenotype is equal in probability, twenty-five percent, and in turn equal to the twenty-five percent probability of the child being BB and brown-eyed or of being bb and blue-eyed. In a sufficiently large population, and assuming no difference in the survivability of the two phenotypes, the expression of a dominant gene for a trait controlled by simple Mendelian genetics should be at or near seventy-five percent and that for the recessive gene at or near twenty-five percent.

In reality, the genetics of few traits have the simplicity of pure Mendelian genetics, and Mendel had to be selective in finding traits that fit the pattern of his theory. The presence of hazel and green eyes in the human population reveal that not even a trait as simple as eye color is transmitted in simple Mendelian ratios. Likewise, traits like height vary continuously over a range rather than having just two sharply divided phenotypes of, say, very tall and very short, and parents often have children that are taller or shorter than either parent. Such everyday observations provided the ammunition for the two decades of debate that followed the re-discovery of Mendel's paper at the dawn of the twentieth century. Eventually, though, geneticists realized, largely through more rigorous mathematical methods, that traits such as eye color could be acted on by separate genes that modified the expression of the simple brown/blue alleles, that single genes could be affected by more than two alleles, and that continuously varying traits like height were the result of the cumulative action of multiple genes, each transmitted more or less in the way Mendel proposed. Mendel selected certain traits to analyze, and was never under the illusion that all traits were inherited in the simple manner he proposed, but it turned out that each gene is affected by Mendelian distribution even when a phenotypic expression of a trait is influenced by multiple genes and multiple alleles.

Chromosomes had been noticed by microscopists in the late nineteenth century, and with the rediscovery of Mendel's work came the realization that his proposal for the distribution of alleles matched the observations of the behavior of chromosomes. That cell nuclei in general and chromosomes in particular contained particularly high concentrations of deoxyribonucleic acid, or DNA, made some suspicious that DNA was the stuff of inheritance, although as late as the 1940s there were many who did not accept that view. A major piece of the puzzle of inheritance was put in place in 1953, however, when James Watson, Francis Crick, and Rosalind Franklin discovered the structure of DNA. Watson, Crick, and Maurice Wilkins, another early researcher on DNA structure who published his results in the same issue of Nature with Watson, Crick, and Franklin, received the 1962 Nobel Prize for Medicine and Physiology; the crucial work of Franklin was, in the view of many, oddly and inexplicably snubbed, and murmured allegations of sexism on the part of the Nobel committee have never entirely subsided.

DNA is shaped as a double helix, like a ladder wrapped in a spiral around a tall tree. The uprights of the ladder are composed of alternating units of a simple five-carbon sugar, called deoxyribose, and phosphates. Attached to each of the deoxyribose segments is one of four nucleotide bases – adenine, thymine, guanine, or cytosine – and each pair of bases, one attached to each of the uprights, makes a rung of the spiral ladder. Because of their shape and binding abilities, adenine is always paired with thymine and guanine with cytosine in making up the ladder rungs. Replication of DNA is as accurate as it is because the natural attraction of adenine for thymine and guanine for cytosine causes them, upon splitting of the molecule up the center of the rungs during duplication, to pair again with the same opposite base and produce a new strand that is a mirror image of itself and a duplicate of the one from which it was separated.

It was soon realized that each series of three nucleotide bases codes for an amino acid. Since there are sixty-four possible three-base sequences using the four bases available to DNA structure, and only twenty naturally occurring amino acids, many amino acids have more than one corresponding sequence. (Leucine is the reigning champion with six three-base sequences. The coding sequences are well defined and available in any number of textbooks and websites.) Messenger RNA is like a single strand of DNA, except that the backbone of the strand substitutes ribose for deoxyribose and uracil replaces thymine in the base sequences. Messenger RNA carries the code for amino acid sequences from the DNA in the cell nucleus to the sites where proteins are assembled. The amino acids prescribed by the code link together in chains and then, because of the shapes and attractions of various amino acids, fold into a multitude of complex shapes that allow them to function as structural components, enzymes, absorption channels, and hormones within and between cells. The DNA code ultimately, then, accounts not just for heredity, but for every function of living organisms.

One of the recent lessons of cellular biology is that a surprisingly small amount of

DNA actually codes for proteins – in humans, only about one and a half percent.[1] DNA also contains sequences that signal the beginning and end of the sequences that code for amino acid chains and the resulting proteins. Other portions of the DNA molecule, by binding corresponding proteins, RNA, and other organic molecules, regulate the transcription and expression of adjacent genes, a process that cellular biologists refer to with uncharacteristic clarity as turning the genes off and on. A surprising amount of DNA has no apparent function, and is frequently referred to as "junk DNA," although it is only fair to note that much of the DNA sequence that is now known to have regulatory functions was once thought to be junk DNA simply because it did not code for a known protein and had no other function known at the time. It seems reasonable to speculate that increased knowledge of cellular mechanisms, the regulation of gene expression, and perhaps of specialized proteins that are only produced in unusual circumstances, may reduce, perhaps markedly, the amount of DNA that is thought to be useless junk.

Any and all of the DNA bases – and they total three billion pairs of bases in human DNA – can be altered by errors in the duplication process. Base substitution, or transcription error, occurs when the pairing process between bases doesn't occur properly, and one of the other three bases takes the place of the original in the chain. Since most amino acids are coded for by more than one three-base sequence, base substitutions may or may not result in an alteration of the resulting amino acid sequence. If one or more bases is skipped and its partner left dangling, or if an extra base or a series of bases is erroneously inserted, the result is called a frame shift, because the deleted or extra base results in a shift in the reading frame, or the grouping of the three-base sequences. (For example, if a four-codon series that originally reads TTT-CCC-GGG-AAA has an extra adenine inserted at the beginning of the chain, the chain would be drastically altered to read ATT-TCC-CGG-GAA, with an extra undecoded adenine dangling at the end inviting yet another misinterpretation of the DNA.) If the sugar-phosphate uprights of the DNA ladder are broken or disrupted, segments of DNA can momentarily float free of their parent molecules, to be lost and deleted, reversed, or reattached somewhere else. And segments of DNA large and small are very frequently duplicated and re-inserted in the genome.

Taken together, all of these errors in the duplication process of DNA are the biochemical sources of mutations and genetic variation. Mutations take place at the rate of approximately one for every one hundred million base pairs per generation, or about sixty new mutations – thirty in the human genome's three billion base pairs

---

[1] Collins, Francis S. *The Language of God: A Scientist Presents Evidence for Belief.* New York: Simon & Schuster, 2006. Pg 124.

received from each parent - in each human baby.[1] Mutations are often, but not always, harmful; in considering that each person averages sixty mutations not present in his or her parents, the relative rarity of genetic diseases leads one to conclude that most mutations are, in fact, quite harmless. New proteins with novel functions can arise by chance substitutions in subscription errors or frame shifts, although most such modifications cripple the function of the resulting protein. Mutations resulting from reversals and transplantations of gene sequences are somewhat more likely to result in functional products, since they often result in the movement of an amino acid sequence with a particular function or binding property (called a domain) to a new location in its original protein or to an entirely new protein. Gene duplications are particularly fortuitous when they occur, because by having duplicates of functional genes, one gene can continue its original function while another might find a new function if altered by any of the processes of mutation. Changes in the regulatory segments of DNA could result in greater or lesser expression of the regulated genes, either of which may be beneficial or detrimental to the organism depending on circumstances.

Traits that are affected by the action of multiple genes can also cumulatively produce a wide range of phenotypes that can be the subject of selection. To take again as an example the mature height of humans, it is a common observation that children can be taller than either parent, or shorter than either parent. The height of mature humans varies greatly. The Dinka of Sudan are commonly cited as being the tallest, with males averaging 1.9 meters (almost six feet three inches) and females 1.8 meters (five feet eleven inches); several populations of people native to heavily forested areas of central Africa, southeast Asia, and several Pacific islands average less than 1.5 meters (four feet eleven inches) in height. There have apparently been selection pressures to produce races of differing heights: it is commonly assumed that the long legs and slender builds of the Dinka is an adaptation to the heat of the open savannah to which they are native, and that the small stature of the several jungle peoples give them greater agility and less body mass to support by the largely jungle environment and hunter/gatherer lifestyles that are their heritage. Regardless of the exact nature of the selection pressures, the very existence of such divergent body types make it plain that selection acting on continuously varying traits can produce phenotypes that both vary widely within a species and are remarkably stable within a local population.

The emerging picture is that DNA provides exactly the kind of genetic material – largely stable to transmit essential traits to subsequent generations, but just labile enough to allow the mutations needed for natural selection to act upon – that is required and predicted by Darwin's theory. Variations in phenotype due to the expression of quantitative traits, together with mutations and changes in gene

---

[1] Collins, Francis S. *The Language of God: A Scientist Presents Evidence for Belief.* New York: Simon & Schuster, 2006. Pg 131.

regulations, provide precisely the heritable variations that, when selected for or against by the very survivability of their hosts and accumulated over successive generations, drive the process of evolution. Like our exponentially greater knowledge of the fossil record, the enormous development of our understanding of genetic and biochemical processes has expanded, validated, and largely completed Darwin's theory.

Homologies, vestiges, and atavisms argue for evolutionary development

The most adamant creationist accepts the central premise of evolution, that of descent with modification, though he may do so unconsciously and be loath to admit it. Evidence for such a bold assertion can be had with a simple exercise of the imagination.

Suppose for a moment that a new island is discovered, previously unknown and unexplored by humankind. There may be excitement at the anticipation of the possibility of discovery of new species of animals, but how different would we expect those animals to be? Would we, in our remotest imagination, expect to find a lizard with six legs, or a bird with its brain in its midsection and spines extending fore and aft, or a frog with a liver inside its skull, or a mouse with an extra eye on the end of its tail? Such designs would be possible if each species is separately designed, and each would have its advantages.

A six-legged lizard could have been created independently of all the vertebrate tetrapods that live elsewhere on earth, and it would have the advantage of being able to use four limbs for a stable platform while using the other two for prehensile tasks. A bird with its brain in its midsection would give its most critical organ the greatest protection by embedding it in the center of its physical structure, protected by a sturdy rib cage and sternum, massive flight muscles, and enfolding wings, instead of protruding awkwardly on a spindly neck, prone to all manner of injury. The brain of a frog, on the other hand, is not a very impressive structure, amounting to little more than a widening at the front of the spinal cord. Pithed frogs were not so long ago used in school anatomy lessons, so that students could see the frog's heart beating; it would continue thumping merrily away after the brain was destroyed, and the students would not be bothered or distracted by movement by the unfortunate object of the day's lesson. Perhaps it would make more sense, then, to use the sturdy skull of the amphibian to protect a more vital organ like the liver. A mouse with an extra eye on its tail could see behind itself to watch for predators, and could point the eye in any direction to stay alert for danger.

The animals proposed in this exercise are fanciful, but not because their design modifications would be impossible to an original designer; indeed, examples of species exist both in the fossil record and in the present day that are nearly as bizarre. A person who knew only the species native to North America would think an elephant with a subtly sensitive and deftly prehensile proboscis reaching two meters (seven feet) to the ground to be beyond belief; early European explorers returning with descriptions of the fauna of Australia were greeted with incredulity; and the indigenous peoples of the new world, unfamiliar as they were with horses, thought mounted cavalry to be miraculous manifestations of an unknown deity. Yet no explorer, whether a believer in evolution or in creation, would expect to find the animals proposed herein on any newly discovered island, because with or without admitting it, he or she recognizes that all animals are related, and that the unique sets of characteristics of each species arise by modification of existing structures rather than spontaneous independent creation. These designs are intuitively impossible, but not because they would fail; rather, the human mind, confronted with all the other evidence of the animal kingdom, recognizes that vertebrates have four limbs rather than six, that the brain of animals is at the front of the spinal cord and the liver in the abdomen, and that eyes are part of the structure of the head, and that all known species display these and a myriad of other commonalities because they have descended with modification from other species that in turn shared the body plan of all vertebrate animals.

Because of that descent, many structures with different functions have developed from the same body part – these are called homologies, and their relatedness argues for descent with modification, and therefore a process of evolution rather than independent design. The forelimbs of vertebrate animals, as diverse as they are, provide an excellent example of homology. The arm and hand of a human being can, with varying amount of talent and training, use a hammer to drive a nail, throw a baseball at speeds approaching a hundred miles per hour, maneuver surgical instruments to produce the miracles of modern medicine, and manipulate paint brushes, carving tools, and musical instruments to create breathtaking beauty. If one needs any further evidence of the marvels of the human appendage, one should spend a few minutes listening to Vladimir Horowitz playing Chopin's *Fantasie Impromptu* or Scriabin's *Etude in D Sharp Minor*, or perhaps the "Traumerei" movement of Schumann's *Kinderszenen* suite. What a miraculous invention is the human hand.

The human hand and arm has the same bones, joints, tendons, and ligaments as that of the great apes, and largely the same as the forelimb of such diverse mammals as dogs, horses, cattle, and rats; even the wings of birds, and the front appendages of reptiles, amphibians, and sarcopterygian fish all have the same basic arrangement of bones, joints, and musculature. The fossil record provides account, with few and inconsequential gaps, of how the simple fleshy fins of fish developed into the diversity of forelimb structures seen in modern terrestrial animals. Such similarity in structure and obvious gradual developmental process is not consistent with independence of design with each new species, but speaks eloquently of the gradual adaptation and change of a structure to fit differing conditions and uses.

The wings of birds not only have the same structures as the human arm and hand, but their development can be accurately tracked in the fossil record. Birds use a markedly elongated second digit as the leading edge and primary support, with the third digit reduced and the first supporting the alula, a small wing appendage that serves a purpose similar to the flaps of airplanes. The equally effective wings of bats use the same structures in a different way to support the membranes of their wing: all five digits are retained, with the first retaining a short claw and the other four being extremely elongated and spread to support the web of the wing stretched between them. The wings of the pterosaurs used the same structures in yet a different arrangement: the fourth finger of the flying reptiles was elongated to support a web that reached all the way in and back to the trunk and the upper portion of the hind legs, and the first three digits remained free for grasping and a quadrupedal gait. It is difficult to understand why a designer would conceive of three separate but effective designs for the wings of vertebrates, each incorporating the same basal structural components used in different ways, and maintain the integrity of each design throughout each of three groups of species that appear to be closely related, and then abandon a proven and successful design in each of the other two groups. It seems enormously more reasonable to suppose that three designs arose at three different junctures, using the same available parts in different ways, and that each of the designs was passed, with modification, to subsequent species that differentiated from the original.

The special cases of homologies that have been reduced to the point that they do not fulfill the same function as is the case in other species are called vestigial structures, and they are many. Vestiges occur because the original structure is, within the behaviors adopted by a species to cope with its unique conditions of life, not used for its original function. The process of natural selection then favors either its conversion to another purpose, or a marked reduction in its size, in either case so the body part is not an unproductive drain on nutrients and metabolic resources of the individual.

The eyes of several species of moles are greatly reduced in size and functionality, a fact that was known to and commented upon by Aristotle. The eyes of many cave dwelling fish are vestigial, and those of several species of cave dwelling salamanders, including *Eurycea rathbuni* of Texas and *Proteus anguinus* of southern Europe, though present as vestiges, are covered with skin. The eyes of at least one species of cave salamander, *Typhlotriton spelaeus*, have been found to fully develop and then regress, all during the larval stage of development.[1]

Pythons have traces of pelvic structures at the appropriate place in their skeleton, though they have no legs to be supported by a pelvis.

Many species of beetles have intact wings, reduced in size to various degrees, beneath fused and immovable wing covers.

The wings of ostriches, rheas, and emus are markedly reduced in size from those needed for flight, and their only remaining use is in display behaviors to threaten other animals and in courtship. The wings of penguins are similarly reduced to a degree that makes them incapable of flight but beautifully adapted to aquatic locomotion.

It is difficult to understand why moles and cave dwelling fish and salamanders would be consciously designed with non-functioning eyes sometimes covered by opaque skin, why a python needs a pelvis if created with no legs, why the perfect model for a beetle is to have wings that can never be used, why the ostrich and similar birds should be planned with flightless wings, or why the original design of penguins should include a derived wing rather than an original flipper. The presence of such vestiges would seem to testify in favor of evolutionary change rather than independent design.

A vestige with one of the most dramatic and thoroughly documented evolutionary paths is that of the splint bones of horses. Although all modern equines bear their weight on canon bones, the third metacarpals and metatarsals, and the associated phalanges, the second and fourth metacarpals and metatarsals are present as narrow elongated bones that run down either side of the canon bones and taper to a point before they reach the fetlock, or first knuckle. Horsemen refer to them as splint bones, and veterinary anatomists allow that they function only in providing a minute portion of the articular surface of the carpus (wrist) and tarsus (ankle). The transition of the second and fourth metacarpals and metatarsals from size and function equal to their fellows in less derived quadrupeds to vestigial status in modern horses is well documented in the fossil record. (See the preceding chapter for a more detailed discussion, with references, of the evolution of *Equus* from its four-toed ancestor *Hyracotherium*.) An evolutionary process, in the most basic sense of gradual change over time, clearly occurred in the reduction of the metacarpals and metatarsals of horses from four equal members to one central member with vestigial remnants on each side. It is reasonable to surmise that such change occurred because the elongation of the

---

[1] Besharse, Joseph C., and Ronald A. Brandon. "Postembryonic eye degeneration in the troglobitic salamander *Typhlotriton spelaeus*." *Journal of Morphology*, vol 144, issue 4, pg 381-405. 6 Feb 2005. Abstract accessed 11 Sept 2008 at <http://www3.interscience.wiley.com/journal/109918467/abstract?CRETRY=1&SRETRY=0>.

limb made locomotion more efficient and speedy in the grasslands that were concurrently developing; no reasonable explanation aside from such a process of natural selection has been proposed for the clearly evolutionary change over time in the limbs of ancestral and modern horses.

As dramatic and telling as is the examination of the details of vestiges, their most striking feature is that they are a stark reversal of the otherwise overwhelming trend towards increased complexity, functionality, and specialization in nearly every aspect of the anatomy of animals. The overall direction of dentition, the integument, the means of reproduction and nurturing young, the nervous system, the digestive tract, and heart and blood vessels, the respiratory system, and the immune system, when considered over spans of genera, families, and orders, has been one of increasing sophistication. The diminution of splint bones in the legs of horses, the reduction and elimination of flight function of the wings of ostriches, and the conversion of the wings of penguins from aerial to aquatic locomotion are notable because they are reversals of a general tendency towards increasing complexity of limb structures; that the vestigial (or, in the case of penguins, modified) structures retain the anatomic elements of the limbs of other closely related animals leads to the conclusion that the modified and vestigial structures are more highly derived rather than less, as an adaptation to the environment and habits of the host animal. Similarly, the fact that the vestigial eyes of some fossorial and cave-dwelling animals assume the anatomic characteristics of the eyes of closely related species at various stages of their embryology or development, rather than taking the form of more primitive eye spots or visual cups, causes them to be regarded in their own way as more advanced adaptations rather than as primitive features. In every case, the reduction of anatomic features to vestiges can be seen to be a purposeful reversal of otherwise inexorable progress towards increasing development of a feature, aimed at specialization of its host species to its ecological niche.

Vestigial structures exist because the genome of the host species includes all the information necessary for the vestigial structure, but either regulatory genes alter the expression or, as has been documented in the case of blind salamanders, other genes are activated that cause the structure to regress. The processes that regulate the full expression of genes for vestigial structures or cause their embryologic degeneration can themselves malfunction, and the results are observable regressions in isolated individuals to a more primitive state, called ativisms.

The coccyx of humans is, under normal development, a vestige of a tail. The human embryo at a gestational age of around a month has a tail with ten to twelve vertebrae and associated muscles, nerves, blood vessels, and skin. In a process much like that observed in the case of the eyes of blind salamanders, the tail regresses before birth to the normal coccyx composed of just three to five vertebrae, each greatly reduced in size and all fused together, hidden under the skin. Several dozen cases have been documented, however, some in related individuals, in which a baby was born with an intact tail. Some human tails have had a normal number of coccygeal vertebrae, but larger and unfused, while others have cartilage supporting structures; skin, muscles, and ancillary structures such as organized nerves and blood vessels are typically present.[1, 2] (Pseudotails have also been documented, without the organization typical of the tails of other animals, and suitably minded authors often falsely dismiss all of the many documented cases of atavistic tails in humans as pseudotails.)

Other rare but well documented atavisms include the occurrences of extra small toes in horses, and wings in normally wingless insects such as earwigs, but among the most spectacular are the atavistic hind limbs, supported by identifiable femurs, tibias, and fibulas, and sometimes tarsal and metatarsal structures, that have been documented in several species of whales and dolphins, betraying their evolution from terrestrial quadrupeds.

Atavisms are a failure of a mechanism for regression of an embryological structure or a mechanism for suppression of a portion of a genome. In all cases of atavism, as in the cases of vestigial structures, one has to wonder why an original design for an animal without precursors would include in its genome the presence of a structure it was not intended to have, and rely on a fallible mechanism of suppression or regression to eliminate the vestige or the rare ativism. It seems far more likely that both vestiges and ativisms betray the presence of genomic material held over from related precursor species.

Evidence supporting evolution from gene sequencing

Since we now know that the growth, development, and metabolism of living things are all governed by the genome, it is reasonable to wonder if vestigial genes are known. A multitude are, and one of them makes vitamin C necessary in the diet of humans.

The disease of scurvy plagued sailors of the fifteenth, sixteen, and seventeenth centuries with bleeding sores, tooth loss, and general debility. When the British navy figured out that scurvy could be prevented by including citrus fruits in the diet of its sailors, it not only gained a significant advantage in keeping its sailors healthier and more able to fight, but it also gained them the nickname of limeys.

---

[1]Bar-Maor, J. A., et al. "Human Tails." *Journal of Bone and Joint Surgery*, vol 62-B, no 4 (Nov 1980), pg 508-510. Accessed 11 Sept 2008 at <http://www.jbjs.org.uk/cgi/reprint/62-B/4/508>.

[2] Dao, A. H., an d M. G. Netsky. "Human tails and pseudotails." *Human Pathology*, vol 15, no 5 (May 1984), pg 449-453. Abstract accessed 11 Sept 2008 at <http://www.ncbi.nlm.nih.gov/pubmed/6373560?dopt=Abstract>, National Center for Biotechnology Information, National Institutes for Health.

But vitamin C is not a dietary requirement for most animals, for most animals manufacture their own; among mammals, only humans, the great apes, guinea pigs, and the Indian fruit bat require dietary intake of vitamin C. Vitamin C, also known by its chemical name ascorbate, is produced from simple sugars in other mammals by a series of five enzymes that includes gulonolactone oxidase. In higher primates, the gene for gulonolactone oxidase, although present in the same region of the genome as in other mammals, fails to function because of several mutations.[1] The gene for the flawed enzyme was not a factor in the survivability of its host, however, because the diet of primates (as well as that of guinea pigs and fruit bats) includes sufficient fresh fruits and vegetables so that vitamin C is supplied in ample amounts by a normal diet. When humans placed themselves in the new environment of long sea voyages and failed to include a sufficient quantity of ascorbate in their diets, scurvy became a significant problem. The gene for gulonolactone oxidase had become vestigial, and mutations had not been affected by natural selection; the gene had, without selection pressure, accumulated several mutations that made it nonfunctional. The fact that the mutations in the gulonolactone oxidase gene are identical among humans and the great apes is yet another indicator that those species shared a common ancestor, implying that the ancestor possessed the vestigial and mutated gene, and passed identical mutations to its descendant species.

Similar evidence is present in the genes for hemoglobin, the oxygen carrying protein of blood. Hemoglobin consists of four iron-containing heme units bonded to four proteins, two each of alpha and beta globins. On human chromosome sixteen reside, due to gene duplication and modification, six copies of the gene for alpha globin – one for embryonic alpha globin, two for fetal alpha globin, two for adult alpha globin, and one, nested in the middle of the other genes that are turned on and off during development, that is not functional. The nonfunctional pseudogene has errors in the regulatory segments that prevent transcription, meaning that it can never be turned on, as well as another that would prevent the use of any messenger RNA transcribed, and four more that would render the protein nonfunctional if it was ever produced.[2] None of this would be remarkable if the pseudogene was present in a single species - gene duplication allows the production of a functional protein, so no selection pressure is present and the pseudogene can, except for the novelty of its sharp similarity to its neighboring genes for alpha globin, recede into the background of junk DNA that comprises over ninety-eight percent of the human genome – but the same pseudogene,

---

[1] Miller, Kenneth R. *Only a Theory: Evolution and the Battle for America's Soul.* New York: Viking, 2008. Pg 97-99.

[2] Chang, L.-Y. Edward, and Jerry L. Slighton. "Isolation and Nucleotide Sequence Analysis of the B-type Globin Pseudogene from Human, Gorilla, and Chimpanzee." *Journal of Molecular Biology,* vol 180 (1984), pg 767-784, in Kenneth R. Miller. *Only a Theory: Evolution and the Battle for America's Soul.* New York: Viking, 2008. Pg 99-103, 229-230.

with the same errors, is present in the same position, surrounded by the same functioning neighboring genes, on the same spot of the same chromosome of chimpanzees and gorillas.[1]

In the cases of both the faulty gene for gulonolactone oxidase that leads to the dietary requirement for vitamin C, and the flawed copy of the gene for alpha globin, the supposition made under the theory of evolution that the mutations were transmitted intact from a common ancestor to humans and their closest relatives is the only reasonable argument. Proponents of any version of a theory that species were independently designed and created must make a case that either their designer had a reason to insert the same non-productive genetic material in the genomes of species that appear to be closely related and no others, or that exactly the same set of mutations from the originally created functional state coincidentally occurred in each of the species of great apes, and in no others.

In another dramatic case of gene duplication and specialization, it has been found that the human genome contains forty genes for twelve different types of myosin.[2] Myosin is a contractile protein that interacts with another protein, actin, to power muscle contractions. Myosin is important in most kinds of movement in living things, from separation of chromosomes to the motion of plants in response to sunlight and in entwining tendrils, to the muscle contractions of animals up to and including humans. The fact that the human genome contains forty genes for myosin is a strong indicator that the mechanisms for gene duplication have been active in its case; it would seem foolish for a designer to have placed forty genes for the same protein in one creature. That the forty genes code for twelve different functioning versions of myosin is another incidence of mutations modifying a functioning protein only slightly, and in ways that are subject to selection. The different types of myosin function in slightly different ways, making them useful in a variety of functions within different cell types, some not fully understood at present.[3] The genetic mechanism of gene duplication followed by the modification and selection of some of the duplicate material for altered functions has worked to produce an array of twelve different but closely related proteins in humans, and a total of eighteen throughout nature.

Unfortunately for the opponents of evolution, the similarity between the human

---

[1] Miller, Kenneth R. *Only a Theory: Evolution and the Battle for America's Soul.* New York: Viking, 2008. Pg 99-103.

[2] Berg, J. S., B. C. Powell, and R. E. Cheney. "A millennial myosin census." *Molecular Biology of the Cell*, vol 12, pg 780-794 (2001). In "The Myosins." Maciver Lab Web Page. 26 May 2002. University of Edingburgh. Accessed 3 Oct 2008 at <http://www.bms.ed.ac.uk/research/others/smaciver/myosins.htm>.

[3] "The Myosins." Maciver Lab Web Page. 26 May 2002. University of Edingburgh. Accessed 3 Oct 2008 at <http://www.bms.ed.ac.uk/research/others/smaciver/myosins.htm>.

genome and that of our closest relatives does not end with two genes suffering from nonfunctional mutations and another bearing unmistakable marks of duplication and functional specialization. Francis Collins, the physicist and geneticist who directed the Human Genome Project, notes that when sequences from segments of DNA that are known to code for proteins are compared to the genome of chimpanzees, all human sequences – one hundred percent - can be matched to a corresponding chimpanzee sequence. When such human sequences are compared to the genomes of dogs and mice, a ninety-nine percent correlation is found, decreasing to seventy-five percent correlation with chickens, and sixty percent correlation with fruit flies. If, however, sequences from DNA segments with no known function is considered (that which is called with some trepidation junk DNA), the correlation of human DNA with that of chimpanzees falls slightly to ninety-eight percent, with dogs to fifty-two percent, with mice to forty percent, with chickens to just four percent, and there is no recognizable correlation with fruit flies.[1]

The significance of these statistics goes far beyond the obvious observation that both functional and non-functional segments of DNA decrease in correlation between humans and animals that are less closely related, although that finding alone is notable. Certain proteins that are constituents of enzyme systems, structural elements, and other universal or near-universal components have been preserved largely intact across the animal kingdom, because most mutations produced loss of function and were not propagated; sixty percent of these functional elements of the genome are shared between animals as disparate as fruit flies and human beings. Mutations in non-functioning sequences of DNA, however, are silent and cause no harm, and are therefore not subject to selection pressure. They can and do accumulate freely with time, resulting in correlation rates that still reflect how closely related animals may be, purely as a function of how recently the species diverged, but with correlation rates that decrease much more rapidly than the sequences from functional DNA. This marked difference in the rates of change between segments of DNA that may be affected by natural selection and the spectacularly higher mutation rates in nonfunctioning DNA is dramatic evidence of the functional competence of Darwinian selection.

As previously noted, many amino acids are coded by more than one three-base sequence within DNA. There are therefore many instances in which substitution of a single base in the DNA sequence will not change the amino acid sequence of the coded protein; for example, changing a single base in a TTA sequence to get either a TTG or a CTA sequence still codes for the amino acid leucine, changing TTT to TTC still codes for phenylalanine, and any sequence that starts with CG – CGC, CGT, CGA, or CGG – codes for arginine. These mutations and many more single-base mutations will

---

[1] Collins, Francis S. *The Language of God: A Scientist Presents Evidence for Belief.* New York: Simon & Schuster, 2006. Pg 127.

be silent in terms of producing any changes in their expression in coding for proteins. The theory of evolution would predict that silent mutations would be expected to be more common than those that cause a structural change in a protein and are therefore subject to selection pressure, and knowledge of the genome of humans and other animals confirms exactly that finding.[1]

The evidence relating the genomes of different animals is as striking as that from paleontology. Chimpanzee and human genomes are identical in fully ninety-six percent of their base sequences.[2] The genome of mammals less closely related show marked but decreasing similarity. The genome of mice is approximately the same size as that of humans, and contains notably similar sections that code for proteins, occurring in the same order, with only the spacing differing slightly. Even long sections of non-functional junk DNA are similar or identical in mice and humans.[3] As mammals, mice are more closely related to humans than, say, the chickens or fruit flies that have also been discussed, but less so than chimpanzees, and analysis of the genomes shows similarities appropriate for the close but less intimate degree of relationship.

One need not restrict one's inquiries to mammals to find evidence of relatedness in genomes. The similarities between the genomes of even far more distantly related species can show striking, although, as expected, fewer, similarities. Hox genes, or homeobox genes, referred to in the discussion of the Cambrian explosion, are significant in ways only recently appreciated. Ed Lewis of the California Institute of Technology does research with fruit flies, one of the classic subjects of genetics researchers, and is widely credited with being the first person to recognize gene sequences that govern the development of segments of fruit fly maggots into appropriate body parts of the adult fly. (Tampering with these genes resulted in bizarre abnormalities such as extra appendages in inappropriate locations.) Further research has revealed that these genes are, in fruit flies, arranged in anatomic order on a single chromosome, with the genes for head parts on one end and those for tail parts on the other end of the sequence. When Hox genes were located in humans and other mammals, it was found that they are similarly clustered on four chromosomes, each gene corresponding to a particular body segment, and each closely similar to the same gene in the fruit fly.[4] Once again, important functional genetic material is consistent across the animal kingdom, with such high correlation in sequence and arrangement as

---

[1] Collins, Francis S. *The Language of God: A Scientist Presents Evidence for Belief.* New York: Simon & Schuster, 2006. Pg 130.
[2] Collins, Francis S. *The Language of God: A Scientist Presents Evidence for Belief.* New York: Simon & Schuster, 2006. Pg 137.
[3] Collins, Francis S. *The Language of God: A Scientist Presents Evidence for Belief.* New York: Simon & Schuster, 2006. Pg 134-137.
[4] Miller, Kenneth R. *Only A Theory: Evolution and the Battle for America's Soul.* New York: Penguin, 2008. Pg 127-130.

to give evidence that they were transmitted and preserved as species descended from species, and families from families, and phyla from phyla.

Arguments against evolution

In spite of over a hundred and fifty years of examination, challenge, and confirmation, opponents of evolution continue to argue against the theory. The most inconsistent feature of their arguments is the widely differing interpretations of scripture; other arguments are remarkable for both their consistency and the thoroughness with which they can be refuted, often enough because of inherent self-contradiction.

Evolution is only a theory

The opponents of evolution frequently point out that it is "only a theory," and go on to conclude from that terminology that the theory is incomplete, tentative, and untested. The word "theory" can be used in such a way, and virtually any dictionary will contain a definition portraying a theory as a speculative thought that awaits further examination.

But such a definition is almost always the second or third definition; the definition that comes first because of being most common and most generally used is more exacting. In science a theory more often and more formally refers to an explanation of facts that brings order and structure to established knowledge and makes consistent and reliable predictions. In the usual context of scientific use, a theory is much more than mere conjecture; rather, it is a system of thought that has been tested and verified, and has proven dependable both in understanding natural phenomenon and in anticipating future observations and experimental results.

It is with that connotation that scientists in various fields refer to the theory of gravity, the atomic theory, the germ theory, the heliocentric theory, the Big Bang theory, and the theory of evolution. For a variety of reasons, none are considered facts, but all fulfill the primary definition of a theory as a well-supported and useful systematization of data.

Gravity is a theory because we can see its effects and formulate mathematical descriptions predicting its actions, but we cannot see or measure either a particle or a wave associated with its action. There are actually two different theories of gravity in current use. Experiments by Galileo Galilei (almost certainly not involving the Tower of Pisa) and mathematical formulations included by Sir Isaac Newton in his milestone *Philosophiae Naturalis Principia Mathematica* (1687) established the theory of gravity for classical mechanics, in which the force of gravity is proportional to the product of the masses of any two objects and inversely proportional to the distance between them. ($Fg=Gm_1m_2/r^2$ where Fg is the force of gravity, G is a gravitational constant, m_1 and m_2 are the masses of the two objects, and r is the distance between their centers.)

The gravitational theory of Galileo and Newton is still in common use, because it explains and predicts almost all astronomical observations – almost, but not all. The planet Mercury has an irregularity in its orbit around the sun that was not explained until Albert Einstein published his theories of special and general relativity early in the twentieth century. Under Einstein's theories, the coordinates of four-dimensional space-time are distorted by the presence of mass, and other objects move along paths that follow the curvature of the space-time continuum. The mathematics of relativity are extraordinarily difficult, and for most purposes the gravitational formulas of Newton provide satisfactory resolutions and predictions, but the relativistic model of Einstein is used when exactitude is critical, and when unusual situations like the orbit of Mercury present themselves. Legitimate science, then, recognizes and uses two fully functional theories of gravity.

Atomic theory is the foundation of all branches of chemistry, but is still properly termed a theory because atoms and their component protons, neutrons, and electrons are too small to be seen. The properties and interactions of atoms are nonetheless predictable, in no small part because Niels Bohr, a friend and contemporary of Albert Einstein, expanded upon one of Einstein's early papers on light quanta to discern, apparently correctly, the characteristics of electrons that govern the interaction of atoms. When Bohr's work is combined with conclusions about the nuclei of atoms gleaned from other sources, there is general satisfaction in the scientific community that atomic theory is valid and that the fundamental nature of matter is understood. That satisfaction arises from the fact that atomic theory can explain and predict experimental observations of chemistry and physics.

A case can be made that the germ theory is the weakest of the several theories mentioned here. The hope of early proponents that all diseases would prove to be caused by microbes has proven false, for disease mechanisms include pathology caused by degenerative processes, genetic abnormalities, nutritional deficiencies and excesses, toxins, immune disorders, parasites, and tumors. Although a few tumors have been found to be associated with viruses, most are not currently known to be thus caused, and the causes of several have been shown to lie in defective regulatory mechanisms in cellular chemistry. Autoimmune and immune mediated diseases are sometimes believed to be caused by abnormal responses by the immune system to microbial antigens, but such involvement by microbes in the pathology of immune mediated diseases is neither certain nor universally suspected. Degenerative processes seldom are directly caused by microbes, although they certainly can be accelerated and complicated by microbes, and there are a wide variety of genetic and nutritional diseases and acute and chronic poisonings in which microbial activity plays no role. Even among known infectious diseases, the interaction between microbes, the immune system, and normal tissue components are frequently complex, and there are differences of opinion among medical researchers about the relative importance of direct microbial activity and the body's response to infection. In spite of these wide-ranging limitations, however, the germ theory is not fully abandoned; the benefits of antimicrobial drugs and food and environmental hygiene continue to be important tools in treating and preventing a wide variety of diseases.

Many readers from outside the science community will be surprised to know that heliocentricity – the concept that the earth and the other planets revolve around the sun – is a theory. The reason is that, under the strictest interpretations of science, the rotation of the planets around the sun has not been directly observed. Although a wealth of observations of the planets are consistent with a heliocentric model, and none inconsistent, heliocentricity will not be considered a fact in the language of science until mankind leaves the solar system and looks back to observe, over a sufficient period of time, the orbits of the planets around the sun.

The theory of evolution is a theory on par with the other foundational theories of science. In the same way that heliocentricity is beyond direct observation, the ancient workings of evolution to form the current diversity of life is beyond direct observation; yet a wealth of modern observations have proven consistent with its premises, and all our observations of living things are understandable under its auspices. Like the germ theory, evolution requires intelligent and rational application, but remains valid when properly considered. Like atomic theory, evolution provides a foundation for understanding a wide variety of phenomenon. Like the theory of gravity, there are sometimes different ways to interpret data under the propositions of evolution. But the theory of evolution has been examined and challenged for over a hundred and fifty years, and remains a valid explanation for observed phenomenon, consistent with the modern findings of paleontology, genetics, cellular chemistry, and even recent developments in fields like anatomy and medicine. It is the cornerstone of our understanding of all branches of the biological sciences; as the renowned geneticist Theodosius Dobzhansky stated in the title of his famous essay, nothing in biology makes sense except in the light of evolution.

Those who proclaim evolution to be a fact are in error to the extent that the prehistoric differentiation of living things was not and can never be observed, but they are closer to the mark than those who commit the more egregious error, through either ignorance or a willful choice to ignore the overwhelming evidence through which the theory has been tested and found valid, of portraying it to be an uncertain and untested hypothesis.

Evolution as dogma

Opponents of evolution portray the theory as dogma held by the scientific establishment to be beyond challenge; investigators in all fields are implied to be either too complacent or too intimidated to question the validity of the theory of evolution. Opponents of evolution portray themselves to be open minded, even revolutionary, in their approach to science, sometimes even alleging a conspiracy among evolutionists to suppress work that challenges evolutionary theory. It is difficult to imagine a position that could misrepresent the process of scientific inquiry to a greater degree.

The advancement of science depends on a process of observation that collects facts, the formation of a hypothesis that explains previous observations and provides a means of making predictions for future observations, and the testing of the hypothesis against its predictions. Any given hypothesis may be confirmed, rejected, or modified upon testing; modification requires further testing.

Scientists, for reasons of both intellect and ego, seek the advancement of science. Those who undertake genuine research seek the satisfaction of advancing mankind's understanding of the world around them and, to an extent greater or lesser and acknowledged or not, to make a name for themselves by their discoveries. Neither cause is advanced by confirmation of already well-established theories; scientists constantly look for the opportunity to challenge established thinking. Such a reality of the scientific process was recognized by none other than Christian apologist C. S. Lewis: "The phenomenon which is troublesome, which doesn't fit in with the current scientific theories, is the phenomenon which compels reconsideration and thus leads to new knowledge. Science progresses because scientists, instead of running away from such troublesome phenomenon or hushing them up, are constantly seeking them out."[1]

As an example, consider again the theory of gravity. The formulas of Sir Isaac Newton were in use for well over two hundred years, with highly satisfactory results, until a young patent office clerk challenged their validity. The name of Albert Einstein became justly famous because he sought and found a more complete theory of gravity that would unify Newton's mechanics with Maxwell's field theories and explain, among other anomalies, the uneven orbit of Mercury. Einstein's theory predicted, among other things, that the observed position of a star whose light passed along the edge of the sun would shift ever so slightly, by just 1.7 arc-seconds (an arc minute being 1/60th of a degree of an angle, and an arc second 1/60th of a minute). Such a star can only be observed during a solar eclipse, of course, and in 1919 exactly the predicted observation was made by Sir Arthur Eddington, and even more precisely many times since. Einstein is a household name and synonymous with genius; Eddington, although knighted, is known mostly to historians and science buffs; the names of others who further confirmed Einstein's theory are even more obscure. Einstein gained fame by

[1] Lewis, C. S. "Christian Apologetics." *God In The Dock*. Grand Rapids: Wm. B. Eerdmans, 1970. Pg 91.

challenging established theories and doing original work, while those who lent proof to his revolutionary theory are little known.

(To be fair, Eddington was in his own right an outstanding man of science who made significant contributions to physics and astronomy, but his is not a household name like that of Einstein. Eddington is also remembered for one of the most famous one-liners of science. He was a life-long Quaker, and is widely said to have displayed humility and kindness in a manner consistent with his faith. An interviewer once asked him if it was true that only three people understood Einstein's general theory of relativity. Sir Arthur hesitated long enough to be gently chided for false modesty, upon which he replied, "On the contrary. I'm just wondering who the third might be." Honesty and humility are both virtues, but they occasionally conflict, and Eddington's evident opinion that only he and Einstein fully understood the theory, at least in the days immediately following its publication, was probably not far off the mark.)

The world of science and scientists is, by its very nature, one of lively debate, where every claim is scrutinized and either verified or attacked. Nothing is accepted without proof, and any theory that expects serious consideration contains a proposal for means of corroboration through further observation or experimentation. The theory of evolution has been tested and examined for over a century and a half and has been enhanced, developed, and modified, but not contradicted or falsified.

The theory of punctuated equilibrium elucidated by Stephen Jay Gould and Niles Eldredge is offered by creationists and their intelligent design surrogates as evidence both of legitimate scientific questioning of the tenets of evolution and, apparently oblivious to the inherent contradiction of their claims, of the alleged suppression of dissent concerning evolution by unidentified arbiters of the scientific establishment. In fact, the concept of punctuated equilibrium has not been concealed, but has been actively discussed and examined since its publication in 1972. Definitions of punctuated equilibrium are contained in most dictionaries and encyclopedias, books by Gould and Niles are still in print and readily available, and a search by a popular internet search engine for punctuated equilibrium on 23 September 2008 yielded one hundred and eighty-six thousand entries – rather ineffective censorship.

The theory of punctuated equilibrium, as originally publicized by Gould and Eldredge, held that species were stable for long periods of time (equilibrium), which were interrupted (or punctuated) by short periods of rapid diversification and speciation. Those seeking evidence of spontaneous supernatural creation of living things pounced on the theory and continue to trumpet it, even though Gould and Eldredge both wrote of their atheism. (Gould would edge gently and somewhat wistfully towards agnosticism as his death from cancer approached in 2002.) Current discussions of punctuated equilibrium by creationists and intelligent design proponents consistently fail to mention that the theory has been incorporated, to the satisfaction of Gould and Eldredge, into the modern synthesis of evolutionary theory. A period during which such factors as climate, food supply, and predation are stable allows relative stability of species and their characteristics. During periods of rapid change in environmental factors, however, natural selection would act on variability to favor new traits that allowed existing species to adapt to new conditions and speciate relatively rapidly. The difference is one of degree and rates of change – the process of evolution was shown not necessarily to progress in a slow, gradual, and uniform manner, but to vary in its rate as environmental stresses give advantage to greater instability and more rapid change in phenotype. Evolution was not abandoned, nor was its abandonment advocated by Gould or Eldredge, although their works are sometimes the subject of quote mining by opponents of evolution that misrepresent them as such; rather, the theory of evolution proved malleable and adaptable to new data analysis that was inherently consistent with its basic premise of descent with modification, and Gould and Eldredge were and are active defenders of evolutionary theory against criticism by proponents of creationism and intelligent design.

The existence of a worldwide conspiracy to quash unfavorable findings and legitimate criticism of the theory of evolution is patently absurd. No such conspiracy could possibly remain a secret, being shared as it necessarily must be by millions of people of diverse nationalities, ethnicities, and religious beliefs. Legitimate scientific journals are refereed, meaning that submissions are reviewed by experts in the field for the integrity of their methods and conclusions. Papers that present false data or unsupported conclusions are rejected, while those that make truthful, reasoned, and well justified presentations of new and even revolutionary ideas are welcomed with enthusiasm and excitement. Proponents of creationism and intelligent design are not published in mainstream journals because their papers contain biased and grossly misrepresented data and unfounded conclusions, as will be evident as the examination of their arguments continues.

The theory that all organisms were created separately, whether presented under the guise of creationism or intelligent design theory, produces no predictions, because every living thing exists at the whim of a creator; without predictions the theory cannot be tested. (Actually, it would seem to predict a high degree randomness in the order, age, and relationship of living organisms that is not reflected in the fossil record or genetic sequences.) It is supported only by those who approach available data with an inherent bias, seeking out only agreeable findings and ignoring, discarding, or spuriously criticizing all of the voluminous data that supports evolution.

The theory of evolution has been scrutinized, evaluated, and debated by legitimate scientific processes for a century and a half. It has incorporated and been verified by all subsequent findings of paleontology, by the discovery of the mechanisms of genetics, and by the still emerging knowledge of the chemistry of cellular processes. It is the largest target in biology for ambitious researchers, but it has survived, modified and updated, largely intact since its first publication.

The evolution of new species have not been observed

The assertion that the evolution of new species has not been observed fails in two ways: it is both an invalid criticism if true, and it is demonstrably false.

The criticism that new species are not observed is often framed as a demand that new species be demonstrated to appear during the lifetime of a human or, somewhat more generously, in the time period since Darwin published his landmark work. Living things have evolved for 3.8 billion years, over twenty-five million times as long as the theory of evolution has been published; Vendian animals appeared six hundred and thirty million years ago, and so are over four million times as old as the theory; vertebrates are five hundred twenty-five million years old, or three and a half million times as old as the theory; *Tiktaalik* is three hundred seventy-five million years old, two and a half million times as old; mammals date to at least two hundred million years ago, over 1.3 million times as old as Darwin's theory; the species *Homo sapiens* is a hundred and thirty thousand years old, meaning that the mind that developed sophisticated enough thought to conceive of the theory is over eight hundred and fifty times as old as the theory itself, and undeniably human creatures existed for 99.9 percent of their history before being confronted by Darwin's theory and beginning to make the observations needed to support or dispute his thesis. The theory does not predict that new species would necessarily be observed in such a short time frame, so any absence of such observations is a failure not of the theory, but of the logical processes of the critic. It is simply not reasonable to demand that new species be constantly produced for the observation of each generation of man.

There are, in fact, reasons within the theory to expect the rate of production of new species to be currently at a nadir. The process of natural selection rewards innovation when ecological niches are available to be filled. It has been over sixty-five million years since the last major extinction event at the Cretaceous-Tertiary boundary, and since that time living things, notably mammals, have diversified extensively to fill available ecological niches. The climate of earth is relatively stable – the last ice age peaked around twenty thousand years ago – and new environments have not developed that are ripe for exploitation by species with new features. The life of earth is, in other words, in one of the states of comparative stability termed equilibrium by Gould and Eldredge. A relative lull in speciation is expected during periods when selection pressures are minimal, and such a finding is consistent with a modern and realistic understanding of the theory of evolution; it is certainly not contravening evidence.

A more enlightening exercise is to ask if any new characteristics have developed in living organisms in the recent past as a result of selection pressures. One of the most obvious answers lies in the problem of antibiotic resistance that is dealt with by practitioners in all branches of medicine. As a practitioner of veterinary medicine, the author has been the recipient of innumerable presentations of new antibiotics by representatives of pharmaceutical companies. Such presentations invariably include charts showing high susceptibility of bacterial isolates to the new antibiotic, and sometimes a claim that no resistance is either present or possible to the miraculous new compound. But as can be testified by any practitioner of human or veterinary medicine who submits cultures to laboratories with any regularity, the incidence of resistance to any and every antibiotic begins to appear after its introduction to regular use and increases with time.

Penicillin is produced by bread mold to eliminate bacterial competition in close proximity to its colonies. When penicillin was first discovered and used medically, it was a devastatingly effective antibiotic, precisely because only the bacteria that had momentarily shared the environment of bread mold had been exposed to it. But its widespread use gave bacteria a selection pressure towards resistance, and its effectiveness soon declined, as has, to a greater or lesser degree, the effectiveness of every antibiotic since. Medicine is now dealing with tuberculosis organisms that require long courses of combinations of exotic antibiotics; populations of bacteria in hospitals, nursing homes, and dialysis centers that, like methicillin resistant *Staphylococcus aureus* (MRSA), have essentially adapted to a medical environment and tolerate a wide variety of antibiotics; even in veterinary medicine, cultures taken from canine ear infections with increasing frequency exhibit multiple antibiotic resistance, making treatment difficult, costly, and prolonged.

Inherent in the use of antibiotics is selection for antibiotic resistance in bacteria. An antibiotic seldom is solely responsible for the recovery of a patient from any bacterial infection, and disease-causing infections are seldom caused solely by the presence of a bacterium. There are millions of bacteria all around us, in every breath we take, on each surface we touch, on everything that we put in our mouths; there are, in fact, more bacterial cells than mammalian cells in the body of a healthy human, dog, or cat. Pathogenic infections occur when a particular bacterium arrives at a site in the body where, because of normal body structures or tissue compromise, it can grow to numbers that cannot be controlled by the immune system. It is more realistic to think of antibiotics as acting by reducing the numbers to tolerable levels that can be controlled by the immune system than it is to conceive of them killing all available bacteria and sterilizing an entire mammalian body. Whether the bacteria are then completely eliminated by the immune system from a sterile site like the kidneys, the brain, or the interior of the eye, or return to the normal commensal populations that are present in the gastrointestinal tract, the respiratory system, or on the skin, any that survive to reproduce have survived the antibiotic. The medical professions have selected for antibiotic-resistant bacteria.

Medical practitioners cannot be condemned for using antibiotics because, of course, the only alternative to selecting for antibiotic-resistant bacteria is to refuse to treat patients with all available resources. Instead, doctors and patients, and the caretakers of veterinary patients, must be aware that antibiotic resistance is an inevitable evolutionary phenomenon and take care to minimize its effects by using antibiotics at a sufficient dose and for a sufficient period to time to maximize their effectiveness and minimize the opportunity for survival of resistant organisms.

The mechanism of antibiotic resistance by bacteria is almost always either a mutation that modifies an enzyme that has been present for another purpose to one that inactivates the antibiotic, and/or a mutation that up-regulates or down-regulates the expression of a gene that affects susceptibility to the antibiotics. (A gene for an enzyme that inactivates the antibiotic may be up-regulated, thus increasing the number of molecules of the antibiotic that can be inactivated by any given bacterial cell, or one that codes for an antibiotic binding site may be down-regulated so that the cell is exposed to lower levels of the antibiotic.) Some of the antibiotic species in which antibiotic resistance is most problematic are those that most readily produce plasmids – strands of DNA independent of chromosomes that can move between bacteria, producing similar opportunities for exchange of genetic material as that afforded by sexual reproduction of higher species. When antibiotic resistance is available through plasmid transmission instead of only by direct descent, antibiotic resistance spreads much more rapidly in a bacterial population, which is of course why plasmid production, as well as antibiotic resistance, is selected for by evolutionary processes.

Since species of bacteria are defined by their biochemical processes – the ability to make use of certain nutrients, produce certain toxins, and so on – a case could be made and considered that the development of resistance to antibiotics may constitute sufficient change to define a new species of bacteria. Bacteriologists have, to date, considered resistant bacteria to be new strains of previously recognized species, but the designation is somewhat arbitrary. There are many instances in nature in which varieties, strains, and subspecies differ enough from one another sufficiently to blur the definition of the word species. Darwin noted in *Origin* that only the elimination of intermediate forms would be necessary in many cases for existing varieties to be considered independent species. Darwin's American defender Asa Gray made similar note of the frequent difficulties of species definitions, along with a certain frustration in dealing with the critics of evolution in his own day:

> The absoluteness of species being the postulate of the science, was taken for granted to begin with; and so all the forms which have been named and admitted into the systematic works as species, are thereby assumed to be completely distinct. All the doubts and uncertainties which may have embarrassed the naturalist when he proposed or admitted a particular species, the nice balancing of the probabilities and the hesitating character of the judgment, either do not appear at all in the record or are overlooked by all but the critical student. . . The patient and plodding botanist spends much of his time in the endeavor to draw specific lines between the parts of a series the extremes of which are patently different, while the means seem to fill the interval. When he is addressed by the triumphant popular argument, "if one form and one species has been derived from another, show us the intermediate forms which prove it," he can only ejaculate his wish that this ideal vegetable kingdom was the one he had to deal with. Moreover when he shows the connecting links, he is told, "Then these are all varieties of one species; species are fixed, only with wider variation than was thought." And when he points to the wide difference between the extremes, as being greater than that between undoubted species, he is met with the rejoinder, "Then here are two or three or more species which undoubtedly have true distinctions, if only you would find them out." That is quite possible, but it is hardly possible that such fine differences are supernatural. . . So I have been at the making and unmaking of far too many species to retain any overweening confidence in their definiteness and stability.[1]

The process described by Darwin and Gray of populations becoming diverse and then separating, through the loss of intermediate forms, into distinct species, is frequently denied by detractors of evolution, but, as is aptly pointed out by Dennis Miller in *Finding Darwin's God*, it is vividly demonstrated in the fossil record by the most plentiful of all fossils, those of diatoms.

Diatoms are single-celled photosynthetic organisms, sometimes forming colonies, that live primarily as free-floating aquatic organisms, and are a major component of plankton populations. They form silicate cells walls that are often quite beautiful when seen under the microscope, and those skeletal remains settle to the sea floor in great quantities. These fossils are so plentiful that deposits are mined as diatomaceous earth and used as filtration media for swimming pools, abrasives in cleaning products, and absorbents in some brands of cat litter.

Of the roughly hundred thousand living species of diatoms in two hundred genera, two species of diatoms of the genus *Rhizosolenia*, *R. praebergonii* and *R. bergonii*, are

---

[1] Gray, Asa. "Natural Science and Religion: Two Lectures, Delivered to the Theological School of Yale College." New York: Charles Scribner's Sons, 1880. Accessed 25 Sept 2008 at <http://home.att.net/~a.caimi/Gray.html>.

differentiated by size. Until about three million years ago, only *R. praebergonii* existed, with measurements of the hyaline component of its shell ranging from 3.5 to just over 5.5 microns. Cores of diatomaceous earth show that over a period of about two hundred thousand years, the range of its size widened, towards the small side, with individual shells as small as 2.5 microns, until a gap occurred in the middle of the size range, leaving two distinct populations with no overlap, that continued to diverge. The result was that by 2.8 million years ago, two distinct species appear with no overlapping size, the larger ranging in size at various times from 3.5 to 6 microns, and the distinctly smaller ranging from less than 1 micron to about 2.5 microns.[1] Speciation occurred in the most plentiful fossils we can observe in exactly the manner predicted by Darwin in the *The Origin of Species*: a diverse population with a range of features, in this case a measurable size characteristic, loses the intermediates of its range and becomes two distinct populations – two distinct species.

But one need not argue for the definition of bacterial species by antibiotic resistance or look to the fossil record for evidence, however plain, of species diversification, for the profession of veterinary medicine has borne dramatic witness to exquisitely documented evolution in the last forty years.

The virus for panleukopenia of cats causes severe vomiting and diarrhea along with a marked decrease in the white blood cell count, and had been known long before the late 1970s, when dogs began becoming seriously ill with similar symptoms caused by a new virus. The virus was isolated in 1978 and determined to differ from the cat virus by just seven amino acids, two of which were in the outer coat of the virus and accounted for its new ability to bind to and infect the cells of dogs. A new virus species had evolved because variations in its genome (a genome of just eight hundred bases) caused new amino acids to be inserted in just two locations in its outer protein. Those new proteins were then, because of the slight alteration, conformed to receptor sites in the cells of dogs and allowed the virus to infect a new host species; it was the first change of viral host species ever documented. The parvovirus of dogs has, in fact, continued to evolve, and strain CPV-2c was isolated for the first time in 2006 by Dr. Sanjay Kapil of the Oklahoma Animal Disease Diagnostic Laboratory.[2]

Some devotees of creationism and intelligent design will argue, of course, that viruses are not living things, since they do not possess all of the mechanisms of a cell, and must rely on host cells for replication in the ultimate of parasitic relationships. Such an argument essentially argues that the line between living things and inanimate chemicals

---

[1] Cronin, Thomas M., and Cynthia E. Schneider. "Climatic Influences on Species: Evidence from the Fossil Record." *Trends in Evolutionary Biology and Ecology.* Vol 5 (1990), pg 275-279. In Miller, Kenneth R. *Finding Darwin's God.* New York: HarperCollins, 1999. Pg 44-45.
[2] Kapil, Sanjay. Personal communication 25 Sept 2008.

is indistinct which, though true, would seem to be an argument inherently in favor of evolutionary descent rather than creationism. In any event, the more important lesson is that the virus, using DNA as its genetic material as do most viruses and all cellular organisms, underwent a mutation of that genetic material that caused it and its offspring to be able to infect a new host species, and thereby become a new species of virus. The mechanism of inherited variation and natural selection of genetic material clearly produced a new species of virus; an argument based on the fact that the genetic material is reproduced by the host cell rather than by the virus itself is moot.

Before moving on to another subject, it should be noted that the argument, false though it is, that new species have not been produced by evolution is not, in fact, an argument against evolution at all, but an argument against the rapid production of new species by any means. Spontaneous creation has not created any more species in the last century and a half than has evolution. Unless one is willing to advocate a position that all known species, living and extinct, were created simultaneously and that the fossil record reflects only the extinction of unfit animals – a position not defensible by a reasonable interpretation of either scripture or paleontology – one must place spontaneous creation and evolution side by side in comparing their rates of development of new species.

Missing links have not been found

As with so many of the complaints about the theory of evolution, Charles Darwin had the foresight to address the assertion that intermediate forms are not found:

> The number of specimens in all our museums is absolutely nothing compared with the countless generations of countless species which have certainly existed. The parent form of any two or more species would not be in all its characters directly intermediate between its modified offspring . . . We should not be able to recognize a species as the parent of another and modified species, if we were to examine the two ever so closely, unless we possessed most of the intermediate links; and owing to the imperfection of the geological record, we have no just right to expect to find so many links.[1]

Researchers in paleontology, have, in fact, recovered a remarkable library of fossils, considering the serendipitous nature of fossil formation. Most fossils are of hard parts – bones, teeth, shells, and so on. Although it may seem intuitive that such hard relics of living things would be easily preserved, they have to first survive predation and scavenging by animals that are capable of ingesting and digesting bones, as are many modern carnivores and, judging from the teeth and jaw structures, many of the past. The prospective fossil then has to either be covered very promptly with sediments,

---

[1] Darwin, Charles. *The Origin of Species.* New York: Gramercy, 1979, Pg 462-463. (Chapter XIV: Recapitulation and Conclusion.)

most commonly at the bottom of a river, lake, or sea, but occasionally by the ash of volcanic eruptions, or in extraordinary circumstances trapped either in tree sap that becomes amber or in the ice of a glacier. The entombment must occur before substantial decomposition or damage occurs from exposure, bacterial degradation, or the actions of insects, worms, crabs, and so on. Once covered, the chemical structures of the bones or shells are replaced by minerals from the surrounding mud and form rock. The fossil then has to survive any distortions or breakage from geological action, the weathering of exposed formations, and finally the often difficult and tedious process of recovery and collection.

Fossil imprints of the soft tissues of plants and animals are, as expected, even rarer than fossilized hard parts because the whole organisms are even more subject to rapid degradation and their imprints even more fragile. The preservation of soft parts is most frequently facilitated by the animal rapidly sinking or being washed into deep bodies of water that have water layers with extremely low oxygen content (or perhaps even being killed by such hypoxic conditions) so that decomposition does not occur before sediment begins to cover the animal. In such unusual but fortuitous conditions, the detail of preserved imprints can be exquisite.

The preservation of whole animals in amber is limited to those of sufficiently small size to be engulfed by sap. Amber-encased fossils are typically small insects, arachnids, and similar creatures. The finds of whole large animals preserved in tar or frozen in glaciers are extraordinary, but extremely valuable; the soft anatomy of such animals very largely confirms the suppositions made by examination of hard fossils, increasing confidence in the interpretive abilities of paleontologists.

The fossil record is, in fact, remarkably complete, considering the rarity of the fossilization process, and its thorough and continuing exploration is due to the admirable dedication and creativity of professional and amateur paleontologists.

Criticism of human evolution

The term "missing link" is often used in connection with the descent of humans from australopithecines, implying unexplained gaps in the paleontological record, yet the fossil record shows a smoothly increasing brain size from brains averaging four hundred and thirty cubic centimeters (cc), only slightly larger than that of chimpanzees, to that of modern man averaging thirteen hundred fifty cc and ranging up to two thousand cc (cf. Chapter 6). Changes in limbs, facial structure, and skull shape develop similarly gradually. The progression includes branches of extinct species, most notably the robust *Paranthropus* genus and Neanderthal man, as expected by a full understanding of the theory of evolution. Most impressively, a number of fossil hominids have intermediate characteristics between species and defy classification even into the well established set of species that lead to *Homo sapiens*.

Opponents of evolution routinely dismiss intermediate fossils as either fully human or fully ape. It is of course a difficult proposition to dismiss as an ape an animal that is fully adapted to walking upright and has a brain size two to three times that of any surviving species of ape besides the naked ones we call humans, but no more difficult than to claim that a species with a brain size half that of modern humans and a markedly prognathic face is fully human; both difficulties arise from a desperate attempt at sharply dividing and discontinuously classifying a succession of species that is, when objectively considered, continuous in nature. It is perhaps most telling that while different anti-evolution authors claim that each of the species is clearly either an ape or a human, with no intermediate characteristics, they cannot agree on which species are so unmistakably apes and which are so obviously human.

A survey of twelve publications by ten authors from 1976 to 2005 considered the classification of six skull specimens, two each from the species *Homo habilis*, *H. ergaster*, and *H. erectus*. Each publication declared that apes and humans were unambiguously distinct, yet the publications were not unanimous in considering any of the six specimens as either human or ape. In ten instances, different specimens of the same species were classified as both apes and humans by the same authors in the same publication, and in three other instances, authors equivocated on the ape/human identity of a single largely complete specimen in spite of maintaining that the distinction between apes and humans were clear and unmistakable.[1] The obvious question is, if apes and humans are so markedly and plainly different from each other, why can the authors neither discern nor agree on which specimens are humans and which are apes? Such profound confusion, disagreement, and self-contradiction leads to the obvious conclusion that the classification of these specimens as either ape or human is problematic, and it is so exactly because the considered fossil specimens are indeed intermediate in nature, representing an evolutionary progression from ape-like ancestors to modern humans.

To all but the most biased observer, there would appear to be no major missing links between great apes and mankind, since a virtual continuum is demonstrated in the key features of brain size, posture, facial features, and limb structure. The exact relationships among the several species and genera that comprise the human family tree are subjects for legitimate and productive debate among experts in the field, but the fact that relationships exist is clear.

---

[1] Foley, Jim. "Creationism and Human Evolution: Comparison of All Skulls." 15 Sept 2005. *Fossil Hominids FAQ, Talk Origins Archive.* 25 Sept 2008. <http://www.talkorigins.org/faqs/homs/compare.html>.

The evolution of horses critiqued

Critics of evolution are nearly as keen to dismiss the paleontological record of the evolution of horses as that of humans. Paleontologist O. C. Marsh collected an impressive collection of equine fossils (as well as those of toothed birds) in working throughout the western United States, and by 1876 he and his fossils had attracted the attention of Thomas Huxley, Darwin's self-proclaimed bulldog. Huxley went on to publicize Marsh's findings and the evolutionary progression of the horse that they suggested. Marsh's findings, and a similar collection and theory by the lesser-known contemporary paleontologist E. D. Cope, were portrayed less than twenty years after the publication of *The Origin of Species* as a devastating example of straight-line, purposeful evolution of a species. The problem with that portrayal is that neither Darwin nor modern evolutionary theory represents evolution as a purposeful process, or as a ladder-like progression of species or characteristics.

Darwin described evolutionary processes as a branching tree, with dead branches of extinctions, twigs that became trunks that support entire classes and families, and a relatively few branches reaching the crown of the tree that represents current populations. Contemporary views of the equine family tree, based on the richness of available fossil evidence, are such a model. The version presented in an earlier chapter of this volume, although it may appear less than concise, is but a brief summary; a recent review of the subject in *Science* discussed no less than twenty-eight genera diagrammed in a branching pattern reaching back fifty-five million years to *Hyracotherium*.[1]

Unfortunately, creationists and proponents of intelligent design are still criticizing the model of equine evolution that was publicized in the late 1870s. Among their criticisms are that a model of linear evolution is presented in many contemporary elementary and early secondary school textbooks; the criticism is valid in that such publications present an antiquated and overly simplified version of the evolution of horses, but such is often true of textbooks aimed at students in the early years of their education. Such texts seldom present any subject in its most recent and fully developed form. Precious few students would comprehend the concept of gravity if it were presented initially as a portion of the theory of general relativity, but Newton's more understandable model, thought incomplete, is sufficient for the initial presentation of the concept of mutual attraction of massive objects for each other. In chemistry education, the motion of electrons is presented as orbits of tiny objects around the nucleus well before the theories of quantum mechanics that govern their wave/particle duality can be comprehended. Multi-volume sets expound every detail of vertebrate

[1] McFadden, Bruce J. "Fossil Horses – Evidence for Evolution." *Science,* vol 307, no 5716 (18 March 2005), pg 1728-1730.

anatomy, but for beginning students learning the names of the large bones and the major organs of the chest and abdominal cavities is a reasonable start. The criticism of a straight-line model of the evolution of the horse is not criticism of the data and theories of current science, but of models over a century old and of material presented to young children in their first encounters with the central theory of the biological sciences; at best, it is a criticism of teaching methods rather than of the theory of evolution as it is currently understood.

The anti-evolution organization Answers in Genesis states on its website, "Informed evolutionists now realize that the picture, even in their own framework, is not a straight line at all. While they still believe in horse evolution, the modern view of the horse fossil record is much more jumpy and 'bushy.'"[1] And it quotes paleontologist David M. Raup of the University of Chicago and Chicago's Field Museum of Natural History, "What appeared to be a nice simple progression when relatively few data were available now appears to be much more complex and less gradualistic."[2] That the picture of evolution of the horse is more complex than thought a hundred and forty years ago, or that it has developed and expanded to accommodate new findings and analyses in that time, is neither a surprise nor a reason to abandon the theory of evolution. It bears repeating that the current model of equine evolution is, in fact, in more intimate agreement with the theory presented by Darwin than was the outmoded and abandoned model of steady linear progression.

The current understanding of the evolution of horses is faulted by opponents of evolution for not accounting for variations in the number of ribs of ancestral species between fifteen and eighteen pairs, but modern horses sometimes vary in their number of ribs, and it is difficult to imagine what selection pressure would exist for or against a particular number of ribs as long as the thorax has adequate protection and integrity of its shape.

The evolutionary tree of horses is criticized on the grounds that the size of ancestral horses does not progress smoothly from small to large, and that modern horses vary widely in size. In fact, the evolutionary tree of horses contains a number of branches, most of which are extinct, that were of various sizes, each advantageous to their own environments. Modern domestic horses vary widely in size because of the selection of

---

[1] Sarfati, Jonathan. "The non-evolution of the horse: Special creation or evolved rock badger?" *Creation*, vol 21, no 3 (June 1999), pg 28-31. Accessed 29 Sept 2008 at <http://www.answersingenesis.org/creation/v21/i3/horse>.

[2] Raup, David M. "Conflicts between Darwin and paleontology." *Field Museum of Paleontology Bulletin* 50:22, 1979. Quoted by Jonathan Sarfati. "The non-evolution of the horse: Special creation or evolved rock badger?" *Creation*, vol 21, no 3 (June 1999), pg 28-31. Accessed 29 Sept 2008 at <http://www.answersingenesis.org/creation/v21/i3/horse>.

humans; populations of wild and feral horses, asses, and zebras vary little in size.

Creationists complain that fossils of species ancestral to horses are found at or near the surface, and allege that such findings belie the antiquity of such samples, but in reality many fossils of ancient forms of life are exposed by geological activity of various sorts. Few would hold that coal is anything but a fossil fuel, but deposits are in many places close enough to the surface to make strip mining economical.

Along the same lines, creationists frequently claim, in print and on internet sites, that fossils of modern horses are found in the same stratum with those of *Hyracotherium*. Extensive investigation, however, fails to find any creationist writing that says where or by whom these fossils are found. No original work can be found referenced; rather, the same claim is repeated and cross-referenced interminably, with no apparent foundation. A patient researcher who followed the meandering trail of references[1] determined that the claim appears to have arisen with Harry Rimmer, a creationist who claimed doctoral degrees in both theology and an unspecified science on the title page of his book *The Theory of Evolution and the Facts of Science* (1935), but whose documented scholastic record consisted only of a third-grade education, a correspondence course in geology, and an honorary doctorate from a conservative evangelical Christian college enamored of his anti-evolution oratory. Adhering to the creationist dogma that all fossils were deposited immediately after the flood of Noah (a theory with enough contravening evidence to fill a book of its own), Rimmer concluded, with no supporting evidence other than his peculiarly circular logic, that because both modern horses and *Hyracotherium* both existed as fossils at all, that they must have lived concurrently.

Opponents of evolution even complain that *Hyracotherium* looks too little like a modern horse to be an ancestor of *Equus*, and that its name reflects a relationship to the rabbit-like hyrax. In fact, *Hyracotherium*, was originally named by a paleontologist named Richard Owen who found only its teeth, and supposed it to be a relative of the hyrax; Marsh found a more complete skeleton and named it *Eohippus* ("dawn horse"), but taxonomists have a simple rule that the first name given a species has priority, so the name *Hyracotherium* officially persists. The argument that *Hyracotherium* is dissimilar to modern horses tacitly acknowledges its small size, primitive limbs, and archaic dentition, while apparently ignoring the intervening twenty-six genera and, most importantly and obviously, the point that evolution is a process of change. *Hyracotherium* naturally enough most closely resembles its successor, as each of the genera in the family tree of horses resembles its predecessor and its successor in turn, in a continuous series of intermediates along the branching tree of evolution.

---

[1] Barber, Jon. "Did *Hyracotherium* and *Equus* Live at the Same Time?" www.talkorigins.org/faqs/horses, 1-3-2002, accessed 1-26-2008.

The evolutionary history of horses is actually well documented, but presentations of the documentation are sometimes oversimplified, as was the original presentation by Marsh and Huxley. A full presentation of the evidence demonstrates the complexity of multiple branches and extinctions, irregular rates of evolutionary change, and independent development of different traits that are the realistic hallmarks of evolution fully considered and understood. Arguments against the evolution of horses are outdated, contrived, and often patently false.

Transitional species are lacking

Those sympathetic to creationism and intelligent design contest every transition of form in the fossil record, but all major transitions are explicable by examining the evidence of living species and the fossil record. The discovery of *Archaeopteryx* was published in 1861, just two years after the first printing of *Origin*, and provided evidence of the link between dinosaurs and birds that has been further clarified by later discoveries. Consideration of *Volvox* brings light to how multicellular organisms with specialization of tissues may have developed. The ancestry of trilobites to horseshoe crabs, crustaceans, arachnids, and insects is readily apparent. Fossil and living echinoderms show the first steps leading to the development of vertebrates, and the hemichordates and cephalochordates demonstrate further progress down that path. Lobe-finned fish, lungfish, *Eusthenopteron*, *Panderichthys*, *Tiktaalik*, *Acanthostega*, and *Ichthyostega* demonstrate in a clear series how vertebrates gradually adapted to moving through shallows, pursuing prey beyond the water line, and colonizing land. The ancestry of whales and dolphins, elephants, and many other modern animals and plants is well established.

It is difficult to understand how much more evidence for descent with modification is required by the opponents of evolution. Few significant gaps exist in the evolutionary history of the major groups of living organisms, and new discoveries are constantly being made that promise to fill those few. For all the reasons foreseen by Darwin, it is not reasonable to expect the fossil record to provide evidence from each generation of life for the last three and a half billion years, but a rational evaluation of the wealth of data that is possessed by humankind finds it to be fully consistent with the evolutionary development of life, and, perhaps against odds, astonishingly complete in its record.

Mutations are always harmful

A common notion exploited by creationists and intelligent design proponents is that all mutations are harmful. It is certainly fair to say that most mutations are deleterious to the survival of the host organisms, but "most" is simply not a synonym for "all."

Because genes code for the production of proteins, those that alter the structure of proteins most often produce a dysfunction in that protein; such is the cause of the overwhelming majority of genetic diseases.

But since much of the DNA of living things does not function in the production of proteins or in the regulation of the segments that code for proteins, mutations in so-called junk DNA do not prove harmful to the survival of its host, and the mutation is propagated freely.

A significant number of mutations are base substitutions that, in the manner previously discussed, produce no change in the amino acid sequence of the resulting protein; such mutations are similarly lacking in impact on the survivability of the host, and are similarly and freely propagated to subsequent generations.

Even mutations that produce an observable change in phenotype may produce little or no change in the capacity of the host to survive and reproduce, and thus perpetuate the mutation. An example of the latter is the common observation of gardeners that a single branch of a plant produces flowers of a different color than the rest of the plant. In the author's own garden, an ixora, a hibiscus, and a bougainvillea plant each exhibits the trait, which is the result of a mutation in the tissue of the branch when it first buds from the stem or parent branch. Unless the color change makes a difference in the attractiveness of the flower to pollination agents, the color change would not adversely affect the likelihood that a flower from the mutant branch would produce viable seeds.

Mutations that produce dysfunction of proteins, then, are in the minority, and although their effects can be dramatically negative, they can also prove serendipitously beneficial to the survival of the organisms bearing the gene. One example of the alteration of a protein to another functional protein has already been provided in the mutation of the surface proteins of the feline panleukopenia virus – a mutation that required a change in just two amino acids - that allowed the mutant virus to attack the cells of dogs and open up for itself a new host environment. The development of antibiotic resistance by bacteria is not beneficial to humans, but it certainly helps the bacteria. Other examples will become apparent as refutations of the arguments against evolution continue.

The rate of evolution

Opponents of evolution hold that the known processes of evolution cannot produce change at a rate sufficient for the differentiation of species demonstrated in the fossil record.

In fact, a review and detailed analysis of a wide range of experimental and observational data by Dr. Philip D. Gingerich, who holds professorships in the departments of geology, biology, and anthropology at the University of Michigan and is the director of the university's Museum of Paleontology, found otherwise. Calculations based on observations of finches, lizards, and house sparrows analyzed by Gingerich document rates of genetic change, expressed in units called darwins, of twelve thousand to two hundred thousand, over one thousand times the rate required for some of the most rapid changes in the fossil record, including those cited as necessitating punctuated equilibrium. Experiments in which plants and animals were observed to colonize new environments yielded rates of change of a similar order, ranging up to 79,700 darwins. The rate of change observed in the rapid radiation of mammals in the Pleistocene Epoch was 0.11 to 32.0 darwins.[1]

Similarly impressive rates of evolutionary change were documented by David N. Reznick of the University of California, Riverside, Frank H. Shaw and Ruth G. Shaw of the University of Minnesota, and F. Helen Rodd of the University of California, Davis, in their observations of native guppy populations in Trinidad. (Trips to Trinidad in winter must have been a terrible sacrifice for the Minnesota-based researchers, but the dedication of men and women of science is frequently inspiring.) Guppies that lived in areas where they were subject to predation reached reproductive maturity earlier and at a smaller size, and produced litters of smaller individual size and greater number, than their counterparts that were not subject to predation. The researchers confirmed that the differences were genetic rather than environmental in origin by raising guppies from each population in laboratory conditions, and indeed, the differences were found to be consistent – predation had selected for animals that reproduced earlier, before they were eaten, and in greater numbers. Seeing the opportunity for a simple but elegant experiment, Reznick and his team transplanted guppies in two different streams from pools at the bottom of waterfalls where they were subject to predation and adapted to it, to pools at the top of the same waterfalls where neither guppies nor significant predators were present.

After observing one site for seven and a half years and the other for eleven years, they saw that both transplanted populations matured at a later age and larger size than their relatives at the bottom of the falls still subject to predation. Only one of the populations showed differences in litter size and numbers – for both populations to have demonstrated the hoped-for changes in all characteristics would have been perhaps a bit too tidy. "The estimated rates of phenotypic evolution range from 3700 to 45,000 darwins. . . They are similar in magnitude to rates that have been obtained by artificial selection and four to seven orders of magnitude greater than those observed in

---

[1] Gingerich, Philip D. "Rates of Evolution: Effects of Time and Temporal Scaling." *Science* , vol 222, no 4620 (14 Oct 1983), pg 159-161. In Miller, Kenneth R. *Finding Darwin's God: A Scientist's Search for Common Ground Between God and Evolution.* New York: HarperCollins, 1999. pg 111. Original paper accessed 29 Sept 2008 at <http://www.sciencemag.org>.

the fossil record."[1] Such a rate is more than rapid enough to account for the bursts of speciation described by punctuated equilibrium or the rapid changes observed in the fossil record of the Cambrian period.

The Reznick paper can hardly be more penetrating in its discussion of its results:

> If evolution is so fast, why does it appear to be so slow in the fossil record? First, evolution is only sustained in response to a changing environment; when a new optimum is attained, no more evolution is expected. . . Second, if environmental conditions vary erratically, so will patterns of evolution, as seen in Galapagos finches. Evaluating evolution with the fossil record averages across intervals of no change, intervals of rapid change, and possibly includes reversals in the direction of change, yielding an estimate of rate averaged over the entire interval. The net effect could well be no measurable change in morphology, or "stasis." On the other hand, sustained directional selection can support far more rapid directional change than seen in the fossil record.
>
> Our work . . . is part of a growing body of evidence that the rate and patterns of change attainable through natural selection are sufficient to account for the patterns observed in the fossil record.[2]

Microevolution has occurred, but not macroevolution

Confronted by demonstrable and measurable evolutionary trends in the characteristics of established species, opponents of evolution concede that microevolution has occurred, but deny the existence of macroevolution.

The prefix "micro" of course means small, and "macro" large; aside from that, the definitions of microevolution and macroevolution are unclear and labile. Microevolution is sometimes used by biologists to describe the alteration of traits within a species, and macroevolution to denote changes sufficient to differentiate species, genera, or higher levels of taxonomy, but such a definition is neither strictly adhered to nor universally accepted. Among those who use the terms it is understood that because speciation, or macroevolution, comes from an accumulation of changes that may in themselves be termed microevolution, microevolution and macroevolution are merely matters of degree of phenotypic change. Many writers and lecturers make a point of avoiding the terms altogether because of their indistinct and unsettled definitions.

Among creationists and intelligent design proponents, the uncertainty of the definitions

---

[1] Reznick, David N. "Evaluation of the Rate of Evolution in Natural Populations of Guppies (*Poecilia reticulate*). *Science*, vol 275, no 5308 (28 March 1997), pg 1934-1937.
[2] Reznick, David N. "Evaluation of the Rate of Evolution in Natural Populations of Guppies (*Poecilia reticulate*). *Science*, vol 275, no 5308 (28 March 1997), pg 1934-1937.

of microevolution and macroevolution is used as an opportunity to sow confusion with their rhetoric. Any evolutionary process that produces observable results can be dismissed as microevolution, and any processes less than fully proven can be categorized as macroevolution. The critic of evolution can then revert to the formal definition of the terms and claim that speciation has not been shown to proceed from evolution. Thus, for example, the evolutionary series that begins with *Hyracotherium* and ends with modern horses, zebras, and donkeys is dismissed as microevolution, implying a diminution and dismissal of the profound changes in equine anatomy over the last fifty-five million years.

The dismissal of observed evolutionary change as microevolution while maintaining that macroevolution has not occurred is, at its root, a mere restatement of the claims that speciation has not been demonstrated and that the rates of evolutionary change are insufficient to account for the radiation and differentiation observed in the fossil record. Both allegations are demonstrably false, and attempts to confuse the issues with rhetorical use and misuse of terms like microevolution and macroevolution do not lend them strength.

Man is a unique and higher species with characteristics unlike animals

Charles Darwin did little to address the origins of man in *The Origin of Species*; his comments were largely restricted to the cryptic prediction that "light will be thrown on the origin of man and his history." Twelve years after the publication of *Origin*, though, with the 1871 publication of *The Descent of Man*, he wryly observed,

> It has often and confidently been asserted, that man's origin can never be known: but ignorance more frequently begets confidence than does knowledge: it is those who know little and not those who know much who so positively assert that this or that problem will never be solved by science.[1]

In one of the more astute deductions he was to make based on his theory, he predicted, in language more modest than its bold content,

> In each great region of the world the living mammals are closely related to the extinct species of the same region. It is therefore probable that Africa was formerly inhabited by extinct apes closely allied to the gorilla and chimpanzee; and as these two species are now man's nearest allies, it is somewhat more

[1] Darwin, Charles. *The Descent of Man, and Selection in Relation to Sex*. New York: D. Appleton, 1897. Pg 2 (Introduction).

> probable that our early progenitors lived on the African continent than elsewhere.[1]

It was, of course, a prediction that would be confirmed decades after Darwin's death. But is the human species something more than a primate with fewer hair follicles than normal? Religious thought from all parts of the world answers yes.

Humans giving serious thought to the origin of their race generally prefer to believe that they differ from animals, as indeed they do in many respects. That desire is not mere vanity, although vanity certainly may play a role. The student of Judeo-Christian scripture is assured in the first chapter of Genesis that man is made in the very image of God (although it does not say by what means man was made, or in what way he is like God), and the Eighth Psalm is quoted in the anonymous Letter to the Hebrews of the New Testament canon, that man is but a little lower than the heavenly beings or angels.[2,3]

And yet man is undeniably an animal. The human animal is a vertebrate, with an embryonic notochord and tail, and with a long flexible spine protecting a concentration of neural tissue that runs the length of the body. The human vertebrate is a tetrapod, with limbs that unmistakably share the bony supporting structures of other four-limbed terrestrial vertebrates. The human tetrapod is a mammal, with a complex skin that includes hair, oil glands, sweat glands, and mammary glands that nourish young after they gestate internally by means of a placenta. The human mammal is a primate, with grasping limbs, and a brain even more extremely developed than those of his fellow primates. Non-human animals can be used as models for the study of anatomy, physiology, and drug metabolism precisely because they are so similar to humans in all aspects.

In what way, then, can man be said to be like God, only a little lower than heavenly beings? The brain of man has, in its development, passed a threshold beyond which it is capable of complex thoughts. The human mind is capable of problem solving, but problem solving on a more rudimentary level can be observed in other animals, up to and including the use of simple tools by chimpanzees; the echidna, the little egg-laying hedgehog-like animal of Australia and New Zealand, primitive in many aspects, was clever enough to stack its food bowls into a ladder-like structure to escape its pen. Chimpanzees and gorillas have been taught to communicate simply but effectively through sign language, and have even appeared to combine signs into new words to express a thought for which they had not been taught a sign. (For example, a gorilla

---

[1] Darwin, Charles. *The Descent of Man, and Selection in Relation to Sex.* New York: D. Appleton, 1897. Pg 155 (Chapter VI – Affinities and Geneology).

[2] Hebrews 2.5-8.

[3] Psalm 8.4-6.

named Koko is said to have combined the signs for "finger" and "bracelet" to name a ring, quite reasonably and creatively, a "finger bracelet.") The human mind, however, is, as far as is known, unique in its ability to think in an abstract manner, to wonder at the workings of the world, to contemplate its own existence, and to consider its own spirituality and its relationship to deity. The results are morality, ethics, altruism beyond what is observed or inferred from the behavior of other animals, as well as religious reflection. By considering the existence of God and, for the believer, the possibility of His pleasure and displeasure at the actions of man and mankind, humans separate themselves from the other animals and take a place a little lower than heavenly beings; it is through the development of the brain that such consideration could develop.

Mankind does not require separate creation to have a special place within creation; the development of his mind is sufficient to assure his status. Asa Gray addressed these same concerns in his address to the students and professors of theology at Yale University:

> In most respects, man is an exceptional creature. If, however, I decline to regard man's origin as exceptional in the sense of directly supernatural, you will understand that it is because, under my thoroughly theistic conception of nature, and my belief in mediate creation, I am at a loss to know what I should mean by the exception. I do not allow myself to believe that immediate creation would make man's origin more divine.[1]

The uniqueness of man is assured, not by the means or the abruptness of his creation, but by the fullness of his mind, the expanse of which can discern and embrace a spirituality that is absent to all other forms of life.

The second law of thermodynamics

Some creationists pronounce the second law of thermodynamics – that the entropy, or disorder, of a closed system will always increase - to be a devastating argument against evolution. They argue that the law precludes the increasing complexity of living organisms described by evolutionary theory, and conclude that because thermodynamics predicts increasing disorder, that each organism, representing as it does an increase in order and a decrease in entropy, is itself a miracle performed by a creator in violation of natural law. The argument fails to recognize the fact, obvious to those who understand the nature of the law and the basics of physics, that neither the earth nor any living organism is a closed system. All living organisms consume energy, either by capturing the radiant energy of the sun, as do photosynthetic plants and algae,

---

[1] Gray, Asa. "Natural Science and Religion: Two Lectures, Delivered to the Theological School of Yale College." New York: Charles Scribner's Sons, 1880. Accessed 25 Sept 2008 at <http://home.att.net/~a.caimi/Gray.html>.

or by ingesting complex molecules that can be metabolized as an energy source, as do animals and some protists. All living organisms expend energy to decrease entropy, by increasing and maintaining order within the boundaries of the organism.

The difference can be seen by a simple example: A cup of sugar and a bucket of water are organized by being separated. If the cup of sugar is poured into the water, it will dissolve, increasing the overall entropy, or disorder, of the system. Depending on the amount of sugar and the temperature of the water, it may take varying amounts of time for the sugar to dissolve, but during the process entropy continually increases until the sugar is all dissolved, at which time entropy is maximized because the molecules of sugar and water are thoroughly and maximally mixed.

As long as the system remains closed, the entropy remains maximized. But with the application of energy to the system, the sugar and water can be separated again, increasing order and decreasing entropy. If the water is heated to boiling, and the resulting steam cooled and condensed again to water, the entropy of the system can be decreased to its original state – dry sugar can be returned to its cup and the water to its own bucket. The key concept to understand in this example is that, by the application of heat to boil the sugar solution, the system is no longer closed. Entropy was decreased and the system was ordered by the application of energy, which is the physicist's definition of work.

If the second law of thermodynamics stated that entropy inexorably increased in all circumstances, regardless of work performed, then it would be impossible for a teenager to clean up a bedroom, or a businessman to straighten his desk, or an author to organize his notes – no amount of work could increase order. But because the law applies only to closed systems, work – the expenditure of energy – can decrease entropy and increase order. Living organisms are systems that expend energy, on the biochemical level, to increase order and decrease entropy. Arguing that the second law of thermodynamics precludes biological evolution is a clumsy misapplication of the law and demonstrates fundamental misunderstanding of basic scientific principles and arguments on the part of creationists.

Information theory

A recent and more sophisticated tactic of intelligent design proponents, but one that springs from similar roots and reflects a similar misapplication of otherwise valid principles, has been to claim that information theory proves that evolution cannot produce and maintain the information content of DNA.

Information theory is the field that mathematically analyzes the storage and transmission of information, and has resulted in such technological advances as DSL lines, MP3 and jpeg files for music and picture storage, and zip files for the compression of computer applications. Intelligent design proponents use misleading and twisted application of information theory, largely originating from William Dembski, to advocate their position.[1] Dembski's "law of conservation of information" states without proof that natural causes are incapable of generating complex specified information.[2] Complex specified information is a term coined by Dembski to include any series of code, such as a credit card number, the digital signal of data transmission for fax machines or modems, or printed words, and DNA. The conclusion of Dembski and his advocates is that cellular apparatuses in general and DNA in particular is incapable of establishing and retaining the information necessary for evolution to proceed effectively. Long technical arguments can counter their argument, but unfortunately for their argument and fortunately for the reader, computer simulations provide more graphic and more easily accessible evidence. Simulations by Thomas Schneider of the National Institutes of Health, Charles Ofria and Richard Lenski at Michigan State University, and Thomas Ray of the University of Delaware demonstrate that the information content of DNA shows significant increases over time, given only an ability to replicate information, a duplication error rate consistent with that of DNA replication, and a selection criterion. In the case of Schneider's NIH program, for example, the selection criterion is conformity of a resulting protein to a collection of binding sites, a criterion realistic to biological systems. The program starts with random sequences, then discards half of the results – the half that produces the lowest degree of conformity to the binding sites – before allowing a certain number of randomized errors in reproducing the sequences in a new generation. With each generation, the conformity and the statistical information content of the sequences increase. When selection pressure is eliminated, the information content of the sequences quickly decreases to near zero.[3, 4]

Intelligent design advocates have misinterpreted even this result, taking the fact that the removal of selection criteria results in a marked decrease of information content of the sequences as evidence that intelligent design is necessary for the maintenance of information content within DNA, but the effectiveness of selection criteria is the central point of both evolution and the simulation. It is meaningless to argue that the decreased information content of the simulators' DNA-like sequences in the absence of

---

1 Schneider, Thomas D. "Dissecting Dembski's 'Complex Specified Information'." 5 Mar 2005. Accessed 6 Oct 2008 at <http://www-lmmb.ncifcrf.gov/~toms/paper/ev/dembski/specified.complexity.html>.
2 Dembski, William A. "Intelligent Design as a Theory of Information." 15 Nov 1998. *Access Research Network*. Accessed 6 Oct 2008 at <http://www.arn.org/docs/dembski/wd_idtheory.htm>.
3 Schneider, Thomas D. "Dissecting Dembski's 'Complex Specified Information'." 5 Mar 2005. Accessed 6 Oct 2008 at <http://www-lmmb.ncifcrf.gov/~toms/paper/ev/dembski/specified.complexity.html>.
4 Miller, Kenneth R. *Only a Theory*. New York: Viking, 2008. Pg 74-78.

selection pressure are proof of intelligent design in the DNA sequences of living organisms. Selection is exactly the element identified by Darwin as the driving force of evolution. Demonstrating that evolution does not work if its central premise of selection is deleted is like "proving" that a car will not run if its engine is removed: true, but unimpressive and pointless, and increasing rather than decreasing one's impression of the importance of that strange and noisy collection of odd-shaped metallic objects.

Irreducible complexity

Creationists and, to an even greater extent, intelligent design advocates, seized on the words of Darwin himself as an opportunity to disprove the theory of descent with modification. In his chapter on "Difficulties on Theory," under the heading "Organs of extreme perfection and complication," Darwin wrote:

> To suppose that the eye, with all its inimitable contrivances for adjusting the focus to different distances, for admitting different amounts of light, and for the correction of spherical and chromatic aberration, could have been formed by natural selection, seems, I freely confess, absurd in the highest possible degree.[1]

Those who sought to disprove the theory of evolution eagerly grasped the prospect of using the words of the author against him. They formulated the doctrine of irreducible complexity – the concept, which intelligent design theorists haughtily proclaim to be a law of nature, that certain systems of anatomic and biochemical parts work so well together that they could not have evolved. Systems are identified as irreducibly complex when two conditions are met: the removal of any component causes failure of the system, and the components have no other use or application that could have provided a source of available materials upon which selection could act. It is the holding of proponents that irreducibly complex systems must have been designed intact, because there is no possible path by which such beautifully integrated systems could have evolved, and that the mammalian eye was correctly identified by Darwin as such a system.

Unfortunately for those who clasp so tightly to the doctrine of irreducible complexity, Darwin continued on the subject of eyes for just a bit longer:

> Yet reason tells me, that if numerous gradations from a perfect and complex eye to one very imperfect and simple, each grade being useful to is possessor, can be shown to exist; if further, the eye does vary ever so slightly, and the variations be inherited, which is certainly the case; and if any variation or modification in the organ be ever useful to an animal under changing

[1] Darwin, Charles. *The Origin of Species.* New York: Gramercy, 1979, Pg 217. (Chapter VI: Difficulties on Theory.)

> conditions of life, then the difficulty of believing that a perfect and complex eye could be formed by natural selection, though insuperable by our imagination, can hardly be considered real.[1]

Those who would evaluate the doctrine of irreducible complexity may then reasonably ask if a progression is present in nature that might satisfy Darwin's criteria. Many small photosynthetic organisms like *Euglena* have eyespots by which they orient themselves to light, and *Volvox* colonies have several cells that are differentiated to perform the same function, with the obvious advantage of positioning the organisms and colonies in light suitable for photosynthesis. Animals whose eye spots are cup shaped, such as flatworms and *Planaria* snails, can sense the direction from which light is coming, because of the relative amounts of light falling on different portions of the cup-shaped receptors. As the cup deepens, the directionality increases, and when the orifice begins to constrict to leave a spherical set of receptors with a relatively small opening, an eye resembling a pinhole camera is capable of forming discernible images; such an eye is present in the nautilus. In annelid worms, a thin transparent layer of skin grows over the pinhole to form a cornea and a closely associated lens. As the lens separates from the cornea, as it does in the eyes of most vertebrates, the image quality improves, as demonstrated by researchers Dan-Erik Nilsson and Susanne Pelger; they even calculated that the entire process of development of an eye with lens from eyespots could, under optimum conditions of maximum selection pressure, take place in just a few hundred thousand years.[2, 3] A detailed proposal for the possible path of evolution of the mammalian eye, encompassing aspects ranging from biochemistry to microanatomy and neuroanatomy, was proposed by Trevor Lamb and his colleagues at the Australian National University in Nature Reviews in 2007.[4]

The flagship example of irreducible complexity, the case cited by Charles Darwin himself as a possible weakness in his theory, resolved in exactly the manner he expected, but undeterred enthusiasts of the doctrine not only continued to proclaim it, in the apparent hope that those ignorant of fact would be convinced, but found other systems to proclaim to be irreducibly complex.

---

[1] Darwin, Charles. *The Origin of Species.* New York: Gramercy, 1979, Pg 217. (Chapter VI: Difficulties on Theory.)
[2] "Evolution of the Eye." WGBH Educational Foundation and Clear Blue Sky Productions. 2001. Accessed 30 Sept 2008 at <http://www.pbs.org/wgbh/evolution/library/01/1/quicktime/l_011>.
3 Nilsson, Dan-Erik, and Susanne Pelger. "A pessimistic estimate of the time required for an eye to evolve." *Proceedings: Biological Sciences* (Royal Society of London), vol. 256, no. 1345 (22 Apr 1994), pg 53-58. Accessed 30 Sept 2008 at <http://www.jstor.org/pss/49593>.
[4] Lamb, Trevor D., et al. "Evolution of the Vertebrate Eye: Opsins, Photoreceptors, Retina and Eye Cup." Nature Reviews Neuroscience 8 (2007):960-976. Quoted by Kenneth A. Miller. *Only A Theory: Evolution and the Battle for America's Soul.* New York: Viking, 2008. Pg 224-225.

Examples of irreducible complexity that are currently favored by intelligent design advocates are those of the bacterial flagellum, the mammalian blood clotting cascade, and the immune system. Kenneth R. Miller is a Brown University professor of biology, and in his research into the biology and biochemistry of cellular membranes, one of the many men and women of faith working at the highest levels of science who reconcile their religious faith with their knowledge of evolution. As presented earlier in this chapter, he is the author of several high school and college biology textbooks as well as two books supporting the concept of theistic evolution and critical of creationism and intelligent design (*Finding Darwin's God* and *Only A Theory*). Miller has, in his books, lectures, interviews, and court testimony, effectively countered each of the three primary examples of irreducible complexity from his extensive knowledge of cellular biology.

Bacterial flagella are composed of thirty to fifty protein parts, and they work together so effectively that the impression of irreducible complexity is, without investigation, understandable. But the doctrine of irreducible complexity holds that none of those parts should have another function, for if another function can be demonstrated, they could have been the subject of selection and been present in the cell performing another function before being coopted and adapted to a new function. The business of science is investigation, and research into the function of bacterial flagella has brought to light other functions for its component proteins and produced a model for its evolution.

When all but ten of its component parts are removed, the base of the flagellum closely resembles, and is made up of the same component proteins as, a structure called the Type III Secretory System,[1] which in turn shares several proteins on the cell surface with the Type II Secretory System.[2] The Type II Secretory System secretes proteins, including toxins, into the environment around bacteria that possess it, while the Type III Secretory System is more aggressive, allowing bacteria such as the causative organisms of bubonic plague, *Yersinia pestis*, the bacterium of typhoid fever, *Salmonella typhimurium*, and disease-causing strains of the gastrointestinal organism *Escherichia coli* to forcibly inject their toxins into host cells. The filament of the bacterial flagellum is composed of proteins collected from other uses within the bacterial cell; in fact, almost all of the thirty to fifty proteins of a functioning bacterial flagellum have functions in other portions of the cell.[3] The flagellum of bacteria is little more than a Type III Secretory System with a filament protruding through its pore.

---

[1] Miller, Kenneth R. *Only a Theory*. New York: Viking, 2008. Pg 57-62.

[2] Hueck, C. J. "Type III protein secretion systems in bacterial pathogens of animals and plants." *Microbiology and Molecular Biology Reviews*, vol 6, no 2 (June 1998). Pg 379-433.

[3] Miller, Kenneth R. *Only a Theory*. New York: Viking, 2008. Pg 61.

The premise of irreducible complexity is that the component parts of complex systems should have no other function, but such is clearly not the case with respect to the bacterial flagellum. It takes little imagination to propose from the known information a plausible scenario for the evolution of bacterial flagella from a basic secretory pore. A Type II Secretory System which acquires the ability for motion in actively injecting its toxins into other cells would provide a significant advantage to a bacterium that feeds on the debris of dead cells, and be subject to selection, leading to the formation of the Type III Secretory System. Since the function of the Type III system is to secrete toxin proteins, the secretion of filamentous proteins could easily have followed, and the apparatus of the active secretion system itself could provide motion. A basal flagellum would be present and functional in at least a rudimentary form, and selection of more efficient and effective forms could progress. The premise that the bacterial flagellum is irreducibly complex fails on investigation.

The blood clotting system of mammals is another example used by proponents of intelligent design to demonstrate irreducible complexity. It is commonly referred to as a cascade, because it is composed of a series of eight reactions, each of which magnify the last. The cascade is initiated when circulating proteins are activated by exposure to tissue enzymes. The activated protein molecule itself acts as an enzyme to cleave several other protein molecules, and that activated protein molecule enzymatically activates many molecules in the next step, and so on. In that way each of the eight steps multiplies the effect of the previous step, until the last enzyme in the chain forms a network of insoluble fibrin strands by cleaving soluble fibrinogen, and all but the most severe bleeding is controlled.

Irreducible complexity is demonstrated to the satisfaction of intelligent design proponents by the existence of hemophilia. Hemophilia A is caused by a deficiency in factor VIII and famously affected the royal houses of Europe, and hemophilia B is caused by deficiency in factor IX; both result in uncontrolled and sometimes fatal bleeding. Irreducible complexity would appear to be present, until one is informed that whales and dolphins lack one of the clotting factors, and some species of fish lack three, and still have blood that clots effectively.[1]

Blood plasma contains a variety of proteins, some of which are soluble in their normal state, but become insoluble upon being cleaved by exposure to serine protease enzymes in the tissues. When there is a break in the wall of a blood vessel, the serine proteases in the surrounding tissues cause some of these proteins to precipitate, sealing the vessel. Such a blood clotting system is used by many invertebrates, successfully so

---

[1] Miller, Kenneth R. *Only a Theory*. New York: Viking, 2008. Pg.

because their blood pressure is low enough that they need nothing else.[1]

Six of the circulating blood clotting factors of mammals (factors IX, XI, and XII of the intrinsic system, factor VII of the extrinsic system, and factor X and prothrombin common to both systems) are all related to each other and share segments of identical or near-identical functional amino acid configurations called serine protease domains.2 Each factor in the cascade is activated when its predecessor removes an amino acid chain that either covers or distorts the active domain, and once active performs a similar function on its successor. A process of gene duplication with retargeting of serine proteases to the bloodstream has been proposed and documented by Dr. Russell F. Dolittle, a research biochemist with University of California San Diego,[3] and as the genome and the amino acid sequences of these proteins have been delineated in recent years, it has become clear that nine of the protein factors of the mammalian clotting cascade could have been produced by only six instances of genetic sequence translocations.[4] Posing even another problem for the claim of irreducible complexity is the fact that thrombin, the last stage of the cascade that converts soluble fibrinogen to clotting fibrin, is highly homologous to pancreatic trypsin, an important digestive enzyme.[5] And the genome of sea squirts, non-vertebrate chordates with no blood clotting mechanism, contains all but two of the protein domains contained in the mammalian clotting cascade.[6]

Hemophilia is a less common clotting abnormality than the less well known and usually less severe von Willebrand Disease. Von Willebrand Disease (vWD) results from deficiency or dysfunction of a protein that causes platelets to adhere to the walls of broken blood vessels and stabilizes circulating factor VII. Since there are several different types of von Willebrand disease, researchers at the Washington University School of Medicine in Saint Louis undertook to determine the gene and amino acid sequences of von Willebrand factor (vWF). The gene is composed of approximately 178 thousand nucleotide bases, making it the largest gene known for blood clotting proteins and "contribut[ing] to the prevalence and heterogeneity of vWD by providing a large target for mutation."[7] "Over 90% of the vWF precursor consists of four

---

[1] Miller, Kenneth R. *Finding Darwin's God: A Scientist's Search for Common Ground Between God and Evolution.* New York: HarperCollins, 1999. Pg 156.
[2] Miller, Kenneth R. *Only a Theory.* New York: Viking, 2008. Pg 63-64.
[3] Miller, Kenneth R. *Finding Darwin's God: A Scientist's Search for Common Ground Between God and Evolution.* New York: HarperCollins, 1999. Pg 156-157.
[4] Miller, Kenneth R. *Only a Theory.* New York: Viking, 2008. Pg 64.
[5] Miller, Kenneth R. *Finding Darwin's God: A Scientist's Search for Common Ground Between God and Evolution.* New York: HarperCollins, 1999. Pg 157.
[6] Miller, Kenneth R. *Only a Theory.* New York: Viking, 2008. Pg 65-66.
[7] Mancuso, David J., et al. "Structure of the Gene for Human von Willebrand Factor." *Journal of Biological Chemistry*, vol 264, no 33 (25 Nov 2989). Pg 19514-19527. Accessed 6 Oct 2008 at <http://www.jbc.org/cgi/reprint/264/33/19514>.

distinct repeated domains present in 2 to 5 copies . . . [The domains] are about 220 amino acids in length and appear to be homologous to segments of complement factor B, complement component C2, cartilage matrix protein, α1-collagen type VI, and the α-subunits of the leukocyte adhesion receptors."[1] Complement is a chemical component of the immune system that enhances cell-killing ability by compromising the cell membrane of targeted cells. Cartilage matrix protein and α1-collagen type VI are structural proteins in connective tissue. Leukocyte adhesion receptors are molecules that help white blood cells stick to subject cells. A component of the blood clotting system is markedly homologous with proteins found in connective tissue and the immune system.

With investigation, it becomes difficult to maintain either that the blood clotting cascade is without function without even one of its components, or that the components have no other function within the organism from which they could be recruited, or that there is no conceivable means by which natural selection could act to provide the mechanism for blood clotting. Irreducible complexity must be rejected.

The ability of the immune system to produce antibodies to the wide array of potentially disease-causing elements in the world, including viruses, bacteria, fungi, cancer cells, bacterial toxins, and even snake venom, is awe-inspiring, and stimulated yet another claim from intelligent design proponents of irreducible complexity; the man who coined the term proclaimed in 1996 that science would "never" demonstrate how it could have evolved. Yet research has demonstrated first that the genes that code for binding sites of antibodies frequently are unstable, constantly shuffling and rearranging their segments so that different binding sites' conformations are constantly available for selection; then that the instability was due to a previously known class of DNA molecules called transposons; and finally in 2005 delineated the exact transposon that accounts for the abilities of the immune system to adapt to changing antigenic stimulants.[2]

Proteins themselves are often said to be enormously complex, and by the estimations of some opponents of evolution, the odds against functional proteins being created by random sequences of DNA are astronomical. The largest known protein, titin, is composed of nearly twenty-seven thousand amino acids (giving its chemical name the arguable status of the longest word: by pasting it in this document, the author found it to run for forty-eight pages, conceded the point, and spared the reader proof), and functions in the regulation and coordination of actin and myosin in muscle

---

[1] Mancuso, David J., et al. "Structure of the Gene for Human von Willebrand Factor." *Journal of Biological Chemistry*, vol 264, no 33 (25 Nov 2989). Pg 19514-19527. Accessed 6 Oct 2008 at <http://www.jbc.org/cgi/reprint/264/33/19514>.

[2] Miller, Kenneth R. *Only a Theory.* New York: Viking, 2008. Pg 70-74.

contractions. The probability of a protein of that size, or, admittedly, of many proteins of more ordinary size, arising from random combinations is small, but with a process of selection favoring function, functional proteins of impressive size and complexity can evolve from simpler versions.

Epinephrine, or adrenaline, is a modification of a single amino acid, either phenylalanine or tyrosine, to a hormone with enormous impact on virtually every tissue of the body. The amino acid praline has been found to have significant catalytic activity in some biological reactions,[1] demonstrating that even minute proteins can have significant function, and therefore be subject to selection.

Several proteins with profound effects are small in size. Substance P is a protein containing only eleven amino acids. It is a neurotransmitter (a molecule active in transmission of impulses between nerve cells) that is essential in transmitting sensations of pain. It also is active in parts of the brain that govern moods, is involved in nausea and vomiting, stimulation of salivation (dogs and cats are often noticed to salivate excessively before displaying more obvious results of nausea), smooth muscle contraction, and regulation of blood pressure. Substance P is regarded as the prototype for approximately fifty neurotransmitters.[2] Several studies have reported increased levels of substance P in fibromyalgia patients. All of its functions are accomplished by a single sequence of just eleven amino acids.

Oxytocin is a hormone that works in the reproductive tract of vertebrates. It promotes uterine contractions that propel eggs along the tract in lower vertebrates and induces birth contractions in the uterus of mammals. After birth, it enhances milk production in mammals and maternal behaviors in most vertebrates. Oxytocin is composed of just nine amino acids, seven of which are identical in all vertebrates. Bony fish differ from mammals in two amino acids, at the fourth and eighth positions. Frogs differ from bony fish in the fourth and fifth positions. Coelacanths, lungfish, birds, reptiles, and many marsupials differ from fish in one; the fifth amino acid has changed to the same amino acid that mammals have in that position. The transformation to the mammalian form is completed by changing just one amino acid in the eighth position.[3] It can hardly escape notice that progression in the short amino acid sequence is remarkably similar to the relatedness of the species.

---

[1] Movasaghi, Mohammad, and Eric N. Jacobsen. "Chemistry: The Simplest 'Enzyme.'" *Science*, vol 298, no 5600 (6 Dec 2002). Pg 1904-1905.

[2] DeVane, C. Lindsay. "Substance P: A New Era, A New Role." *Pharmacotherapy*, vol 21, no 9 (2001). Pg 1061-1069.

[3] Archer, R., and J. Chauvet. "The neurohypophysial endocrine regulatory cascade: precursors, mediators, receptors, and effectors." *Frontiers in Neuroendocrinology*, vol 16, no 3 (July 1995), pg 237-289.

A related hormone has vastly different effects. Antidiuretic hormone (ADH, or vasopressin) differs from oxytocin by only two amino acids, in the third and eighth positions.[1] It functions in the maintenance of body water content by stimulating the kidneys to make the urine more concentrated and conserve fluids, hence the name antidiuretic hormone. At higher doses it causes enough constriction of arterioles to raise the overall blood pressure, accounting for its synonym, vasopressin.

It will come as no surprise to a vigilant reader that each of the amino acid substitutions by which the various versions of oxytocin and vasopressin differ from each other can be accomplished by the change of a single base pair in the DNA code, save one: frog oxytocin differs from fish oxytocin by two base pairs. The oxytocin/vasopressin family of peptide hormones provide graphic evidence that the simplest possible mutation, the substitution of a single base pair, can produce proteins with enhanced function (in the case of oxytocin) and widely varying activity (in the comparison between oxytocin and ADH).

Insulin is fifty-one peptides in length, still relatively small by the standards of proteins, but large enough to make its spontaneous appearance from random sequences unlikely, and it exhibits obvious homology between species. Strikingly similar hormones are produced by animals ranging from nematodes to domestic animals and man. Bovine insulin differs from human in only three amino acids, porcine in only one; both are functional, but to differing degrees, when administered to diabetic humans, dogs, and cats. Functionality, in the form of conformance between the shape of the protein hormone and its receptors in various species, is consistent across much of the animal kingdom, with minor species-specific variations, in a protein of significant size.

Somatostatin provides a clear example of how functional proteins can increase in size. It is a regulatory hormone that inhibits excessive secretion of growth hormone and thyroid stimulating hormone from the pituitary, both insulin and its opposing glucagon from the pancreas, and several hormones of the gastrointestinal tract. Somatostatin has been identified in two forms, one just fourteen amino acids in length, and the other twenty-eight; the latter is simply composed of two units of the former linked together.

A variation of the argument of irreducible complexity is applied to living cells, in that opponents of evolution sometimes argue that living cells are too complex to have originated by chance. Mammalian cells in all their complexity are not likely to have spontaneously originated from random combination of molecules, but the evolution of increasingly complex cells, like increasingly complex organisms, from more primitive examples, is not only much easier to conceive, but well supported by observations.

---

[1] Archer, R., and J. Chauvet. "The neurohypophysial endocrine regulatory cascade: precursors, mediators, receptors, and effectors." *Frontiers in Neuroendocrinology*, vol 16, no 3 (July 1995), pg 237-289.

Self-replicating proteins have been recently identified which may have provided the earliest cells with the means of accurate reproduction without incorporating DNA and RNA. The development of more complex genetic material may have been a later development, supported by natural selection. Once even the most rudimentary cells had formed, selection of cells more survivable could frequently and easily equate to selection of cells more complex and therefore more versatile.

The human hand was discussed as an example of homology, but it works equally well as an anatomic example of irreducible complexity. Its multitude of bones, ligaments, and tendons, all supplied by an intricate network of blood vessels and sensory and motor nerves, combine to produce a delicacy and precision of both movement and sense that would, if observed in isolation, lead to incredulity that an evolutionary process could lead to its creation, and should therefore qualify as a design of irreducible complexity. Intelligent design advocates have never (to this author's knowledge) presented it as such, of course, because its evolutionary roots are well known and fully understood. It is only in areas that remain unexplored that the argument of irreducible complexity can be maintained; examination has repeatedly falsified claims of irreducible complexity.

Microbiologists, because of the short generation times of their subjects, have observed numerous instances of new biological systems emerging by natural selection. Among the most dramatic is an example that would, if its development had not been directly observed, provoke the argument of irreducible complexity. A microbiologist, in the course of studying the evolution of antibiotic resistance, deleted the gene for galactosidase, an enzyme that splits the disaccharide lactose into the simple sugars glucose and galactose which can be used by the bacteria. He then grew the altered bacteria on a medium that contained only lactose as an available energy source. Under observation, the bacteria evolved not just a new galactosidase (which arose by selection for a mutation in another enzyme), but an adjacent regulatory segment that switched the new gene on and off when stimulated by the presence or absence of lactose, and a cell membrane component to enhance lactose absorption with its own regulatory segment that activated its expression in the presence of lactose.[1] The entire system would almost certainly be considered by intelligent design advocates to be irreducibly complex had its evolution not been directly stimulated and observed under laboratory conditions.

---

[1] Hall, Barry G. "Evolution on a Petri Dish. The Evolved β-Galactosidase System as a Model for Studying Acquisitive Evolution in the Laboratory." *Evolutionary Biology,* vol 15 (1982). Pg 85-150. And Barry G. Hall. "Evolution of New Metabolic Functions in Laboratory Organisms." *Evolution of Genes and Proteins,* edited by M. Nei and R. K. Koehn. Sunderland, MA: Sinauer Associates, 1986. In Miller, Kenneth R. *Finding Darwin's God: A Scientist's Search for Common Ground Between God and Evolution.* New York: HarperCollins, 1999. Pg 145-147.

Irreducible complexity is, as of this writing, the central argument of the intelligent design movement. The doctrine is, at its heart, an argument of incredulity: "Because I cannot conceive of it, it cannot be so." The argument of incredulity is not a valid logical argument, however, for it is merely a rejection without consideration of anything one does not understand. If the argument of incredulity was to stand valid, one would refuse to avail themselves of modern medicine without the years of study required to fully understand the anatomy, physiology, and biochemistry of the human body (and even then, there are some aspects of medical care that are successful without being fully understood). If everyone who does not fully understand how a sewing machine works to produce, with one needle moving up and down, the same kind of stitches produced by a tailor moving a needle back and forth through the fabric, refused to wear the produce of such marvelous machines, the results would be ugly and embarrassing (not to mention entailing some very uncomfortable sunburns). Few who operate a computer or any of the myriad of everyday devices that contain a processing chip undertake to understand silicon-based microcircuitry. The list of everyday experiences that do not survive the argument of incredulity can go on and on.

A logical reply to an argument of incredulity from a professing theist is to ask, "If I find the existence of a god to be incredible, does that prove that your God does not exist?" Are those who hold scriptures to be true and sacred willing to abandon them because someone finds it difficult to conceive of their antiquity? Such questions are not sacrilegious – they merely apply the same standards of proof and logic to the arguments against evolution and those against the existence of God. It is simply not true that everything that one does not understand requires direct divine intervention to operate; nor is it theologically sound to proclaim so, for in that case the power of God varies inversely with the knowledge and inquisitiveness of each human, and few Christian theologians would brook such a consideration of their deity. The argument of incredulity inherently professes satisfaction with ignorance, thereby stifling investigation, learning, and progress.

As a direct result of the argument of incredulity that is at the heart of the doctrine of irreducible complexity, the theory of intelligent design inherently stifles research, and is thereby self-fulfilling. We will soon see that the expressed purpose of the primary organization supporting intelligent design theory is to identify systems to which the argument of incredulity may be convincingly applied. The individuals and foundations associated with intelligent design theory are then in a position to argue that the identified natural phenomenon is explained by the supernatural, and therefore needs no further investigation, and since no further investigation is needed or performed, the supernatural explanation can never be challenged.

Alternative theories

The only alternatives to the evolutionary development of living things are creationism and its offshoot, intelligent design. Treating creationism and intelligent design as scientific theories, by testing their predictive ability, leaves them wanting.

Theorizing that each species was an independent creation of an intelligent designer would appear to predict a randomness of complexity and relatedness relative to time. There is no need for an intelligent designer of infinite knowledge to gradually increase the complexity of design over millions of years, or to develop anatomic characteristics by minute gradations, or to progress by small degrees from one related species to another; such a designer should be fully capable of designing a fully functional mammal, for example, contemporaneously with the first prokaryote, or a terrestrial weight-bearing limb without it being modified from a fin. Neither the fossil record nor methods of genetic and biochemical analysis demonstrate random patterns or spontaneous appearance of unrelated species or characteristics, however. The argument that a sovereign God could choose to create living organisms and anatomic characteristics in any order that He chooses, in this instance in a progressive manner that mimics evolution, while theologically valid, renders the theories without testable predictions in this regard and therefore outside of the realm of science. (As we shall see in a later chapter, it also begs some difficult questions about the nature of God.)

Proponents of intelligent design state that their theory "begins with the observation that intelligent agents produce complex and specified information (CSI)"[1] and propose that "One easily testable form of CSI is irreducible complexity . . .When ID researchers find irreducible complexity in biology, they conclude that such structures were designed."[2] Such testing has several problems. First, CSI is ill defined. Attempts to define CSI rely on complexity and specificity giving the appearance of design, rendering the definition both circular and dependent on the opinion of an observer. Spider webs and bee hives might appear to be designed by a higher intelligence if one does not consider the source. Secondly, there is a logical flaw in reasoning that because intelligence produces complexity and information content, intelligence is the only source of complexity and information. The observation that humans produce hair does not lead to the valid conclusion that a bearer of hair is necessarily human. Bees and ants convey complex and specific information about the location of food sources

---

[1] "The Theory of Intelligent Design: A Briefing Packet for Educators." Undated. The Discovery Institute. 29 May 2013. Pg 6. <http://www.discovery.org/scripts/viewDB/filesDB-download.php?command=download&id=1454>.

[2] "The Theory of Intelligent Design: A Briefing Packet for Educators." Undated. The Discovery Institute. 29 May 2013. Pg 6. <http://www.discovery.org/scripts/viewDB/filesDB-download.php?command=download&id=1454>.

through elaborate sequences of movements in the former case and through chemical markers in the latter case, but lack the intelligence of higher animals, let alone that ascribed to a creator. Thirdly, since intelligent design theorists have to date not produced an example of irreducible complexity that survived scrutiny, one should be led to the conclusion that a theory so tested was falsified rather than confirmed.

The Discovery Institute, one of the leading organizations promoting intelligent design, describes the scientific method quite reasonably as "a four step process involving observations, hypothesis, experiments, and conclusion,"[1] but states that its purpose is to "seek evidence of design in nature."[2] It is notable that in the methodology of intelligent design, a conclusion is reached first, and then evidence to support the conclusion is sought, in an absolute reversal of what the Institute itself defines as scientific method. The disregard of evidence contradicting the pre-ordained conclusion is implied and practiced.

One example of that approach is displayed in the published views of the Institute and its fellows regarding the Cambrian period, which seek to portray the Cambrian as an instantaneous appearance of essentially modern animal forms. Less biased accounts show the Cambrian to be 54 million years in length, preceded by an important extinction event, accompanied by a rapidly increasing atmospheric oxygen content, and encompassing the development of the Hox gene sequence which enabled and regulated the development of the segmental body plans that characterize higher animals. A wealth of ecological niches were open to exploitation at the same time that the animal life of the planet had the tools of enlarged and increasingly complex body features and improved respiratory resources to support them. The resultant burst of diversity is neither inexplicable nor without equal, being one of several increases in speciation that occurred after extinction events.

As the diversification of the Cambrian is not without identifiable cause, neither can evolution since the Cambrian be dismissed as inconsequential. While it is true that almost all surviving animal phyla made their first appearance in the Cambrian, it is a gross misrepresentation to imply that the fauna of the earth was essentially modern at the end of the period. Cambrian arthropods were dominated by trilobites, which although highly successful were only distant precursors of modern insects, arachnids,

---

[1] "The Theory of Intelligent Design: A Briefing Packet for Educators." Undated. The Discovery Institute. 29 May 2013. Pg 6. <http://www.discovery.org/scripts/viewDB/filesDB-download.php?command=download&id=1454>.

[2] "The Theory of Intelligent Design: A Briefing Packet for Educators." Undated. The Discovery Institute. 29 May 2013. Pg 6. <http://www.discovery.org/scripts/viewDB/filesDB-download.php?command=download&id=1454>.

and crustaceans. The graptolites and acorn worms of the early Cambrian are only remote ancestors of modern fish, amphibians, reptiles, and mammals.

Discussions of the Cambrian "explosion" by intelligent design proponents sometimes lead one to believe that they theorize that their designer acted in the early Cambrian at the levels of phyla, but at other times their rejection of later phases of the evolutionary process seem to belie that opinion. The theorists of intelligent design have, unlike publishing scientists of other disciplines and opinions, not proposed a way to test their predictions other than the continuing search for irreducible complexity. That is, of course, understandable, since it is difficult to imagine what other predictions are possible from a premise that an unidentified deity acts at its whim, in deliberate violations of natural law, in designing new aspects of life ranging from biochemical systems to entire phyla.

In their more candid moments, intelligent design proponents acknowledge difficulties in supporting their theory, and even admit that they do not, in fact, have a viable theory. A 2004 issue of *Touchstone* magazine that was largely sympathetic to intelligent design, containing articles by such ID leaders as William A. Dembski and Phillip E. Johnson, quoted Discovery Institute fellow Paul A Nelson: "Easily the biggest challenge facing the ID community is to develop a full-fledged theory of biological design. We don't have such a theory right now, and that's a real problem. Without a theory, it's very hard to know where to direct your research focus."[1] Phillip E. Johnson is a retired Berkeley law professor who is widely acknowledged as the father of the intelligent design movement, wrote or co-wrote at least seven books critical of evolution and modern science, and was a principal author of the Wedge Document (and, incidentally, authored at least five articles arguing that the Human Immunodeficiency Virus, or HIV, is not the cause of Acquired Immune Deficiency Syndrome, or AIDS[2]). In an interview published by the *Berkeley Science Review* in 2006, he said, "I also don't think that there is really a theory of intelligent design at the present time to propose as a comparable alternative to the Darwinian theory, which is, whatever errors it might contain, a fully worked out scheme. There is no intelligent design theory that's comparable."[3]

Intelligent Design on trial

As we have seen, the Christian fundamentalist movement was a reaction to the

[1] "The Measure of Design." *Touchstone*, vol 17 issue 6 (July/August 2004). Accessed 31 Aug 2008 at <http://touchstonemag.com/archives/article.php?id=17-06-060-i>.

[2] "Phillip Johnson." Undated. *Virusmyth: a rethinking AID$ website.* 31 Aug 2008. <http://www.virusmyth.com/aids/index/pjohnson.htm>.

[3] D'Agostino, Michelangelo. "In the matter of Berkeley v Berkeley." *Berkeley Science Review*, vol 10 (Spring 2006), pg 31. Accessed 31 Aug 2008 at <http://sciencereview.berkeley.edu/articles.php?issue=10&article=evolution>.

perceived twin threats to Christian faith from higher criticism of scripture and the theory of biological evolution most famously stated by Charles Darwin. School science curricula quickly became the most contested territory in a war for the mind of America, and the first attempt by fundamentalists at defense of their interpretation of Christian scripture involved the criminalization of the teaching of evolutionary theory; the most famous result was the Scopes trial of 1925, in which high school teacher John Scopes was convicted of violating the Tennessee statute prohibiting the teaching of evolution. Similar statutes survived in various states until 1968, when in the case of *Epperson v Arkansas* the United States Supreme Court overturned the Arkansas statute on the grounds that it was an improper result of government promoting religious views. Fundamentalists continued to espouse a conservative Biblical interpretation as an alternative to evolution, however, and changed tactics to demand balanced treatment; the result was that a Tennessee statute requiring that equal amounts of classroom time be devoted to the scientific theory of evolution and the religion-based model of creation were overturned by a United States Court of Appeals in 1975. Undaunted creationists then turned to a tactic of using scientific language to describe their religion-based views, which resulted in a series of trials of scientific creationism that culminated in *Edwards v Aguillard*, a 1987 Supreme Court ruling again finding it improper for public schools to interfere in religious issues, even though they be disguised by scientific terminology.

Opponents of evolution, weary of so many court defeats, again changed tactics. Philip Johnson, a retired University of California, Berkeley law professor, led the Discovery Institute in identifying several weaknesses in the presentation of Genesis-based creation doctrine and the writing, in 1998, of a strategic paper referred to as the "Wedge Document" or the "Wedge Strategy." Although its existence was denied for some time, the Wedge Document was eventually acknowledged and published by the Discovery Institute. The Wedge Document is so named for its declared intention of being "a 'wedge' that, while relatively small, can split the trunk"[1] of a materialist or empirical approach to science. It equates Charles Darwin to Karl Marx and Sigmund Freud in "portray[ing] humans not as moral and spiritual beings, but as animals or machines"[2] and bemoans the social and political results of that view. The document portrays intelligent design proponents less as scientists in the traditional sense of persons who examine and explain the working of nature, than as social reformers who seek to overthrow scientific methods because of their perceived political, economic, and moral consequences. Since its aims are political and social rather than scientific, the Discovery Institute has made a practice of filling its top leadership positions with

---

[1] "The Wedge Strategy." *Center for Renewal of Science and Culture, Discovery Institute.* Pg 2. Accessed 3 Oct 2008 at <http://www.antievolution.org/features/wedge.html>.

[2] "The Wedge Strategy." *Center for Renewal of Science and Culture, Discovery Institute.* Pg 1. Accessed 3 Oct 2008 at <http://www.antievolution.org/features/wedge.html>.

people whose training and career experience are in politics, government, and policy rather than science, and has adopted strategies of appealing to the popular press as opposed to scientific journals and downplaying any comparison of intelligent design to creationism.

Although it has since attempted to disavow significant involvement in the case, the Discovery Institute filed a brief of *amici curiae*, a so-called "friend of the court" brief by which those in sympathy with a litigant weigh in with their opinions, evidence, and legal arguments, in the 2005 case of *Kitzmiller v Dover.* In that case a group of parents in Pennsylvania (two of which were also teachers) sought to reverse an order by the board of the Dover Area School District instructing ninth-grade biology teachers to read to their classes a statement critical of the theory of evolution and endorsing intelligent design. Two of those offering testimony in support of the board and intelligent design were senior fellows of the Discovery Institute: Dr. Michael Behe is a professor of biology at Lehigh University with a Ph. D. in biochemistry, is recognized as the originator of the term "irreducible complexity," and has authored *Darwin's Black Box* and a number of articles in the popular press in support of intelligent design; Dr. Scott Minnich is an associate professor of microbiology at the University of Idaho. The presiding judge was John E. Jones, a 2002 appointee of President George W. Bush, who publicly supports the teaching of intelligent design in schools.

Dr. Behe and Dr. Minnich had difficulty supporting their positions with sworn testimony. Judge Jones wrote in his opinion:

> Professor Behe conceded that there are no peer-reviewed papers supporting his claims that complex molecular systems, like the bacterial flagellum, the blood-clotting cascade, and the immune system, were intelligently designed. In that regard, there are no peer-reviewed articles supporting Professor Behe's argument that certain complex molecular structures are "irreducibly complex."[1]

Judge Jones' opinion quoted Dr. Minnich's testimony regarding his research into the relationship between the bacterial flagellum and secretory system: "Professor Minnich testified about his research as follows: 'we're looking at the function of these systems and how they could have been derived one from the other. And it's a legitimate scientific inquiry.'"[2]

Evidence for the irreducible complexity of the blood clotting cascade was similarly found lacking by Judge Jones, and he seemed to find Dr. Behe's testimony regarding the immune system to be vexing, if not a bit obdurate:

---

[1] *Kitzmiller v Dover.* Case No. 04cv2688. US District Court, Middle District of Pennsylvania. 20 Dec 2005. Pg 87-88. <http://www.pamd.uscourts.gov/kitzmiller/kitzmiller_342.pdf>

[2] *Kitzmiller v Dover.* Case No. 04cv2688. US District Court, Middle District of Pennsylvania. 20 Dec 2005. Pg 77. <http://www.pamd.uscourts.gov/kitzmiller/kitzmiller_342.pdf>

> Professor Behe was questioned concerning his 1996 claim that science would never find an evolutionary explanation for the immune system. He was presented with fifty-eight peer-reviewed publications, nine books, and several immunology textbook chapters about the evolution of the immune system; however, he simply insisted that this was still not sufficient evidence of evolution, and that it was not "good enough."[1]

Jones' conclusion was that "irreducible complexity has been refuted in peer-reviewed research papers and has been rejected by the scientific community at large."[2]

The trial also addressed the legitimacy of intelligent design as a scientific theory. The judge noted that scientific activity is characterized by research and publication. At trial, the only example of a peer reviewed publication supportive of intelligent design that was cited by the experts in the field was a paper authored by Dr. Minnich on bacterial flagella which was presented to an engineering conference, and Minnich described the review as "minimal." Judge Jones then again turned to the testimony of the expert witnesses called to support intelligent design:

> The evidence presented in this case demonstrates that ID is not supported by any peer-reviewed research, data or publications. . . Professor Behe admitted that: "There are no peer-reviewed articles by anyone advocating for intelligent design supported by pertinent experiments or calculations which provide detailed rigorous accounts of how intelligent design of any biological system occurred." . . . In addition to failing to produce papers in peer-reviewed journals, ID also features no scientific research or testing.[3]

In a position that should trouble believers of most religions, intelligent design theorists deny that the designer that they propose is God. Documents published by the Discovery Institute state that, "Unlike creationism, the scientific theory of intelligent design does not claim that modern biology can identify whether the intelligent cause detected through science is supernatural."[4] Similar denials were voiced at trial, but the judge also noted that "Professor Behe remarkably and unmistakably claims that the plausibility of the argument for ID depends upon the extent to which one believes in

---

[1] *Kitzmiller v Dover.* Case No. 04cv2688. US District Court, Middle District of Pennsylvania. 20 Dec 2005. Pg 78. <http://www.pamd.uscourts.gov/kitzmiller/kitzmiller_342.pdf>

[2] *Kitzmiller v Dover.* Case No. 04cv2688. US District Court, Middle District of Pennsylvania. 20 Dec 2005. Pg 79. <http://www.pamd.uscourts.gov/kitzmiller/kitzmiller_342.pdf>

[3] *Kitzmiller v Dover.* Case No. 04cv2688. US District Court, Middle District of Pennsylvania. 20 Dec 2005. Pg 87-88. <http://www.pamd.uscourts.gov/kitzmiller/kitzmiller_342.pdf>

[4] "The Theory of Intelligent Design: A Briefing Packet for Educators." 13 Nov 2008. The Discovery Institute. 18 Aug 2008. Pg 6. <http://www.discovery.org/scripts/viewDB-download.php?command=download&id=1453>.

the existence of God"[1] and that "not one defense expert was able to explain how the supernatural action suggested by ID could be anything other than an inherently religious proposition."[2] Judge Jones was led to conclude that "the writings of leading ID proponents reveal that the designer postulated by their argument is the God of Christianity,"[3] and that "the overwhelming evidence at trial established that ID is a religious view, a mere re-labeling of creationism, and not a scientific theory."[4]

Conclusion

It is sometimes astonishing how many people are eager to debate *The Origin of Species* without reading it or understanding its contents. Its representation by atheists as justification for their belief is untrue to its content, and to Darwin's expressed intent, and is strangely echoed by Christian fundamentalists. Those who use it to rationalize their atheism are often more familiar with its contents than are the conservative Christians who proclaim its atheistic nature, although neither are accurate, and the latter are frequently adamant in proclaiming the false impression that they hear from their leaders. Many of those who read his works are surprised at the humility of Darwin, the thoughtfulness of his presentation, the depth of his supporting evidence, and most especially by the complete absence of atheistic statement or implication in *Origin*.

As a scientific theory, evolution by means of descent with modification has been highly successful. Our understanding of biological systems is yet incomplete, but every finding of the biological sciences, from the wealth of paleontological findings that have been discovered and elucidated since 1859, through the uncovering of the genetic apparatus of inheritance, to the most recent findings of cellular biochemistry and gene sequencing, coincide with the substance and predictions of the theory of evolution. The most serious challenge came from the theory of punctuated equilibrium in the 1970s, but even that was, upon evaluation, found to be nothing more than variability in the rate of evolution caused by alternating periods of environmental stability and stresses, and was absorbed into the theory to the satisfaction of its authors.

Unlike the successful testing of the theory of evolution over a period of a century and half, the opponents of evolution have proposed no theory that can be evaluated. The theories of creationism and intelligent design are identical in their approach to the independent origination of species. Of the two predictions conceivable from those

---

[1] *Kitzmiller v Dover.* Case No. 04cv2688. US District Court, Middle District of Pennsylvania. 20 Dec 2005. Pg 28. <http://www.pamd.uscourts.gov/kitzmiller/kitzmiller_342.pdf>
[2] *Kitzmiller v Dover.* Case No. 04cv2688. US District Court, Middle District of Pennsylvania. 20 Dec 2005. Pg 31. <http://www.pamd.uscourts.gov/kitzmiller/kitzmiller_342.pdf>
[3] *Kitzmiller v Dover.* Case No. 04cv2688. US District Court, Middle District of Pennsylvania. 20 Dec 2005. Pg 26. <http://www.pamd.uscourts.gov/kitzmiller/kitzmiller_342.pdf>
[4] *Kitzmiller v Dover.* Case No. 04cv2688. US District Court, Middle District of Pennsylvania. 20 Dec 2005. Pg 43. <http://www.pamd.uscourts.gov/kitzmiller/kitzmiller_342.pdf>

theories, the random and spontaneous appearance of species throughout geologic history, without relationship to temporally and geographically adjacent species, is consistently and dramatically belied by the fossil record; implacable adherents are forced to assert that such was simply the will of their God, an untestable corollary with uncomfortable theological implications. The second prediction, that of irreducible complexity found in anatomic or biochemical systems, has never been found true, and many proposed instances have been falsified by investigation. Because of the depth of the modern understandings of science, arguments against evolution are in essence arguments that the laws of chemistry and physics do not apply to biological systems, and such an argument is inherently insupportable.

It is surpassingly strange that American Christian fundamentalists so readily agree with atheists that a true theory of evolution implies a universe absent a higher power. Anti-evolution rhetoric is almost entirely an American phenomenon. Many Jewish and Christian believers in the United States and Canada, and virtually all abroad, including some working at the frontiers of the biological sciences, have come to accommodate their faith with the theory of evolution. They do so by simply recognizing that a fair, reasonable, and supportable interpretation of Judeo-Christian scripture does not insist on either a time frame or a mechanism of theistic creation. The truth of scripture is resolved with the truth of the material world, and both can be seen as revelatory of the nature and mind of God.

Of the extent of evolutionary processes, Darwin wrote:

> If man can by patience select variations useful to him, why, under changing and complex conditions of life, should not variations useful to nature's living products often arise, and be preserved or selected? What limit can be put to this power, acting during long ages and rigidly scrutinizing the whole constitution, structure, and habits of each creature, favoring the good and rejecting the bad? I can see no limit to this power, in slowly and beautifully adapting each form to the most complex relations of life.[1]

In the last hundred and fifty years, science has, indeed, found no reasonable limit to the theory of evolution, either in its ability to adapt species to their environment, or in its ability to explain the biosphere. Evolution is, in the strictest sense, not a fact, but it is a theory that has been tested and found both true and powerful. Truth and power, in the belief systems of Judaism and Christianity, belong to God, and the truth and power of evolutionary descent with modification must be ascribed to God for Judeo-Christian thought and faith to remain relevant to modern man.

---

[1] Darwin, Charles. *The Origin of Species.* New York: Gramercy, 1979, Pg 467. (Chapter XIV: Recapitulation and Conclusion.)

Chapter 8

A Modern Interpretation of the Biblical Creation Stories

Truth cannot contradict truth. Does the material truth provided by God in His creation then demand that we abandon the scriptural truth that Judeo-Christian tradition maintains was provided by His inspiration? Or can scriptures be interpreted in such a way that they accommodate the truth of the material world, and so preserve our acceptance of their spiritual and moral truth?

To remain relevant, scripture must be interpreted in light of certain knowledge. Children who are accustomed to playing with puzzles notice that the eastern coast of the Americas appears to fit against the western coast of Africa and Europe, and the theory of plate tectonics explains that observation. The gradual development of life is equally obvious upon rational consideration of the fossil record, and the modern synthesis of evolutionary theory explains that body of facts like no other theory. As Saint Augustine wrote of scriptural interpretation, "[W]e should always observe that restraint that is proper to a devout and serious person and on an obscure question entertain no rash belief. Otherwise, if the evidence later reveals the explanation, we are likely to despise it because of our attachment to our error, even though this explanation may not be in any way opposed to the sacred writings of the Old or New Testament."[1]

One can, with a basic understanding of the primary scientific theories of the origins of

[1] St. Augustine. *The Literal Meaning of Genesis.* Translated and annotated by John Hammond Taylor. New York: Newman, 1982. Vol 1 of 2, pg 73 (2.18.38).

the universe, the earth, and terrestrial life, and availing oneself of the expertise of those scholars of ancient languages who have translated and annotated the scriptures, interpret the creation stories of Genesis and the comments regarding creation in other locations of the Bible in an enlightened way. Such an interpretation is not, as it is cast by some, an assault on the authority of the scriptures; rather, it is a measure of the timelessness of the Bible that it remains validly engaged and interpretable in the light of new knowledge.

To a person of faith, the most significant words concerning the creation are contained in the first verse of the Bible: God was the Creator. Remembering that these words originated with the ancient Hebrews, the importance of these words, and elaborations that follow, is that those things that were deified by other cultures with which the ancient Jews had contact – the sun, the moon, the leviathan of the sea – were created, not the creators as other cultures believed.

The nature of God, matter, and time

The very fact that the Creator God of the Hebrews was invisible put him in the realm of the spiritual, rather than a heavenly body, an animal, or a carved or cast image. The spiritual nature of God is given further emphasis in the first creation story by God's portrayal as one who creates by command, and by the sense of God's transcendence of time and matter itself in the first two verses. God was not a part of creation – He was present and powerful at the beginning of time, the I Am, the Creator observing the initial formlessness.

This portrayal is consistent with the Big Bang hypothesis, in that no material being could have existed within the primordial singularity. Matter was infinitely compressed, so that even space and time were infinitely curved and, therefore, did not exist in a form recognizable outside of the most advanced and difficult theorems of modern physics. The placement of God outside the Big Bang singularity means that He himself is outside of the confines of space and time, a characteristic that may therefore be seen as being consistent with the teaching of Judeo-Christian theologians that God transcends not just matter, but time and space, as well.

Further concurrence with the overall theories of heavenly bodies being formed by cosmic expansion, gravitational attraction, and cooling, can be found in the description of formlessness given to the initial state of creation. This does not support the interpretation that God created the currently observed universe from nothing (referred to by theologians as *creatio ex nihilo*), but that He gave to it a previously absent order. The initial formlessness of creation in the first Genesis account can be convincingly interpreted as a description of the early state of the earth in its molten state; a reference to the chaotic condition of the dispersed matter of nebulae, supernovae, and aboriginal hydrogen as it began to condense into the sun and its planets; or most dramatically as a portrayal of the Big Bang singularity, containing as it did an enormous quantity of matter still in the disorganized form of unrelated quarks, not structured even to the level of protons and neutrons, let alone that of atoms.

The age of creation

The issue of time is of great concern to some readers of Genesis, chiefly those who have been influenced by "Young Earth" theorists. The Young Earth Theory is the most extremely literalist interpretation of Genesis, adherents of which insist that God created the universe in six twenty-four hour periods of intensely miraculous undertaking, that the genealogies of the Pentateuch are complete and inerrant, and that from those premises they can accurately calculate that the universe is around six thousand years old. (Although Youth Earth adherents insist that their calculations are accurate with absolute certainty, various adherents curiously cannot seem to agree precisely on that absolutely certain date.)

The arguments against literalism and inerrancy have been discussed earlier, and the theological implications of the Young Earth Theory will be discussed in a later chapter, but the issue of the time frame of the first creation story, Genesis 1.1 through 2.4a, deserves addressing, because the time frame of creation is not an issue of mere semantics or petulance. The process of natural selection has necessarily taken the billions of years of the earth's existence to produce the current crop of inhabitants. If the earth could be shown to be only a few thousand years old, the process of natural selection would be insufficient to account for the diversity of life on the planet; if the scriptures provide a clear declaration that the earth is only a few thousand years old, they are inconsistent with the physical findings and theories of the scientific process, and one would be forced to choose between the truths made apparent by God in His creation and those provided by Him by His inspiration of scripture.

Most modern-day printings of the Bible with significant annotations acknowledge that the Hebrew word translated as "day" is, in fact, a word of indistinct meaning. *Yôm* can indeed mean a twenty-four hour day, but it can also refer to a period of time bounded by events, and in that meaning can be just as correctly translated to the word "era." It may seem odd that such an indistinct word would be chosen by the original author of this passage, but as Robert Alter noted in his translation of Genesis, a certain degree of ambiguity is inherent in the Hebrew writings, and is so widespread as to appear to be a deliberate device of either literary choice or to reflect the inherent mystery of divinity itself.[1]

---

[1] Alter, Robert. *Genesis: Translation and Commentary.* New York: W. W. Norton, 1996, xii of "To The Reader".

The fact that a word with such an indistinct meaning would exist in Hebrew, then in the ancient Greek of the Septuagint, then in the Latin of Jerome's Vulgate, may also seem peculiar, until one considers the use of the word "day" in English. When a speaker or writer makes a statement like, "In my grandfather's day, horses and mules were used by farmers to work their land," no one interprets the word day as a twenty-four hour period in which the speaker's grandfather was born, reached maturity, fathered children, completed a life's work, and died. The word "day" in that context denotes an era bounded by the working life of the grandfather, just as "the day of the steam engine" or "the days before penicillin" denote indistinct eras bounded not by the time it takes for the earth to rotate on its axis, but by the events and characteristics of an otherwise indistinct period of time. This work referred to a six-week long trial (*Kitzmiller v Dover*, Chapter 7) as a "day in court" without fear of being misunderstood. It is, then, reasonable and appropriate to translate the Hebrew *yôm* to the English word "day," in that both have a second indistinct meaning more closely related to the word "era." Consideration of the possibility that the days of the first creation account in Genesis may represent something other than the period from dawn to dusk is not, as is sometimes claimed by young earth theorists, a distortion of the actual words of the scripture; rather, it is a legitimate and commonplace interpretation of both the Hebrew *yôm* and the English "day."

The word "day" is, in fact, used in numerous other places in scripture without being interpreted literally. First Samuel 8.8 refers to the forty-year exodus from Egypt as a day; verse 18 of the same chapter refers to the day of the reign of the kings of Israel. The twenty-second and twenty-third chapters of Second Samuel and the Eighteenth Psalm quote an essentially identical song, attributed to King David and written in the first person, referring to the time when Saul sought his death as "the day of my calamity." The book of Isaiah refers repeatedly to times of disaster as a day. The "day of the Lord," a concept denoting not only a day of judgment but the initialization of a reign by God in the earthly realm, is referred to in at least nine locations in the prophetic writings of the Old Testament[1] and in at least seven locations in the canon of the New Testament[2] without the phrase being interpreted to mean that the reign of God will last for less than an earthly day.

The phrase "the evening and the morning" linked to the description of each of the six days of the first creation story would seem, at first glance, to argue for interpreting *yôm* as a twenty-four hour day. Similar imagery is used poetically, however, in each of the Thirtieth, Fifty-ninth, and Ninetieth Psalms. The motif of evening and morning as beginning and end of a time period, a day or a longer period, is common in Hebrew

---

[1] Jeremiah 46.10; Joel 1.15, 2.31; Amos 5.18, 20; Obadiah 1.15; Zephaniah 1.14; Zechariah 14.1; Malachi 4.5

[2] 1Corinthians 5.51; 1 Thessalonians 5.2; 2 Thessalonians 2.2; 2 Peter 3.10; Revelation 16.15

writings and in the tradition of beginning the observance of the weekly Sabbath, and of longer festivals spanning several days (Yom Kippur and Hanukkah, to cite widely familiar examples), at sunset and ending them at the sunrise following the last day of observation.

It is, of course, entirely possible that the writer of the first creation story of Genesis recorded an oral tradition that erroneously believed that the world was created in six calendar days. It is equally possible that the original intent of the storytellers, with regards to the time frame of the story, was not clear after centuries of repetition and transmission, and that the writer of the first creation account deliberately used the word *yôm* because of its ambiguity. In either event, it is not reasonable to expect a writer several centuries before the beginning of the Christian era to comprehend and record the vast time scale involved in the evolutional birth of the universe; indeed, such a time scale was not perceived by mankind until the nineteenth century, and is fully comprehended by few even in today's world.

The Ninetieth Psalm is referenced incompletely in the New Testament in Second Peter. Second Peter is the source of the phrase often quoted by apologists seeking to resolve the time issue in Genesis, "with the Lord one day is like a thousand years, and a thousand years are like a day."[1] The Ninetieth Psalm is more poetic:

> Before the mountains were brought forth,
> Or ever you had formed the earth and the world,
> From everlasting to everlasting you are God.
> You turn us back to dust,
> And say, "Turn back, you mortals."
> For a thousand years in your sight
> Are like yesterday when it is past,
> Or like a watch in the night.
> You sweep them away; they are like a dream,
> Like grass that is renewed in the morning;
> In the morning it flourishes and is renewed;
> In the evening it fades and withers.[2]

Taken in the larger context of the Psalm, it is clear that the intention is to portray God, due to His essential nature as a being outside of time and limitless in His lifespan and His vision, as being inconsiderate of human measures of time. A millennium is a period of time outside the experience of a man or woman, over ten times a normal lifespan. Modern men and women speak of thousands of years without personalizing the elapsed time. Americans of the twenty-first century cannot honestly comprehend, in a personal way, the two hundred fifty year history of their nation. A thousand years was

[1] 2nd Peter 3.8. New Revised Standard Version.
[2] Psalm 90.2-6, New Revised Standard Version.

almost certainly intended by the author to represent an incomprehensible length of time, and even an incomprehensible amount of time is to God like a mere day to a human. That a thousand years are to God "like yesterday when it is past" is reminiscent of the observations of parents reflecting on how quickly their children have grown. ("It seems like yesterday that . . .") Night watches were commonly divided into thirds,[1, 2] shorter than daytime watches so that soldiers could stand night watch and still be rested enough to continue other duties; in other words, standing a night watch was intended to be inconsequential to the schedule of a man at arms. A thousand years can be lost to God as quickly as a dream is lost on awakening. Grass, in the hostile environment of Israel, clung tenuously to life, and often could be seen to wither in the heat of the day and to hydrate and freshen in the morning, after a period of cool during the night, as a means of surviving. The overall impression intended by the author's poetic language is to convey that time periods that seem immense to men are inconsequential to God.

Attempts by some to use the words of the Ninetieth Psalm and the Second Epistle of Peter to create a sort of second layer of literalism, by creating mathematical formulas from the obviously poetic language of those passages, are awkward and unproductive to the resolution of science and faith. Whether asserting that each of the Genesis days are exactly one thousand years (leading to a calculation that the age of the earth is six thousand years plus whatever ages are discerned from the various genealogies of the Bible), or inexplicably and randomly deciding that each of the Genesis days represents a year and that each of the days of those years represents a thousand earthly years[3] (leading to a calculation that each Genesis day represents 365,000 years, so that creation was effected 2.2 million years before the genealogies begin), the resulting time line does not correspond to the ages of the earth demonstrated by geological findings and radiologic dating methods. Still others have embarked on calculations based on unfounded premises that the hours, minutes, or seconds of the days of Genesis each represent a thousand years, but such calculations, based as they are on pseudo-literal interpretations of the scriptures as science texts rather than as documents focusing on the spiritual, are inherently clumsy and fruitless.

The division of the time of the formation of the cosmos into days has for centuries been seen as an allegorical device applied to bring order to the events of creation. In *The Literal Interpretation of Genesis* Saint Augustine of Hippo (354-430) wrote extensively of his difficulty in interpreting the creation stories. Convinced as he was that the stories of Genesis should be interpreted literally, he was equally convinced that the six

[1] Alter, Robert. *The Book of Psalms: A Translation with Commentary.* New York: W. W. Norton, 2007. Pg 318.

[2] *New Interpreter's Study Bible.* Nashville: Abingdon Press, 2003. Pg 834.

[3] *New Interpreter's Study Bible.* Nashville: Abingdon Press, 2003. Pg 834.

days of creation were not, in fact, intended to be taken as six calendar days. Augustine's concept of literal interpretation was to conclude that the terms of light, day, evening, and morning bore "spiritual, rather than physical, meaning," and that the six days of creation was an organizational device.[1] He wrote:

> That day in the account of creation, or those days that are numbered according to its recurrence, are beyond the experience and knowledge of us mortal earthbound men. And if we are able to make any effort towards an understanding of the meaning of those days, we ought not to rush forward with an ill-considered opinion, as if no other reasonable and plausible interpretation could be offered. Seven days by our reckoning, after the model of the days of creation, make up a week. By the passage of such weeks time rolls on, and in these weeks one day is constituted by the course of the sun from its rising to its setting; but we must bear in mind that these days indeed recall the days of creation, but without in any way being really similar to them.[2]

Consideration of Saint Augustine's treatise leads to several interesting realizations: First, his and other ancient scholars' idea of a literal interpretation of scripture differs widely from the modern concept of literalism. Second, he was imminently conscious, even in his age, of the continual progress of science, and warned against dogmatic positions by Christian individuals and institutions that could be overturned by developing knowledge, and the inherent threat of such dogmatism to the credibility of the witness of the church, a position that will be discussed further in a later chapter. Third, Augustine was remarkably prescient in recognizing that creation included a potential for the development of new forms. Fourth, unlike many current creationists who proclaim their sure knowledge of the meaning of scripture, the greatest Christian scholar of his time, a time nearly sixteen hundred years closer to the origin of the scriptures than modern man, readily admitted that the interpretation of Genesis is difficult, not at all obvious, and subject to various possibilities at any number of points.[3]

The interpretation of the Hebrew *yôm* as an era rather than as a solar day is referred to as the Day-Age Hypothesis. It recognizes, like Saint Augustine, that the six days of creation can be seen as a logical framework for understanding the stages of creation, similar to the framework provided by the current descriptions of the ages and periods of earth history. Both are somewhat arbitrary - both the Biblical days and the ages and periods of geological history are based on human-selected milestones in the development of the earth and its living inhabitants – but, in the context of their time,

---

[1] Young, Davis A. "The Contemporary Relevance of Augustine's View of Creation". *Perspectives on Science and Christian Faith* 40.1:42-45 (March 1988), American Scientific Affiliation.
[2] St. Augustine, *The Literal Meaning of Genesis*, translated and annotated by John Hammond Taylor, vol 1 of 2. New York: Newman, 1982. Pg 135 (4.27.44).
[3] Young, Davis A. "The Contemporary Relevance of Augustine's View of Creation". *Perspectives on Science and Christian Faith* 40.1:42-45 (March 1988), American Scientific Affiliation.

equally useful as a framework for understanding the events of earth history.

The time frame in which creation occurred has been discounted as unimportant by commentaries by Christian scholars from Augustine until the modern day. The commentary of The New Interpreter's Study Bible is concise: "The miracle of creation consists not in God's speed, but in God's sovereign power and control."[1]

The first Genesis account – Genesis 1.1 to 2.4

With the subject of the time frame of creation being resolved or set aside, the chronology of the first Genesis account is quite strongly concurrent with current scientific knowledge.

The initial state of the cosmos is chaotic and formless, whether the formlessness refers to the initial conditions after the Big Bang, to the disorganized state of matter early in the formation of the solar system, or to an earth still in a molten state and suffering constant bombardment by meteors and comets. God begins his creation by gradually, in a stepwise fashion, bringing order to chaos. Throughout the account, the language of the Hebrew and Greek texts speaks of God organizing and separating rather than creating from nothingness (*creatio ex nihilo*).[2, 3, 4]

On the first day, God separated day from night, corresponding to the establishment of planetary rotation from the first moments of the earth's history, along with an obvious light source, the sun.

The second day saw the separation of the waters above the earth from the waters below by a dome called the sky. While this can be seen by moderns as corresponding to the formation of an atmosphere, it also betrays an erroneous cosmology present in Jewish thought. The Jews of the era saw the earth as a bubble in the waters of the universe, with the waters of earth, the subterranean, the sea, and the above-sky cosmos being seen as threatening, chaotic, and malevolent. Both the description of the waters being loosed from windows of the sky in the flood of Noah's time,[5] and the reference in Job to the waterskins of the sky from which rain comes,[6] refer to this mistaken concept of the earth's place in the universe. It would seem unnecessary to adopt this obviously erroneous and outdated cosmology in order to accept the spiritual truths of the Bible.

---

[1] *New Interpreter's Study Bible.* Nashville: Abingdon Press, 2003. Pg 834.

[2] Coogan, Michael D., editor. *New Oxford Annotated Bible.* 3rd ed. Oxford: Oxford University Press, 2001. Hebrew Bible Pg 11.

[3] Whybray, R. N. "Genesis". *Oxford Bible Commentary.* Oxford: Oxford University Press, 2001. Pg 42-43.

[4] *New Interpreter's Study Bible.* "Excursus: Creation: Ordering Chaos." Nashville: Abingdon Press, 2003. Pg 5.

[5] Genesis 7.11. New Revised Standard Version.

[6] Job 38.27. New Revised Standard Version.

On the third day, the separation of waters continued with the separation of land from sea, corresponding roughly to the formation of a crust on earth's surface and the accumulation of bodies of water necessary to the ecology that could support life. Also on the third day, God commanded the earth to bring forth plant life of various sorts, corresponding to the beginnings of life in photosynthetic organisms of the Archean Eon, colonies of which grew to considerable size. The only specific plants mentioned – seed-bearing plants and fruit-bearing trees – are both among the flowering plants, the most evolutionarily advanced and diverse family of the plant kingdom, which date to the middle of the Cretaceous Period. Anthropocentrism is evident in the fact that the only plants deemed worthy of specific mention are those with food value; grains and fruits were important to hunter-gatherer societies and were the first crops cultivated by early agrarian societies. The seed-bearing plants are referred to as grasses in some translations, which is appropriate since cereal grains, including wheat, rice, maize, barley, oats, and rye, are all grasses.

On the fourth day of Genesis, God made the sun and moon. This would seem problematic when considering that the first day of creation saw the separation of light from darkness, but can be resolved (with just a bit of a stretch) by equating this step of creation with the clearing of the earth's atmosphere, which would have made the spheres of sun and moon visible from the earth's surface, and could also have coincided with an increasing atmospheric oxygen level that made animal life possible. The literal interpretation that the sun and the moon did not exist until the fourth day, as is often pointed out, makes the measurement and definition of the first three days impossible, and begs the question of the source of the daylight clearly identified on the first day and presumed to continue on the second and third days. Strict literalism, as defined by modern-day evangelicals, is again difficult to sustain. Although the description of the sun and the moon seem clear, the absence of their specific names in the text is seen by commentators as a snub to other cultures known by the Jews to worship the sun and the moon as deities.[1, 2]

The fifth day, after the presumed clearing and increased oxygen content of the atmosphere, saw the first animal life develop in the seas and in the air. The obvious correlation with evolutionary theory is that the first animal life is known to have developed in the rich environment of the sea. The reference to birds, apparently preceding terrestrial life, has two possible resolutions: Since birds themselves are direct descendants of dinosaurs, the placement of birds early in the creation chronology may reflect suspicion (or revelation, if the reader prefers) of the relationship of birds to earlier more primitive life forms. There is also a notion, one that finds but little

---

[1] Coogan, Michael D., editor. *New Oxford Annotated Bible.* 3rd ed. Oxford: Oxford University Press, 2001. Hebrew Bible page 12.

[2] *New Interpreter's Study Bible.* Nashville: Abingdon Press, 2003. Page 6.

support among Hebrew scholars and translators, that the passage refers to flying animals in general rather that to birds in particular, and acknowledges insects as being among the earliest animal life to colonize dry land. Most plausible, probably, is that this detail of the first Genesis chronology defies resolution, and that the passage reflects a mistaken notion by the early Jews of the order of the appearance of living things.

The sixth day of creation was devoted to terrestrial animals. Animals wild and domestic, creeping and grazing, are declared by God to be good, in the same language that has ended other creative acts, before mankind is created. The creation of mankind is specifically noted to include male and female created concurrently, and man is granted dominion over all other animals, as the apparent pinnacle of God's creative effort, and a worthy regent for God in ruling the earth.

Genesis 1.27 states, in the paired verse structure common to the Psalms, that God created mankind in His own image. Only a small minority of interpreters have taken this to mean that God has a corporeal existence in a human-like body. It is a more orthodox interpretation to regard this as a statement of mankind's spiritual nature. The phrase "in his image" is reminiscent of the Platonic Theory of Forms, by which all material things are a form, or imperfect replica, of a perfect form in the realm of the ideal. Thus, each horse, for example, is an attempt by the material world to reproduce the perfect horse, and each flower is a flawed replica of a perfect flower. Alexander the Great was a student of Aristotle, who was in turn a student of Plato, so knowledge of the great philosopher spread with Helenism. It is easily conceivable that Jewish writers after the fourth century BCE, including a possible editor or redactor of the Genesis accounts, could have had knowledge of Plato's writings. That man is made in the image of God would mean, in the Platonic sense, that man is an imperfect replica of a perfect God, as expressed in his spiritual awareness, his intellect, and his delegated dominion over the earth and its life. (Later but similarly pervasive Helenistic influence can be supposed in the striking similarity to Stoic philosophy of the many New Testament admonitions to be content in one's circumstances and to trust that all earthly political, economic, and social developments are in accord with God's will and plan.)

Overall, then, the reader of the first Genesis account sees increasing order in the universe and the earth, as the earth and sun are formed from existing matter. Life arises, then progresses from simple to complex, and from sea to land. Dry land is first colonized by plant life, then by an increasingly diverse variety of animals. Mankind is a special creation, the last, and recognized by God as being advanced in intellect, in its ability to control and modify the environment, and in its awareness of self, others, and the spiritual realm. Each of these major assertions of the first creation account of Genesis is in accord with modern scientific theories.

A striking feature of this account that escapes most readers is the fact that plants, sea animals, and terrestrial fauna are all created by means of a command from God that the land or the sea, as appropriate, bring them forth, as opposed to God either creating them from nothing or crafting them from pre-existing matter. Thus, the first Genesis story itself appears to provide for the properties of matter and earth to play their role in the process of creating life. God, conspicuously and consistently, does not work to create life independent of the earth itself; rather, He provides for the earth to become the source of life in all of its varieties.

Yet another notable feature of the first Genesis account is that the creative process of God was limited to an initial foundational period and did not resume. The seventh day of creation, the day of God's rest, is a particularly thorny problem for creationists, one that is seldom addressed. If, as creationists hold, each entity and each characteristic is a separate miraculous creation of God, rather than the result of the continued action of natural laws, a period of God's rest should coincide with a period of stasis of the biosphere, weather, the geological features of the earth, and the heavens. If the six days of the first Genesis account were earthly days, followed by the command to follow God's example of resting and hallowing one day of each seven, then unless God uncharacteristically violates His own precepts, a day of stasis should be observable once a week, in which no births or deaths occur and bacteria stop dividing, wind and weather are calm, heavenly bodies stop moving and changing, and the geological forces of earth are frozen. If each of the six days is interpreted as an age of creation, and an eighth day of creative activity by God has not ensued undeclared by scripture, we are living in God's day of rest and such stasis should be the order of our age.

As fruitless as it is to argue that such stasis is observed, it is equally fruitless to hold that the instruments of change in the world around us, the laws of physics and chemistry, do not affect living things: the law of gravity equally affects living and inanimate matter, laws of heat transfer make us cold and hot and even burn us when we are not careful, and the motion of the wind musses our hair, all under the auspices of physics; every reaction and system of living things among the myriad examined, however simple or complex, obeys the rules of chemistry. Changes in the biosphere are documented in extinctions, in the development of new characteristics like antibiotic resistance in bacteria, and in new species like the canine parvovirus; wind and waves, volcanoes and glaciations, earthquakes and storms, reshape the earth; comets and asteroid impacts and star formation and supernovae are observed by astronomers. The only reasonable conclusion that maintains theism is that the universe was created with an inherent capacity for change and is unfolding according to the ordination of God.

This first creation account has a certain symmetry that has been noted by many commentators. The first and fourth days mark the separation of light from darkness and the creation of the sun and moon, respectively. The second and fifth days are distinguished by the separation of the waters and the creation of the sky on the second day, and the population of these domains by creatures of the sea and the air on the fifth day. The third and sixth days are similarly parallel, with the creation of dry land on the third day, and the population of the land on the sixth. The third and sixth days also contain two distinctive creative acts each; the text separates the creation of dry land from the creation of plants on the third day, and the creation of terrestrial animals from that of mankind on the sixth day, each with the benedictory observation that "It is good." The symmetry of these passages has been compared to the rhythmic repetition that is typical of Hebrew poetry,[1] lending credence to a literary interpretation of the entire account, and making further argument against a strict literal interpretation, especially as regards the time frame of creation.

Although some recent translations (including most notably the New Revised Standard Version) translate verses 11, 12, 21, 24, and 25 of Genesis 1 without making the distinction that each plant and animal reproduces "according to its own kind", as do most older versions (including the venerable King James Version), commentators note that the language of these verses in Hebrew does, indeed, support an awareness on the part of the writer that each kind of plant and animal only produced offspring of its own species.[2, 3] While this observation may seem readily apparent to modern readers, it should be remembered that cultures later than that of the Hebrew authors, including the Greeks and Romans, did not understand this principle and as a result populated their mythology with animals such as centaurs, resulting from bestiality between humans and horses, and fauns from humans and goats; gryphons resulted from breeding between eagles and lions, and hippogryphs arose from breeding between gryphons and horses. The recognition that animals and plants reproduced only their own species was a fairly advanced observation for the time.

The second Genesis account – Genesis 2.4 through 4.26

Consideration of the second creation account must begin with the acknowledgement that it is, indeed, a separate, independent, and fundamentally different account than the first. The first account is attributed to the Priestly source under the classic version of the Documentary Hypothesis, while the second account is considered to have originated in the Jawhist source. The first creation account contains a notable amount of material consistent with modern scientific knowledge and theories. The second creation account includes intriguing details that cause a careful reader to wonder at the understanding of the writer, but the chronology is markedly different than the first

---

[1] Alter, Robert. Introduction: III. The Poetry of Psalms. *The Book of Psalms: A Translation with Commentary.* New York: W. W. Norton, 2007. Pgs xx-xxviii.

[2] Whybray, R. N. "Genesis". *Oxford Bible Commentary.* Oxford: Oxford University Press, 2001. Pg 41.

[3] *New Interpreter's Study Bible.* Nashville: Abingdom Press, 2003. Pg 6.

account and cannot be rationally resolved with modern scientific findings.

Robert Alter, one of the most respected modern authorities on Hebrew scripture and literature, writes in the notes of his original translation of Genesis: "In this more vividly anthropomorphic account, God, now called *YHWH 'Elohim* instead of *'Elohim* as in the first version, does not summon things into being from a lofty distance through the mere agency of divine speech, but works as a craftsman, fashioning (*yatsar* instead of *bar'a*, "create"), blowing life breath into nostrils, building a woman from a rib."[1] Other commentators and translators join Alter in noting distinct differences in style, rhythm, vocabulary, and syntax, comparing the first account to a formal liturgy and the second to a casually told folk tale. The scope of the story narrows just as abruptly from consideration of an entire cosmos to a tale of two people.

Commentators who strive to maintain inerrancy of scripture have attempted to resolve the two creation accounts by asserting that the second is an elaboration of the details of the first, but such attempts fail with an objective reading. The first half of Genesis 2.4 is a benedictory statement closing the first narrative. In the middle of the verse, the book of Genesis abruptly starts over with a new sentence (one that wanders through the seventh verse) as it begins a new account with an arid and desert land. Both literalism and unification are dealt a serious blow with the observation that any land from the first account would have emerged from the sea on day three, less than seventy-two hours before the creation of man, and would have been muddy rather than arid on the sixth day, when humans were created. In the first account, God orders the earth to produce plant life immediately after separating sea and land on day three and man is created last, on day six, but in the second an already arid land has yet to produce any vegetation when man is created as the first living thing.

The second account clearly places mankind second in creation, after only the earth itself. God fashions a man, *'adam*, from the soil, *'adamah*. The word *'adam* is a Hebrew word meaning simply "human;" it is neither a proper noun, nor even necessarily male. Early translators mistakenly interpreted it as a given name, and the error has been perpetuated for centuries; modern translators render *'adam* as "a man" or "a human," since neither the male *ish* nor the female *ishshah* appears at this point in the text. Thus a nonspecific human being, or *'adam* is formed by God from *'adamah*, a soil suitable for cultivation, in a pun-like play on words. (Alter cleverly imitates the word play by pairing "human" with "humus" in his translation.)[2]

To provide for His new creation, God plants a garden (note that He planted it rather than created it), and installs the human as both gardener and consumer. The location

---

[1] Alter, Robert. *Genesis: Translation and Commentary.* New York: W. W. Norton, 1996, Pg 8.
[2] Alter, Robert. *Genesis: Translation and Commentary.* New York: W. W. Norton, 1996, Pg 8.

of this garden is unclear. The text describes the garden as including four major water courses. The Tigris and the Euphrates rivers are in Mesopotamia, modern-day Iraq, and in fact reach their point of closest proximity in the area of Baghdad. The Gihon, however, is a spring in Jerusalem; moreover, the land of Cush with which the Gihon is associated in this passage is most commonly associated with Ethiopia or the Arabian peninsula. Neither the Pishon nor its land of Havilah are known.[1, 2]

After installing his *'adam* as the caretaker and beneficiary of His garden in the second creation account, God recognizes that His human is in need of companionship in a world with no other animal life. He begins to fashion animals from *'adamah*, presenting each to the *'adam* human to be named and evaluated. Man and every animal are thus said by the writer of this second account to be composed of the same fine particulate matter that makes up the earth itself.

This material unification of earth, animals, and man, each composed of the same minute particles, has been interpreted as a primitive statement of atomic theory. In the New Testament book of Hebrews we find a statement that can be similarly interpreted: "the worlds were prepared by the word of God, so that what is seen was made from things that are not visible;"[3] the worlds (intriguing plurality) were made from invisibly small atoms, according to this interpretation. While few would assert that either writer understood atomic structure in the same sense that it is taught to modern chemistry students, the realization that elements were common to earth, animals, and humans is a precursor to the more exacting modern theory. Although Greek philosophers of the fifth through third century BCE are commonly credited with the earliest atomic theories (mostly encompassing as elements earth, water, fire, and air), the second Genesis account may reflect similar thoughts pursued by its author, indicating either a high level of thought and perception equal to his more famous Greek contemporaries, or very early knowledge of the developing Greek theory.

Although the first account, as previously noted, clearly asserts that the male and the female of the human species were created concurrently, the creation of the animal kingdom in the second account is for the express purpose of finding a companion for the created human. It seems rather bizarre for a wise and understanding God to create creatures ranging from snails and lizards to cattle, deer, and the predator big cats, all in a misguided attempt to create a companion for the lonely human. Nonetheless, the animals of the earth and air and sea are created in a process that must have been as frustrating as it was fruitless.

---

[1] Coogan, Michael D., editor. *New Oxford Annotated Bible.* 3rd ed. Oxford: Oxford University Press, 2001. Hebrew Bible pg 13.

[2] *New Interpreter's Study Bible.* Nashville: Abingdon Press, 2003. Pg 9-10

[3] Hebrews 11.3. New Revised Standard Version.

The ultimate resolution for the dilemma of human companionship is one of the most bizarre episodes in scripture. God causes the *'adam* to fall into a deep sleep, with obvious parallels to general anesthesia. (General anesthesia is deeper than ordinary sleep – if someone cut you with a scalpel while you were napping on the couch, you would not be unresponsive.) A rib is removed and the incision closed in what passes for a terse description of a surgical procedure, and the removed rib is fashioned into a woman. It has been correctly noted that in removing a rib, the surgeon chose to harvest one of the few bones that can be spared without producing significant disability to a patient, and with it a significant amount of the versatile cells of bone marrow along with the adjacent muscle tissue and parietal pleura. It follows then to represent the production of a female human from the rib and its adjacent tissue as an instance of cloning, but such attempts fail to take into account the fact that the genome of the harvested tissue would have the male XY chromosomal structure rather than the female XX. Intracellular surgery to replace Y chromosomes of germinal tissue with Xs from discarded cells would be required, but of course is no less plausible than placing the technology of cloning in the Bronze Age in the first place.

The similarities of the description to modern anesthesia and surgery are intriguing, even without speculation about the use of cloning. General anesthesia was not used in western medicine until the nineteenth century; a Chinese physician named Hua Tuo is said by some to have developed a protocol for general anesthesia in the third century, but even he would be antedated by several centuries by any writer of Genesis. The application of the same sewing techniques that go into the construction of garments to the healing of living flesh is so intuitive that it arises in nearly all known cultures. Evidence of intentional surgical procedures, mostly skull trephinations, exists in the archeological findings from many cultures of prehistoric Europe, Asia, and the Americas. Contact with these cultures by the very early Hebrews has not been documented and seems unlikely, however, so the origin of this short but credible description of an inexplicable surgical procedure remains as much a mystery as why God did not create a woman from dusty soil, as He did the man and all the other animals.

The teaching, blessedly rare at the time of this writing but encountered in the youth of the author, that the account explains the "fact" that men have an odd number of ribs, one fewer than women, is false. Both men and women have twenty-four ribs, arranged in twelve pairs; there is no difference between the sexes to explain. At the other end of the interpretive spectrum are those who take this as a description of general anesthesia, surgery, and cloning performed in the earliest moments of the human race, and count it, along with such reports as Elijah's departure from earth in a fiery chariot,[1] as the remembrances by primitive humans of contact with advanced extraterrestrials. The

[1] 2nd Kings 2.11.

evidence for such an interpretation is thin at best, but the parallels to modern anesthesia and surgery are as striking as they are mysterious.

It is difficult to give serious credence to the assertion that the first woman was created by a process that involved general anesthesia, surgery, chromosome manipulation, cloning, tissue culture, and organogenesis, with or without the visitation of extraterrestrials, but it is striking that the human female had a means of creation entirely different from that of every other living thing. Is this a reflection of the protected status of women in human societies, a status that is frequently more marked in primitive cultures including that of the early Hebrews? May it be a foreshadowing of the unique status of Mary as the earthly virgin mother of a component of the triune God? Might it mark Eve and Mary as types in parallel to the philosophical type shared by Adam and Jesus, as visited by Paul in the fifth chapter of Romans and slightly less explicitly late in the fifteenth chapter of his first letter to the Corinthians? The entire episode of the creation of the first woman in the second creation account is in contrast to the simplicity of the first account in stating that humankind was created male and female like other species, and defies confident explanation.

The development of permanence of human marriage is reflected in words at the end of the second chapter, which are part of many Christian and Jewish wedding ceremonies: "Therefore a man leaves his father and mother and clings to his wife, and they become one flesh."[1] Permanent coupling is a behavioral advance that provides obvious benefits to the survivability of offspring by the more certain provision of food and security inherent in the ongoing presence of the male parent.

Immediately following the strange story of the woman's creation and her acceptance by the *'adam* comes the story of the first temptation and the first sin. The woman, still nameless, is confronted by a talking snake (not identified in the scripture as Satan – that is a tradition that arose independent of scripture) who points out the delights of the fruit from the forbidden tree of knowledge. The woman then demonstrates the first instance of scriptural interpretation: in Genesis 2.17 God said that *'adam* should not eat the fruit, but in her response to the serpent in 3.3 she says that she and her husband were commanded to neither eat nor even touch it. Still, she succumbs to the arguments of the serpent, and the equally nameless man in turn succumbs to the arguments repeated by the woman, and the forbidden fruit is plucked and consumed, and imparts knowledge and wisdom to the couple.

The most immediate result of the acquisition of knowledge by these first humans, said by the scripture to be heretofore unashamed of nakedness, was the desire to practice modesty by clothing themselves. (In yet another example of figurative language taken

[1] Genesis 2.24. New Revised Standard Version.

so by self-proclaimed literalists, the actual words are "the eyes of both were opened,"[1] but no one infers that they were previously groping about the garden blindly.) Although the standards of modesty vary enormously between cultures, inherent in the inclusion of such a sentiment in the stories of the origins of mankind is the tacit acknowledgement that humans originated from more animal-like forebears that neither clothed themselves nor burdened themselves with the thought that a lack of clothes was immodest, immoral, or in any other way troubling. As the narrative continues, God, portrayed in very human form, takes an evening stroll in His garden. Apparently without the omniscience with which He is later credited, He is at first quite unaware of the human transgression, and notices only the absence of the human couple. Quickly deducing what has happened, God extracts a confession (along with a comically childish round of a very human blame game) and banishes them from His garden with curses of fruitless toil and increasingly painful childbirth. He then replaces their fig-leaf clothes with a new set made Himself from animal skins.

The account of original sin is obviously highly allegorical. No fruit, of course, bestows knowledge, intelligence, or wisdom by being consumed; neither is it likely or even reasonable to suppose that another undiscovered fruit will confer physical immortality. The notion that the depiction of a fruit bearing moral or material knowledge is intended to be symbolic rather than literal finds further encouragement in the book of Proverbs, which urges the pursuit of wisdom by referring to it, in language that strongly parallels that of Genesis, as "a tree of life to those who lay hold of her."[2] Some preachers argue that man's sinful nature, a necessary element of Christian belief, arises from the consumption of the forbidden fruit by the first human couple, and that all of their descendants are therefore tainted, genetically as it were, by their sin. To one not formally trained in theology, a plainer reading would seem to be that sin originated not from the specific act of consuming a piece of fruit, but in the attitude and actions that arose from selfish ambition and disobedience. As Augustine said, "We must not imagine that the tempter would have caused man to fall unless there had arisen in the man's soul a proud spirit that needed to be checked, so that the humiliation of his sin would teach him how wrong he was in relying on himself."[3] The concept of man's sinful nature would seem to survive intact by interpreting this passage as an allegory acknowledging that the mind of man was from its beginning inherently selfish, ambitious, and rebellious, and that disobedience to God's principles of right and wrong proceed from that inherent defect. That the psyche of mankind was so flawed from its beginning should be neither a surprise nor a hindrance to the understanding of the relationship between God and man by theologians or laymen. Given the concept that

---

[1] Genesis 3.7, New Revised Standard Version.

[2] Proverbs 3.18. New Revised Standard Version.

[3] Saint Augustine. *The Literal Meaning of Genesis.* Translated by John Hammond Taylor. New York: Newman Press, 1982. Vol 2 of 2, pg 138 (11.5.7).

the sin of *'adam* became a sin that was bequeathed to each subsequent human, it makes much more sense to consider that sin to be that encompassed by disobedience, selfish desires, and arrogant ambition than to attempt to show that all of mankind harbors the guilt for a specific act of pilfering fruit. The first sin, the one that became a part of the human spirit, was not petty larceny, but self reliance that led to defiance of God's will.

Augustine, while maintaining that the tree was real enough, explained its importance by emphasizing the use to which it was put by God:

> It was proper that man, placed in a state of dependence upon the Lord God, should be given some prohibition, so that obedience would be the virtue by which he would please his Lord. . . The tree, then, was not evil, but it was called the tree of the knowledge of good and evil because, on the supposition that man would eat of its fruit after the prohibition, there was within it the future violation of the command, and because of this transgression man would learn by undergoing punishment the difference between the good of obedience and the evil of disobedience.[1]

The punishment imposed upon the first man and woman for their disobedience is less clear than supposed by many. While it is commonly stated that the punishment for the woman was pain at child birth, the text actually says that the pain of childbirth would increase, implying that birth pain already existed. Further punishments were imposed in the form of linking libido to the pain of child birth, and in submission to her husband. Labor is the sentence supposedly imposed upon the man, but the purpose of his being placed in the garden was to "till it and keep it;"[2] it may be that his punishment was in increase in his labor and a decrease in his productivity, akin to the increased pain of childbirth for his mate. We learn from His punishment, however, that God has expectations for the behavior of humans and that there are consequences to transgressions, but in His reconciliatory provision of animal skin clothing far superior to the fig leaf coverings the rebellious couple provided for themselves, we see God's forgiveness and continuing loving care for the race that He created for His communion.

As the narrative resumes, the male human, still lacking a proper name for himself, names his wife Eve, and she bears to him two sons, Cain and Abel. Cain becomes a crop farmer and Abel an animal husbandman before Cain, in a fit of jealousy over the inexplicable favoritism shown by God towards Cain's offering, kills his brother.

The ensuing passages of the second creation story provide several arguments for the presence of other humans living concurrently with those central to the related story.

---

[1] Saint Augustine. *The Literal Meaning of Genesis.* Translated by John Hammond Taylor. New York: Newman Press, 1982. Vol 2 of 2, pg 42 (8.6.12).

[2] Genesis 2.15. New Revised Standard Version.

Cain marries and begets a child in Genesis 4.17 with no mention of Eve having a daughter. Either another human family provided a wife for Cain, or, if Eve delivered a daughter without it being noted in the text, he entered into an incestuous relationship, which was at least as severely proscribed by the ancient Hebrews as it is by modern western societies. Cain also builds a city, which would seem extravagant with a world population of five – at the time, only Adam, Eve, Cain, Cain's unnamed wife, and his son Enoch are reported being alive. Both Cain's marriage and his founding of a city would appear to argue that the origins of humans were monophyletic (originating from a group or a population with similar traits) rather than monogenetic (originating from one couple); such a finding would be consistent with the human origins proposed by modern scientific understandings.

Similarly, a direct descendant of Adam, Lamech, later boasts of revenge killings, with no apparent effect on the population or genealogy of his immediate family, which again argues for the existence of a human populace outside the family of the central story line and a monophyletic origin of humanity.

Several generations after Adam – seven by the genealogies of the fourth chapter of Genesis, but such genealogies are widely thought to skip generations – Jabal is said to be the "ancestor of those who live in tents and have livestock"[1] and his brother Jubal "the ancestor of all those who play the lyre and pipe."[2] Another brother, Tubal-cain, is said to have "made all kinds of bronze and iron tools."[3] Just before the second creation account ends with a long genealogical section at the beginning of the fifth chapter, Eve bears Adam a son, Seth, who himself has a son named Enosh, and "at that time people began to invoke the name of the LORD."[4]

It can hardly be argued that all keepers of livestock are genetically descended from Jabal, or that all musicians are genetically descended from Jubal; rather, it appears clear that they founded traditions, and later practitioners of their professions are their descendants in the sense of adopting and developing their arts and abilities rather than in the sense of being their biological offspring.

It seems similarly clear that mankind can be considered the spiritual offspring of Adam and Eve without necessarily being their biological descendants. The presence of other human beings seems to be strongly implied in a number of details of the scripture, as has been noted. The fact that intermarriage between the line of Adam and other humans began with Cain, the first generation after Adam and Eve themselves, means that a true human line descending from Adam cannot be separated from other humans,

---

[1] Genesis 4.20. New Revised Standard Version.
[2] Genesis 4.21. New Revised Standard Version.
[3] Genesis 4.22. New Revised Standard Version.
[4] Genesis 4.26. New Revised Standard Version.

and if it could, Christianity would be forced to deal with the questions of whether such traits of spiritual humanity such as an awareness of God, the presence of an inherent sinful nature, and the available forgiveness by God, are present in any humans not genetically descended from Adam and Eve.

Regarding all of mankind as the spiritual descendants of Adam resolves all these issues even if humans are monophyletic rather than monogenetic. If the original sin of selfish ambition is a property of the human spirit common to Adam and any contemporaries, all of humanity can be the heir of Adam in inheriting a spirit of disobedience by spiritual rather than by genetic transmission. If an awareness and communion with God, and a realization of the forgiveness available from Him, are spiritual qualities learned by Adam and taught by him to his contemporaries as well as his and their descendants, then all who reach similar realizations are the spiritual descendants of Adam, and genetic descent ceases to be of importance. Such an interpretation is consistent with a view of the Bible as a document of spiritual and theological significance rather than one complete in its portrayal of either science or genealogy. The spiritual dimensions of man, rather than his genetic makeup, should be the primary concern of faith and the documents of faith. The first real human, in his awareness of his spirituality, began a tradition and a process of spiritual growth and evolution that makes all humans of religious thought his heirs and descendants.

Anatomically modern man, identifiable by paleontologists as *Homo sapiens*, appeared approximately two hundred thousand years ago, in a gradual transition from previous species, and has continued to develop anatomically. Mankind has also continued to develop socially and spiritually. In a document of primary spiritual and religious emphasis such as the Pentateuch, it is reasonable to ask how man is defined. Anatomic features would reasonably be expected to be less important than intellectual, social, and spiritual features in defining humankind. In a book about the developing relationship between man and God, man's awareness of God and of His intentions for mankind can be expected to define his humanity.

The social and spiritual characteristics of humanity that are apparent in the second creation account are several. Of primary importance, appropriate to a work with the development of the relationship between God and man as its subject, is man's awareness of God. The first humans were defined by their recognition of God. In this account, an anthropomorphic God converses with humans, physically walks in the garden that He entrusted to them, and in many ways seeks their companionship.

The question of what role religious thought and awareness of the divine played in the development of mankind is difficult, but not wholly unapproachable. Religious thought seems to be an inherent quality of the mind of humans, as evidenced by psychological studies that show that children, with or without religious training, seek explanations of natural phenomenon that encompass both teleology (a sense of purpose, such as clouds existing for the purpose of providing rain) and a supernatural agent of causality.[1, 2, 3, 4, 5, 6, 7] Psychologists have also observed that, in their early years, children ascribe omniscience to virtually all adults, but after the approximate age of five they begin to realize that adults do not in fact know everything while still attributing omniscience to God.[8] These observations have led at least some psychologists to

---

[1] Kelemen, D. "Are Children 'Intuitive Theists'?: Reasoning about Purpose and Design in Nature." *Psychological Science* 15: 295-330, 2004. Cited by Joseph A. Bulbulia in *Oxford Handbook of Evolutionary Psychology*, Chap 36, "Evolution of Religion." Louise Barrett and Robin Dunbar, ed. New York: Oxford Univ Press, 2007. Pg 621-638. Accessed 9 March 2008 at <http://www.victoria.ac.nz/religion/downloads/OXFORD_CHAPTER36_BULBULIA.pdf>.

[2] Kelemen, D. "Why are rocks point? Children's preference for teleological explanations of the natural world." *Developmental Psychology* 35:1440-1453, 1999. Cited by Joseph A. Bulbulia in *Oxford Handbook of Evolutionary Psychology*, Chap 36, "Evolution of Religion." Louise Barrett and Robin Dunbar, ed. New York: Oxford Univ Press, 2007. Pg 621-638. Accessed 9 March 2008 at <http://www.victoria.ac.nz/religion/downloads/OXFORD_CHAPTER36_BULBULIA.pdf>.

[3] Kelemen, D. "British and American children's preference for teleo-functional explanations of the natural world." *Cognition* 88: 201-222, 2003. Cited by Joseph A. Bulbulia in *Oxford Handbook of Evolutionary Psychology*, Chap 36, "Evolution of Religion." Louise Barrett and Robin Dunbar, ed. New York: Oxford Univ Press, 2007. Pg 621-638. Accessed 9 March 2008 at <http://www.victoria.ac.nz/religion/downloads/OXFORD_CHAPTER36_BULBULIA.pdf>.

[4] Evans, E. M. "The emergency of beliefs about the origin of species in school-age children." *Merrill Palmer Quarterly* 46:221-254, 2000. Cited by Joseph A. Bulbulia in *Oxford Handbook of Evolutionary Psychology*, Chap 36, "Evolution of Religion." Louise Barrett and Robin Dunbar, ed. New York: Oxford Univ Press, 2007. Pg 621-638. Accessed 9 March 2008 at <http://www.victoria.ac.nz/religion/downloads/OXFORD_CHAPTER36_BULBULIA.pdf>.

[5] Evans, E. M. "Cognitive and contextual factors in the emergency of diverse belief systems: Creation versus evolution." *Cognitive Psychology* 42: 217-266, 2001. Cited by Joseph A. Bulbulia in *Oxford Handbook of Evolutionary Psychology*, Chap 36, "Evolution of Religion." Louise Barrett and Robin Dunbar, ed. New York: Oxford Univ Press, 2007. Pg 621-638. Accessed 9 March 2008 at <http://www.victoria.ac.nz/religion/downloads/OXFORD_CHAPTER36_BULBULIA.pdf>.

[6] DiYanni, C., and D. Kelemen. "Time to get a new mountain? The role of function in children's conception of natural kinds." *Cognition* 97: 327-335, 2005. Cited by Joseph A. Bulbulia in *Oxford Handbook of Evolutionary Psychology*, Chap 36, "Evolution of Religion." Louise Barrett and Robin Dunbar, ed. New York: Oxford Univ Press, 2007. Pg 621-638. Accessed 9 March 2008 at <http://www.victoria.ac.nz/religion/downloads/OXFORD_CHAPTER36_BULBULIA.pdf>.

[7] Kelemen, D., and C. DiYanni. "Intuitions About Origins: Purpose and Intelligent Design in Children's Reason About Nature." *Journal of Cognition and Development* 6(1): 3-31. Cited by Joseph A. Bulbulia in *Oxford Handbook of Evolutionary Psychology*, Chap 36, "Evolution of Religion." Louise Barrett and Robin Dunbar, ed. New York: Oxford Univ Press, 2007. Pg 621-638. Accessed 9 March 2008 at <http://www.victoria.ac.nz/religion/downloads/OXFORD_CHAPTER36_BULBULIA.pdf>.

[8] Barrett, J. L., and R. A. Richert. "Anthropomorphism or Preparedness? Exploring Children's God Concepts." *Review of Religious Research* 44(3): 300-312, 2003. Cited by Joseph A. Bulbulia in *Oxford Handbook of Evolutionary Psychology*, Chap 36, "Evolution of Religion." Louise Barrett and Robin Dunbar, ed. New York: Oxford Univ Press, 2007. Pg 621-638. Accessed 9 March 2008

conclude that children are "born to believe."[1]

Given that religious thought, in the form of ascribing both a sense of purpose and a causal agent to the features of the natural world, is such a universal and congenital trait of the human mind, the next question that must be asked within the framework of evolutionary understanding is, "What selection pressure exists to favor the development of the capacity for religious thought in humans?" The most plausible answer is that enhanced cooperation within communities with similar religious values increases the probability of survival. It has been proposed that, under the Nash Equilibrium components of game theory (named for mathematician John Nash, made popularly famous by the book and movie *A Beautiful Mind*), the hope of reward and fear of punishment by a deity changes the social behavior of most people by shifting the expectation of the greatest benefit from dishonorably selfish actions to behavior that is, if not magnanimously altruistic, at least ethical. In other words, the fear of hell and hope of heaven in the tradition of Jews, Christians, and Muslims, or the concept of karma and its effect on the states of future incarnations in other traditions, provide a motivation for individuals to conform to social norms of commerce and government and to avoid behaviors (such as abrogation of contractual obligations, infidelity to marriage, or murder of societal equals) that may otherwise provide individual advantage but damage the welfare and survivability of the community.[2] Within this theory, religious ritual provides a setting for individuals to both display and observe displays of pious devotion, many of which expressions are difficult to imitate or falsify by those not fully committed to religious belief, and thereby assess the reliability of social contracts with each other.[3] Such theorization is given credence by functional magnetic resonance imaging studies that have demonstrated that the consideration of religious statements and questions induces activity in the same regions of the brain that process complex social interactions such as the identification of emotion and evaluation of the intent of others and the subsequent appraisal of the relative risk and benefits posed by

---

at <http://www.victoria.ac.nz/religion/downloads/OXFORD_CHAPTER36_BULBULIA.pdf>.

[1] Bulbulia, Joseph A. Chap 36, "Evolution of Religion" in *Oxford Handbook of Evolutionary Psychology*, Louise Barrett and Robin Dunbar, ed. New York: Oxford Univ Press, 2007. Pg 621-638. Accessed 9 March 2008 at <http://www.victoria.ac.nz/religion/downloads/OXFORD_CHAPTER36_BULBULIA.pdf>.

[2] Bulbulia, Joseph A. Chap 36, "Evolution of Religion" in *Oxford Handbook of Evolutionary Psychology*, Louise Barrett and Robin Dunbar, ed. New York: Oxford Univ Press, 2007. Pg 621-638. (Pg 10-13 of 25 as displayed online.) Accessed 9 March 2008 at <http://www.victoria.ac.nz/religion/downloads/OXFORD_CHAPTER36_BULBULIA.pdf>.

[3] Bulbulia, Joseph A. Chap 36, "Evolution of Religion" in *Oxford Handbook of Evolutionary Psychology*, Louise Barrett and Robin Dunbar, ed. New York: Oxford Univ Press, 2007. Pg 621-638. (Pg 13-15 of 25 as displayed online.) Accessed 9 March 2008 at <http://www.victoria.ac.nz/religion/downloads/OXFORD_CHAPTER36_BULBULIA.pdf>.

interactions with them.[1] The reader should note that these findings of psychology and neuroanatomy are not unique to Judeo-Christian religious thought; rather, they explain and encompass the apparently universal seeking of deity by humankind as expressed by religions ancient and modern throughout the world, and the adoption of any particular religious belief, including Christianity, remains a choice of faith.

Within the theology of Judeo-Christian tradition, concurrent with mankind's awareness of God came a certain independence of thought – an ability to choose whether or not to adopt belief in God and the social responsibilities that are at the heart of religious ethics - that is characterized as a free will. Inherent in the principle of free will is the concept that God desired mankind to be willing participants in their relationship to Him. Biologically, free will is constituted by the ability of conscious thought and reasoning to overcome instinctive behaviors, processes located in the frontal lobes of the cerebrum. Theologically, a free will is a necessary condition for God's desire for communion with mankind, in that He does not desire the worship of automatons, but of people who choose to obey, follow, and commune with Him. This very independence is demonstrated, for both good and ill, in the story of early man's disobedience in eating the forbidden fruit of knowledge.

Basic to the inception and maintenance of human society was the foundation of the family unit. With permanent pairing came shared responsibilities and combined ingenuity in the procurement of resources, securing shelter, defense, child rearing, and so on. The family unit also became the central element in transmitting the wisdom and knowledge necessary for survival to a new generation, and the provision for the elderly emerged as a means for preserving their accumulated knowledge. Thus the ethic of fidelity, which would at first glance seem antithetical to natural selection by restricting the distribution of the male genome, undergoes a positive selection pressure by enhancing the survivability of larger units of human society.

Also visible in the second creation account is a transition from a society of hunters and gatherers, portrayed by Adam and Eve's life in the garden, to one based on fixed agriculture and cultivation of food crops and animals, by Cain and Abel. With this transition came a division of labor that is first delineated by Cain's specialization in cultivation and Abel's specialization in animal husbandry, and within a few generations, the development of craftsmen such as the smithy Tubal-cain. Mention of the musician Jabal demonstrates that the development of the arts was linked to the early history of humanity, and may suggest that at least the art of music was valued enough to be an occupation supported by the community, since no other gainful employment is

---

[1] Kapogiannis, Dimitrios, et al.. "Cognitive and neural foundations of religious belief." *Proceedings of the National Academy of Sciences (early edition).* 3 Feb 2009. Accessed 9 Mar 2009 at <www.pnas.org/cgi/doi/10.1073/pnas.0811717106.>

mentioned in connection with Jabal. As communities became more diverse and individuals more specialized, an increased interdependence between various skills made it increasingly practical for people to gather together to exchange the produce of the various trades; hamlets, villages, towns and cities were born of the mutual need among the budding professions.

The Sumerians are widely regarded as the first human civilization. Sumer began as a cluster of loosely affiliated city-states, as often at war with each other as not, in the southeastern alluvial plain of the Tigris and Euphrates rivers, where the rivers approach their terminus in the Persian Gulf. (One of these city-states was Ur, which according to Genesis 11.31 was the hometown of Abraham.) The Sumerian culture began to develop around 5000 BCE, the principal cities were in existence around 4000 BCE, and later kings unified the cities into a manageable realm, beginning around 2800 BCE. Sumerian writing had progressed from pictographs to cuneiform script by around 3000 BCE. The Sumerians employed a primitive but effective irrigation system and working animals to enhance and stabilize agricultural production. Trades and crafts flourished in the Sumerian culture – men practiced carpentry and building trades in the cities, and crop farming and animal husbandry in rural areas; women practiced spinning and weaving. Goods and materials were imported from other portions of the Middle East and the nearby coast of southern Asia. The Sumerians invented bureaucracy – the earliest known human writings are records of the exchange of goods and services overseen by Sumerian authorities. Later Sumerian writings include stories, including the widely known Epic of Gilgamesh, populated by a variety of deities, in the first clear demonstration of religious thought by humans. Sumerian law institutionalized marriage. Sumerian cities were decorated with sculptures and relief carvings. Lyres are found in royal tombs and musicians are depicted in Sumerian carvings; a Sumerian king of circa 2100 BCE boasted of his skill in composing songs.[1, 2]

Although the references to Jerusalem's Gihon spring and the unknown Pishon River confuse the issue, the clear reference in Genesis to the Tigris and Euphrates Rivers in association with the major developments of civilized man – religious thought, the founding and advancement of fixed agriculture, division of labor, the development of artisan knowledge and abilities, urban living with its necessary system of exchange, and the practice of visual and musical arts – is remarkable, especially considering that the Sumerians were not known to archeologists until the nineteenth century.[3]

---

[1] Guisepi, Robert A., and F. Roy Willis. "Ancient Sumeria." *International World History Project.* 2003. History World International. 24 Feb 2008. <http://history-world.org/sumeria.htm>.
[2] Hooker, Richard. "The Sumerians." *World Civilizations.* 6 Jun 1999. Washington State University. 24 Feb 2008. <http://www.wsu.edu/~dee/MESO/SUMER.HTM>.
[3] Guisepi, Robert A., and F. Roy Willis. "Ancient Sumeria." *International World History Project.* 2003. History World International. 24 Feb 2008. <http://history-world.org/sumeria.htm>.

The Psalms

The two creation accounts of Genesis are the longest and best-known creation stories in the Bible, but shorter references to creation occur in numerous other locations in Judeo-Christian scripture. The Psalms contain several references to creation, as do the books of Isaiah and Job. Most New Testament allusions to creation quote or cite an Old Testament reference.

The 102nd Psalm concludes with a testimony to the immortality of God, quoted inexactly in the New Testament book of Hebrews:

> In the beginning, Lord, you founded the earth,
>   And the heavens are the work of your hands;
> They will perish, but you remain;
>   They will all wear out like clothing;
> Like a cloak you will roll them up,
>   And like clothing they will be changed.
> But you are the same,
>   And your years will never end.[1]

The passage makes it clear that the writer saw the earth and the heavens as temporal in their existence, the creation of an eternal God. In modern parlance, we once again see a God dwelling outside the space-time continuum. The concept that time may have had a beginning is a very recent development in western thought, with serious consideration beginning in the nineteenth century, and confirmation and wide acceptance coming about in the last half of the twentieth century with the acceptance of the Big Bang Theory. Yet this passage clearly refers to both a beginning and an ending of time and existence, and places God as Creator outside of the dimensions of space and time.

The quotation in Hebrews contains a line which is not found in the current version of the Psalm, but which may have been present in another version available in the first century: "Like a cloak you will roll them [the heavens] up." In modern cosmological models that include sufficient dark matter to stop the expansion of the universe by gravitational attraction, the universe contracts to an ending singularity similar to the Big Bang singularity at the beginning of time. Although such models are currently in disfavor, their very existence is a result of advanced work in astrophysics, and the concept of a contracting universe and a resulting end of time itself would hardly seem likely to Bronze Age man. The allusion is admittedly vague, but could represent a consideration by writers soon after the time of Christ of the possibility of such a turn of events.

---

[1] Hebrews 1.10-12. New Revised Standard Version.

The 104th Psalm is a song praising the Creator God, and largely reflects the cosmology of the first creation account of Genesis in more poetic language. It is by no means clear whether the first Genesis account or the Psalm were written first; either could have influenced the other, and some analysts feel strongly that the Psalm was known to the writer of the first Genesis account. The language of the Psalm is that of a hymn, rich in imagery (and the dead horse of literalism is flogged again.): God "stretches out the heavens like a tent,"[1] and "makes the clouds his chariot and rides on the wings of the wind."[2] At several points the Psalm reflects the Jewish cosmology of an earth surrounded by waters above and below, with the waters possessing an ominous and threatening character. The Psalm seems to find value in the beauty and sustaining characteristics of creation independent of anthropocentrism.

The fifth verse grants permanence to the earth in a manner that is quite opposite to the view of the 102nd Psalm that the heavens and the earth are a passing phenomenon: God "set the earth on its foundations; it can never be moved."[3] Such permanence is much more in line with the thought of western man prior to the nineteenth century; it was then the common holding of both science and philosophy that the earth had always existed and was both immortal and unchangeable. This and a few similar scriptures were once used to defend geocentric models against the heliocentric theory originated by Copernicus and expounded upon by Galileo, as will be discussed in more detail in a later chapter.

The 104th Psalm also makes repeated reference to water covering the land. This is of course reflective of the first Genesis account and the process of separation and sorting by which God parted the seas from the land. The more specific and complete description present in the Psalm, however, brings to mind the large inland seas which are known by the fossil record to have existed in ages past. It is within reason to wonder if fossils of obviously aquatic life forms may have been known to the early Jews, since they are easily recovered in many areas of the world, and the lands known to the Hebrews were frequently deeply cut by wadies. (Other prehistoric peoples are known to have taken an interest in fossils. An archeological site in Canada, rich in stone implements, also contained a fossil trilobite that had been transported 500 kilometers, or a little over 300 miles, across a major mountain range and a highland plateau, from its origin.[4]) The knowledge of such fossils could easily lead to a folk tradition that includes land emerging from the sea, as depicted in the Psalm; indeed,

---

[1] Psalm 104.2. New International Verision. . (The New Revised Standard Version differs only in being written in the second person rather than the third.)

[2] Psalm 104.3. New International Version. (The New Revised Standard Version again differs only in being written in the second person.)

[3] Psalm 104.5. New Revised Standard Version.

[4] "The Fraser River trilobite." *Past lives: Chronicles of Canadian Paleontology.* 7 Feb 2008. Geological Survey of Canada. 16 Mar 2008. <http://gsc.nrcan.gc.ca/paleochron/12_e.php>.

hardly any other conclusion is possible when sea shells are found in the desert.

Although some portray the event of God's breathing life into man in Genesis 2.7 as man's receipt of a spirit or soul from God, Genesis 1.30 refers to God's breath of life in the animal kingdom, and this Psalm uses identical language in reference to the life of animals. Life in terrestrial animals as well as man, then, is linked by common observation to the act of breathing. Of the animals it is said in the 104th Psalm: "When you take away their breath, they die and return to the dust. When you send forth your spirit, they are created, and you renew the face of the earth."[1] The Hebrew word rendered here as "breath" and "spirit" is the same; life is the presence of breath and spirit, and death is its absence. The Psalm eloquently acknowledges God's sustenance as well as His hand in the birth and death of all living things.

It is noteworthy that the ongoing birth of animals is described by the Psalm as creative activity by God in renewing the earth. That birth is honored as a creative act of God belies the insistence of creationists that each new species was a separate creative act. If each birth is a creative act guided by God's spirit or granted by God's breath, spontaneous creation of new species is not necessary to an interpretation of the creation stories of Genesis; rather, the process of change delineated in modern theories of evolution and genetics can be seen as a tool, itself created and guided by God in a series of births progressing towards God's intended end. Similarly, if God has a hand in death and, by extension, extinctions, then His guidance can be considered in that aspect of the evolutionary process, and the death of individuals, genera, and phyla can be seen as part of the creative process designed, foreseen, and guided by God. In the 104th Psalm, God is seen to create through the processes of birth and death, rather than through spontaneous generation of new forms, completely in compliance with current biological theories.

The Books of Job and Isaiah

In the course of its consideration of the enigma of theodicy (the allowance of the existence of evil by a good and just God, a subject that continues to engage writers of theology, philosophy, and popular works), the book of Job records long, and at times angry and accusatory, conversations between God and Job. Among the subjects that are touched upon is God's role in creation, most especially in the thirty-eighth chapter. Therein God defends His sovereignty in a speech dripping with sarcasm, and challenges Job's qualifications to dispute Him by reviewing His own credentials as creator and omnipotent deity. In so doing, God analogizes earth to a building, with features including a foundation, a cornerstone, and a construction process involving measurements and stretching a line to assure straight and square dimensions. The

[1] Psalm 104.29-30. New International Version.

imagery conveys a sense of an involved deity taking action in the manner of a craftsman, as does the second creation story, as well as a sense of permanence of the earth.

The now-familiar Jewish cosmology, of waters above and below the earth as well as in the seas, appears again in God's homily. Following the foundation of the earth, He again takes a workmanlike approach, now to restraining the chaotic waters, by building doors with bars to contain them.

The text also refers to storehouses of both snow and hail, again consistent with Jewish cosmology. A reference to cutting channels for rain and lightning in the twenty-fifth verse reflects a belief that the sky was a solid dome, and that rain, as well as snow and hail and the poorly understood phenomenon of lightning, need passageways from the outer waters to the realm of the earth and its atmosphere.[1]

In verses thirty-one through thirty-three God mocks Job's inabilities to control the movement of the constellations. Modern translators typically substitute the names of current constellations in this passage for the unknown ones imagined and named by the early Hebrews, but the very fact that they had names for constellations means that they made observations of the heavens and recognized that various stars were visible in different seasons of the year.

In the thirty-seventh verse, clouds are paired with "the waterskins of the heavens" in a poetic doublet. The reference itself does not make clear that the reference to waterskins is figurative, but since it is clear that rain was associated with clouds by common observation, and by similar observation the Jews could observe both ground fog and the nature of clouds clothing mountains, it is reasonable to assume that the language is purely metaphorical.

The discourse emphasizes God's power and knowledge as creator and sustainer of the earth and its biosphere with example after example, and by implication establishes Him as the ultimate source of wisdom and authority. In contesting the right to determine what is just in life, Job and his friends do not fare well in their argument with God.

Like the references in Job and brief allusions in other parts of scripture, creation is cited in the Book of Isaiah as a means of establishing the credentials of God as unique in power and authority. In Isaiah 45.12-13, for example, God, speaking in the first person, establishes His ascendancy by proclaiming His creation of the earth and the heavens, and then uses His divine prerogative, thus established, to commission and endorse the actions of Cyrus in repatriating the Jews from Babylon and rebuilding

---

[1] Crenshaw, James. "Job." *Oxford Bible Commentary.* Oxford: Oxford University Press, 2001. Pg 352.

Jerusalem and the Temple. Later in the same chapter (verses 18 and 19), the narrator similarly establishes God's credentials as creator before quoting His claim to monotheistic holiness. The narrator includes an unusual note that the purpose of God's creation of earth was to provide for its inhabitation, implying that the earth is unique in its ability to support life. The proclamation of His status as creator to establish the authority of God is also a feature in chapters 40, 42, and 44 of Isaiah.

New Testament

The Judeo-Christian God has two primary roles in scripture – that of creator and that of the author and judge of moral and ethical values. The scriptures often present the former as a source of authority for the latter; God was the planner and designer of all that is, and because of His infinite knowledge of His creation, is qualified both to define the principles by which He expects mankind to govern himself and his charge, and to serve as judge of how well mankind in general and individuals in particular have conformed to God's will in their duties to each other and the world at large. The motif of God's authority stemming from his role as creator continues into the New Testament in the many expressions of praise and frequent parallel declarations of His authority.

In the last book of the Christian Bible, the fourth chapter of the Revelation to John describes a scene from the throne room of God. The throne of YHWH is central, and surrounded by seven torches, four winged animals covered with eyes who continuously sing a song of praise, and twenty-four lesser thrones held by "elders," who intermittently prostrate themselves and sing their own song, "You are worthy, our Lord and God, to receive glory and honor and power, for you created all things, and by your will they existed and were created."[1] It is beyond the subject of this tome to discuss the many and varied means of interpreting the many difficult aspects of Revelation, among them the identity and roles of the twenty-four elders, but two observations would seem critical to understanding the concept of the twin roles of God as creator and judge. First, the glory and honor and power of God, including presumably the power and authority of the judgment of mankind imminent in the Revelation, again stems from His role as Creator. Secondly, all things were created and continued to exist by His will. Absent is any mention of creative physical activity; the power of His will, with the wisdom and omniscience inherent in His being, were sufficient to initiate and sustain His creative act. The ongoing physical formation of new characteristics and species is not endorsed by this passage.

Further thoughts by Augustine

Saint Augustine of Hippo wrote extensively about his interpretations of the creation

---

[1] Revelation 4.11. New Revised Standard Version.

accounts, his largest work on the subject being *De Genesi ad litteram*, or *The Literal Interpretation of Genesis*. As has been touched upon, Augustine's idea of literalism was drastically different from that of modern-day creationists, and his work, while justifying the actual occurrence of biblical events, did so within the framework of fifth century science with the admission that his opinions may need to be modified by scientific advancement. His thoughts on the scriptures are filled with proposals for symbolic and allegorical interpretations of events and complex speculation about the intended and hidden meanings of scripture. His work can hardly be summarized briefly, but one of the most remarkable contentions of Augustine in *The Literal Meaning of Genesis* is his extensive argument that the scriptures reflect two stages of creation for each created entity. By Augustine's reasoning, God first creative act in each instance was to create a cause (in philosophy, a concept of the created thing and the impetus for it to come into being), and only in a second creative act, attributed to the actions of angels or the processes of nature, to give it material form.

> Thus, God by His almighty power made what would appear in the future, and when He who is before the ages created the beginning of the ages, in what we might call the germ or root of time, He created man to be formed later in due time.
>
> Some creatures, indeed, precede others either by reason of time or by reason of causality. But God precedes all that He made not only by reason of His superiority as the Author of all, even of causes, but also by reason of His eternity.[1]
>
> Nevertheless, under one aspect these things are in the Word of God, where they are not made but eternally existing; under another aspect they are in the elements of the universe, where all things destined to be were made simultaneously; under another aspect they are in things no longer created simultaneously but rather separately each in its own due time, made according to their causes which were created simultaneously – among which was Adam, formed from the slime and animated by the breath of God, like the grass sprung from the earth; under another aspect they are in seeds, in which they are found again as quasi-primordial causes which derive from creatures that have come forth according to the causes which God first stored up in the world – and thus we have the crops from the earth, and the seed from the crops.
>
> In all these things, beings already created received at their own proper time their manner of being and acting, which developed into visible forms and natures from the hidden and invisible reasons which are latent in creation as

[1] St. Augustine. *The Literal Meaning of Genesis.* Translated and annotated by John Hammond Taylor New York: Newman, 1982. Vol 1 of 2, pg 187 (6.8.13).

causes.[1]

By Augustine's theory, all that would ever develop has existed forever in the mind of God, and was in that sense created before the beginning of time, even though many creations would exist in a material way only much later.

> According to the division of the works of God described above, some works belonged to the invisible days in which He created all things simultaneously, and others belong to the days in which He daily fashions whatever evolves in the course of time . . .[2]

The use of the word "evolves" by Augustine does not, of course, indicate foreknowledge of Darwin's theory over a thousand years later, but is used only in the sense of gradual development; nevertheless, it clearly troubled Augustine not at all to see that the physical world around him was changing, or to attribute the developments and transformations to the wisdom and planning of God.

Summary and conclusions

In considering the Biblical accounts and comments on creation, it must be remembered that the Hebrew words that are variously translated as "earth" and "land" in English versions of the Bible are nearly always the same word, *eretz*. No scriptural author had a concept of the earth as a sphere spinning in space. The earth they knew was the land that they saw, and the understanding that they needed was an understanding of their own observations and experiences.

That the known world of the authors of Genesis and other works of scripture was so limited makes it all the more remarkable that so many parallels exist between their writings and the observations and theories of modern science.

Although the erroneous Jewish cosmology that sees the earth as an island of inhabitable space surrounded by menacing waters above, below, and surrounding it is pervasive in the scriptures, the first Genesis account validly describes the primordial state of the cosmos and the earth as disorganized and chaotic before embarking on a reasonable and organized chronology of the evolutionary development of the earth and the biosphere. Unlike their contemporaries, the Jews recognized that individuals reproduced only with their own species and produced offspring of the same species.

The second creation account of Genesis is insupportable in its chronology of the origin of animal species, in the light of either modern scientific knowledge or of the first

---

[1] St. Augustine. *The Literal Meaning of Genesis.* Translated and annotated by John Hammond Taylor New York: Newman, 1982. Vol 1 of 2, pg 189 (6.10.17).

[2] St. Augustine. *The Literal Meaning of Genesis.* Translated and annotated by John Hammond Taylor New York: Newman, 1982. Vol 1 of 2, pg 183-184 (6.6.9)

creation account, but it contains tantalizing hints of understanding beyond that expected of an author of an age several centuries before the birth of Christ. The early Israelites seemed to understand that the human body and the animal kingdom are made of the same elements as the earth, an understanding that can plausibly be interpreted as a nascent atomic theory, in the same vein as that of the later Greeks. The account seems to define mankind by his spiritual and cultural dimensions, as could be reasonably expected in a religious document, and to correctly place the development of such hallmarks of civilization as fixed agriculture, division of labor, urbanization, the institutionalization of marriage, and the development of the arts, along with the onset of religious thought, in the Fertile Crescent, even though the Sumerian civilization was not otherwise known until the nineteenth century. The advanced concept of a beginning and an ending to time was a part of Jewish thought, and even a vague but intriguing reference that may allude to the idea of a contractile universe finds mention. The most specific of the references to land emerging from waters can be interpreted as knowledge of the pre-historic existence of inland seas.

Other portions of early Jewish scripture are equally intriguing. The food hygiene practices of the ancient Israelites are so effective that in the modern day, many non-Jews regard the kosher designation as an assurance of food quality and safety. The Jewish proscription against the consumption of pork protects against infection with trichinellosis, the serious parasitic disease that causes cooks to insist on the thorough cooking of pork products even with modern farming practices. Although true leprosy is less contagious that commonly believed, Jewish law provided for quarantine of suspected cases, a diagnostic period for the disease to declare itself, and options for restoration or continued quarantine of the much-feared disease after a positive diagnosis. Modern medical authorities point out that the Jewish criteria could erroneously diagnose a variety of diseases with skin lesions, including the plague, as leprosy, but the result of the restrictions was the containment of contagious disease almost three thousand years before western medicine understood the germ theory of infectious disease transmission. As a matter of fact, the rabbinical laws regarding personal and food hygiene resulted in such a marked decrease in the incidence and death rates of the Black Plague among Jewish communities of the middle ages that the Jews were accused of causing the disease by poisoning public wells and were thought to be Satanically protected from the disease; such accusations provided a pretext for pogroms in many locations in Europe. Jewish writers no later than the fifth century BCE can thus be seen to have codified practices to contain the spread of contagious disease that have been proven effective in the most extreme circumstances; by contrast, Louis Pasteur is widely considered to be the father of the germ theory in western medicine after his work in the middle of the nineteenth century.

How did an ancient Semitic people acquire the knowledge of cosmology, geology, archeology, biology, and microbiology displayed in Jewish scripture? Were they more keen observers than they have been given credit for? Was their thinking more advanced that later Greeks, Romans, and early European cultures? Did they retain within their folk traditions knowledge of earlier cultures such as the Sumerians? Did they have contact with other advanced civilizations, perhaps some still undiscovered? Were they, as some of the more imaginative theoreticians would have us suppose, visited by extraterrestrials? Or was their knowledge divinely revealed?

The answer to these questions cannot be known with certainty. What is certain is that the Jews believed fervently in a single powerful God who created all that is in existence, and who favored their nation with special attention for good and for ill. For all the hints and allusions to advanced knowledge, the Bible remains a document focused on faith. The ancient Jews sought to understand the world around them in terms of their relationship to God.

Little accommodation is necessary to interpret Judeo-Christian scripture in a manner consistent with contemporary scientific knowledge. Yet, because the Bible is a collection of documents of religious intent, the scriptures do not speak of the mechanisms of physics, chemistry, or biology. Geological and biological evolution is neither described nor explicitly ruled out by scripture. Only the arguments of man make science either theistic or atheistic.

Chapter 9

The God of Uncertainty

The preceding chapters have presented condensed versions of what is known and suspected of the human history of scripture, cosmology, and the evolution of life, and proposed a means based on those considerations of interpreting holy writ in a manner consistent with the findings of science. All was to provide a foundation for reflection on the impact of science on faith and the human conception of the nature of God.

There are four possible reactions to the faith founded by the Judeo-Christian scriptures and the facts and well-founded theories of twenty-first century science: faith without science, science without faith, faith and science reconciled, or rejection of both. If the faith and authority of scripture is rejected, one may either hold to atheism or find solace in another religious tradition, and in either case still face the choice of whether to accept or reject the findings of science. Faith remains a choice of the spirit, outside of rational confirmation or denial. Attempts to prove the existence of God from reason, though admirable and at their best convincing, fall short of the strict standards of proof; attempts to disprove the existence of God through similar means are similarly doomed by the laws of logic, for one can never conclusively prove the non-existence of anything, only that such has not been discovered. The doctrine that God, and faith in God, is beyond rationality was a theme of Danish theologian and philosopher Søren Kierkegaard, who went on to assert that doubt is a necessary part of faith, that a faith that has not been doubted and examined is not worth holding, and that a faith without doubt is not a faith at all. If proof exists, faith is not required. By the measure of Kierkegaard and a great many other Christian thinkers, God asks for our belief without proof precisely because He wishes for us to choose a belief in Him rather than to be confronted with such evidence that no faith is required for our belief.

For one who chooses faith based on the scriptures and traditions of Judaism and/or Christianity, the choice remains of whether to embrace the findings and theories of science. Such a choice would seem to many, with and without faith, to be an easier choice than the choice of whether or not to hold to faith, for the proofs of science are so much more tangible and overwhelming. It is a measure of the strength of the faith of some, admirable in some ways, that they would seek a means to dismiss material evidence that they consider threatening to their choice of faith. Yet one is left to wonder if those who do so consider the cost exacted by that choice to their faith and to the institutions of their faith.

It is the purpose of the remaining chapters of this book to examine and compare the impact on the perceived characteristics of God, and on the institution of the church, made by the holdings of creationism and intelligent design on one hand, and by a synthesis of theistic evolution on the other.

Is there room for God in the minds of those who accept the theories of science as they exist in the early years of the twenty-first century? If there is a God, does He have a continuing role in the universe, or is He a God of deism, setting the universe in motion and then making Himself a mere observer of results? Is there, then, in a world governed by the known laws and theories of science, no personal aspect to God, no possibility of knowing Him, no reason to think that He has a purpose for the lives of those who choose to acknowledge and serve Him? Is there, in a world consistent with physical reality, no forgiveness available consistent with the traditions of Judaism and Christianity?

Seeking truth

Few fundamentalist Christians, laity and clergy alike, are aware that their interpretation of scripture, especially as it relates to the origins of the earth and its life, is a relatively late invention, dating primarily to the nineteenth century and the reactionary stance against higher criticism of scripture and Darwin's theory of descent with modification by means of natural selection. As we have seen, St. Augustine of Hippo (354-430) not only wrote of the Genesis creation stories being highly symbolic, but considered his symbolic interpretation to be literal.

Similarly few Christian fundamentalists are aware of the long tradition of regarding the natural world and its exploration as being revelatory of the nature of God. Paul's letter to the Romans includes these words: "Ever since the creation of the world his eternal power and divine nature, invisible though they are, have been understood and seen through the things he has made."[1] The scriptural admonition, originating in the

[1] Romans 1.20. New Revised Standard Version.

Pentateuch,[1] that the proper worship of God involved heart, soul, strength, and mind was confirmed by Jesus in all three of the synoptic gospels.[2]

The examination, debate, and elaboration of the Torah that gave rise to the Talmud and continues in the study and scholarly deliberations of modern students of Judaism constitutes an act of worship in Jewish tradition, as does the observation and investigation of the world around us. The multitude of scripture verses that equate the wonders of creation to the glory of God are too numerous to mention, and each student of the Torah and the Bible has his or her favorites. Together with the traditions of Judeo-Christian thought, the dual scriptural admonitions to use the mind in worship and in the observations of nature cause the activities of science to be seen as an alternative and supplemental means of knowing the mind of God.

The monasteries of Europe answered those admonitions by becoming, along with courts so disposed, the repositories of knowledge, literature, and basic literacy during the middle ages. In the millennium between the fall of Rome and the flowering of the Renaissance, monks not only preserved the available writings, but multiplied them by laborious (and often lovingly artistic) hand copying, and studied their contents. The canonical Christian scriptures, which in that day included the works now regarded by most Protestants as apocryphal, were included, but were by far not the only works preserved in the monasteries; works by early Christian writers such as Augustine were similarly preserved and transcribed, as were the surviving writings of luminaries such as Plato and Aristotle and the works of scholars in the fields of mathematics, astronomy, and geometry. These monasteries continued in their role as centers of learning and research into the modern era, as evidenced by the role of Gregor Mendel in unlocking the mysteries of genetics. Many of the most prestigious universities and libraries of Europe are direct descendants of Christian monastic communities that considered learning and scientific exploration to be an act of worship.

Martin Luther (1483-1546) wrote forcefully of the need for Christians to be well educated, arguing for their need to understand both the revelations of God and the world in which those revelations were made manifest. Luther's contemporary Nicolaus Copernicus (1473-1543), the Catholic clergyman who originated the theory of heliocentricity, is widely quoted, "To know the mighty works of God; to comprehend His wisdom and majesty and power; to appreciate, in degree, the wonderful working of his laws, surely all this must be a pleasing and acceptable mode of worship to the Most High, to whom ignorance cannot be more grateful than knowledge." John Calvin (1509-1564) often spoke of creation being a "second book" of divine revelation. Mark Noll, in his critique of trends in Christian thinking *The Scandal of the Evangelical Mind*,

[1] Deuteronomy 6.5.

[2] Matthew 22.35-29, Mark 12.28-31, and Luke 10.25-28.

noted that, under the teaching of Calvin, "Protestants were encouraged to labor as scientists so that their scientific work could rise to the praise of God. By so doing, the early Protestants expressed their belief that God had made the natural world to be explored and that the results of such exploration showed forth his glory."[1]

A prominent nineteenth-century professor of theology at Princeton University, Charles Hodge, wrote in 1863,

> Nature is as truly a revelation of God as the Bible; and we only interpret the Word of God by the Word of God when we interpret the Bible by science. . . . When the Bible speaks of the foundations, or the pillars of the earth, or of the solid heavens, or of the motion of the sun, do not you and every other sane man, interpret this language by the facts of science?. . . Shall we go on to interpret the Bible so as to make it teach the falsehood that the sun moves around the earth, or shall we interpret it by science, and make the two harmonize?[2]

The Belgic Confession, dating back to 1561, is equally explicit:

> We know [God] by two means: first, by the creation, preservation, and government of the universe, which is before our eyes as a most elegant book, wherein all creatures, great and small, are as so many characters, leading us to contemplate the invisible things of God, namely, his eternal power and Godhead, as the Apostle Paul saith (Romans 1:20). All which things are sufficient to convince men, and to leave them without excuse. Secondly, he makes himself more clearly and fully known to us by his holy and divine Word; that is to say, as far as is necessary for us to know in this life, to his glory and our salvation.[3]

And the seventeenth-century Westminster Confession of Faith begins with the words, "the light of nature and the works of creation and providence manifest the goodness, wisdom, and power of God."[4]

Sir Isaac Newton, whose invention of calculus and breakthrough theories in gravity and optics are still revered and used, is said to have written more about religion than on math and science. His writings clearly reveal that he regarded his seeking for scientific

---

[1] Noll, Mark A. *The Scandal of the Evangelical Mind.* Grand Rapids, MI: William B Eerdmans, 1994. Pg 39.

[2] Hodge, Charles. "The Bible in Science." *New York Observer.* 26 Mar 1863. Pg 98-99. Quoted in Noll, Mark A. *The Scandal of the Evangelical Mind.* Grand Rapids, MI: William B Eerdmans, 1994. Pg 184-185.

[3] Belgic Confession, article 2, Reformed Standards of Unity, 2nd edition. Grand Rapids: Rose, 1952.

[4] Westminster Confession of Faith, Modern English Study Version, 1.1. Accesed 25 Nov 2008 at <http://www.opc.org/documents/MESV_frames.html>.

truth as indivisible from his search, as a devout Christian, for knowledge of God.

French physicist Pierre Simon, the Marquis de Laplace, often referred to as the French Newton, made contributions to celestial mechanics, mathematical physics, and probability theory that are still highly respected, conceived of the possibility of black holes, and, ironically for one who is widely credited with the development of scientific determinism, suggested an interplay of probability and physics that vaguely presaged quantum theory. He clearly had theistic thoughts when he wrote near the turn of the nineteenth century:

> Given for one instant an intelligence which could comprehend all the forces by which nature is animated and the respective situation of the beings who compose it - an intelligence sufficiently vast to submit this data to analysis - it would embrace in the same formula the movements of the greatest bodies of the universe and those of the lightest atom; for it, nothing would be uncertain and the future, as the past, would be present in its eyes. . . All these efforts [of science] in the search for truth tend to lead it back continually to the vast intelligence that we have just mentioned, but from which it will always remain infinitely removed.[1]

Fellow Frenchman Blaise Pascal, whose contributions to mathematics and physics in the seventeenth century are still revered, wrote extensively on Christian theology. After his death, a piece of paper was found sewn into the lining of his coat. The writing that he so treasured was a record of a religious ecstasy, referred to since as Pascal's Memorial:

> The year of grace 1654, Monday, 23 November, . . .
> From about half past ten at night until about half past midnight,
> FIRE.
> GOD of Abraham, GOD of Isaac, GOD of Jacob
> not of the philosophers and of the learned.
> Certitude. Certitude. Feeling. Joy. Peace.
> GOD of Jesus Christ.
> My God and your God.
> Your GOD will be my God.
> Forgetfulness of the world and of everything, except GOD. . . .
> This is eternal life, that they know you, the one true God, and the one that you sent, Jesus Christ.
> Jesus Christ.

---

[1] Laplace, Pierre Simon. *A Philosophical Essay on Probabilities*, translated by F. W. Truscott and F. L. Emory. London: Chapman & Hall, 1902. Pg 4. Accessed 20 Nov 2008 at <http://books.google.com/books?id=WxoPAAAAIAAJ&dq=laplace+essay+on+probabilities&pg=PP1&ots=_L5_GZ5NfK&source=bn&sig=xCFPZsOB85stKAdxhQMo61g3_CY&hl=en&sa=X&oi=book_result&resnum=4&ct=result#PPP5,M1>.

> Jesus Christ. . .
> May I not forget your words. Amen.[1]

Albert Einstein, though untraditional in his religious thinking and rejecting the existence of a personal God, nevertheless famously quipped "I want to know God's thoughts; the rest are details." And in an article in Nature entitled "Science and Religion," he opined, "Science without religion is lame. Religion without science is blind."[2]

Advocates of theistic evolution, from Asa Gray to Theodosius Dobzhansky , Pierre Teilhard de Chardin, George Coyne, Ken Brown, and Francis Collins, all active and publishing research scientists, join many of their colleagues in regarding their exploration of the natural world as a form of worship. Stephen Hawking, wavering as he continues to do between atheism and agnosticism, closed his popular book *A Brief History of Time* with words that seem to betray a certain longing:

> If we do discover a complete theory [unifying physics], . . . [t]hen we shall all, philosophers, scientists, and just ordinary people, be able to take part in the discussion of the question of why it is that we and the universe exist. If we find the answer to that, it would be the ultimate triumph of human reason — for then we would know the mind of God.[3]

The effect of creationism and intelligent design on the nature of God

If science is a window on the mind, character, and nature of God, what effect does the rejection of such a vast body of knowledge as that which supports modern theories of cosmological, geological, and biological evolution have on the perception of God?

A God of deceit

Creationism requires belief in a god that consciously designed his creation to cruelly deceive and mislead the created mind of man in every way.

Young earth creationists would have us believe that God created light from each star and galaxy to be already en route to earth, giving the deliberately false appearance that it had traveled for thousands and millions and billions of years from its source when observed from earth. Alternatively, they propose that the speed of light was several orders of magnitude faster in the past than now, or that the speed of light is inexplicably different in other regions of the universe.

---

[1] Pascal, Blaise. "Pascal's Memorial." Translated by Elizabeth T. Knuth. 1999. Accessed 31 May 2009 at <http://www.users.csbsju.edu/~eknuth/pascal.html#English>.

[2] *Einstein, Albert. "Science and religion". Nature, vol 146 (9 Nov 1940). Pg 605–607.*

[3] Hawking, Stephen W. *A Brief History of Time.* New York: Bantam Books, 1988. Pg 175.

Since time exists as the fourth dimension of the space-time continuum, those arguments are, contrary to the claims of young earth creationists themselves, identical. To look across space is to look across time, since even light takes time to travel. The things we see across the room happened an infinitesimally short period of time before we sensed them, those across a football field a little longer, but still an immeasurably small time. Events on the moon are seen a little more than a second after they happen, events at the surface of the sun around eight minutes later. Light, and therefore sense and knowledge, takes over four years to reach us from the nearest star, Alpha Centauri, and around two million years from the nearest galaxy, Andromeda. There is no reason, beyond the choice of beliefs by those young earth creationists who hold these unsupported hypotheses, that any of the laws of physics or chemistry are different in other parts of the universe, and abundant evidence to the contrary. The fact that spectral bands of the various elements are visible in the light of distant stars means that matter exists there with the same atomic structure as the matter in our portion of the universe, because the spectral bands depend upon the energy status of the electrons of the atom, unique to each element because of the uniqueness of the atomic nuclei that attract the electrons. The fact that the spectral bands and all other forms of radiation are red-shifted by degrees appropriate to their distance from the earth means that Doppler's law, as an example of other physical laws governing energy and mass that can be assessed from across vast reaches of space, holds true at great distances from earth. Every measurement of the nature, path, frequency, direction, and origin of radiant energy from all parts of the universe – the only means of making observations from so great a distance, since the only other material component of the universe is matter - corresponds to those predicted by the laws of physics formulated by observing our region of the universe. All observations of the universe testify to a uniformity of the laws of physics and chemistry, and with that uniformity an immense age.

The falsehoods of God continue, according to creationists, on the earth itself. Some explain the presence of the fossils of extinct organisms as an *in situ* creation by God – that God created the earth's crust with the false evidence of fossils in place. Others claim that all the layers of sedimentary rock ever discovered and examined were deposited in the forty to one hundred days of the Biblical flood, even though many laws of physics would have to be suspended for the deposition of millions of layers of sediment reaching depths of over a mile in so short a time in locations like the Green River formation and the Grand Canyon. Some creationists dispute the validity of radiocarbon dating with spurious pseudo-scientific theories about accelerated and variable rates of decay, and claims that God created rocks of the earth, like the light from stars, in a state that not only falsely indicated their age, but with characteristics that caused the decay series of the several radioactive elements that are measured to falsely corroborate each other.

The theory of intelligent design as promoted by the Discovery Institute, its fellows, and its admirers, requires similar manipulation on the part of a creator. Under that theory, the overwhelming appearance of relatedness among living things, pervasive on the anatomic, genetic, and biochemical levels, was a deliberate creation by their unnamed designer-creator that gives the false appearance of descent with modification. The many transitional species are not transitional at all, but are independent and spontaneous creations designed to give the appearance of transition. Even DNA was designed to give a false appearance of being an agent of inheritance with variability, false because they hold (although the holding has been disproved) that it is incapable of generating and transmitting sufficient information content under their version of information theory.

A persistent proponent of creationism or intelligent design may argue that God in his omnipotence could have chosen to create any or all of these falsehoods according to His sovereign will. Conceding the sovereignty and omnipotence of God, one must then ask for what purpose He would will such, for a will must certainly have a purpose, whether selfish or benevolent. The Judeo-Christian concept of God is of One who is omniscient as well as omnipotent. A God with perfect knowledge and perfect foresight by definition foresaw the development of the human mind, and with it the perceptions of the human mind and the theories that it would derive from the material evidence. Under the theories of creationism and intelligent design, God even created the mind of man in such a way that it would find the false evidence of His creation and lead itself to false conclusions. If the fossil record is untrue, it is an element, along with the apparent age of the universe and the speed of light, the transmission time of light from distant stars and galaxies, the apparent constancy of the Doppler effect, and the presence of background microwave radiation consistent with an initial explosive event at the beginning of time, in a great lie by God, with no apparent purpose other than to crush the faith of men and women who, by using the intellect given them by God, seek to understand Him and His creation. The inescapable conclusion is that the God of creationism and intelligent design created a universe, a planet, and a biosphere knowing that it would mislead and deceive the mind of man, and concurrently created the mind of man to be susceptible to His lies.

Creationists and proponents of intelligent design hold that their theories of origins are the only true interpretation of scripture, and to reject such theories is to reject the very word of God, thereby God Himself, and the availability of forgiveness. They damn evolutionists to eternal punishment by God. The issue of priority of origin theory over salvation through grace will be dealt with a bit later, but even deferring that exploration leaves us with the inevitable conclusion that, in the logic of the opponents of evolution, God provided material evidence that He knew would lead to the damnation of human beings, with perfect knowledge of the consequences.

Does a God who is so bent on deceit that He creates in the universe a great lie, supported as lies so often are by a vast network of smaller lies, retain the moral authority to be the judge of mankind? An earthly judge who exhibited the same disregard for truth would justly suffer impeachment. The author of lies cannot be the ultimate Truth. A creator who deliberately, with perfect foresight, gives mankind both the evidence and the thought processes that lead to his damnation can no longer profess to love mankind as a whole or humans as individuals. Can God be just in condemning humans for merely believing the evidence that He Himself provides? He would have created the mind of man, capable with centuries of observation of comprehending a profoundly powerful and far-reaching set of physical, chemical, and biological laws, only to then confound mankind's mind with a crushing body of evidence specifically designed to lead it to false conclusions. If the purpose of man's creation was to be a companion and worshipper of God, why would God provide such overwhelming evidence that ends in the separation of man from God that is inherent in His condemnation? The creationist or defender of intelligent design who answers blithely that such is the will of the sovereign God that they worship admits that they worship a God of treachery, cruelty, and malevolence rather than the God of love and justice portrayed by Christianity.

An inept designer

Even further problems in the conception of God await opponents of evolution in considering the meaning of extinction. The problem of extinctions became a significant issue in theology when, in the early nineteenth century, mankind began to realize that animals had once existed that are now extinct. How, theologians asked, could a perfect God exercising His perfect judgment in the design and creation of living things, have failed in His design? If a being perfect in knowledge and foresight designed and created every element of the cosmos, the earth, and the biosphere, one could reasonably expect it to be a perfect creation. A perfect creation would not only not need to change, but would prohibit change, because any change from created perfection would be, by definition, an imperfection. If on the other hand one holds that a causal being created and executed an imperfect design, then one has to question the perfection of his knowledge and foresight.

If one accepts the obvious conclusion that the universe, the earth, and the life of earth has changed and continues to change, one must necessarily conclude that any conscious effort at independent design of the elements of creation by an intelligent designer was hesitant, frequently unsuccessful, and, to be honest in one's assessment, bumbling.

If such an assessment seems harsh, consider the evidence in the fossil record. We now understand that approximately four trillion species of living things have existed during the history of the earth.[1] Approximately 1.7 million species are now known and catalogued; estimates of currently surviving species range from two million to a hundred million. If two million species are currently in existence, 0.00005% of the species of living organisms resulting from design have survived; 9,999,995 of every ten million created species were failures and just five succeeded. Using the most generous estimate of a hundred million surviving species improves the success rate of the designer to 0.0025%; still, 999,975 of every million designs have failed and just twenty-five succeeded. If one contests the estimate of the number of species that have existed in the history of earth, and lowers it by a factor of ten, twenty-five out of a hundred thousand species still failed for a success rate of 0.025%.

Aside from the startling lack of survivability of the designed organisms, proponents of design must account for why so many species, genera, and families of organisms were initially so successful, yet became extinct. Dinosaurs were the dominant terrestrial vertebrates for a hundred and sixty million years, then became rapidly extinct just sixty-five million years ago at the K-T boundary. Trilobites were plentiful for a hundred and eighty million years, and then avoided complete extinction for another hundred million years, but they are gone now. Millions and billions of other genera that were less spectacularly successful than dinosaurs and trilobites, from the soft-bodied Vendian ancestors of modern sponges to saber-tooth tigers and mammoths, thrived for their own time before suffering extinction. Paleontologists recognize at least five major extinction events in earth's history, at the end of the Ordovician Period, the late Devonian Period, the end of the Permian Period, the Triassic-Jurassic boundary, and the Cretaceous-Tertiary (Cenozoic) boundary. While the so-called Cambrian Explosion produced the earliest examples of most surviving animal phyla, it also produced many entire phyla that went rapidly extinct. Twenty-first century advocates of creationism and intelligent design must, even more than similar thinkers of the early 1800s, answer how the original designs of an omniscient creator could suffer such a spectacularly high failure rate, and how such enormous numbers of extinctions fit into a creative plan that does not include natural selection.

It is common for intelligent design proponents to answer that plants and animals suffered a sort of reverse evolution from an initial state of created perfection – that they were created in a perfect form, but because of the instability of DNA, degenerated to forms that were unfit and in many cases became extinct. The argument begs the question of why God would then have created a means of inheritance that allowed for variation at all. If a living thing is created perfect, would not any deviation from the original design vary from perfection and be, by definition, imperfect? And if the design carried the inherent potential for variation, and therefore for imperfection, the design

[1] "The Great Tree of Life." *Virtual Fossil Museum.* Undated. VFM. 9 Apr 2008 <http://www.fossilmuseum.net/Tree_of_Life/tree_of_life_home.htm>.

itself could therefore not be considered perfect.

A similar argument is sometimes applied to the existence of intermediate forms and well-delineated lines of descent such as those known for humans and horses. Intermediate forms are said to be degenerations from the more advanced and perfect species. The species *Homo erectus*, *H. habilis*, and *H. ergaster*, and genera such as *Australopithecus* and *Paranthropus* are said to be populations of *H. sapiens* that degenerated in characteristics leading to their extinction, just as the genera identified as ancestors of equines are said to have degenerated from modern horses and zebras to become extinct. In addition to the case that mutability of the genome constitutes an inherent imperfection of design, the temporal relationship of fossil species poses an impassable problem for the argument. The simple finding that, in both cited circumstances and in the paleontologic record in general, the fossils with more primitive features are older than those more advanced belies the theory that the primitive forms are degenerative. Further confounding the argument of degenerative forms is the direction of the branching pattern of descent – degeneration would generate branching forms of degeneration descending from the perfect created form, but what is almost universally observed in the fossil record is a branching genealogy progressing from a primitive form to several successors with more advanced adaptive traits, closer to the modern forms.

The belief that God created each species of living thing independently, regardless of its time frame, necessarily portrays God as being a designer with an extremely poor record, and therefore something far less than omniscient and far less than perfect, in diametric opposition to traditional Christian theology.

A god of stasis

The second theological problem posed by the nineteenth-century recognition of the phenomenon of extinction was that the earth and its residents were changing at all. As naïve as it may sound in the early twenty-first century, the prevailing scientific opinion until the 1800s was that the earth and the cosmos had always existed and were unchanging, as were the flora and fauna that populated the earth. The problem of extinction, and of the parallel recognition of geological changes over time, created the need to explain why a perfect creation would change. The dilemma is similar to that stated with respect to individual animals: if creation as a whole was perfect at its inception, any change would be a corruption of that perfection, and the very capacity for change would be an imperfection.

The problem remains in the arguments of creationists and proponents of intelligent design. The concept of the independent design and creation of the universe, the earth, and each member of the biosphere forces its adherents to make an uncomfortable choice between advocating the existence of an unchanging universe, or admission that their concept of a creator is of a being less than the omniscient God of Judeo-Christian tradition.

An assertion that the earth and the surrounding universe is static, of course, defies both the verifiable observations of science and the experiences of everyday life. The atmosphere of the earth is sufficiently unstable that the weather changes not just with the seasons, but day by day and hour by hour, including such extreme events as thunderstorms, blizzards, floods, tornados, and hurricanes. Erosion, both rapid processes resulting from severe weather events and the slower but still observable effects of wind, rain, flowing water, and waves, alter the contours of beaches, the courses of rivers and the shape of their banks, the distribution of soils, and the shapes, sizes and very existence of dune structures on shorelines and in deserts. Hurricanes and typhoons commonly wash away small islands, split existing islands with new inlets and channels, and create new islands by means of new and altered distribution of sediments and sand bars. On a longer time scale is the common observation that stones large and small are round when exposed to the erosive effects of running water or wave action, but more angular when freshly exposed. It requires only a little attention to news media or mild curiosity during travel to recognize that the face and contours of the earth are changed by earthquakes, that volcanic islands are rising and falling from the sea floor and being augmented and expanded by lava flows, that seashores are altered by tsunamis, and that the size and shapes of mountains continue to change by erosion, by the slow and inexorable motion of tectonic plates, and by the sudden events of volcanic activity with its explosive eruptions, magma extrusions, and ash distribution. The biosphere has been altered in historic times by extinctions, the observed development of new species, and ongoing adaptations such as antibiotic resistance among bacteria.

The observations of experts in various fields of the physical sciences, although second hand to most people, nonetheless verify evidence of changes. Astronomers regularly observe novae and supernovae, and the impact of meteors on planets within the solar system. All observed stars and galaxies are documented to be moving away from the sun and away from each other, leading to the conclusion that the universe is continually expanding. Radioactive decay, resulting in changes in the essential character of the atoms that make up all known matter, is measurable. The chemical and crystalline compositions of the various kinds of metamorphic rocks have, by definition, been changed by immense temperature and pressures of the earth's crusts. The earth's crust bears evidence that layers of sediment have accumulated and been turned to stone; some of those sediment layers bear evidence that the flora, fauna, and climate of earth have changed drastically over the four billion years of its existence. Individuals, species, genera, families, classes, orders, and phyla are born, live, and die, and, under the unusual circumstances required for fossilization, leave their remains in the earth to testify to their existence.

The position that the earth and the universe is in stasis is insupportable without rejecting virtually every finding in every field of science, the reporting of current events in the world's news media, and one's everyday observations of the world around them. Once again, however, the claim that creation was perfect is belied by the very fact that it has the capacity for change; that capacity embodies an inherent defect of design that allows degeneration from perfection, and therefore renders the design itself imperfect. The only alternative within creationism or its surrogate intelligent design to asserting stability of cosmological, geologic, and biological systems, against all observations of science and everyday life, is to admit that creation is an imperfect product of a designer equally imperfect in knowledge and foresight, inconsistent with Judeo-Christian theology.

The limits of God

The God conceived by the doctrine of theistic evolution uses the laws of chemistry, physics, and biology as tools of His creation. In opposing theistic evolution, adherents of creationism and intelligent design proclaim, or at least imply, that God is not capable of having worked by the means known to science.

Man cannot fully know God within the Judeo-Christian system of beliefs. Even were God not a spirit being, beyond the material senses and the probing measurements of scientific instrumentation, the fullness of God cannot be embraced by the human intellect. The mind of One who possesses all knowledge cannot be comprehended by a mind, however well educated, that is finite in its experience and learning. The power of an omnipotent Creator cannot be conceived by a being limited by the abilities of humanity and his inventions. The existence of an I Am who transcends the boundaries of time and space, though time is measured in billions of years and space is ever expanding without apparent limit, cannot be grasped by one created to live in three dimensions for a period measured in years and decades, as a member of a race just a few thousand years old. Because of our limitations, we can know only a portion of the reality of God. The God we know and worship is, then, only a part of the God of Truth, a portion encompassed by the beliefs we choose and the bounds of our minds and our experiences.

The disciplines of modern science can be considered by men and women of faith to be an exploration of that portion of the God of Truth that is material, and therefore observable. The observations and theories of science are, therefore, a part of the knowledge of God - but again only a finite part, both because human knowledge of science is finite, though ever expanding, and because science cannot explore the spiritual dimensions of existence. An infinite One in whom all truth, material and spiritual, is contained is beyond examination and measurement by the tools of science and beyond the comprehension of the mind of man.

Those who deny the principles and underlying observations of celestial, terrestrial, and biological evolution seek, consciously or unconsciously, to worship a god like themselves – finite in intellect, knowledge, capability, and time. On one level, it is easier to think of the creation of stars and planets *ex nihilo* than it is to attempt to comprehend the vastness of space, its inexorable expansion, and the immense but patient forces that cause matter to form first protons, then atoms, then stars and planets. On that same level, it is easier to think of plants and animals as being sculpted and animated in an inventive moment by a divine hand than it is to reflect on the ability of living things to adapt, expand, and develop by means of inheritable variation and selection over countless generations. It is without doubt easier to conceive of a god who has lived and worked for just a few generations of men than to comprehend a God who is outside of space and time itself - One who sees spread before Him the nearly incomprehensible four billion years of the earth's history, the unfathomable fourteen billion years of the universe, and a future of unknowable scale.

To choose such beliefs, however, is to limit the God of one's belief to the boundaries of the mind of the believer. Underlying many, if not all, of the religious arguments against the theories of contemporary science is the difficulty of comprehending the vast scale of time inherent in the action of the theories, as well as the full understanding of the theories themselves. To believe that God can only work by means easily comprehensible to mankind is to deny His omniscience and omnipotence, and to limit His abilities to those of the human mind. Such a god is not God at all, but mankind clothed in a false deity.

The God of theistic evolution

In contrast to the God conceived and characterized by the theory that He created each element of the cosmos *ex nihilo* and each species independently without relationship to or descent from other species, the God envisaged by embracing modern theories of cosmic, geologic, and biological evolution is consistent with the concept of a God that is, in the largest sense, omniscient, as well as unimpeachable in integrity.

The God proposed by advocates of theistic evolution is an intelligent designer, in a sense at once more basic, more profound, and more elegant than that version of intelligent design that insists on the independent creation of species. Those men and women of faith who embrace the wealth of available scientific knowledge and the theories that arise from its thoughtful consideration see God as the Creator of a system of chemical and physical laws governing all aspects of the interactions and conversions of matter and energy. The same laws apply to the matter and energy within living things, with the result that even these, the most complex systems of reactions known, are, within the ever expanding limits of human knowledge, understandable and predictable. The God who created the system of laws created it in such a way that it would fulfill His plan for the development of atoms, stars, planets, life, and a reflective intelligence worthy of communion with Him. The laws of chemistry, physics, and biology, are not hindrances to His creation, but tools of His creation.

The adoption of theistic evolution solves all the problems of creationism and intelligent design in the conception of God.

The God of theistic evolution is no longer a creature of deceit, but one of integrity. The characteristics of God revealed in the words that He inspired in the many authors whose works are now canonical no longer conflict with those characteristics revealed in the "second book" of His creation. The conflict between scripture and science, born not by the actual content of scripture but by a rigid interpretation by man, is fully resolved, and the consistency of truth is restored to the conception of God. The evidence that leads intelligent minds to conceive and support the theories of the Big Bang and biological evolution need not be manipulated into tortured and contrived theories that portray God as the greatest liar in the cosmos.

With the restored honesty of God is a restored benevolence. Where the God of intelligent design seeks to malevolently condemn mankind for believing the evidence of his own eyes, the God of theistic evolution, by maintaining the consistency and integrity of His own testimony, invites mankind to know Him through His words and His works, as proposed in Romans 1.20. With knowledge of the God of theistic evolution comes the opportunity to know His grace and forgiveness rather than an inexplicable and pitiless desire to mislead and condemn.

Under theistic evolution, we can see the perfection of God's plan. Extinctions are no longer evidence of imperfection of design, but are part of a perfect system that led to God's intent of a companionable reflective being. The God of intelligent design, when confronted with the need for a bacterial flagellum, a blood clotting cascade, or an immune system, is forced to intervene and revise His plan in violation of the very laws of nature that are at the heart of His creation, to accommodate that which He did not foresee. The God of theistic evolution, on the other hand, watches contentedly as His plan unfolds, because His plan included a provision for the adaptability of living things (and, as we shall see, a parallel provision for His guidance of their adaptations). A God with perfect foresight and perfect knowledge would not have needed to practice and test designs for structures like spines, jaws, lungs, limbs, and brains. A God who creates a mechanism for the development of those structures regains, in measure greater than even a perfect spontaneous creation without precedent could give, the characteristics of foresight and planning implied by the concepts of omniscience and omnipotence.

With the restoration of God as the ultimate planner comes restoration, missing in the God of intelligent design and creationism, of an intellect of a higher power, superior to the collective intellect of mankind. The mind of God is no longer limited to simple human comprehension. Instead, the mind of man has spent its entire history seeking, with the increasing but still incomplete knowledge and theories of science, to understand the enormity of the intellect of God. If He planned and executed the theistic evolution of everything from the atom to the cosmos, including the evolution of life on at least this one planet, and we humans have spent our entire history striving to understand the means of His creation that are encompassed in the laws of physics, chemistry, and biology, who can be said to have the greater intellect? Magicians can cause objects to appear to vanish and materialize, and although we find entertainment and even amazement in their illusions, they inspire no thoughts of deity and no cause for worship. Is not a God who, with perfect foresight, instituted in the chaos of the Big Bang a system of laws that would take ten to seventeen billion years to fulfill His purpose, more awe-inspiring than one who can only work by making things appear on His whim? A God who had the knowledge and foresight to see that the creation of the rules governing matter and energy could act over lengths of time beyond the concept of any mortal to result in the cosmos, biosphere, intellect, and spirituality of today is infinitely more wise, insightful, and powerful than a God who can only create by miraculous intervention.

An analogy

Consider two homeowners who each decide to build a backyard shed for their lawn mowers and tools. Lou begins by pouring a concrete slab floor, and as he begins building the frames for the walls, he realizes that he needs a means to anchor the walls to the slab. He takes a break from his construction efforts to make a trip to the local home improvement store, purchases the proper hardware, and drills holes in the cured concrete to firmly affix the walls of his shed to the foundation. Tom, too, starts with a slab, but before he pours his concrete, he purchases J-shaped anchor bolts, and he pushes them into the wet concrete at the proper intervals before finishing the concrete surface, so his anchors are ready when he begins framing the walls. Lou frames up his walls and covers them with his chosen siding, then considers that he would like a window over his workbench. He cuts an appropriately sized hole in the siding and the frame members, retrofits the necessary sill, header, and side supports, and installs his window. Tom, on the other hand, anticipates the place where he wants a window, builds the frame of that wall to accommodate the later installation of the window, then completes the siding and installs the window at the site that was prepared according to his blueprint. Lou finishes his roof, then realizes that the shed would be cooler if he put in a ridge vent, so he removes a few rows of shingles, cuts notches in the roof decking, installs the vent, and re-shingles up to the new vent. Tom, of course, includes a ridge vent in his original planning, cuts the roof decking appropriately before he nails it down to the trusses, installs the ridge vent, and then works his way up the roof with tar paper and shingles.

A visitor admiring the finished products might see no substantial difference in the two men's sheds once they are finished and painted. But a friend of both men who has stopped by on frequent Saturday afternoons to check on the construction progress knows that, even though both are equally skilled with tools, Tom is the better planner, and so has built his shed more efficiently, in less time, and quite likely at a bit less expense than has Lou.

Which God is more worthy of respect, awe, and worship – one who works like Lou in constantly altering His creation to make up for His own lack of planning and foresight, or one like Tom who, with thought and care, anticipated every aspect of His creation in His design?

Advocates of creationism and intelligent design wish the world to believe in a God who, after creating a universe and a world governed by laws of physics and chemistry of His own authorship, had to time and again intervene miraculously in a manner inconsistent with His own laws as His plan went awry, in order to create each of the millions of species that inhabit the earth, and each of the billions more that are extinct.

Advocates of theistic evolution wish the world to believe in a God who, with unimaginable planning ability that comes from complete knowledge and perfect wisdom, created a universe and a world governed by laws of physics and chemistry, laws so perfectly formulated that they lead unhindered and unmodified to the creation that He intended, including the origination of a species capable of reflective thought and communion with its Creator.

God as lawgiver

In the book of Revelation, as we have seen, God's role of creator is given as justification for worship and, by implication and by temporal proximity, His role in the coming apocalyptic judgment. The nineteenth Psalm links the dual roles by moving smoothly from the laws governing nature and the knowledge of God to be gained in observing them, to those governing human behavior and the benefits of their obedient observance. It thus proposes that "[n]ature and law are both needed for a full revelation of God."[1]

> The heavens are telling the glory of God;
> and the firmament proclaims his handiwork.
> Day to day pours forth speech,
> and night to night declares knowledge. . . .
> The law of the LORD is perfect,
> reviving the soul;
> The decrees of the LORD are sure,
> making wise the simple;
> The precepts of the LORD are right,
> rejoicing the heart;
> The commandment of the LORD is clear,
> enlightening the eyes;
> The fear of the LORD is pure,
> enduring forever;
> The ordinances of the LORD are true
> and righteous altogether.[2]

The book of Isaiah similarly links creation with forgiveness, and proclaims that salvation and righteousness are a part of God's creation: "Shower, O heavens, from above, and let the skies rain down righteousness; let the earth open, that salvation may spring up, and let it cause righteousness to sprout up also; I the LORD have created it."[3] In the words of a well regarded commentary, "Righteousness and salvation . . . are envisaged as flowing out from God's created order."[4]

The role of God as a giver of natural law is consistent with the first creation story of Genesis, in that God therein creates by bringing order; the establishment of natural laws brings order to the material world. In the same way, and in a continuum of authority within the Hebrew scriptures, God brings order to human society by moral law.

Under theistic evolution, that continuum of authority as a giver of laws is maintained and enhanced. Moral law provided for the survival and advancement of the human race by establishing family units for the nurture and protection of offspring, protecting property rights through entreaties against covetousness, and establishing the foundation for systems of exchange that eventually included contractual arrangements by valuing integrity in word and deed. The codification of ethical behavior by the Hebrews (and

---

[1] Rodd, C. S. "Psalms." *Oxford Bible Commentary.* Oxford: Oxford University Press, 2001. Pg 173.
[2] Psalm 19.1-9. New Revised Standard Version.
[3] Isaiah 45.8, New Revised Standard Version
[4] Coggins, R. "Isaiah." *Oxford Bible Commentary.* Oxford: Oxford University Press, 2001. Pg 471.

other ancient cultures) is an inevitable result of the recognition of these natural moral behaviors, themselves inherent in the evolutionary creative process. The creator God is seen to establish a continuum of natural laws that meld smoothly, as portrayed in Jewish scripture and philosophy, into moral law. Even forgiveness of God, the acceptance of which is essential to both Jewish and Christian concepts of righteousness, is incorporated in the evolutionary plan of creation.

The doctrine of theistic evolution, by maintaining God's role as the ultimate creator (not incidentally regaining the characteristics of omniscience and perfect wisdom), maintains His worthiness as an object of worship and His credentials as the giver and judge of moral and ethical law, whereas within the belief system of creationism God necessarily and frequently takes the corrupting action of violating His own laws, thereby eroding trust in His authority as lawgiver and judge.

The uniqueness of earth

The earth is, within the solar system, uniquely suited to the development of advanced forms of life, chiefly due to the presence of large quantities of water in a liquid state. Venus is thought to have only a small amount of water in an atmosphere otherwise consisting of clouds of sulfuric acid swirling in carbon dioxide, and surface temperatures over 470 degrees Celsius (880 degrees Fahrenheit). The surface of Mars bears evidence of extensive flooding and flowing water at a time three and a half billion years past, but the only water known to exist in the present day is in the form of minute ice crystals mixed in the soil, beginning at depths of about a meter, over the areas of the poles. Europa, one of over sixty moons of Jupiter, is slightly smaller than earth's moon, and is composed like earth of a rock mantle over an iron core. It has enough water to completely cover its surface, but Europa is so far from the sun that the water is perpetually frozen to a depth of several kilometers. Europa's orbit around Jupiter is sufficiently elliptical that the tides resulting from the varying distance from the massive planet churn the water or slush beneath the surface adequately to heat it and keep it at least partially liquid. Other moons of Jupiter - Ganymede and Callisto, for example – have large quantities of solid ice, as do some of the over fifty moons of Saturn. Among the latter, Enceladus is thought to have a thick crust of ice and an underlying slush like Europa; volcanic activity has been observed as the thick sheets of ice composing its crust move, crack, and collide like the stony tectonic plates of earth.[1]

Such observations demonstrate that water molecules are more common, at least in the solar system and probably in the universe at large, than are the conditions under which water can exist in a liquid state in quantities sufficient to allow the development of advanced forms of life. Although we may be blinded by our understanding of the

[1] *Solar System Exploration.* 13 Aug 2008. National Aeronautics and Space Administration. Accessed 2 Nov 2008 at <http://solarsystem.nasa.gov/planets/profile.cfm?Object=SolarSys>.

biology of our planet and ourselves, viable alternatives to carbon-based biochemistry functioning in a hydrated environment have not been demonstrated. It therefore seems likely that the development of complex organisms, especially animals, is limited to sites with large quantities of liquid water and abundant carbon-containing molecules. Although microbial life forms are known to live in extreme environments on earth and may exist on other planets and moons, it is difficult to imagine how complex multicellular organisms would adapt to life in the subterranean icy slush believed to exist on Europa or Enceladus, or in the mixture of soil and ice crystals of Mars. The geologic features of Mars that appear to betray the presence of large quantities of liquid water three and a half billion years ago are the only evidence that such conditions have ever existed within the solar system other than on earth, and although that evidence is intriguing, it is not at all certain that such conditions existed for a sufficient period of time for significant evolution to take place; such questions will probably have to await human exploration of Mars, because paleontological investigations are beyond the current capabilities of robotics, especially given the size limitations imposed by the need for transportation and landing on Mars. If multicellular organisms have existed on Mars at all, it is safe to believe that they were extinct before any similarly complex life arose on earth.

The characteristics of earth that allow the presence of vast quantities of liquid water include not just its relative distance from the sun, but also the velocity of its rotation on its axis. The earth, of course, orbits the sun at a distance that allows temperatures to remain between the freezing and boiling points of water for long periods of time. The rotational velocity is similarly significant, sufficient that the temperature differences between day and night are not too extreme, yet low enough to not substantially counteract the effects of gravity by centripetal force or cause an undue amount of turbulence in the atmosphere. While the earth contains vast bodies of water, portions of the earth of course have dry land. The complex terrestrial environment with its attendant challenges of seeking hospitable dwelling sites, pursuing food, and avoiding predation appear to be an environment in which thought and reasoning are favored, since terrestrial animals (and their descendants who readapted to an aquatic lifestyle) show a pronounced tendency towards brain development. The earth has the right mass (a property that is in turn decided by its density, the highest of any planet in the solar system, and it size) so that its gravity is strong enough to retain its atmosphere but weak enough to allow the development of land animals of sufficient size to carry a brain. The difficulties that would be attendant to a stronger gravitational field are demonstrated by the elephant, which has to have legs so thick as to be unwieldy in order to support its weight. A land animal much heavier than an elephant would have to have legs thicker and wider than its body to support itself and walk.

The elements that make life possible – the iron in the earth's core, the oxygen of the atmosphere, and the carbon whose tetravalent chemistry makes it uniquely suited to forming the variety of bonds that are necessary to biochemistry – are only present after succeeding generations of stars have forged them and distributed them in the massive explosions of supernovae. And while the future course of the universe remains theoretical, most scenarios develop conditions under which planets with the characteristics necessary for life become increasingly less likely. In cosmological terms, the earth exists in a window of time unique in its ability to develop a life-sustaining planet. It may have originated rather early in that window, given the calculated lifespan of stars of sufficient size to produce the heavier elements and the age of the universe; in any event, it has been stable enough for long enough for evolution to produce beings of sufficient intellectual capacity to reflect on their own origins and their relationship to the universe.

It is easy, at first glance, to suppose that there are a myriad of inhabitable worlds among the hundred billion stars in each of the hundred billion galaxies, and yet when one considers all the properties of earth – a solid, dense core; of the right size to retain an atmosphere without a crushing force of gravity; with the right amount of water to be abundant yet not cover the surface entirely; orbiting its star at the right distance to allow the water to be, in large part, in a fluid state; with the right period of rotation so that temperature fluctuations are moderate yet the atmosphere is not unduly turbulent nor the carefully balanced gravity counteracted – one begins to realize that the combination of conditions conducive to the development of sentient beings is imposing and may not be common. In a substantial number of galaxies (elliptical galaxies), the motion of stars is so chaotic that stable planets are unlikely, with any planets present being buffeted by changing gravitational fields and the forces and radiation of colliding stars. Near the center of spiral galaxies, stars are so close together that any surviving planets would be similarly unstable. Among the remaining stars, binary systems are relatively common, presenting complex gravitational fields that may not be conducive to stable planetary orbits. Some stars appear to be orbiting nothing; these are thought to be binary systems one component of which has collapsed into a black hole, presenting even greater challenges to planetary stability.

Only in the outer arms of spiral galaxies is it likely that planets can circle single stars with relative stability. Planets have been detected in the region of a number of stars, however, by the alteration of the star's position by its orbiting planet. Remember that gravity is a force that works in both directions, so a star is attracted to its planet with the same force that a planet is attracted to its star. The motion of stars relative to their planets is most often imperceptible because the enormous mass of the star is not moved substantially by the gravitational force of an ordinary sized planet, but when a planet the size of Jupiter orbits close to a star, the star appears to wobble ever so slightly as the massive planet circles it. In most instances it is this wobble that has been detected in a number of distant stars and leads astronomers to conclude that they have planets; the direct observation of planets is far less common.

While one cannot look up on a starry night and suppose that each of the stars has an earth orbiting it, one can neither be certain that the earth is as unique within the galaxy or the universe as it is within the solar system. The characteristics of earth that make it hospitable to complex multicellular organisms are so specific that they are probably highly unusual, but when one considers the vastness of the known universe, it remains entirely possible that another planet circling one of the billions and billions of stars may have similar conditions.

Whether the earth is unique or merely rare, the system of physiochemical laws that are, in the mind of theistic evolutionists, the governing creation of God, provided at least once for the evolution of a planet with the necessary properties to originate and nurture living things. There remain within those laws mysteries that affect the development and existence of planets, stars, galaxies, and the universe itself. And, as we will see, the most advanced theories of science provide an inherent latitude for God to influence the outcome of events in a manner imperceptible to man and within the boundaries of His natural laws.

Mysteries of creation

The most basic forces of physics have absolute values that are independent of each other and cannot be derived from any currently accepted equation, yet they are so finely tuned that minute changes would make a universe containing life completely impossible. The most familiar forces are gravity and the electromagnetic force that causes like charges to repel each other and opposite charges to attract. Physicists also refer to the strong and weak nuclear forces. The strong force works over very small distances to holds proton and neutrons together to form nuclei of atoms, even though the positive charges of protons would otherwise repel each other and force the nuclei apart. It is the strong nuclear force that is released in nuclear explosions. The weak force is involved in radioactivity and the radioactive decay of nuclei. Some physicists postulate the existence of a fifth force, a repulsive force observable only over immense cosmological distances, referred to by the Greek letter lambda (λ). These values, or more properly the relationships between these values, are the subject of some of the most intense work currently being done in physics.

Gravity is amazingly weak compared to the other primary forces of physics. Electromagnetism is 1,000,000,000,000,000,000,000,000,000,000,000,000 (10^{36})[1] to

[1] Rees, Martin. *Just Six Numbers: The Deep Forces That Shape the Universe.* New York: Perseus Books Group, 2000. Pg 33. Originally published 1999 by Weidenfeld & Nicholson, Great Britain.

1,000,000,000,000,000,000,000,000,000,000,000,000,000,000 (10^{42})[1] as powerful as gravity. We think of gravity as being powerful in everyday life because the force of electromagnetism is neutralized by the balance of electrons and protons in everyday objects, but when we recall how heavy metallic objects can be lifted by magnets of modest size and how powerful electric motors can be in overcoming gravity to lift heavy objects, we gain a clearer perception of the relative power of gravity and electromagnetism. In fact, the only reason that the earth and other heavenly bodies do not completely collapse, taking us and all our possessions with them, is that the electromagnetic repulsion of the electrons in the outer shells of atoms overcomes gravity; electromagnetism is what makes solid objects solid, including the ground we stand on, and thereby keeps us from being drawn all the way to the center of the earth. Since gravity provides the compression that powers the nuclear reactions in stars, including our sun, though, weaker gravity would produce more feeble reactions generating less heat and light, which would in turn limit the size and complexity of the biomass of any life-sustaining planet. Even more dramatically, a slight increase in the force of gravity would cause stars to form, burn out, and collapse more rapidly, not allowing time for the evolution of life.

The strong force of atomic nuclei is equally important and equally sensitive. When two hydrogen atoms fuse into one helium atom, the change in mass is 0.007 percent. Under Einstein's famous equation $E=mc^2$, the change in mass, m, relates directly to the energy released, E, in nuclear reactions. The difference in the masses of two hydrogen nuclei and one helium nucleus, which is represented by ε, is therefore a direct measure of the change in the energy content of the nuclei, and in turn is a measure of the strong nuclear force. If the strong force was weaker by an amount that made ε equal 0.006, fusion of hydrogen to helium would not occur under gravity, stars would not produce heat or light, and the only elements that would exist would by hydrogen along with the small amount of helium and trace amounts of lithium and beryllium that were produced in the Big Bang. If ε was 0.008, all of the hydrogen would have been consumed by the formation of heavier elements in the Big Bang, and there would still be no stars, no light, no heat, and no opportunity for life.[2]

The force of cosmic expansion represented by λ was originally conceived by Albert Einstein to make stable the universe conceived by his equations. At the time, the expansion of the universe had not been recognized – in fact, the universe was believed to contain only the Milky Way galaxy and to be static in size - and Einstein, mindful that gravity would necessarily lead to the collapse of the universe if it was not

---

[1] Greene, Brian. *The Elegant Universe*, 2nd ed. New York: Random House, 2003. Pg 12.

[2] Rees, Martin. *Just Six Numbers: The Deep Forces That Shape the Universe.* New York: Perseus Books Group, 2000. Pg 52-57. Originally published 1999 by Weidenfeld & Nicholson, Great Britain.

counteracted, invented a force, referred to by him as the "cosmological constant," to oppose gravity. When the ongoing expansion of the universe was recognized by the work of Edwin Hubble and others, Einstein renounced his cosmological constant in technical and popular works,[1] and referred to λ as his "biggest blunder."[2] For several decades, the story of Einstein's "blunder" was a cautionary tale told to warn against introducing "fudge factors" into theories and calculations, and a quaint reminder of how even the greatest minds can go astray. In the waning years of the twentieth century, however, astronomers began to report observations of distant supernovae that were consistent with an expansion of the universe that was not decelerating as it would if it was influenced and regulated solely by gravity, but was actually accelerating, and interest in Einstein's cosmologic constant was reawakened. The existence of an antigravity force or dark energy, while not universally accepted pending further observations, is a subject of significant discussion in circles of astrophysicists and astronomers. If the value of λ is not zero, it is small enough to make Einstein's cosmological constant the weakest force of physics and therefore observable only over immense distances of intergalactic space. It has to be minute because if it counteracted gravity too strongly it would prohibit the formation of stars and galaxies, but an absolute value has not been determined.

One of the several difficulties in determining the value of λ is the evidence for a considerable amount of dark matter in the universe. The motion of stars within galaxies and the motion of galaxies relative to each other are not consistent with the gravitational forces that can be calculated from objects visible with telescopes. Stars consistently orbit the centers of their galaxies at speeds notably higher than expected. Stars on the outer edges of our own and other galaxies are moving at speeds that excel the escape velocity for the galaxy unless gravity is stronger than expected. Gravity can only be increased by increases in mass, as far as we know, so the presence of large quantities of matter not observable by telescopes – dark matter in quantities of around ten times the amount of matter thought to exist in stars, planets, and interstellar gas clouds – is inferred. Observations of the gravitational effects of distant galaxies and galaxy clusters on light lead to similar conclusions that their mass is around ten times that expected by the amount of visible matter. Little is certain about dark matter – even its nature is unknown. Brown dwarf stars, planets and comets not in orbit around a star, and black holes could all account for portions of dark matter, but exotic particles of non-atomic matter, including neutrinos and perhaps some undiscovered particles of considerable mass (even atom-sized black holes dispersed widely in space) are thought

---

[1] Einstein, Albert. "Appendix Four: The Structure of Space According to the General Theory of Relativity." *Relativity: The Special and the General Theory,* 15th edition. Authorized translation by Robert W. Lawson. New York: Random House, 1961. Pg 152-154.

[2] Gamow, George. *My World Line.* New York: Viking, 1970. Pg 149. Quoted by Walter Isaacson in *Einstein: His Life and Universe.* New York: Simon & Schuster, 2007. Pg 355-356.

by many physicists to contribute a major portion of the mass of dark matter.[1] What is certain is that dark matter is present in an amount that makes the total mass of the universe very close to that critical mass where the balance is tipped between continued expansion and eventual gravitational collapse. As Cambridge Royal Society Research Professor and Astronomer Royal Sir Martin Rees writes, "[T]he required precision is astonishing: at one second after the Big Bang, Ω [the ratio between the actual mass of the universe and its critical mass] cannot have differed by more than one part in a million billion (one in 10^{15}) in order that the universe should now, after ten billion years, still be expanding and with a value of Ω that has certainly not departed wildly from unity."[2] Dark matter and its interaction with dark energy is currently an area of active research and discussion.

The laws of physics beginning somewhere around a thousandth of a second after the Big Bang are understood with reasonably high confidence, but the earliest events in the first tiny fractions of the first second of time are not understood with certainty, because every particle in the then-existing universe had higher energies than mankind has been able to generate with particle accelerators. We currently have no way of understanding or predicting the initial rate of expansion of the universe, or even why it should expand at all beyond our intuitive suspicion that such a large mass of unstructured matter might be unstable, yet as pointed out by the imminent physicist Stephen Hawking, "If the rate of expansion one second after the big bang had been smaller by even one part in a hundred thousand million million [10^{17}], the universe would have recollapsed before it reached its present size."[3] Similarly, the unevenness of the distribution of matter and energy in the earliest moments of expansion, which produced the gravitational centers that would eventually allow the formation of galaxies, stars, and planets, can be calculated from its results to be about one part in a hundred thousand, but that value likewise cannot be predicted by any current theory.[4] Quantum mechanics predicts that the distribution will be uneven, but not to what degree.

Even the minute mass of the electron is critical, for if electrons were only slightly heavier, they would bind with available protons to form neutrons rather than hydrogen atoms, leaving, within moments of the Big Bang, no fuel for stars and few or no

---

[1] Rees, Martin. *Just Six Numbers: The Deep Forces That Shape the Universe.* New York: Perseus Books Group, 2000. Pg 80-101. Originally published 1999 by Weidenfeld & Nicholson, Great Britain.

[2] Rees, Martin. *Just Six Numbers: The Deep Forces That Shape the Universe.* New York: Perseus Books Group, 2000. Pg 99. Originally published 1999 by Weidenfeld & Nicholson, Great Britain.

[3] Hawking, Stephen W. *A Brief History of Time.* New York: Bantam Books, 1988. Pg 121-122.

[4] Rees, Martin. *Just Six Numbers: The Deep Forces That Shape the Universe.* New York: Perseus Books Group, 2000. Pg 115-129. Originally published 1999 by Weidenfeld & Nicholson, Great Britain.

hydrogen atoms available for fusion into heavier elements.

The universe would be very different from the one we see, and unable to develop or sustain intelligent life, if any of the critical values for the four primary forces, the initial expansion rate after the Big Bang, the degree of unevenness of the distribution of matter and energy, or possibly the expansion constant λ, was not established at its current value within very narrow tolerances. The mysterious exactness of these inexplicable and apparently independent values give theists of all bents cause to contemplate the possibility that they were set by a creator God for the purpose of creating a universe in which contemplative beings can exist.

God of the gaps

Even such contemplation carries risk to the interplay of faith and reason. Some Christians have followed a line of logic, justly derided as "God of the gaps," that identifies as the providence of God anything not understood by science. Evolution could be accepted as a general principle, but gaps in the fossil record proved the action of God. The motion of the stars and planets could be ascribed to gravity, but their creation and existence was inexplicable before the elucidation of the Big Bang Theory, and demonstrated the hand of a Creator. In such a faith, God exists only in the gaps of human knowledge.

The obvious problem in such an understanding of God is that God becomes smaller as human knowledge grows greater. God cannot reside permanently and exclusively in ignorance; the God of theistic evolution can and does revel in the exercise of the human mind that is supported by scripture and tradition and results in progress by mankind in understanding the works and mind of God. Both atheists and thinking Christians, respectively with contempt and sadness, justifiably view a "God of the gaps" approach to a resolution between faith and science as diminishing the personal and cultural perspective of God.

Just as faith cannot be dependent on a false or uninformed premise that the mammalian eye, the bacterial flagellum, or the vertebrate immune system requires the miraculous intervention of God, it likewise cannot be dependent on a hope that the critical values of physics will remain forever independent and inexplicable. Physicists have for several decades sought a unified theory to relate and merge the primary forces of nature. Einstein spent the last twenty years of his life in the unsuccessful pursuit of a theory that would unify gravity and electromagnetism (the only two forces known until the late stage of his career) by reconciling general relativity with quantum mechanics.

The most promising area of research towards a unified theory is thought by many to be string theory. String theory is a complex set of equations requiring at least ten dimensions, and as many as twenty-six.[1] The first of the equations was conceived by Leonhard Euler over two hundred years ago and published by Gabriele Venazia in the late 1960s when he realized that it described the strong nuclear force. Mathematicians and theoretical physicists intermittently toyed with the equations until Leonard Susskind became the first to describe the equations in terms of strings, or strands. Interest in string equations was intensified by the realization by John Schwartz that a description of gravity was also present in the equations. The understanding of black holes and the Big Bang singularity had been limited in no small part by the problem that they are at once small, requiring consideration of quantum mechanics, and massive, requiring consideration of general relativity; general relativity and quantum mechanics contradict each other and produce irresolvable anomalies at such points. The development of equations that described both the strong nuclear force acting in the quantum realm and gravity acting in the relativistic realm meant that they held promise for resolving the conflicts between the two major theory sets, and string theory continued to develop in the hands of many theoreticians, including such luminaries as Michael Green, who was instrumental in unifying particles and forces under string theory.

Strings themselves are mathematical constructions representing submicroscopic, almost infinitesimal, strands of energy that take on the characteristics of each of the basic particles and fundamental forces by vibrating in different ways. The dimensions of string equations include the three bidirectional spatial dimensions, the unidirectional time dimension that itself requires the use of imaginary numbers under relativity, and at least six more dimensions. The extra dimensions are spoken of as being "rolled up" or "curled up," in a manner perhaps not terribly unlike the intense curvature of the other four dimensions in the regions of black holes and at the initial singularity of the Big Bang, into a form not recognizable by common observation from a universe of three spatial dimensions. As string theory developed, five major versions emerged that differ mathematically and occasionally contradict each other in their details, such as whether strings are open-ended or closed loops. In 1995 Edward Witten of the Institute for Advanced Study (the home of Einstein in the last decades of his life), introduced M theory, which unifies and incorporates the five major string theories by introducing an eleventh dimension to the ten of most previous versions of string theory.[2, 3, 4] M theory considers the strings of the five basic string theories to be cross-sections of

---

[1] Hawking, Stephen, with Leonard Mlodinow. *A Briefer History of Time.* New York: Random House, 2005. Pg 117-137.

[2] Witten, Edward. "Unraveling string theory." *Nature,* vol 438, no 2, 29 Dec 2005. Accessed 13 Nov 2008 at <http://www.sns.ias.edu/~witten/papers/Unravelling.pdf>.

[3] Witten, Edward. "Universe on a string." *Astronomy,* June 2002, pg 42-47. Accessed 13 Nov 2008 at <http://www.sns.ias.edu/~witten/papers/string.pdf>.

[4] Hawking, Stephen, and Leonard Mlodinow. *A Briefer History of Time.* New York: Random House, 2005. Pg 117-137.

membranes; each of the five theories works because each examines different cross-sections of the membranes of M theory.

String theory, primarily in the form of M theory, continues to develop as an undertaking of mathematics without physical confirmation. Proposals for experimental testing in ten and eleven dimensions have so far been lacking, and string theory has been heavily criticized by its detractors for developing no testable predictions. Its proponents nonetheless see in it an elegance in uniting theories and values that were previously frustratingly independent and contradictory, and hold hope that string theory may yet be the single unifying theory of physics. A leading string theorist wrote of his field that it is "not . . . a theory that has been completely worked out, confirmed by vigorous experimental tests, and fully accepted by the scientific community. . . [S]tring theory is such a deep and sophisticated theoretical structure that even with the impressive progress that has been made over the last two decades, we still have far to go before we can claim to have achieved full mastery."[1]

The mathematics of string theory, incorporating as it does multiple dimensions, opens the possibility of other universes existing in other sets of dimensions. There is mathematical support for the possibility that Big Bangs occur within black holes, originating other universes obscured from our view by the event horizon surrounding the singularity. It is not clear what other universes may look like if they exist. Would other dimensions be uncurled? Might more than four dimensions uncurl in some universes? If so, the extra dimensions would lead to such extreme instability in the primary forces that neither atoms nor stars would be stable.[2] If time is a dimension that remains curled up in another universe, might an intelligent resident of that universe see all of the events in that universe concurrently, in a manner similar to that in which the Judeo-Christian God is said to transcend time? Might other sets of dimensions, combined with such a non-functioning dimension of time, have properties that allow a resident there to see and perhaps even influence events in the dimensions of our universe in unseen ways? Would not such a being have, then, all the qualities that Judeo-Christian theology attributes to God?

The support for such conjecture about multiple universes, like that for string theory that gives it sustenance, is mathematical rather than experimental or observational. Whether string theory develops into the long-sought unifying theory of physics, becomes yet another step in the process of approaching that unity, or turns out to be an extremely advanced mathematical wild goose chase remains to be seen. Since the speculated parallel universes are beyond the event horizons of black holes, there is an

---

[1] Greene, Brian. *The Elegant Universe* 2nd ed. New York: Random House, 2003. Pg 18.
[2] Hawking, Stephen, and Leonard Mlodinow. *A Briefer History of Time.* New York: Random House, 2005. Pg 131-132.

inherent difficulty – by current standards and means, an inherent impossibility – in confirming or denying their existence. String theory itself is presently beyond proof or falsification for similar reasons. The singularities of black holes demonstrate the essential dichotomy of physicists in considering string theory: on one hand, proponents are encouraged that the mathematics remain without anomalies where other theories have broken down or been found incompatible; but on the other hand, detractors point out that the predictions made by string theory are beyond the event horizon and therefore unverifiable. Although the eventual detection of certain particles by large particle accelerators that are, at this writing, nearing completion, may be consistent with string theory, it is not clear that string theory is the only explanation for those particles, or that their detection will mean that any more than a narrow portion of string theory is correct in describing actual physical phenomenon. Conversely, the lack of detection of the predicted particles does not doom string theory, because it may mean nothing more than that our technology is not as good as we think it is at generating or detecting the particles.

In no case is the faith of a believer threatened by string theory, or by the Big Bang, biological evolution, or any other development of science if the believer includes in his or her concept of God that He is the creator of all the marvels that science discovers and explains. If string theory is one day confirmed and accepted by physicists, any debased sense of awe at the precision of the fundamental values of the universe may justly be replaced by what may perhaps be a deeper sense of awe that all of the particles and forces of the universe could originate from the same building blocks, that the very nature of their existence could generate that precision of interrelated values, and that they could contain within the infinitesimal such enormous complexity, existing as they do in their multiplicity of dimensions. It will, after all, have taken the best minds of mankind all of the history of the species to discern and delineate the concept underlying the structure of a universe created by God, a creation foreseen by Him over a period exceeding ten billion years to have led to our comprehension of His work.

The life and death of scientific determinism

As ambitious as is the current search for an all-encompassing unified theory, such a quest is modest compared to earlier goals of science. Beginning in the late eighteenth century, prominent scientists and philosophers, including most famously Pierre Simon, the Marquis de Laplace, held that all future events could be calculated and predicted given knowledge of the state of everything at any given moment and an understanding of the laws governing them. In today's terms, the doctrine of scientific determinism maintains that if the location and velocity of each particle of matter and each quantum of energy could be known, the laws of science, if fully understood, could calculate every future event between them, and therefore predict the future course of stars, planets, living things, and even the thoughts and decisions of each human mind.

The necessary theological consequence of scientific determinism is clear: a universe governed by immutable laws leaves no room for action or intervention of a deity. A deterministic world is necessarily either atheistic or deistic, and deism was in fact a popular religious philosophy of the eighteenth century, ascribed to by many of the American founding fathers: Thomas Paine, Benjamin Franklin, John Adams, Thomas Jefferson, and by some accounts, George Washington. Deism holds that a creator God set in motion the physical universe and observes it without interference; miracles and scriptural revelations are rejected, but the value of ethical behavior and repentance is maintained. Prayer for the intercession of God in the physical universe is anathema to deism and to scientific determinism; at their greatest extremes, both would hold that even a prayer of repentance is an act foreordained by the chemistry and physics of the brain.

Judeo-Christian theology rejects deism on a number of grounds, not the least of which is that intercessory prayer – prayer by the faithful to God asking for His intervention in the world, in such diverse forms as protection from a perceived threat, the healing of physical ailments, providing for temporal needs, or influencing the thoughts and actions of others – is the subject of instruction and confirmation, in the form of stories of affirmative and frequently miraculous answer to such prayers, in both the Old and New Testaments. Among the former are passages such as Psalm 102.17 ("He will regard the prayer of the destitute, and will not despise their prayer."), Proverbs 15.8 ("The sacrifice of the wicked is an abomination to the Lord, but the prayer of the upright is his delight."), the words of Jesus in Matthew 21.22 ("Whatever you ask for in prayer with faith, you will receive.") and Mark 11.24 ("So I tell you, whatever you ask for in prayer, believe that you have received it, and it will be yours."), portions of epistles to the Romans (12.12) and the Philippians (4.6), and the letter to Jewish Christians attributed to the apostle James (James 5.15-16: "The prayer of faith will save the sick, and the Lord will raise them up; and anyone who has committed sins will be forgiven. Therefore confess your sins to one another, and pray for one another, so that you may be healed. The prayer of the righteous is powerful and effective."). (All quotes are from the New Revised Standard Version.) Examples of answered prayers are many and often miraculous. The prophet Elijah defeated four hundred and fifty prophets of Baal by challenging them to have their god accept their sacrifice via fire induced by prayer, mocked their failure, and then successfully prayed for fire from YHWH to consume his own water-soaked sacrifice.[1] In the New Testament, the prayers of Jesus were answered in healings and in the raising of Lazarus,[2] and His disciples continued to perform miracles through prayer in the book of Acts.[3] Determinism and deism rejects any intervention by God in the material universe,

[1] 1st Kings 18.20-40.

[2] John 11.1-44.

[3] Acts 3.1-10, 5.12-16, 8.13, 9.32-41, 13.6-12, 14.8-10.

whether induced by prayer or His sovereign will.

Judeo-Christian thought correctly rejected determinism, but often for incorrect reasons. Many in the Christian community felt it necessary to reject science and scientific theory to preserve their theology. In reality, science itself, in the twentieth century, provided its own defeat of determinism, on three valid grounds: the lack of sufficient computing power to make meaningful predictions, and the related discoveries of quantum mechanics and the uncertainty principle. Few theologians, authors, or pastors in the Christian community seem to have understood the theological implications of these three pillars of the demise of determinism.

The first failure of determinism is the astounding complexity of the calculations necessary to make the most basic predictions. Stephen Hawking, the preeminent physicist, states that "in practice, we cannot solve the equations for any atom besides the simplest one, hydrogen, which has only one electron, and we use approximations and computers to analyze more complicated atoms and molecules."[1] There are on the order of 10^{78} atoms in the observed universe, with most being hydrogen atoms in stars,[2] but larger atoms and the molecules of which they are a part increase the complexity of such calculations exponentially. Glucose ($C_6H_{12}O_6$) has ninety-six electrons interacting with twenty-four nuclei composed of a total of ninety-six protons and eighty-four neutrons; the calculations of the exact state of all the components of this quite simple organic molecule are beyond comprehension. The simplest living cell contains millions of molecules, many of them far more complex than glucose. Vertebrates contain billions of cells, each interacting with each other based on the chemical properties of their components. The technology to perform the calculations necessary to fully predict the performance of even a single cell has not even been imagined.

The human body is said to contain around one hundred trillion (100,000,000,000,0000) cells.[3] The human population of earth is 6.7 billion (6,700,000,000). The biosphere, of course contains not just humans, but every living species. A human body, like those of most mammals, contains a population of microbes larger than the census of host cells. When one considers the earth's population of plants and animals ranging from the simplest green algae and sponges to flowering plants, trees, and the modern reptiles and mammals that inhabit the planet, as well as the immeasurable population of microbes, the complexity of the interactions of each with each other and their environment is

---

[1] Hawking, Stephen, and Leonard Mlodinow. *A Briefer History of Time.* New York: Random House, 2005. Pg 100-101.

[2] Rees, Martin. *Just Six Numbers: The Deep Forces That Shape the Universe.* New York: Perseus, 2000. Pg 94.

[3] *The Nobel Prize for Physiology or Medicine 2001.* 8 Oct 2001. Nobel Foundation. 2 May 2008. <http://nobelprize.org/nobel_prizes/medicine/laureates/2001/press.html>.

unfathomable. Characterizing and calculating the effect of each of the interactions between the component cells and molecules of this multitude of organisms would appear to be impossible.

Judeo-Christianity in general, and Christian evangelicalism in particular, has largely failed to realize the significance of this point. The calculations required to predict the workings of an infinitesimal part of the universe for a fraction of a second are beyond the capabilities or even the imagination of man's most creative minds and most advanced technology. The conclusion is inevitable that the intellect of a Judeo-Christian God who created by means of theistic evolution, who could not only foresee all of the physiochemical events of the universe for a period of at least ten billion years, but plan the laws governing matter and energy to achieve a desired end, must be an intellect itself beyond human comprehension. The knowledge of the enormity of God is expanded by endorsing the findings of science.

Even considering the complexity of the interactions between 10^{78} atoms, it remains that a deistic God of inconceivable intellectual and computational capacity could have planned and created a universe governed by His own laws which was fully deterministic while still remaining beyond the finite ability of mankind to calculate the enormous multiplicity of exchanges and relations between matter and energy. Such a universe, because of its determinism, would have no role for God except that of a spectator.

The theory of quantum mechanics and its component uncertainty principle, however, spelled the death of scientific determinism, and by doing so provided a means within the laws of science for the ongoing activity of a non-deistic God.

Quantum mechanics arose from the early work of Albert Einstein, much to his later discomfort. His famous creative flurry of 1905, which included the special theory of relativity, also included a less celebrated but by many measures equally important paper in which he built on the work of Max Planck to propose that electromagnetic energy, including light, existed in discrete packets, or quanta, later called photons. The existence of photons caused light and other radiation to behave with particulate characteristics that complemented the classic wave characteristics that were at the time more well defined. Neils Bohr, in his turn, built on the 1905 paper of Einstein by discerning that the existence of irreducible quanta of energy meant that the electrons orbiting the nuclei of atoms could exist only in energetic states corresponding to those quanta, and proposed the existence of electron shells that remain central to chemistry. (To understand the genius of this work, it should be recalled that the very existence of atoms was at the time not universally accepted.) In defining the structure of atoms, though, Bohr's work included the disquieting conclusion that, although electrons could reach a higher energy state by absorbing a photon and a lower state by emitting one, the time and direction of photon emission could not be predicted; an absolute prediction was replaced by a probability formula.

The wave/particle duality of light is easy to perceive: its existence in the quantum packets of photons is particle-like in character, and the variation of wavelengths that is perceived as colors is a property of a wave. The effects of such a dual nature become a bit disconcerting in considering units of matter that had been more traditionally considered particles, however, as demonstrated by the classic two-slit experiment, the results of which have been so comprehensively addressed by physicist and author Richard Feynman that the demonstration itself is sometimes referred to as the Feynman experiment.

If a light with a single wavelength is shined on a partition with a slit, an image of the slit will, to no one's astonishment, appear on a screen behind the partition. When the experimenter opens a second slit in the partition parallel to the first, however, the result is a bit of a surprise: not the image of two slits, but an alternating series of light and dark bands fading into each other, with the center bands more intense and the outer bands growing fainter and wider.

The surprising pattern of bands occurs because of the wave nature of light. When the peaks of waves coincide with each other, they are said to be "in phase" and they enhance each other. When the peak of one wave overlaps the trough of another, they cancel each other out. The distance from each of the slits to each point on the screen behind varies slightly, so the light waves passing through the two slits are in phase at some points on the screen, creating light bands, and out of phase in others, creating dark bands. The bands fade into each other and repeat as the waves transition gradually from being in phase to out of phase and back again.

Once the pattern is understood, it is easy to accept the banding pattern as a property of the wave character of light. It is a bit disconcerting to know that the same banding pattern appears when photons are sent through the slits one at a time, but the wave nature of light is so well accepted that seeing an interference pattern under those conditions does not greatly disturb our intuition. When electron beams are projected through similar slits onto detector plates, however, a more remarkable result is obtained: the interference pattern of alternating bands appears, confirming that electrons have a wave component of their nature, even though they are commonly thought of as particles and have a small but demonstrable mass. An even more unsettling observation is made when electrons are sent towards the slits one at a time: they continue to produce the banded pattern of wave interference. A single electron is thus demonstrated to have passed through both slits at once, and its waves to interfere with each other. Clearly, the wave/particle duality of quantum mechanics is confirmed with respect to electrons, and the position or path of a single electron at any moment cannot be ascertained. Instead of absolute positions, physicists find that they must speak of the position of subatomic particles in terms of probability. Minute particles like electrons and photons are regarded as following all possible paths at once in accordance with their wave characteristics, and their waves as corresponding to the probabilities of various paths.

Quantum mechanics recognizes a wave/particle duality in all matter and energy. The duality of electrons and photons is demonstrable, and similar dualities are perceived for gravitons carrying the force of gravity (not yet detected experimentally, perhaps because gravity is so weak relative to other forces), gluons carrying the strong nuclear force, and weak gauge bosons, with small but detectable masses, carrying the weak nuclear force. Quantum mechanics becomes progressively less significant in the macroscopic world as mass increases, because wavelength is inversely proportional to mass. Billiards is a game of particle interaction, and it remains a game of skill rather than chance because the mass of a billiard ball particle is sufficient to make its wave one of extremely short wavelength and low amplitude, so that the courses of the balls and the results of their interactions with each other and the cushions is limited only by the player's proficiency in planning and executing their interaction.

On the level of atoms and subatomic particles, quantum mechanics predominates. The movements and actions of such particles are predictable as averages and probabilities applied over large populations, but the course of an individual particle is not predictable. Human prediction of the status of such particles is further frustrated by a component of quantum mechanics called the Heisenberg uncertainty principle, after physicist Werner Heisenberg, the associate of Neils Bohr who first thoroughly elucidated it. The uncertainty principle acknowledges that, by the very act of measuring, we interfere with the object of our measurements and cause inherent inaccuracies in our own measurements.

To understand this principle, consider the problem of measuring the diameter of an inflated balloon. One may begin by laying the balloon down on a ruler. The person doing the measurement may close one eye and squint while trying to line up one edge of the balloon, then move to the other side of the balloon and attempt the same measurement, intending to subtract one value from the other, but one quickly realizes air currents, including those generated by the person doing the measurement moving from one side of the balloon to the other, will change the position of the balloon relative to the ruler. One can, of course, hold the balloon down against the ruler, but pressing down on the balloon widens it and changes the very measurement the operator intends. Using tape to fix the balloon to the ruler similarly distorts it, even if only slightly, and similarly changes the diameter. Calipers may improve the measurement, but they cannot give a perfect measurement either, because the operator has to either read the measurement just before it touches the balloon, or tighten the caliper until it evidences contact by indenting the balloon perceptibly; neither results in a completely accurate measurement. One could even argue that, even if the measurement instruments are sufficiently accurate, handling the balloon in the act of measuring it causes it to lose a minute amount of air, itself resulting in a change in the measurement of its diameter.

If the accurate measurement of the diameter of a balloon begins to seem daunting, consider the measurement of the position and velocity of an electron. The mass of an electron is so small that the impact of a single photon of light, necessary to its observation, changes its velocity. As a matter of fact, in the two-slit experiment, whenever a detector of either electrons or photons is installed in one of the slits to determine whether the projected element is in fact passing through that slit, the wave interference pattern disappears, a casualty of the interaction between photon or electron and its detecting apparatus. It can be proven mathematically that increasing the accuracy in the measurement of the position of a particle decreases the accuracy of the measurement of its velocity, and vice versa. The essential components of any motion, position and velocity, can never both be measured with complete accuracy for the same object.

The net effect of quantum mechanics and its subsidiary uncertainty principle is that the position and velocity of small particles like electrons cannot be measured and their future course cannot be predicted with certainty. Determinism, in the absence of either a reliable measurement of the beginning status of a particle or an absolutely defined future course, cannot be supported.

Quantum mechanics and matter

Given that the positions and velocities of electrons, being governed by the indeterminate laws of quantum mechanics, are not individually predictable, and that the interaction of electrons with the nuclei of atoms is the basis for chemical reactions and the stability of atoms and molecules, it follows that there is no certainty that any one atom will interact with others in its neighborhood in any one particular or predictable way.

It is commonly known that water is a liquid between its freezing point of 0 centigrade or 32 Fahrenheit degrees and its boiling point of 100 centigrade or 212 Fahrenheit degrees. While we know that this is generally true, we also know that small amounts of water evaporate at temperatures far less than the boiling point – washed dishes dry in a drying rack, and clothes can be dried on clotheslines. Evaporation, or drying, is the same process as boiling, in that individual water molecules gain enough kinetic energy to leave the liquid state and enter the gaseous state of steam. When those molecules evaporate in an unrestricted space, we lose track of them, but if we put plastic wrap over a glass of water at room temperature, we soon see that those same water molecules are just as capable of losing energy and returning to a liquid state, as evidenced by the condensation that is visible on the underside of the plastic wrap.

One milliliter (or cubic centimeter) of pure water has a mass of one gram and contains 3.348×10^{22} (33,480,000,000,000,000,000,000) water molecules. That or any population of water molecules will, as a group, behave in predictable ways; the evaporation rate and the ratio of molecules that exist in the liquid versus the gaseous state can be calculated as long as such variables as temperature and surface area are known. But the behavior and fate of any one of that multitude of molecules can be neither predicted nor measured. The very light that our eyes sense in observing the water sample is energy, and the energy of light may or may not be absorbed by the molecule of water that we choose to observe and thereby increase its motion, or energy status, and thus cause it to move from the liquid to the gaseous state, in accordance with the uncertainty principle. Quantum mechanics recognizes that we cannot foresee which if any among the thirty-three thousand billion billion molecules in that small amount of water will absorb and become energized by any particular photon, be it a photon of light or of electromagnetic radiation of other wavelengths, or when any given molecule may interact with a photon to reach the threshold that causes it to be transformed from the liquid to the gaseous state. Similarly, the fate of an evaporated molecule cannot be predicted – there is nothing but a set of probabilities to determine whether it resides at any given moment in one corner of the room or another, or when it will return to the less energetic state defined as water.

Since the interactions of electrons with each other and with atomic nuclei determine the stability and interactions of atoms and molecules, chemical reactions are similarly subject to quantum mechanics. Large populations of atoms and molecules react in a manner that is predictable in terms of ratios and probabilities, but the actions of individual atoms and molecules cannot be forecast. Chemical reactions are properly seen as being states of equilibrium in which individual atoms move in and out of chemical bonds in proportions that are specific to the chemical formula and dependent on the conformation of electrons of the component atoms; the status of any particular atom in that equilibrium cannot be discerned or predicted any more than can the phase status of any given molecule in a milliliter of water.

Every object we see in the world around us is composed of atoms and molecules with various degrees of stability, and every process we see is composed of chemical reactions. Biological functions are chemical equilibria governed by the laws of quantum mechanics; at their most complex they are composed of layer upon layer of biochemical reactions occurring both sequentially and concurrently, but each individual reaction is still ruled by the laws of chemistry and physics. The forces that match DNA base pairs to their mirror image during the duplication and transcription processes are weak chemical bonds governed by physiochemical laws. When DNA is altered by base substitution, frame shifts, duplication, transposition, reversal, or deletion, the resulting mutation is nothing more or less than the application of quantum mechanics to one or more steps in the complex biochemical process of DNA strand duplication. Each of the multitude of chemical reactions inherent in DNA duplication is governed not by an absolute outcome that would prohibit variation through mutation, but by a set of probabilities attached to every possible outcome. For each reaction, every result is possible; accurate reproduction of any given segment of DNA is the most probable outcome, but each kind of mutation is possible and occurs with certain frequencies governed by quantum mechanics.

The development of quantum mechanics meant the end of determinism, a development that was not accepted by Albert Einstein even though quantum mechanics was an outgrowth of his own theories. In the last thirty years of his life, Einstein spent any time not devoted to his unrequited quest for a unified theory inventing arguments against the indeterminate results of quantum mechanics. His famous retort against the uncertainty of quantum mechanics was "God does not play dice." (Einstein's lifelong friend and intellectual sparring partner Neils Bohr is said to have answered on at least one occasion, tongue no doubt planted firmly in cheek, "Einstein, stop telling God what to do!") Einstein's sense of order was offended by the failure of determinism, and he could not free his mind of the concept. Since the ultimate goal of a unified theory is to find a resolution between general relativity and quantum mechanics in accounting for all the primary forces, it may be that his failure to embrace quantum mechanics hindered his approach to a unified theory.

Quantum mechanics and theology

Although it has not been widely appreciated within the faith community, the falsification of determinism that disquieted Einstein's concept of God is a boon to traditional Judeo-Christian theology.

The God to whom Einstein made obeisance was the result of a meld of deism and pantheism. Like many in the modern age, Einstein thought of God as an impersonal creator who inhabits his own creation, but does nothing to influence it. For those who believe in that manner, God is largely encompassed in a sense of order, and order is central to whatever awe they feel and whatever worship they contemplate. In such a belief system, indeterminism means randomness, which in turn implies a lack of purpose; hence Einstein's protest that "God does not play dice."

The consequences of indeterminism to conventional theology are quite different, however. The indeterminate outcomes of quantum mechanics provide room within the exactness of scientific theory for God to wield an unseen hand in shaping events in the universe of His creation. The thoughtful theist allows that, contrary to Einstein's favorite remonstration, God does play dice, and that the He chooses moments to bend the rolls to His purposes.

Quantum mechanics demonstrates that the most basic building blocks of the universe – electrons, quarks, and the primary forces of physics – move and interact in ways that can be neither measured nor predicted. Probabilities rather than absolute outcomes govern every interaction of matter and energy, every basal element of the material universe. It is an essential characteristic of creation that every outcome is possible, and among the untold billions and billions of interactions that make up even the simplest event, even the most wildly improbable will occasionally occur.

In a universe governed by probabilities, it is just possible that a planet, having condensed at the right time in the development of the cosmos to be rich in water and carbon-based molecules, could be at the right distance from its star to keep the water in a liquid state over much of its surface, and be of the correct size and density that its gravity could retain an oxygen-rich atmosphere without crushing living inhabitants beyond the miniscule.

In a world governed by probabilities, it is possible, even if unlikely, that organic chemicals could form primitive amalgams that reproduced themselves and, by so doing become subject to natural selection and establish the roots of a biosphere.

Within living things governed by probabilities, any mutation is possible. In the same way that the behavior of a population of water molecules is predictable given such factors as temperature and surface area, genetic mutations occur at a relatively predictable rate given such factors as generation times and the exposure to electromagnetic radiation. But in the same way, too, that the fate of a single water molecule cannot be predicted, we cannot predict what mutations will occur at what site in a genome. Mutations good and ill can be sorted by the probability of their own survival, and the evolutionary development of living things can occur in a universe governed by probabilities.

Quantum mechanics insists that every outcome is possible, even the improbable. At every event, the God conceptualized by Judeo-Christian tradition can influence the observed outcome within the realm of possibilities described by quantum mechanics and, without violating the physical laws He authored, exercise His sovereign will in the material universe. The creation of God is found to contain in its very fabric a degree of uncertainty that allows Him to guide it with His unseen hand, while still preserving the free will of mankind to choose or deny belief in Him.

The impact of quantum theory on the religious debate about evolution was elucidated by Kenneth Miller in *Finding Darwin's God*:

> Remarkably, what the critics of evolution consistently fail to see is that the very indeterminacy they misconstrue as randomness has to be, by any definition, a key feature of the mind of God. Remember, there is one (and only one) alternative to unpredictability – and that alternative is a strict, predictable determinism. The only alternative to what they describe as randomness would be a nonrandom universe of clockwork mechanisms that would also rule out active intervention by any supreme Deity. Caught between these two alternatives, they fail to see that the one more consistent with their religious beliefs is actually the mainstream scientific view linking evolution with the quantum reality of the physical sciences.[1]

Since quantum mechanics provides the necessary uncertainty within which God can exert undetected influence, prayer is no longer an ineffectual murmuring against deterministic fate; rather, it is an entreaty for God to affect a desired outcome from among the realm of probabilities available under His laws of physics. Miracles are believable as the realization of outcomes that are among the least likely of a multitude of probabilities. The Judeo-Christian God, by including uncertainty in the laws that govern His creation, dealt determinism a fatal blow and preserved His own capacity to work His will and answer prayers, while keeping His own existence beyond proof and therefore in the realm of faith. The sovereignty of God remains unchallenged by science, because although the outcomes of the most basic material events are uncertain to the mind of man, God can both foresee and affect every event. In the prescient words of the seventeenth-century Westminster Confession of Faith, "In his sight all things are open and manifest; his knowledge is infinite, infallible, and independent of his creatures; so that nothing to him is contingent or uncertain."[2]

Science and God

The renowned and prolific Christian apologist C. S. Lewis wrote,

> As far as I understand the matter, Christianity is not wedded to an anthropocentric view of the universe as a whole. The first chapters of Genesis, no doubt, give the story of creation in the form of a folk-tale – a fact recognized as early as the time of St. Jerome – and if you take them alone you might get that impression. But it is not confirmed by the Bible as a whole. . . We are in no position to draw up maps of God's psychology, and prescribe limits to His interests. . . . The doctrines that God is love and that He delights in men, are positive doctrines, not limiting doctrines. He is not less than this. What more He may be, we do not know; we know only that He must be more than we can conceive. It is to be expected that His creation should be, in the

---

[1] Miller, Kenneth R. *Finding Darwin's God.* New York: Harper Collins, 1999. Pg 213.

[2] Westminster Confession of Faith, Modern English Study Version, 2.2. Accessed 25 Nov 2008 at <http://www.opc.org/documents/MESV_frames.html>.

> main, unintelligible to us.[1]

An informed understanding of scripture and the facts and theories of science finds the two testimonies of God's nature to be essentially compatible, as indeed they must be if God is to be the God of Truth. An event in the Gospel of Matthew[2] records that Jesus Himself regarded the scriptures to be specific to context and situational in nature. In the course of tempting Jesus to demonstrate His deity by throwing Himself from the top of the temple, Satan quoted Psalm 91.11-12: "He will command his angels concerning you to guard you in all your ways. On their hands they will bear you up, so that you will not dash your foot against a stone." Jesus replied by quoting Deuteronomy 6.16, "Do not put the LORD your God to the test," simultaneously rejecting the inappropriate use and interpretation of scripture to justify irrational actions and arguments, and confirming the value of its guidance when interpreted with appropriate contextual sensitivity. Jesus did not reject Satan's quotation as untrue, but as inapplicable to the moment, and countered by arguing the larger principle of the sovereignty of God.

The collective mind of man has made enormous progress in the last few centuries in the quest to understand the universe around us so that it is ever less unintelligible. The believer in theistic evolution can justifiably argue the larger principle of unity between the revelation of God in scripture and that contained in the consistent and overwhelming evidence present in God's creation in support of the modern insights of science. It is perhaps somewhat ironic that the agnostic Stephen Hawking so accurately captured the mindset of theistic evolutionists:

> Some people . . . regard the question of the initial situation [of the universe] as a matter for metaphysics or religion. They would say that God, being omnipotent, could have started the universe off any way He wanted. That may be so, but in that case God also could have made it develop in a completely arbitrary way. Yet it appears that God chose to make it evolve in a very regular way, according to certain laws.[3]

God in His transcendence saw in the present tense all of the developments of cosmology, geology, biology, and intelligence at the moment He created the laws of science, and in the same way He saw the explorations of those laws by the mind of man. The laws of the natural world are laws of God just as surely as are the laws of human behavior and ethics that govern the human conscience. Nature and natural laws are not the enemies of God, but are His creation; knowledge of the laws of nature are

---

[1] C. S. Lewis. "Dogma and the Universe." *God in the Dock: Essays on Theology and Ethics.* Edited by Walter Hooper. Grand Rapids: William B. Eerdmans, 1970. Pg 42-43.
[2] Matthew 4.3-7.
[3] Hawking, Stephen, and Leonard Mlodinow. *A Briefer History of Time.* New York: Random House, 2005. Pg 15.

not a threat to God, but an exploration of His nature by the understanding of His works. Any theological argument that rejects nature's laws rejects the creative acts of God and the evidence of Himself that He included therein. Materialism, defined as the search for natural causes for all observed phenomenon, is only a threat to theism if one considers God to be outside and alien to nature. Many modern scientists rejoice in God's creation by seeking understanding, and regard their work as worship and their results with a sense of awe.

Other scientists, of course, see in the facts and theories of modern science a cause to espouse their atheistic beliefs. They err in logic, however, in asserting that God does not exist merely because they have not found or proven Him. Many of the same scientists believe in string theory or in parallel universes with no more experimental or observational evidence than that available for theism. Stephen Hawking gave an honest assessment of the role of science in evaluating the belief in God: "What I have done is to show that it is possible for the way the universe began to be determined by the laws of science. In that case, it would not be necessary to appeal to God to decide how the universe began. This doesn't prove that there is no God, only that God is not necessary."[1] But the God of Judeo-Christian tradition, in the manner of Søren Kierkegaard, does not claim to be "necessary" in the sense that His existence is an inescapable conclusion; rather, it is essential to His nature that He remains beyond attestation, so that belief in Him is a choice of faith.

Theists of all stripes must not reply to atheism with concepts of God that introduce limits to His perceived power, knowledge, or wisdom. The arguments of creationists and intelligent design proponents, however, often do just that in implying (and, occasionally, overtly stating) that God is incapable of having acted by means of the mechanisms of chemistry and physics that are incorporated in cosmological, geological, and biological evolution. Any who consider such arguments must ask whether the God conceived by such advocates lacks the patience, foresight, or knowledge that is present in the theories of science. A God who is omniscient is not limited by human comprehension or time constraints. There is no reason except the limits of the human mind to prevent him from possessing the foresight and patience to work over periods of billions of years to achieve His ends, by creating a universe with inherent capabilities for change and development, and with an equally inherent capacity to submit to His guidance. The God of theistic evolution designed the laws of the universe, including indeterminism, in such a way that it had the capacity to develop life, intelligence, reflection, and spirituality, all under His subtle direction.

---

[1] "Was war vor dem großen Knall?" ("What was before the Big Bang?") *Der Spiegel* 42 (17 Oct 1988). Pg 246-249. Accessed 28 Nov 2008 at <http://wissen.spiegel.de/wissen/dokument/dokument.html?id=13531415&top=SPIEGEL>.

Stephen Jay Gould, a paleontologist and evolutionary biologist and prolific author, famously argued that, due to indeterminism, evolution could just as easily have had widely different outcomes. He proposed that if evolution was a videotape that could be rewound and replayed, that it would come out different each time, and that results would not necessarily include intelligent beings capable of religious thought.[1] Atheists embrace the argument as making a case against the existence of God, which is consistent with Gould's intent and writings, and anti-evolutionists regard the argument as proof of the atheistic nature of evolution; in fact it is neither.

Gould's evolutionary tape has been rewound, at least part way, with each major extinction event, the last of which was the K-T event that exterminated the dinosaurs. Pierre Teilhard de Chardin convincingly argued that the trend of living things, indeed the apparent teleological trend of the universe as a whole, is to develop ascending awareness, cognizance, consciousness, reflection, and thus resulting spirituality. Although the K-T extinction event opened a variety of ecological niches that were then populated by mammals, from which developed the human animal with its religious tendencies, there is no reason to assume that dinosaurs, being predominantly bipedal and tending towards endothermy (a trend that, as previously noted, was completed in their avian descendants), would not have developed intelligence sufficient for reflective thought; nor is there any reason to assume that God requires His worship to arise from beings with hair rather than scales or feathers.

If the evolutionary tape, rewound and replayed, produced a different species with the reflective cognition that theologians refer to as a soul, the purpose of God in designing a universe capable of producing a race worthy and desirous of communion with Him would still be served, and that species would be, in the spiritual sense, an image of God. To a Judeo-Christian believer, the very fact that physiochemical laws lead to intelligent beings that can discover and comprehend both the natural and the moral laws of God, including the indeterminacy that permits God the latitude to guide the results of His creation, is evidence of the intent and fulfillment of the God of their faith. Such a result is itself not a foregone conclusion, as Stephen Hawking notes in considering the exactness of the primary values of physics:

> [I]t seems clear that there are relatively few ranges of values for the numbers that would allow the development of any form of intelligent life. Most sets of values would give rise to universes that, although they might be very beautiful, would contain no one able to wonder at that beauty.[2]

---

[1] Gould, Stephen Jay. *Wonderful Life: The Burgess Shale and the Nature of History.* New York: W. W. Norton, 1989.

[2] Hawking, Stephen W. *A Brief History of Time.* New York: Bantam Books, 1988. Pg 125.

The nature of faith is that it embraces as truth that which cannot be verified or tested. The nature of science is that it embraces as truth *only* that which can be tested and verified; any conclusions that result from the organization and consideration of those facts are theories that undergo constant challenge and verification. Science fails to prove the existence of God, but fails, too, to deny Him. The most advanced theories of science leave room for action by God to influence which of the seemingly haphazard outcomes of the untold number of indeterminate events actually occur. When outcomes of low probability occur, it remains to the mind of the observer to see in the result either an inherent randomness or the guiding hand of a deity. To a man or woman of faith, the laws created by God to govern His universe leave opportunity for Him to work His will. Although it is sometimes easier to believe in a burst of creative energy, God reveals in his creation that He is immensely patient, having created a complex mechanism of physical laws and guiding it to produce stars and planets and life and, finally, in mankind, a species worthy of knowing and communing with Him. The choice of belief or unbelief remains a choice of the soul of man, but regardless of the chosen belief, the universe is most assuredly not determinate.

Four choices remain to the soul of man regarding the testimonies provided by God of His nature.

Adherents of creationism within other religious traditions reject both that portion of God revealed in Judeo-Christian scripture and that revealed by the thoughtful consideration of His creation.

One who chooses to accept the revelations of creation but reject the revelation of scripture must profess either atheism or a version of deism that excludes determinism. In either case, one must accept that the material universe is governed by the randomness of fully undirected probabilities, abandoning the millennia-old quest for meaning and purpose that is at the center of human spirituality.

In accepting the revelation of scripture but rejecting the well-supported observations and theories that are the result of human inquiry into the revelation of God in His creation, a believer chooses to worship a God who is deceitful in providing highly corroborative but false evidence both in His creation and, by creating the misleading appearance of compilation from various sources writing at different times, in his revealed word; inept in creating such a vast multitude of unsuccessful species of life; unjust in condemning souls of men for using the intellectual gifts He provided in striving to understand the false evidence of His creation; and diminished by being thought incapable of creating through the patient means discovered by science. Such a God would seem to be little improved in character over any of a multitude of false pagan deities.

By embracing the realities of revealed scripture and created material testimony, one may choose belief in a God worthy of worship. He is a God of truth, consistent in the integrity of His message to mankind. He is a God of justice, with the authority to make and judge moral law. He is a God of omniscience, having foreseen from the earliest moment of time every material event of at least ten billion years now past and a future knowable only to Him. He is a God of uncertainty, for only in the uncertainty of indeterminism can He touch and guide the progress of His creation and the minds and hearts of man. Science has, in quantum mechanics, discovered that the genius of His creation included just the necessary uncertainty for Him to act unseen, and perhaps, in string theory, the dimensions in which He can dwell in transcendence.

The God of Uncertainty is a God greater than anything the mind of man can comprehend, and so immense in His intellect that the accumulated thought and wisdom of all the millennia of mankind is just beginning to understand that which He conceived and created before the beginning of time.

Chapter 10

The Case for Reconciliation

> Usually, even a non-Christian knows something about the earth, the heavens, and the other elements of this world, about the motion and orbit of the stars and even their size and relative positions, about the predictable eclipses of the sun and moon, the cycles of the years and the seasons, about the kinds of animals, shrubs, stones, and so forth, and this knowledge he holds to as being certain from reason and experience. . . . If they find a Christian mistaken in a field in which they themselves know well and hear him maintaining his foolish opinions about our books, how are they going to believe those books in matters concerning the resurrection of the dead, the hope of eternal life, and the kingdom of heaven, when they think their pages are full of falsehoods on facts which they themselves have learnt from experience and the light of reason? Reckless and incompetent expounders of Holy Scripture . . . recite from memory many passages which they think support their position, although they understand neither what they say nor the things about which they make assertion.[1]

Thus wrote Saint Augustine near the dawning of the fifth century in *The Literal Meaning of Genesis.* While the observations and theories of science have surely changed markedly, the issues confronting the church in its encounters with the learning of science have apparently changed little. More than thirteen hundred years before the publication of *The Origin of Species* and well over a millennium before higher criticism of biblical texts was seriously deliberated, Augustine identified and considered the pitfalls of maintaining the position that scriptural truth contradicts scientific truth. He recognized that true knowledge is evident from study of the physical realms and that

---

[1] St. Augustine. *The Literal Meaning of Genesis.* Translated and annotated by John Hammond Taylor New York: Newman, 1982. Vol 1 of 2, pg 42-43 (1.19.39).

the authority of scripture is misappropriated in challenging empirical observations; he referred to such misuse of scripture as disgraceful, dangerous, and embarrassing to the faith. Augustine warned that such interpretations damaged the credibility of the scriptures, the church fathers who authored and interpreted them, and all who persist in nonsensically proclaiming a contradiction between the rational interpretation of physical evidence and their interpretation of scripture. By such compromises to the credibility of the message and messengers of Christianity, and by provision of unnecessary distractions from the significance of the central doctrines of the faith, the introduction of invented conflicts between science and Christianity make more difficult the task of proselytizing, even for those who personally avoid such fallacies.

It is little wonder that Augustine concluded this, one of his most quoted passages, by using the words of First Timothy 1.7, in which Paul admonishes his protégé to recognize and reject false teachings and their proponents among believers in Ephesus. Augustine used the same words applied by the apostle to Gnostics and ascetics to condemn those who hold positions giving ascendancy to scripture over empiricism in scientific matters. The same concerns expressed by the Bishop of Hippo over a millennium and a half ago continue to affect that segment of the church that in the twenty-first century erroneously teaches its adherents both to reject the current knowledge of science and to condemn those who understand and accept the well-supported theories of modern scientific endeavors. The effects on the church, foreseen by Augustine and continuing to be realized today, include corruption of its ethics, a diminution of its message, and a wholly avoidable impediment in proselytizing.

A lesson from history

Whether his thoughts were due to divine inspiration, shrewd perception, or bitter experience, the concerns expressed by Augustine were manifest in dramatic fashion in the Renaissance.

Nicolaus Koppernigk was born in 1473 and lost his father at the age of ten. He became the ward of a maternal uncle who was a high official in the Catholic church, and who reached the rank of Bishop while Nicolaus was still a young man. His uncle encouraged the young Nicolaus in the pursuit of his education and urged him toward a career in the church. Nicolaus Latinized his surname to Copernicus and studied canonical law in addition to Latin, mathematics, philosophy, astronomy, and, later, medicine. With, no doubt, the assistance of his influential uncle, Copernicus secured a position as a canon of Frauenburg Cathedral, a position which assured him of an ongoing stipend in return for rather light administrative and advisory duties, and which thus provided him with a secure income while he pursued studies and observations in his chosen fields.

The lively mind of Copernicus had many interests, but he was particularly fascinated by astronomy and became a keen observer of the heavens. Copernicus had been schooled in the geocentric models of Aristotle and Ptolemy, which had been accepted for nearly two millenia, but his observations (which were made sans telescope, that instrument not having been invented) led him to believe that the sun was the center of the solar system, and that the planets orbited the sun rather than the earth. By 1514 he felt sufficiently confident in his new heliocentric ideas that he circulated among his friends a short hand-written and unsigned manuscript, now referred to as *The Little Commentary. The Little Commentary* contained a remarkable and haunting passage: "Here, for the sake of brevity, I have thought it desirable to omit the mathematical demonstrations intended for my larger work."

The "larger work" of Copernicus, *De revolutionibus orbium coelestium*, was not published until 1543, near the end of Copernicus's life; its deferral may have been due to the expectation of the rejection by church authorities clearly anticipated by Copernicus or, as seems more likely by his many and ongoing revisions, a perfectionist's dissatisfaction with his work. Even after decades of delay, the original preface was removed by a Lutheran clergyman in whom its first printing was entrusted and replaced with a disclaimer stating that the contents were to be considered only an easier mathematical model for calculating the position of the planets rather than a truthful representation of the actual state of the cosmos.

The Copernican theory was, as expected by its author, the subject of condemnation by the Church, and therefore a source of controversy for several more decades. An early proponent, Giordano Bruno, was condemned by the Inquisition and burned at the stake in 1600. Galileo Galilei, who did not invent the telescope but certainly did much to refine it and was the most diligent and productive of those who first applied it to astronomy, used the new instrument to discover four moons orbiting Jupiter, and to observe that Venus, when viewed from earth, progressed through a full set of waxing and waning phases like the moon; both observations were inexplicable under geocentric models. Galileo published his findings in 1610, accompanied by both his defense of Copernican theory and obeisant words directed to the Church and its leadership, and thus soon became the most visible proponent of heliocentricity. (A letter from Galileo to a noblewoman is available online at www.fordham.edu/halsall/mod/galileo-tuscany.asp and is a worthwhile read due to its articulate and timeless discussion of the relationship between faith and reason, particularly in regard to the interpretation of scripture, in the course of defending heliocentricity.)

In 1616, the cardinals of the Inquisition formally held Copernican theory to be heresy, on the basis of testimony from theologians who opined that only the earth, as the home of mankind, the pinnacle of God's creation, could be the center of a universe created by God. Inquisitors justified their geocentric beliefs with scriptures such as

Psalm 93.1 (the second sentence of which is "He has established the world; it shall never be moved), Psalm 96.10 and 1 Chronicles 16.30 (each of which reads in part "The world is firmly established; it shall never be moved."), Psalm 104:5 ("You set the earth on its foundations, so that it shall never be shaken."), and Ecclesiastes 1:5 ("The sun rises and the sun goes down, and hurries back to where it rises.) (All quotes are from the New Revised Standard Version.) Even after the heresy declaration Galileo found favor with the pope and his close advisors, and enjoyed the honor of several papal audiences. Amid mixed signals, then, Galileo in 1632 published *Dialogue Concerning the Two Chief Systems of the World - Ptolemaic and Copernican*, in which he presented a convincing case for Copernican heliocentricity and named the advocate for Ptolemaic geocentricity "Simplicio," as in simpleton. The views of the church were then made crystal clear – Galileo was convicted by a church court of heresy in 1633 and forced to recant his support of heliocentricity under threat of being burned at the stake. His publications were banned and he was sentenced to a lifetime of imprisonment, a sentence which was enforced as house arrest. He continued writing in favor of a Copernican model of the solar system and about other matters of astronomy and physics, but his later works had to be smuggled out of the country for publication, and he died in relative isolation, disgraced and humiliated.

Nevertheless, neither the fervency of their belief nor the majority of their opinion made true the arguments of the persecutors of Galileo. The physical reality and the material evidence derived therefrom proved heliocentricity to be correct, vindicated Copernicus and Galileo, and condemned those who suppressed the candid exploration of God's creation.

Galileo Galilei, one of history's most revered scientists, was buried in secret by his family, and when his remains were moved to a church tomb in 1737, it was still over the objection of many church authorities. It was not until 1992 that the Catholic Church, represented then by Pope John Paul II, publicly admitted that its theologians erred in advising it in Galileo's Inquisition trial. The papal statement declared closed the case of Galileo, then 350 years dead, but interestingly contained neither an apology nor any direct admission that the Church had been wrong to convict him for defending the Copernican theory with his observations and reason. Galileo's rehabilitation appears to continue, however, as the Associated Press reported in December 2008 that Pope Benedict XVI had publicly credited Galileo with enabling men and women of faith to "contemplate with gratitude the Lord's works," and that certain Vatican officials favor making Galileo a patron of the interaction and dialogue between faith and reason.[1]

The story of Galileo is apropos to the discussion of modern theories of cosmological and biological evolution precisely because it contains so many of the elements warned against by Augustine. That the top leadership of the Catholic Church felt compelled to address the subject three hundred and fifty years after Galileo's death is ample evidence that the affair remains a source of embarrassment for Christianity in general and for Catholicism in particular. In taking a position favoring geoentricity over heliocentricity, Inquisitors interpreted scriptures narrowly, ignoring and excluding the possibility of any artful literary interpretation and adhering to strict literalism. They then gave their own rigid interpretation ascendancy over the empiric observations, calculations, and rationale of Nicolaus Copernicus and Galileo Galilei. The Church thus put itself in the untenable position of suppressing concrete facts and persecuting those who knew the truth and used it to reach rational conclusions. The difficulty in that position is reflected in the statement of Pope John Paul II that there was a need to reopen the case of Galileo in order to "dispel the mistrust that still opposes, in many minds, a fruitful concord between science and faith. . . By virtue of her own mission, the Church has the duty to be attentive to the pastoral consequences of her teaching. Before all else, let it be clear that this teaching must correspond to the truth."[2] In other words, the pontiff recognized that the Church's role in opposing scientific truth had placed in the minds of some an impediment to faith of the very sort predicted by Augustine.

Pope John Paul II also made it clear that he recognized that the proximate cause of the Church's difficulties in the famous case of Galileo was its own narrow interpretation of scripture. In his remarks he quoted with approval a letter from Galileo to his friend Benedetti Castelli, a Benedictine mathematician, "If Scripture cannot err, certain of its interpreters and commentators can and do so in many ways."[3] The Pope similarly recognized the wisdom of Saint Augustine on the same subject: "If it happens that the authority of Sacred Scripture is set in opposition to clear and certain reasoning, this must mean that the person who interprets Scripture does not understand it correctly. It is not the meaning of Scripture which is opposed to the truth but the meaning which

---

[1] Winfield, Nicole. "Good heavens: Vatican rehabilitating Galileo." 23 Dec 2008, Associated Press. Accessed 8 Jan 2009 at <http://www.huffingtonpost.com/2008/12/23/vatican-rewrites-history_n_153232.html>.

[2] Pope John Paul II. Address to Pontifical Academy of Sciences 31 Oct 1981. English translation accessed 8 Jan 2008 at <http://www.its.caltech.edu/~nmcenter/sci-cp/sci-9211.html>.

[3] Galileo Galilei. Letter to Benedetto Castelli, 21 Nov 1613, in Edizione nazionale delle Opere di Galileo Galilei, A. Favaro, ed. 1968., Vol V, pg 282. Quoted by Pope John Paul II in address to Pontifical Academy of Sciences 31 Oct 1981. Accessed 8 Jan 2008 at <http://www.its.caltech.edu/~nmcenter/sci-cp/sci-9211.html>.

he has wanted to give it."[1]

More lessons

If the long and difficult case of Galileo is the most egregious instance of the church embarrassing itself and making more difficult its own mission of evangelism by taking unfounded positions, it was, alas, not to be the last. The number of preachers, evangelists, and authors who have professed to have deciphered from scripture the date of divine judgment is too large to consider. An honest reading of the several epistles of the New Testament and other early Christian writings reveals that the return of Christ to earthly dominion was expected to be eminent even then, and each generation has produced proponents of the same hopes and fears. The author's father recalls confident declarations from the pulpit that Benito Mussolini was the Antichrist of Revelation; books and sermons predicting apocalyptic events in the closing years of the twentieth century were common. Seldom do the purveyors of such predictions seem to consider the damage to the credibility of the pulpit or the faith done when their deadlines pass uneventfully. In fact, wars and natural disasters are considered fodder for apocalyptic prophesies only because of apparent misinterpretation of words of Jesus that, when considered more carefully, appear to actually disavow any connection of such events to end times: "And you will hear of wars and rumors of wars*; see that you are not alarmed*; for this must take place, but *the end is not yet*. For nation will rise against nation, and kingdom against kingdom, and there will be famines and earthquakes in various places: *all this is but the beginning* of the birth pangs (emphasis added)."[2] The Eastern Orthodox churches wisely condemn speculation about the date of the end of time as dangerous and unreliable, both because of the potential damage to the credibility of the churches and priests who endorse such predictions, and more importantly because of Jesus' several warnings against such attempts. The Gospels of Mark and Matthew relate that Jesus answered disciples' queries on the subject by abjuring: "But about that day or hour no one knows, neither the angels in heaven, nor the Son, but only the Father."[3] Jesus' relentless disciples continued to press the subject, until just moments before His ascension, he was forced to again reply, "It is not for you to know the times or periods that the Father has set by his own authority."[4]

It is little known in the twenty-first century that it was once a common belief of Christians that the moon, the other planets of the solar system, the sun, and the largest

---

[1] Saint Augustine. Epistula 143, n 7 PL 33, col 588. Quoted by Pope John Paul II in address to Pontifical Academy of Sciences 31 Oct 1981. Accessed 8 Jan 2008 at <http://www.its.caltech.edu/~nmcenter/sci-cp/sci-9211.html>.

[2] Matthew 24.6-8. New Revised Standard Version. Emphasis added. The Gospel of Mark, which is widely believed to have been a source for the writing of Matthew, is virtually identical in 13.7-8.

[3] Mark 13.32. New Revised Standard Version.

[4] Acts 1.7. New Revised Standard Version.

of the asteroids were inhabited by intelligent beings. Although a significant number of churchmen seem to have long held that the human race and its home planet occupied unique places as the pinnacle and central goal of God's creative effort, that opinion was, as late as the nineteenth century, diametrically opposed by sizable numbers of Christian philosophers, theologians, and their devotees who reasoned that God would not have created other worlds without also creating intelligent creatures to appreciate their beauty. Christian pluralism was so pervasive and so well accepted that its truth was presumed in many works of the eighteenth and nineteenth centuries. *The Christian Philosopher; or, the Connexion of Science and Philosophy with Religion*, was a book by clergyman and amateur astronomer Thomas Dick, well meaning in its object "to illustrate the harmony which subsists between the subject of Nature and the subject of Revelation; and to show, that the manifestations of God in the material universe ought to be blended with our views of the facts and doctrines recorded in the volume of Inspiration."[1] (Although the present volume has similar goals, it is to be hoped that its science is more well-founded and resilient, being based more on observation and less on philosophical speculation.) Dick's book was so popular that it was printed in at least twenty-five editions from 1823 until 1869. It refers repeatedly and confidently to the inhabitants of the moon, planets (including several large named asteroids), and sun; so firmly convinced of pluralism was Dick that he calculated the population of the solar system to be nearly twenty-two trillion at a time when the human population of earth was, by most estimates, less than 1.2 billion.[2]

The Great Moon Hoax was authored by Richard Adams Locke (a descendant of philosopher John Locke) and published in the New York *Sun* in 1835. Locke reported in a series of articles that astronomer Sir John Herschel had used a telescope of revolutionary design and size to observe the inhabitants of the moon. In addition to blue unicorns, bears with horns, and spherical amphibious animals that rolled themselves around as a means of locomotion, the moon was said to be populated by a race of humanoids with bat-like wings that built extravagant temples and were fond of prolific public procreation. Herschel was a very real astronomer of excellent reputation, but was unaware of the *Sun* serial at the time of publication, and was at least initially amused by the furor over the findings falsely attributed to him. While the primary motivation for the sensational series may have been to increase sales of the *Sun*, it was also a sharp-edged satire of *The Christian Philosopher* in particular and of

---

1 Dick, Thomas. *The Christian Philosopher; or, the Connexion of Science and Philosophy with Religion*, 25th ed. London: Charles Griffin & Co., 1869. Pg 5. Accessed 12 Jan 2008 at <http://books.google.com/books?hl=en&id=LTUXAAAAYAAJ&dq=thomas+dick+christian+philosophy&printsec=frontcover&source=web&ots=v-qzVY9Hed&sig=KMQzfDi-XQdvd6oVVBkAyoxIlgA&sa=X&oi=book_result&resnum=1&ct=result>.

2 "Historical Estimates of World Population." U. S. Census Bureau, Population Division. 12 Dec 2008. Accessed 13 Jan 2009 at < http://www.census.gov/ipc/www/worldhis.html>.

Christian pluralism in general.

The satirical hoax of Locke and the pluralistic beliefs of Christian philosophers that inspired it are amusing to readers of the twenty-first century, but they join the apocalyptic predictions of innumerable evangelical authorities and the distressing persecution of Galileo and others who dared defend heliocentric theory in demonstrating the dangers of staking the credibility of the faith on uncertain conclusions. In the case of geocentricity and each of the multitude of end-time prophecies, the authors and defenders sincerely believed that their opinions were grounded in scripture. Christian philosophers were no less sincere in their belief that their pluralistic opinions were well grounded in reasoning based on their concept of God. Galileo's opponents, untold numbers of apocalyptic visionaries, and Christian pluralists all forgot that sincerity of belief does not sufficiently substitute for factual observations, and truth is therefore not affected by belief. All staked the credibility of their faith on their personal opinions – a narrow and debatable interpretation of scripture in the case of apocalyptics and Ptolemaic astronomers, and their estimations of the nature of God in the case of the pluralists. The credibility of the witness of representatives of the faith, even of those who do not hold the debated views, is inevitably compromised when such certain proclamations are proven false. The evidence for that injury to the perceived integrity of Christianity is contained in the satire of Locke, the ridicule directed towards the endless repetition of end-time prophesies, and the ongoing effort of the Catholic Church to redress its condemnation of Galileo.

Remarkably, proponents of creationism and intelligent design are willing, once again, to needlessly stake the credibility of the Christian faith and scripture on outdated, ill-conceived, dubious arguments against well-founded and generally accepted scientific observations and theories. They persist in the same error of giving their narrow interpretations of scripture ascendancy over empirical data and conclusions drawn therefrom, making their positions clearly and easily falsified, and incredibly expecting to win and retain devotees with their arguments against observation and reason. No enemy of Christianity could create a device better suited to portraying the religion as foolish and lacking in credibility than the tactic of those ardent but misguided believers who reject reason and observation in favor of insupportably narrow interpretations of scripture.

The ethics of integrity

The difficulties in maintaining a stance rejecting the findings and theories of modern science go far deeper than mere image and presentation of the faith; rather, it demands that adherent individuals and assemblies take tenuous ethical positions that betray basic tenets of Judeo-Christian principles.

Few would contest the premise that honesty is a foundational value of Judeo-Christian ethics. An admonition against lies is contained in the Ten Commandments (Exodus 20.1-7 and Deuteronomy 5.6-21), arguably the most basic statement of principle in Judeo-Christian thought and, alongside the Code of Hammurabi, one of humanity's earliest legal conventions. Nearly every religion embraces integrity as an essential underlying principle of human society. The development of civilization was in large part dependent on the exchange of goods and services, in that such exchanges allowed individuals to move beyond subsistence activities to develop specialties, with their resultant artisanship and technologies, and the humanities. The exchange of goods and services is dependent in turn upon the truthful representation of the exchanged commodities. All contract law, from the most complex corporate transaction to the simplest consumer purchase is contingent on the honest depiction of the characteristics of the elements of the exchange. The price of purchased goods is a measure of the value of their promised performance, and the fee affixed to a service is its perceived worth in relation to the labor, skill, and education that is offered and professed by the party who tenders himself for employment. Money itself is merely a physical symbol of a promised purchasing power, and vehicles such as checks and credit accounts have no inherent value other than the pledge of funds behind the vehicle. Untruths or misrepresentations of elements of exchange, real or imagined, are the proximate causes of every business disagreement and lawsuit, and those untruths and misrepresentations are onerous to society because they each represent, to a greater or lesser extent, a disruption in the system of exchange upon which civilization is built.

It is no coincidence that most English translations render the commandment not to lie as an admonition not to "bear false witness," for the oldest Greek and Hebrew texts most literally prohibit bringing or supporting false charges in courts.[1] One of the primary functions of legal systems is to ensure fair business transactions by assuring the truthfulness of representations and the fulfillment of obligations under contracts. Since Jewish courts had the death penalty at their disposal for punishment of a variety of crimes against person, property, and societal norms, the prohibition against taking fraudulent legal actions and giving false testimony also reflected a respect for human life.[2, 3] As noble as that reverence for life may be, even it has its roots in commerce; working men were protected by society from death and injury so that they could provide for their families and contribute their skills and labor to the community, and even in the twenty-first century civil awards for injury and wrongful death are based in

---

[1] Houston, Walter. "Exodus." *Oxford Bible Commentary.* John Barton and John Muddiman, ed. New York: Oxford University Press, 2001. Pg 82.

[2] Houston, Walter. "Exodus." *Oxford Bible Commentary.* John Barton and John Muddiman, ed. New York: Oxford University Press, 2001. Pg 82.

[3] Bultman, Christoph. "Deuteronomy." *Oxford Bible Commentary.* John Barton and John Muddiman, ed. New York: Oxford University Press, 2001. Pg 141.

large part on earning potential lost to victims, dependents, and heirs. In the centuries since the codification of the Decalogue, extension of the value of integrity from the legal arena to all aspects of life has become commonly accepted as virtuous in Judeo-Christian thought, and for similar reasons. The only situation in which a lie is commonly accepted as an ethical act is when the truth would put another person in immediate and unjust danger. (The example that comes immediately to mind is that of a person providing shelter to Jews during the Holocaust, stating to Nazi raiders that there are no Jews on the premises; few would consider it morally right to tell the truth by turning in people who sought one's help in a time of such an enormous threat, the threat being rooted in clear injustice.)

No such ethical dilemma is readily apparent in the stance of those who reject cosmological and biological evolution, yet they support their arguments with lies of commission, omission, and implication.

Creationists begin by misrepresenting the nature and words of the Bible. As has been discussed, there is ample evidence that the Pentateuch is a compilation of the work of several authors. The teaching that it was received intact as a single revelation from God is not consistent with the characteristics of the text or the narrative flow, and is not asserted by the Pentateuch itself except for a very few short passages in which God is said to have revealed moral law to the Israelites through Moses. Efforts to resolve conflicting accounts – most pertinent to the consideration of the issue of reconciling the Bible with modern scientific theories, the two distinct creation accounts contained in Genesis 1.1 through 2.3 and 2.4 through 3.24 – are far more tortured and inconsistent than the simple acknowledgement that two different creation myths were both considered valuable enough to the knowledge of God, the origin of mankind, and the relationship between humans and God, to be preserved and recorded by early Hebrews. The presentation of the Bible as a simplistic document subject to a single undisputed interpretation is equally false. It is, in fact, rich in meaning and often ambiguous, sometimes apparently deliberately so. Episodes in the New Testament itself, particularly in the letters of Paul, demonstrate that layers of literal and allegorical meaning were attached to scripture in the time of Christ, and Jesus' participation in discussions and debates about the scripture reveal that He saw complexity in the words of the Pentateuch, the books of wisdom, and the works of the prophets; if such complexity was lacking and the meaning of scripture was beyond debate, neither the commentary that would eventually be recorded as the Talmud nor Jesus' contribution to the scholarly deliberations of the time would have been necessary or fruitful.

The fruitfulness and necessity of such discussions arises, in large part, from the ambiguity of words. The fact that the earliest complete manuscripts date only to the seventh to eleventh century Masoretic reconstructions, themselves replete with notations of alternate versions, render spurious any claim to exact authenticity of the scripture, even before the process of translation and paraphrase that produced modern versions of the Bible. The English of modern translations is, contrary to the assertions of fundamentalists, frequently subject to different interpretations. The translation of the Bible into modern languages was entirely necessary to its being accessible to the masses, but as noted by scholars of ancient languages, the process of translation involves a certain inherent degree of interpretation, and efforts to clarify difficult passages involve even more. As a result of the long process of transmission and translation of scripture, modern readers can hardly claim to capture the subtleties of the original text, much less the underlying oral traditions. Thus, for example, the markedly indistinct Hebrew *yôm* became the Latin *diem* and then the English word "day" in the process of translation; "day" still has the possibility of different meanings, but all those except the twenty-four hour period in which the earth rotates once on its axis are stripped away by confident fundamentalist interpreters. Translations vary in their degree of interpretive predisposition, and there is irony in the fact that the more scholarly and literal translations are disregarded by erstwhile fundamentalists, literalists, and creationists, in favor of translations that demonstrate more narrow and biased viewpoints. The argument that any translation that does not support evangelical viewpoints should be discarded as being inherently in error is both circular and empty, because scholarly effort at approximating the original meaning of scripture should not be a threat to those who seek to interpret scripture with candor and probity. Paraphrases of scripture such as *The Living Bible* and the more recently fashionable *The Message* are popular among evangelicals, and while the increased accessibility is admirable and provides a good starting point for the understanding of scripture by those unfamiliar with its content, it comes at a cost: the removal of mystery, the forfeiture of depth and layered meaning, the loss of the elegance, nobility, and majesty of the language, and frequent oversimplification are necessary casualties of the process of making the texts more understandable and approachable. The assertion that the meaning of interpretation of scripture is consistently simple and clear is itself inherently false.

Besides misrepresenting their own holy writ. creationists also misrepresent the revelation of God in His creation. Frequent and persistent misrepresentations are made regarding the physical evidence of the fossil record. Opponents of evolution widely proclaim that there is no evidence in the fossil record of evolutionary processes or, specifically, of intermediate species. A rational consideration of the fossil record, however, clearly demonstrates a gradual progression of living things from simple to complex, and intermediate species are known for every major transitional phase in the development of animals from single-celled organisms to humans. The first *Archaeopteryx* skeleton, intermediate between dinosaurs and birds, was discovered in 1861, less than two years after the original publication of *The Origin of Species*. The intervening years have produced a steady stream of specimens demonstrating the intermediate characteristics expected of other transitional fossils, the most important of which were enumerated previously in this volume. The discovery of *Triktaalik* dramatically demonstrated that knowledge of the continuum of evolutionary development was so complete that paleontologists could find transitional anatomic features that they desired to examine by proactively excavating geological deposits of the appropriate age (a technique that has been repeated innumerable times with less fanfare).

The broad evolutionary trend towards increasingly complex structure and function is visible in the most durable of hard parts, teeth. A tooth from a Great White Shark (top right, below) bears a strong resemblance to the scale from which it is derived. The tooth of *Tyrannosaurus* (replica, left) is more specialized to function as a tooth, but still simple in structure. The carnassial tooth of a modern dog (bottom right) has multiple roots and a distinct crown shaped for the specialized task of shearing. (The irregularities on the surface of the dog tooth are tartar deposits. The tooth was extracted from a patient by the author due to periodontal disease in the course of clinical practice.)

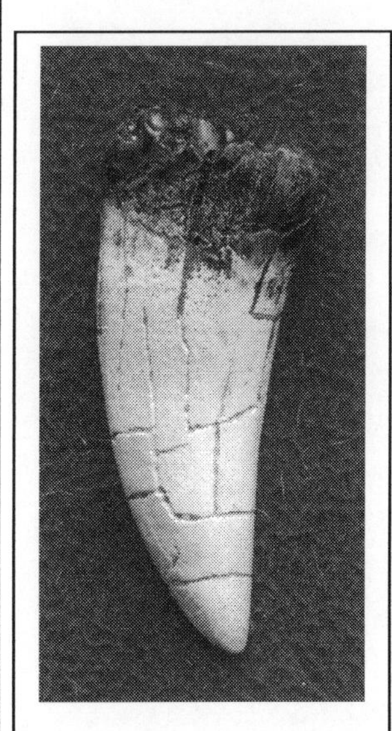

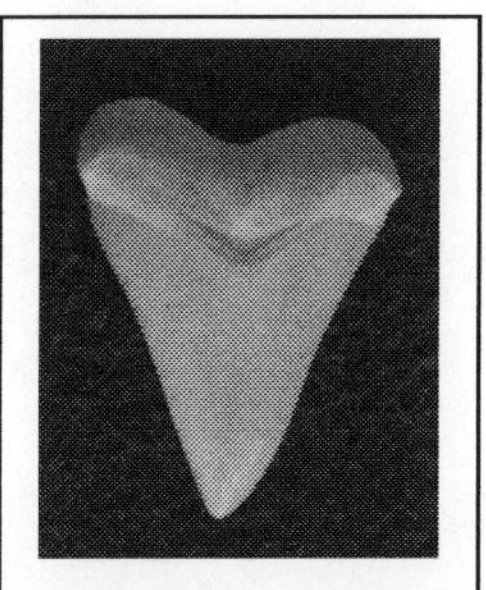

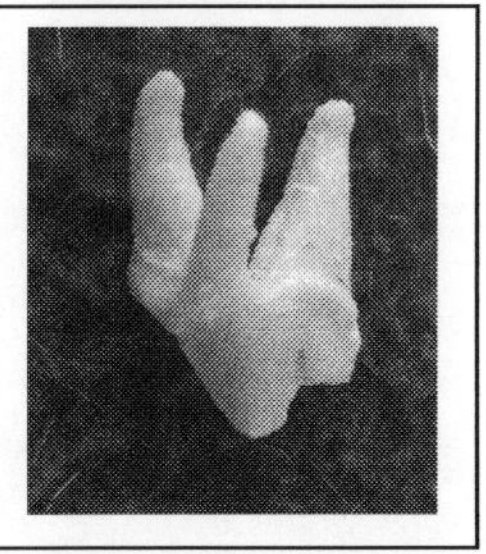

Failing to plausibly deny the existence of transitional fossils, opponents of evolution then seek to falsely deny the transitional nature of specimens. Thus *Archaeopteryx*, to return to a prominent example, is portrayed as being undeniably bird-like in its features, displaying no resemblance to the therapod dinosaurs from which it, under evolutionary theories of descent, arose. Such arguments correctly assert that *Archaeopteryx* had feathers, webbed wings, an opposable hallux (big toe), and a furcula (prominent fused clavicles, the wishbone) like modern birds; they ignore or deny, however, a multitude of other features that clearly link *Archaeopteryx* to its reptilian forebears. The animal that creationists and intelligent design theorists regard as just another typical bird had toothed jaws with no beak; nostrils placed well forward, separated from the eye sockets by large fenestra like reptiles, rather than placed close to the eyes like modern birds, which have either no or minimal fenestration in that location; a skull that attaches to the spinal column at its back like a terrestrial tetrapod with a horizontal neck, rather than at its bottom like a bird with its neck held vertically; a vertebral column that is jointed and flexible through the thorax and abdomen, rather than the largely fused and immobile spine of birds; a relatively flat sternum quite unlike the keel-shaped bone that anchors the well-developed flight muscles of modern birds; ribs that lack uncinate processes, protrusions that brace ribs against each other, making the rib cage of *Archaeopteryx* flexible like those common to terrestrial vertebrates rather than rigid like that of birds; gastralia, rib-like structures that guard the abdomen of theropods, some other dinosaurs and modern crocodilians, but are absent in birds; a long jointed tail quite unlike the tail of birds, which is composed of several vertebrae fused into the pygostyle; grasping fingers and a mobile wrist joint lacking the extensive fusion present in other birds; and a similar lack of fusion in the bones of the foot and ankle that is present in other birds.[1] These and other anatomic details cause current taxonomists to conclude that *Archaeopteryx* is, in fact, more closely related to its therapod ancestors than to modern birds, quite contrary to the opinions arrived at by the superficial and biased consideration of creationists. Without even quibbling about the degree of resemblance to either group, however, the presence of such a striking mixture of avian and reptilian characteristics would seem to provide the very definition of a transitional species, the existence and characteristics of which are falsely denied by opponents of evolution.

The interpretation of fossil evidence is frequently challenged by those who question how so much can be known about extinct animals by the examination of only hard parts – the bones and teeth that are most commonly preserved. It is a valid observation that impressions of soft tissues are relatively rare and are not known for the vast majority of fossil species, and the direct preservation of abdominal and thoracic organs, brains, and muscles occurs only in extraordinary circumstances that occur when living or very recently dead animals are entrapped in glacial ice or tar pits. It is not valid, however, to assume that nothing is known about soft tissues that are not directly preserved, and such assertions are blatantly false. The places where muscles attach to bone are well-defined anatomical features that are consistent between species; the size and shape of the resulting bony processes are very highly correlated with the strength of the attached muscle. The musculature of an animal can therefore be deduced from its skeletal structure with an exceptional degree of accuracy. To illustrate the point from the example already developed, the pectoral flight muscles of *Archaeopterix* can be said with certainty to be considerably weaker than those of modern birds, because calculations of bioengineers demonstrate that its sternum, lacking the well developed keel-shaped protrusion of modern birds and the rigidity of the rib cage of which it is a part, has neither adequate surface area for muscle attachment nor, even

---

[1] Nedin, Christopher. "All About *Archaeopteryx*." Talk Origins Archive. 15 Jan 1999. Accessed 25 Jan 2008 at http://www.talkorigins.org/faqs/archaeopteryx/info.html.

more convincingly, the structural strength to anchor such powerful muscles without crumbling. Fossilized skulls, too, necessarily contain a cast of the brain, from which much can be said about the size and structure of the brain, and from which in turn much can be inferred about the sensory, motor, and cognitive abilities of the examined fossil animal. More subtle but still valid correlations exist between the structures of ribs, vertebrae, pelvis and limbs and the anatomy of internal organs of the thorax and abdomen. Such anatomic clues are combined with strongly correlated relationships between tooth structure and diet, the contents of coprolites, knowledge of concurrently available food sources, and the digestive processes necessary for the extraction of nutrients from various types of food, to deduce much about the diet, digestive system, and feeding behaviors of extinct animals.

Even hard evidence is frequently denied in arguments countering geological and biological evolution. As we have seen, opponents of evolution deny that either speciation or the development of new biological systems have occurred, even though they are clearly represented in both the fossil record and in the observation of living viruses and bacteria. The existence of atavisms is frequently denied, and atavistic human tails are falsely asserted to be pseudotails. Creationists desperately deny the unambiguous evidence of human evolution by futilely attempting to classify fossil hominids as either fully human or fully ape-like in character; the futility and falsehood of their exercise is embarrassingly evident in their inability to agree on the placement of individual specimens in what they claim to be a well defined classification scheme, and by their placement of different individuals of the same species in different categories. Even the nature of the radioactive decay that is the basis of dating of rocks and minerals is denied by opponents of science, even though the several radioactive decay series are well known, thoroughly documented, and mutually confirmatory.

The very fact that religious opponents of evolution are willing to challenge the interpretation of anatomic evidence in living and fossil animals implies criticism of the qualifications, veracity and objectivity of experts who are the primary researchers, criticism which is almost universally false. Unlike the pronouncements of creationists and intelligent design proponents, the work of paleontologists, zoologists, botanists, anatomists, geologists, astronomers, and physicists is carefully scrutinized. Papers are published in refereed journals, submissions to which are appraised for factual accuracy, rationality of arguments, and validity of and support for stated conclusions. The methods of observation are made available to colleagues so that the observations themselves may be confirmed or challenged. Publication of new observations stimulates debate and discussion among experts in the field regarding the validity of the data, its applicability and significance, and the weight of the support that it lends to the resulting theory. Reputations are made by those who break new ground and challenge the status quo; endless confirmations of proven and well accepted theories elicit yawns and difficulty in publication. Falsification of findings or conclusions ends careers in disgrace, and attempts are rare because researchers in every field fully expect their work to be scrutinized by others of high expertise in the same and related fields. Statement and implications that data and conclusions contradicting evolution are suppressed are belied by a system that is inherently open and actively stimulates debate and innovation.

Opponents of evolution, on the other hand, restrict their publications to non-refereed journals, frequently of their own creation. They interminably cross-reference each other so that unsubstantiated opinions appear to be supported by hard data and primary research, when in reality the references are themselves unsubstantiated, opinionated, and biased. Authors frequently refer to themselves as a "doctor," implying credentials in their subject, when their degrees are actually in far different fields. The implication that people with doctorates in unrelated domains have the expertise to challenge the data and interpretations of highly specialized experts in complex disciplines such as paleontology, cellular biology, and astrophysics is as insulting as it is false. Although they claim that censorship is the reason that their views are not published in mainstream scientific journals, the actual reason is that their misrepresentations of data, conclusions, author qualifications, and scholastic recognition constitutes academic fraud. The case of Harry Rimmer, the preacher with the third-grade education who falsely claimed doctorates in theology and science, and who erroneously concluded that all species of fossil horses since *Hyracotherium* lived concurrently, may seem extreme, but the troubling fact is that Rimmer's unsubstantiated and absurdly false claims are still directly and indirectly cited by proponents of creationism and intelligent design.

As an apparent part of their strategy to counter biological evolution, opponents misrepresent the nature of the theory itself, its current status, and its author. While such a strategy certainly makes the theory easier to dispute, it is inherently dishonest and renders moot the arguments based on the misrepresentation. Evolution is portrayed as being inherently atheistic, even though Darwin's writings refer frequently to divine providence, a large number of scientists, prominent and not so prominent, find reconciliation between Christian and other faiths and scientific theory, and even courts have found that evolution is compatible with theistic beliefs. As a part of his ruling in Kitzmiller versus Dover, Judge John E Jones III wrote,

> [M]any of the leading proponents of ID make a bedrock assumption which is utterly false. Their presupposition is that evolutionary theory is antithetical to a belief in the existence of a supreme being and to religion in general. Repeatedly in this trial, Plaintiffs' scientific experts testified that the theory of evolution represents good science, is overwhelmingly accepted by the scientific community, and that it in no way conflicts with, nor does it deny, the existence

of a divine creator.[1]

Darwin himself is falsely portrayed both as vociferously atheistic and as a late convert to Christianity, but neither is true. In both published works and in private correspondence, Darwin was deeply and humbly respectful of the beliefs of others, and in at least one instance, in a letter to Asa Gray, explicitly rejected the idea that his theory supported atheism. Darwin remained agnostic, and he neither converted to Christianity nor renounced his biological theories on his deathbed, even though both are widely reported as facts by his detractors. Anyone who seeks familiarity with Darwin's writings quickly realizes that his words are in fact far more modest, circumspect, and respectful than those of his critics. And although atheists often use evolution as a premise in arguing their belief, the resulting claim made by religious opponents of evolution that all who endorse evolution are atheists is clearly and profoundly belied by the many scientists, including such notables as Asa Gray, Theodosius Dobzhansky, Francis Collins, Ken Miller, George Coyne, and Pierre Teilhard de Chardin, who publicly state their Christian faith.

Evolution is commonly referred to by its opponents as a random process, but properly defined and considered, natural selection is a force that brings order and gives direction to the variation that is inherent in biological systems. Opponents argue that all mutations – in essence, all genetic variation – is harmful, but such an argument is absurd on its face and clearly false; otherwise, every surviving living thing could only be an exact clone of the other members of its species. Legitimate scientific discussion of the mechanism and rate of evolution, and of the place of individual species in the tree of life, are misconstrued by creationists and intelligent design proponents as criticism of the basic premises of the theory itself. Punctuated equilibrium, touted as a challenge to the foundational tenets of evolutionary theory, was never conceived or presented as a such, but as a refinement in the understanding of the rates of evolution at various times under various conditions. The concocted theory of irreducible complexity is presented as a law of nature, but in reality no example of genuine irreducible complexity has been presented, and the evidence supporting it is full of half-truths, denials of observable facts, and outright fabrications. Legitimate work in information theory, genetics, and biochemistry is distorted and misconstrued to suit the arguments against science and mislead the unknowing. In the cases of the evolutionary history of horses, opponents argue against outdated models of linear evolution from the nineteenth century, knowing that their arguments are invalid against present day data and the more refined models that they support. Even the very definition of the word "theory" contained in virtually every dictionary, the definition that is commonly used by persons in all branches of science, is falsely denied and corrupted in a way that is laughable to people

[1] *Kitzmiller v Dover.* Case No. 04cv2688. US District Court, Middle District of Pennsylvania. 20 Dec 2005. Pg 136. <http://www.pamd.uscourts.gov/kitzmiller/kitzmiller_342.pdf>

who work in scientific disciplines.

Some of the most blatant falsehoods perpetrated by the opponents of modern scientific theory are in the form of "quote mining," a practice by which the original meaning of an author's words are misrepresented and often completely reversed by selective editing. By such means Charles Darwin is made to sound as if he condemned his own theory because he found the mammalian eye to be inexplicable; an examination of the context of his words in a previous chapter of this book revealed that he wrote that his theory would fail if precursors to the mammalian eye could not be found in nature, but that such precursors were well documented even in his time. Similarly, the sixth chapter of *Origin* is quoted, "If it could be demonstrated that any complex organ existed, which could not possibly have been formed by numerous, successive, slight modifications, my theory would absolutely break down." Conveniently omitted are the next words, "But I can find out no such case."[1]

Darwin, though a frequent victim of quote mining, is certainly not alone in having his words misconstrued. Evolutionary biologist Douglas Futuyma would appear to think that the fossil record does not support the theory of evolution if we consider only the two sentences quoted by creationists: "Undeniably, the fossil record has provided disappointingly few gradual series. The origins of many groups are still not documented at all." But noting that the title of the book is *Science on Trial: The Case for Evolution* causes us to wonder at the context, and our curiosity proves justified as it turns out Futuyma has a rather different overall opinion:

> Contrary to Creationist claims, the transitions among vertebrate species are almost all documented to a greater or lesser extent. *Archaeopteryx* is an exquisite link between reptiles and birds; the therapsids provide an abundance of evidence for the transition from reptiles to mammals. Moreover, there are exquisite fossil links between the crossopterygian fishes and the amphibians (the icthyostegids). Of course, many other ancestor-descendent series also exist in the fossil record. I have mentioned (Chapter 4) the bactritid-ammonoid transition, the derivation of several mammalian orders from condylarthlike mammals, the evolution of horses, and of course the hominids.
>
> Undeniably, the fossil record has provided disappointingly few gradual series. The origins of many groups are still not documented at all. But in view of the rapid pace evolution can take, and the extreme incompleteness of fossil deposits, we are fortunate to have as many transitions as we do. The creationist argument that if evolution were true we should have an abundance of intermediate fossils is built by denying the richness of paleontological

[1] Darwin, Charles. *The Origin of Species.* New York: Random House, 1979. Pg 219

> collections, by denying the transitional series that exist, and by distorting, or misunderstanding, the genetical theory of evolution.[1]

The writings of Stephen J. Gould are mined for quotes with surprising frequency. An example:

> The absence of fossil evidence for intermediary stages between major transitions in organic design, indeed our inability, even in our imagination, to construct functional intermediates in many cases, has been a persistent and nagging problem for gradualist accounts of evolution.[2]

Those familiar with the work of Gould and Eldridge as the originators and vocal proponents of punctuated equilibrium (the uneven progress of evolution) recognize that Gould is arguing against gradualism (the slow and even change of genotype and phenotype) in defense of his own theory, but those unfamiliar with the nature of the debate at the time are easily duped into thinking that he argues against evolution itself.

Francis Crick, the molecular biologist who, with James Watson and Rosalind Franklin made the landmark discovery of the structure of DNA, is quoted thus: "An honest man, armed with all the knowledge available to us now, could only state that, in some sense, the origin of life appears at the moment to be almost a miracle."

The period at the end of the sentence is not there in Crick's writing, though; a comma is in that place, and those misusing the quote are not even honest enough to acknowledge the continuation with an ellipsis. Crick continues on to a vastly different theme than that of his opening phrase:

> An honest man, armed with all the knowledge available to us now, could only state that, in some sense, the origin of life appears at the moment to be almost a miracle, so many are the conditions which would have had to have been satisfied to get it going. But this should not be taken to imply that there are good reasons to believe that it could not have started on the earth by a perfectly reasonable sequence of fairly ordinary chemical reactions. The plain fact is that the time available was too long, the many microenvironments on the earth's surface too diverse, the various chemical possibilities too numerous and our own knowledge and imagination too feeble to allow us to be able to unravel exactly how it might or might not have happened such a long time ago,

---

[1] Futuyma, Douglas J. Science on Trial: The Case for Evolution. New York: Pantheon, 1982. Pg 190-191)

[2] Gould, Stephen J. "Is a new and general theory of evolution emerging?" Paleobiology. Vol 6(1), Jan 1980. Pg 127.

> especially as we have no experimental evidence from that era to check our ideas against.[1]

As a last example of quote mining, it is interesting to consider the treatment of a less well-known scientist, Edmund J. Ambrose, a Professor Emeritus of cellular biology at the University of London. He is repeatedly quoted in creationist literature:

> At the present stage of geological research, we have to admit that there is nothing in the geological records that runs contrary to the view of conservative creationists, that God created each species separately, presumably from the dust of the earth.[2]

But once again, an author portrayed as a creationist more fully states his case: creationism is seen differently when the entirety of his statement is considered:

> We need to remember that the only evidence about the way events occurred in the past is found in the geological records. . . . At the present stage of geological research, we have to admit that there is nothing in the geological records that runs contrary to the view of conservative creationists, that God created each species separately, presumably from the dust of the earth. My own view is that this does not strengthen the creationists' arguments.

Elsewhere in the same volume Abrose demonstrates both a clear understanding of evolutionary theory and reverence for Judeo-Christian faith:

> It is strikingly clear in the geological records, when life had reached the stage where organisms were capable of living in a previously unoccupied region of the planet, such as the move from estuaries to dry land, the appearance of plants growing to great heights which provided a location (habitat) for climbing animals, or when birds and insects actually moved up and flew in the air above the earth's surface. Large numbers of new species appeared at these times; this has been called radiation, a spreading out of life. . .
>
> Surely it is not unreasonable to suppose that the Creator utilised existing life forms to generate new forms. I have already suggested that the Creator would operate within the framework of the universe He had created in forming the physical world. May this not be the same for the biological world?[3]

---

[1] Francis Crick. Life Itself, Its Origin and Nature. New York: Simon & Schuster, 1981. Pg 88.

[2] Dr. Edmund J. Ambrose. The Nature and Origin of the Biological World. Oxford: John Wiley & Sons, 1982. Pg 164.

[3] Ambrose, Edmund J. *The Nature and Origin of the Biological World.* Oxford: John Wiley & Sons, 1982. Pg 103.

If not for the steadfast pronouncement by opponents of evolution that such a position is impossible, one might think that Dr. Ambrose holds to theistic evolution! At the very least, he does not dismiss biological evolution in the manner attributed to him by creationists.

The misrepresentation by creationists of the nature and history of scripture, scriptural texts and their interpretation, empiric facts of the physical sciences, the theories they criticize, and the qualifications and words of their opponents, violate the honesty that is central to Judeo-Christian ethics. Moreover, any opponent of modern scientific theories, including contemporary theories of biological evolution, must consider whether a scientific position that can only be maintained by denial of material evidence, falsehoods, half truths, and rampant misrepresentations can itself be true. Any who base such opposition on religious beliefs must ask if their religion can be true and still demand adherence to such untruth, or if distortions and misrepresentations of the nature and words of their own scriptures should be necessary to support a true position, or if indeed the tenets of the faith can be maintained while such a basic principle as integrity is consistently violated. As we have seen, proponents of intelligent design have gone so far as to deny, in publications, on web sites, and even in court, that the intelligent designer that they proclaim is the Judeo-Christian God, yet they strangely have the support of multitudes of evangelicals in their misinformation campaign countering biological evolution. Taking into consideration the overwhelming physical evidence in support of modern theories – evidence included by God in His creation – and the consistent and reasoned interpretations of scripture that can accommodate those theories, is there a sound reason why theistic evolution must be proscribed?

Turning again to Augustine, we read:

> [T]he credibility of Scripture is at stake, and, as I have indicated more than once, there is danger that a man uninstructed in divine revelation, discovering something in Scripture or hearing from it something that seems to be at variance with the knowledge he has acquired, may resolutely withhold his assent in other matters where Scripture presents useful admonitions, narratives, or declarations. Hence, I must say briefly that in the matter of the shape of heaven the sacred writers knew the truth, but that the Spirit of God, who spoke through them, did not wish to teach men these facts that would be of no avail for their salvation.[1]

The ethics of ignorance

Witnesses in modern courtrooms give an oath that their testimony will be "the truth, the whole truth, and nothing but the truth." The whole truth is the only truth, because,

---

[1] St. Augustine. *The Literal Meaning of Genesis.* Translated and annotated by John Hammond Taylor. New York: Newman, 1982. Vol 1 of 2, pg 59 (2.9.20).

as both the law and common sense acknowledge, the presentation of select portions of the truth can distort truth into deceit. Creationists tell a partial truth – the portion contained by their interpretation of the Pentateuch – but by denying the physical evidence presented by God in His creation and dismissing close and thoughtful examination of scripture, they confine themselves to partial truth. Creationists join intelligent design proponents in ignoring or misrepresenting empirical data unfavorable to their own views, again limiting themselves and their audiences to incomplete truth.

Untruth supported by partial truth carries a double ethical danger: besides the dishonesty inherent in considering and presenting only that portion of the facts that favors one's own views, one is forced to work to maintain ignorance in others in order to support one's opinion. Suppressing knowledge is the only way to support a position made untenable by knowledge of the full truth, but encouraging and enforcing ignorance, like promoting and sanctioning falsehood, creates an ethical conflict for those of Judeo-Christian faiths.

Championing ignorance is a relatively new role for the church. As previously discussed, the early and medieval church was a repository of knowledge, and the church took a major role in educating and supporting generations of scientists in all fields. Major figures of the Reformation incorporated the view that scientific research and education, undertaken in the context of understanding the works of God's creation, were means of knowing and worshiping God. Sunday schools originated as an opportunity to teach basic literacy skills to children at a time when child labor was unregulated and a commonplace way for the poor to make ends meet.

With the publication of *The Origin of Species* and the erroneous notion that its theory was inherently atheistic, certain segments of the church began choosing to reject and deny the empirical data of science along with atheistic arguments based on scientific findings, and to assume that any exploration of the physical world would both be motivated by atheistic thought and result in the promulgation of atheistic ideas. Scientific learning became and remains anathema to many conservative evangelical branches of the church, as evidenced by frequent disparaging and condescending remarks from pulpits. ("Book-learning fools" is one unfortunate phrase by which the author has commonly heard men and women of science referred to in contemporary times.) Ephesians 3.19 reads in part "[T]he love of Christ . . . surpasses knowledge;" First Corinthians 8.1-3: ". . . Knowledge puffs up, but love builds up. Anyone who claims to know something does not yet have the necessary knowledge: but anyone who loves God is known by him;" Matthew 11.25-26: ". . . [Y]ou have hidden these things from the wise and learned, and revealed them to little children;" First Corinthians 1.26-28: "Think of what you were when you were called. Not many of you were wise by human standards; not many were influential; not many were of noble birth. But God chose the foolish things of the world to shame the wise; God chose the weak things of the world to shame the strong." A passage that bridges the eighteenth and nineteenth verses of the third chapter of First Corinthians: "If you think that you are wise in this age, you should become fools so that you may become wise. For the wisdom of this world is foolishness with God." Pulpiteers have used these texts to devalue learning, particularly in scientific fields, when in fact they do not refer to scientific knowledge at all; rather, they endorse values of humility and consideration for the feelings and beliefs of others. When Paul closes his first epistle to Timothy with a warning, "Timothy, guard what has been entrusted to your care. Turn away from godless chatter and the opposing ideas of what is falsely called knowledge, which some have professed and in so doing have wandered from the faith,"[1] he is not warning against knowledge of the physical realities of God's creation, but against the doctrine of Gnosticism.

The portrayal of knowledge as an impediment to faith is not consistent with much of scripture. When Solomon ascended the throne of the kingdom unified by his father David, he prayed for "wisdom and knowledge, that I may lead this people,"[2] and was subsequently revered for his wisdom. The book of Proverbs, which is attributed to Solomon (but more likely is a compilation of the sayings of multiple sages and traditions), frequently links knowledge, wisdom, and godliness (19.2: "It is not good to have zeal without knowledge." 15.14: "The mind of one who has understanding seeks knowledge, but the mouths of fools feed on folly." 18.15: "An intelligent mind acquires knowledge, and the ear of the wise seeks knowledge."), and the Psalms exhort the faithful to the study and understanding of creation (111.2: "Great are the works of the Lord, studied by all who delight in them."). In the fourth chapter of Hosea, the prophet pronounces God's "indictment against the inhabitants of the land"[3] that includes, alongside swearing, lying, murder, theft, and adultery, promoting ignorance. In addressing the priests, Hosea says, "My people are destroyed for lack of knowledge; because you have rejected knowledge, I reject you from being a priest to me."[4] Malachi similarly charges the priesthood: "For the lips of a priest ought to preserve knowledge, and from his mouth men should seek instruction – because he is the messenger of the LORD Almighty."[5] Those with contempt for knowledge fare no better in the New Testament. In his letter to the Colossians Paul wishes for his disciples to "have all the riches of assured understanding and have the knowledge of God's mystery," and refers to Christ as the One "in whom are hidden all the treasure of wisdom and knowledge."[6] Second Peter 1.5-7 lists knowledge among the virtues for which Christians should strive, along with goodness, self-control, endurance, godliness, and love for one

---

[1] 1st Timothy 6.20-21. New Revised Standard Version.

[2] 2nd Chronicles 1.10. New Revised Standard Version.

[3] Hosea 4.1. New Revised Standard Version.

[4] Hosea 4.6. New Revised Standard Version.

[5] Malachi 2.7. New International Version.

[6] Colossians 2.2-3. New Revised Standard Version.

another. Second Peter goes on to condemn the narrow interpretation both of Paul's letters and of earlier scriptures: "There are some things in them [Paul's letters] hard to understand, which the ignorant and unstable twist to their own destruction, as they do the other scriptures."[1]

Encouraged by church leadership, an increasing number of fundamentalist Christians are turning to home schooling. From 2003 to 2007, the number of students in kindergarten through twelfth grades being homeschooled increased from 1.1 million to 1.5 million, an increase from 2.2% to 2.9% of the student population. Eighty-three percent of parents of homeschooled children cited a "desire to provide religious or moral instruction" as a primary reason for the decision to home school.[2] Based on the plethora of creationist study courses available, it is safe to assume that a significant number of home schooled students receive the incomplete science curriculum that is consistent with such views; ignorance of scientific theories and the evidence that supports them passes for religious instruction. Colleges and universities supported by fundamentalist churches, denominations, and ministries also commonly modify their biology curriculum to either not acknowledge biological evolution or to present it in a negative light. It is entirely possible for a young person to receive a college degree in almost any field without being confronted by a true representation of the central theory of modern biology, the overwhelming evidence in its favor, or the very real biochemical mechanisms to which it is inextricably linked. Neither student nor parent can of course be blamed for having information and conclusions withheld from them; the ethics of leaders and institutions that withhold and deny scientific data in the name of religious indoctrination must be questioned, however.

Creationists are gleeful that a 2009 Gallup Poll reported just thirty-nine percent of Americans, and only twenty-four percent of those who attend church weekly, believe in evolution,[3] and that a 2008 survey by the same organization showed that fully forty-four percent of Americans believe that God created mankind in its present form less than ten thousand years ago.[4] Creationists may well gloat at the success of their strategy, but majority opinions do not constitute truth, especially in the realm of science. Geocentricity, abiogenesis, and Lamarckism (the inheritance of acquired traits) were all widely held opinions in their day, and all false. Evolution will eventually be as well understood and accepted as heliocentricity, biogenesis, and genetics, and the

---

[1] 2nd Peter 3.16. New Revised Standard Version.

[2] "1.5 Million Homeschooled Students in the United States in 2007." 23 December 2008. National Center for Education Statistics, Institute of Education Sciences, U.S. Dept of Education. Accessed 8 Feb 2008 at <http://nces.ed.gov/pubs2009/2009030.pdf>.

[3] Newport, Frank. "On Darwin's Birthday, Only 4 in 10 Believe in Evolution." *Gallup.* 11 Feb 2009. Accessed 19 Feb 2009 at <http://www.gallup.com/poll/114544/Darwin>.

[4] "Evolution, Creationism, Intelligent Design." *Gallup.* 2009. Accessed 19 Feb 2009 at <http://www.gallup.com/poll/21814/Evolution>.

current stance of creationists will be looked upon as an embarrassment to the faith and the church equal to that felt due to its persecution of Galileo for defending Copernican theory. Outside the circle of American fundamentalists and the overseas missions they support, the vast majority of Christendom already feels that embarrassment, along with an attendant bafflement at the stubbornness of their American brethren in resisting such an obvious resolution as theistic evolution. The evidence of a parallel trend between education and acceptance of evolution is already present in the United States: only twenty-one percent of Americans with a high school education accept the theory of evolution, but the proportion more than doubles to fifty-three percent of college graduates (which includes graduates of evangelical colleges where evolution is denied), and seventy-four percent of those with postgraduate degrees.[1] Education is clearly anathema to creationism, and those who promote creationism and intelligent design for their own purposes engage in an effective strategy by promoting ignorance and spreading misinformation among the less learned. There is a danger, though, that Christianity, or at least those evangelical branches that promote a belief in creationism and intelligent design over theistic evolution, will come to be perceived as and exist as a religion of ignorance, with the ignorant and dishonest leading the ignorant innocents.

The same leaders and institutions who press their adherents to remain ignorant of science apply a similar ethic of promoting ignorance in the consideration and teaching of their faith. Even among laymen who have spent their lives submitting to the religious instruction of evangelical churches, the number of those who are aware of the documentary hypothesis is miniscule. The Pentateuch is presented as having been dictated intact by God to Moses, and neither the inconsistencies of that view in the narrative, nor the variety of styles, vocabularies, and syntax present in the writings, nor the many duplications of text, nor even the simple fact that the Pentateuch as a whole makes no such claim of direct word-for-word revelation (excepting only short segments), is acknowledged. Other portions of the Bible receive similarly shallow treatment. The history of oral and written transmission and translation is not spoken of, with the result that the known history of holy writ is not a subject for discussions, discrepancies between different texts are not admitted, and any difficulty or uncertainty of translation or interpretation goes unrecognized. In much the same way that half truths are used to support dogmatic stances of creationism and intelligent design, ignorance of the history and nature of scripture is used to maintain a simplistic approach to holy writ.

Evangelical laymen remain almost entirely uneducated by the church regarding the writings of the fathers of the faith, and evangelical clergy often appear to have little or no knowledge of them, either. The name Saint Augustine, for most evangelicals, recalls

---

[1] Newport, Frank. "On Darwin's Birthday, Only 4 in 10 Believe in Evolution." *Gallup*. 11 Feb 2009. Accessed 19 Feb 2009 at <http://www.gallup.com/poll/114544/Darwin>.

a small Florida city that is the site of the famous fort Castillo de San Marcos and the oldest permanent European settlement in North America. Few pause to consider that it is the namesake of arguably the most important Christian writer and theologian subsequent to the Apostle Paul, or that his voluminous writings are readily available in modern translations. His works are as inspirational as they are thoughtful and deeply pious, and they consistently recognize in scripture a depth and complexity that is almost wholly absent in modern evangelical writings. Central to Augustine's thoughts was the idea that the authors of the Bible worked under inspiration to provide moral and spiritual instruction, and that other matters were not only subject to interpretation, but to multiple interpretations. Unlike many modern preachers and writers, Augustine guarded against over-confidence in his exegesis:

> In matters that are obscure and far beyond our vision, even in such as we may find treated in Holy Scripture, different Interpretations are sometimes possible without prejudice to the faith we have received. In such a case, we should not rush in headlong and so firmly take our stand on one side that, if further progress in the search of truth justly undermines this position, we too fall with it. That would be to battle not for the teaching of Holy Scripture but for our own, wishing its teaching to conform to ours, whereas we ought to wish ours to conform to that of Sacred Scripture.[1]

Holding such opinions of the veracity and ethics of scriptural interpretation, it is little wonder that evangelicals in particular and creationists and intelligent design proponents in particular would not want their adherents to know or read Saint Augustine. Creationists portray themselves as guardians of scripture, but they really guard their own beliefs, which are not only unsupported by scripture, but contrary to legitimate and thoughtful interpretations. In their role as guardians, they take it upon themselves to suppress and deny inconvenient passages, and to appoint themselves as arbiters of which portions of scripture are to be literally interpreted and which are not. They represent themselves as having certain knowledge of the means God used for creation, even though their certainty is contradicted by the evidence provided by God in His creation.

Saint Augustine is perhaps fortunate to have a famous town named after him, however; the names of other important early Christian writers such as Irenaeus and Origen, men who played major roles in shaping Christian theology in the second and third centuries, are completely unknown to the overwhelming majority of evangelicals. Martin Luther and John Calvin are shadowy historical figures, and few evangelical clergy and even fewer laymen have clear ideas of either their teachings or the conditions that prompted their rebellion against the dominant church teachings of their day and the advent of

---

[1] St. Augustine. *The Literal Meaning of Genesis.* Translated and annotated by John Hammond Taylor. New York: Newman, 1982. Vol 1 of 2, pg 41 (1.18.37).

Protestantism. The names of other figures important to the foundation of Protestantism such as John Wycliffe, John Hus, and Ulrich Zingli are hardly recognized. Powerful and elegant statements of faith like the Apostles' Creed, the Nicene Creed, and the Belgic Confession are almost entirely ignored by most evangelical denominations, and those who worship in their churches are most often ignorant not only of their content but of their very existence.

One can only wonder at the motivation of clergy and other leaders who choose to remain ignorant and to promote and enforce ignorance in their parishioners in subjects like church history, the history of canonical writings, and the principles of scriptural interpretation, along with knowledge of the work of God in the physical realm. The effect is in some ways a reversal of the effects of the Reformation, in that one of the key criticisms of the Catholic Church of that day was that the Church and her priests restricted access to the scriptures; within twenty-first century Christian fundamentalism, the clergy does not restrict access to the words of the scripture, but attempts to control how scripture is interpreted and considered, and therefore what thoughts the scriptures inspire. Whether or not their sole motivation is the enhancement to their own power and influence, the means of ignorance and untruth cannot be ethically justified, and is wholly inconsistent with the ancient Hebrew tradition, given voice by Christ Himself, of worshipping God through activities of the mind.

Humility abandoned

There is arrogance inherent in such attempts at controlling the thoughts of men and women. It is difficult to imagine a position more distant from the humility to which Christians are called than to claim an exclusive ability to interpret scripture and know the mind of God. What modicum of modesty is there in the assertion that you and you alone, among the thousands of learned and dedicated and pious scholars who over the centuries have studied and discussed holy writ, and proposed layer upon layer of literal and allegorical meaning for passage after passage, are privy to the incontestably true and authoritative meaning of scripture? Alternate interpretations of the Genesis creation stories arising from various means of considering scripture are legion – an interpretation consistent with the current state of science is contained in this tome, and Augustine proposed in his landmark *De Genesi ad litteram libri duodecim* (*The Literal Interpretation of Genesis*) at least one, and more often several, interpretations of each passage consistent with the state of scientific understanding in his day, which included belief in the Greek elements of earth, water, air, and fire, the existence of dragons, abiogenesis, and a defense of the dome cosmology of the Hebrew writers. So by what light do creationists declaim their interpretation to be uniquely true? What measure of meekness is there in the contention that they fully understand the mysteries of God and His creation, mysteries that are referred to as such in scripture and in the commentary of centuries of devout scholars? Is there not an implied claim to deification in the assertion that one knows fully the mind and will of God? Can God remain sovereign in the mind of those so convinced?

Creationism, cultism, and credibility

The unfortunate answer to these questions is that adherence to creationism or its recent surrogate, intelligent design, requires behaviors and thought patterns characteristic of cults. Devotees must accept oracular pronouncements of truth from their leaders, without questioning or researching the abundantly available scientific or scriptural resources. Those pronouncements must, in order to preserve their stance, be composed of falsehoods and half truths and delivered by persons of dubious academic credentials and authority, and yet still be unconditionally accepted by cult affiliates. The rejection of outside truth, in the realms of both science and in that of the history and interpretation of scripture itself, must be complete and decisive. Serious and substantive consideration of either physical evidence or scriptural exegesis cannot be tolerated, lest the weakness of the cultic stance be revealed. Neither honesty, nor education, nor humility can be tolerated, let alone viewed as virtues, within the creationism or intelligent design cults. Leaders and peers exert overt and subtle pressures for conformity.

Cults typically remain relatively small, ineffectual, and fragile in their existence, precisely because consideration of outside knowledge and opinions weakens their attractiveness to all but the most single-minded devotees. Creationists of all ilk, including intelligent design proponents, remain a relatively small proportion of the worldwide Christian religion; they are more visible and proportionally more numerous in the United States than in any other part of the world by a considerable margin. Whether or not they consciously relate the thinking and actions of creationists to cultism, people outside of creationist circles and those within creationist denominations and congregations who begin to question creationism find the process of excluding unfavorable knowledge and interpretive opinions to be unattractive and troubling.

The inherent weakness of cultism is that knowledge makes adherence to the cult problematic, and ignorance cannot be maintained indefinitely. In the case of creationism, both the raw scientific data and the theories that are derived from the rational consideration of that data are readily accessible to anyone who, stimulated by schooling, casual reading, educational television programs, or even the frantic tone of creationists themselves, feels a moment of curiosity. All of the scientific information presented in this tome is available to any reader who desires to confirm its validity or to seek deeper knowledge of a particular subject. Footnotes are intentionally extensive and include websites, books of significant distribution and therefore readily available in libraries, bookstores, and by delivery from web-based retailers, and respected professional journals; the most exotic sources are articles and papers in specialty journals that are available for viewing and printing through purchase from internet sources. Similarly, information regarding the origins, history, preservation and transmission, translation, and interpretation of scripture are presented in commonly available Bibles, accompanying essays and notes, and commentaries. The works of prominent theologians and Judeo-Christian thinkers and philosophers can be read online, checked out from libraries, and purchased from booksellers.

In this period of history in which knowledge and opinions are so easily disseminated, anyone who indulges their moment of curiosity is capable of discovering that the clergy, religious leaders, and authors who endorse and advocate creationism do so out of ignorance at best and deceit at worst. A crisis of credibility immediately and necessarily follows. When a person or institution maintains its integrity scrupulously and to the point of stubbornness, a high level of trust is established with all who come in contact. Conversely, when one is found to be false, whether deliberately or by attempting to speak authoritatively about a subject in which knowledge is lacking, trust is eroded, and even truthful statements are questioned and challenged by those whose trust has been violated. In exactly the manner predicted by Augustine, the credibility of the church and its servants is damaged by creationists; because they lack integrity in addressing issues related to modern science, creationists and their institutions, and also other Christian individuals and institutions that are tainted by peculiar and unjustifiable positions that they do not share, lose standing and authority with many who may otherwise benefit from the ethical, moral, and spiritual teachings that are the legitimate domain of religion and the church.

Even more perilous than the plight of adults who feel their trust violated by the church and its agents is that of youth who, having grown up in conservative churches and been kept ignorant of the depth of both scientific knowledge and scriptural exegesis, are abruptly confronted, in college classes or dorm room discussions, with the knowledge that has been withheld from them; the false simplicity of their faith and their view of the world around them and their place in it are shaken in the same moment that they come to grips with the realization that the churches and pastors and lay leaders (including in many instances their own parents) in whom they have placed their trust have misled them. In either case, evangelicals who confront the evidence for evolution and find it credible are too frequently challenged by demands that they choose between their religious faith and current scientific theories. Since science provides verifiable evidence in published photographs, descriptions, astronomical observations, and experimental and theoretical physics, erstwhile believers choose to believe their own senses and reason, and either abandon faith entirely, choose a denomination and congregation more tolerant of knowledge, or guiltily keep their convictions a secret to remain among people who are familiar but who they know are not accepting of them and their core beliefs. What science is contained in the Bible is from the Bronze Age of its writers; demanding that it be regarded as a science text, ignoring two thousand years of scientific observations and conclusions, demeans its value as a document of enormous ethical, legal, spiritual, and theological importance and compromises the credibility of both scripture and those who make spurious demands of it.

Mark Noll, an evangelical Christian who spent twenty-seven years as a professor in the history and theology departments at Wheaton College before joining the faculty of Notre Dame University, began his book *The Scandal of the Evangelical Mind*, a study of the origins and causes of anti-intellectualism in American evangelicalism, with the sentence, "The scandal of the evangelical mind is that there is not much of an evangelical mind."[1] If that is the scholarly assessment of the quality of thought - the worship of and by the mind - from within the evangelical community, what must be the assessment of fellow Christians outside the more overtly evangelical denominations, of potential converts to the faith, and of the God who commands the service of our minds along with that of our flesh and our spirit? Christians not under the proximate influence of creationists are aghast at the stubbornness, ignorance, and falsehood that are presented in the name of their faith. Prospects who are told that they must ignore several millennia of learning and progress and adhere to scientific understandings of the Bronze Age in order to enter into the fellowship of Christians justifiably reject fundamentalist faith; atheists are delighted by creationist rhetoric, and progressive churches, some of which are criticized by more conservative denominations for liberal teachings in ethical and social issues, accept those who are alienated or rejected by congregations and clergy who proclaim or imply that creationism is an essential belief of their brand of Christianity. No mere mortal should presume to fully understand and predict the thoughts of God on this or any matter, but it is at least reasonable to wonder if God feels well served by ambassadors who represent His word as simple and backward, His work as misleading and illogical, and the witness of His truth encompassed in His two-fold revelation to mankind as self-contradictory and unworthy of our trust.

Interestingly, thirty-six percent of Americans report that they believe in theistic evolution, and only twelve percent believe that God had no role; i.e., three times as many people believe in theistic evolution as in atheistic evolution.[2] That means that the legitimate beliefs of over a hundred and ten million Americans, nearly as many as the estimated hundred and thirty million who report regular church attendance,[3] are rejected by creationists, even though those believers encompass in their faith a belief in

---

[1] Noll, Mark A. *The Scandal of the Evangelical Mind.* Grand Rapids: William B. Eerdmans, 1994. Pg 3.

[2] "Evolution, Creationism, Intelligent Design." *Gallup.* 2009. Accessed 19 Feb 2009 at <http://www.gallup.com/poll/21814/Evolution>.

[3] Newport, Frank. "No Evidence Bad Times are Boosting Church Attendance." 17 Dec 2008. Accessed 19 Feb 2009 at <http://www.gallup.com/poll/113452/Evidence-Bad-Times-Boosting-Church-Attendance.aspx>.

God, and the rejection of those beliefs by creationists is for reasons that are incompatible with scripture and the witness of God's creation. Creationists assert that evolution is inherently atheistic, but only one out of four people who accept evolution consider it to be atheistic. Is it a right or power of any man to reject or discourage the faith of another when that faith is consistent with a reasonable interpretation of scripture?

Dilution of the gospel message

Clearly, opportunities for ministry are lost by the baseless insistence on creationism and intelligent design as a component of Christianity. Three-quarters of the people who believe in evolution believe that it was a tool used by God in creation, yet instead of embracing those believers and their faith, welcoming them in the fellowship of worship, and making use of their talents and abilities as they pursue opportunities to deepen their faith, creationist laymen, clergy, congregations, and denominations choose to devote their energy to convincing the believer in theistic evolution to deny the evidence of their own senses and reason or, failing to thus convince them, to alienating and ostracizing them.

The founding impetus for evangelicalism is found in the words of Jesus just before His ascension, charging his followers to bear witness of His life, death, and resurrection "to the ends of the earth."[1] The central message of Christianity is that the Creator God, the great I Am, is a loving God who offers forgiveness, earthly peace, and eternal rest to all who accept His grace; all else is extraneous. Salvation is not found in loud music with guitars and drums or in the mellow tones of a pipe organ; it does not depend on standing, dancing, clapping, waving hands, or ecstatic utterance, any more or less than on the staid contemplation of liturgy. Neither the rejection nor the acceptance of scientific observations and theories is a precondition to the love or mercy of God, although the case can certainly be made that participation in scientific research and debate is more in keeping with the exhortations of scripture than is an effort to mislead and misinform the flock regarding the testimony of God's creation. The debate about the means of creation, contrived as it is, is a pointless distraction from the vital knowledge that the one true God was the Creator, and the unfathomable mystery that that same God became man and took upon Himself the sins of mankind along with propitiating punishment, all out of love for His created creature.

God's role as creator is not inconsequential to His role as a law-giver and judge, and as the agent of moral mercy in turn. As previously discussed, God's authority derives at least in part from His credentials as creator. God's undertaking as the sole creator in Judeo-Christian tradition and scripture establishes His oneness, in contrast to the

[1] Acts 1.8. Multiple translations.

polytheism of cultures surrounding ancient Israel and many other cultures worldwide. (Recall the proclamation of Deuteronomy that was and is a part of Judaic worship: "Hear, O Israel, the LORD our God, the LORD is one."[1]) With His role as sole creator established, His sole authority as the author and arbiter of physical and ethical law follows, and from the oneness of that role arises His power to fully forgive. If another deity performed any task in creation, it would likewise share authority with God, based on its knowledge of the design of creation, in establishing the laws governing creation. If any such deity existed, the authority of God to forgive would necessarily be similarly shared, and the forgiveness of God would be incomplete insofar as another offended deity would retain the discretion of his or her own forgiveness. With the oneness of God established by His role in creation, the completeness of God's forgiveness is assured. His righteousness is similarly established by His solitary role as creator, since in His oneness He has no rival in establishing or judging moral law; the justice of His judgments are therefore without challenge, and His mercy uncontested. Had one or several other deities established their authority by sharing in the tasks of creation, the forgiveness of God would have required concurrent forgiveness for the other deity for any offense perceived by it in order to be complete, and every merciful judgment of God would be equally incomplete until it accommodated the verdict of His co-creator.

God's oneness as creator is necessary in establishing His authority, but both the means and the time frame of His creation are irrelevant. Whether He created all that is in a moment, in six revolutions of the earth on its axis, or over a period of fourteen billion years, His authority is established by His agency in creation. Whether he created by the instantaneous fabrication of finished entities or by providing the apparatus for a prolonged course of sustained development, He is One. His knowledge and wisdom, displayed in the creative process of a moment or an age, establishes his credentials as the one true God with the authority to judge and forgive. Once His oneness is established by acknowledging His role as creator, debate about the means and time frame of His creative influence is a mere distraction to the consideration of His grace.

As the contrived debate about evolution contributes nothing to the knowledge or acceptance of God's mercy, so it likewise contributes nothing to the understanding of God's nature. True and valid arguments cannot be based on false premises; any deliberation or contemplation of the constitution or quintessence of God based on creationist arguments is invalid because of being rooted in the false premises of denial, incomplete consideration, and falsification of the material evidence present in the testament of God's creation.

One of the chief concerns expressed by religious critics of biological evolution is its sociopolitical impact. They feel that mankind's relationship to animals debases humans

---

[1] Deuteronomy 6.4. New International Version.

and devalues human life, and blame all manner of modern problems on the teaching of evolution. The causes of society's many current ills are beyond the scope of this work, but knowledge of modern scientific theories need not be counted among them. In the first place, it is highly debatable whether human life has been devalued in the years since the publication of *The Origin of Species*. Human savagery does not seem to have an historical boundary: wars, motivated by territorial disputes, the possession of resources, and ethnic hatred, permeate our history; the examples of despotism among rulers ranging from petty feudal lords to the greatest monarchical houses are too many to count or even know; horrific regimes like that of Pol Pot show no evidence of being governed by knowledge of either Jesus or Darwin; acts of the Inquisition and the Crusades are not a credit to Christianity, but predate Darwin by centuries. Secondly, there is no rational reason why evolution should debase humanity. Whether the change developed gradually or was instilled abruptly, to be human is to possess conscience, intellect, appreciation for beauty, and spirituality that surpasses that of all other animals; only in the realm of intellect is the human species even remotely rivaled. That the meritorious training of those gifts is deficient in modern society is an arguable point; an argument that they are of value only if they are instantaneously delivered to the human race and somehow compromised by being gradual in their prehistoric development is fatuous.

The spiritual cost of the distraction from the central message of Christianity and the contemplation of the nature of God cannot be measured, but the cost in human and material resources give cause to question the stewardship of those who promulgate the creationist and intelligent design message. The man hours, energy, dedication, thought (however misapplied), and effort that goes into the baseless and unproductive arguments of creationism is enormous but difficult to quantify. Tax documents in the public record reveal that the Discovery Institute, Answers in Genesis, and the Institute for Creation Research combine to raise tens of millions of dollars each year, with assets also reaching into the tens of millions.[1,2,3] These and other similar organizations refer to the gospel frequently in their publications, but seldom mention love, forgiveness, or the simple means of accepting God's grace that is central to Christian theology and the Biblical presentation of the gospel as good news for mankind. Instead, the gospel they refer to is the gospel of creationism, with all its divisiveness, exclusionism, and misrepresentations of both material evidence and scriptural exegesis, diverting attention

---

[1] IRS form 990, 2006, filed by Discovery Institute 21 Nov 2007. Accessed 24 Feb 2009 at <http://dynamodata.fdncenter.org/990_pdf_archive/911/911521697/911521697_200612_990.pdf>.

[2] "Answers in Genesis/AiG/Ken Ham." Ministrywatch.com. Undated. Accessed 24 Feb 2009 at <http://www.ministrywatch.com/profile/Answers-in-Genesis.aspx>.

[3] "Institute for Creation Research/ICR." Ministrywatch.com. Undated. Accessed 24 Feb 2009 at <http://www.ministrywatch.com/profile/Institute-for-Creation-Research.aspx>.

and consideration from the real gospel of Christ's living example and the redeeming sacrifice of His death. What could be the impact if the human resources and voices of these organizations were devoted to evangelizing the cause of Christianity instead of erecting barriers to the birth and maturity of faith by expounding the necessity of creationist beliefs to Christian doctrine? What good could be done in meeting humanitarian needs for medical care, food, shelter, and clothing by redirecting the fund raising capabilities and reserves of these organizations?

Proselytization

Creationism impedes the adoption of Judeo-Christian faith by men and women of science. No less a personage than Albert Einstein rejected traditional religion because of fundamentalist interpretations of scripture. Although he was raised in a highly secular Jewish family, the adolescent Einstein became enamored of traditional Judaism and was for a time highly observant of Jewish law, custom, and ritual. At the age of twelve, however, he later wrote, "through the reading of popular scientific books, I soon reached the conviction that much in the stories of the Bible could not be true."[1] Although he would retain a lifelong belief in a deity who brought order and harmony to the universe that he so skillfully explored, Einstein would never again embrace organized religion or formal worship.

The defining characteristic of evangelicalism – the commitment and effort devoted to presenting Christianity to the mass of humanity and to convert others to the faith – is compromised by creationism. Christians have, indeed, good reason to offer their religion as a balm to modern man. The life of Jesus provides an enduring example of tolerance, respect, compassion, and grace, and His words provide inspiration, comfort, and theosophy. To become Christian, which means most literally to become like Christ, to embrace the values lived and spoken by Jesus, is to change one's life and lifestyle, often radically, from one of selfishness and greed to one of selflessness, generosity of spirit, humility, and concern for others. A person who is truly Christian, and not embracing a false mantle of Christianity either on his own or under the auspices of an organized church, becomes more fully human – more fully realizes the human traits of conscience, intellect, appreciation of beauty, spirituality, and humility - as he approaches a fuller knowledge of God.

Insisting on creationism as a central component of Christianity is, besides being false to both scripture and the evidence of the created universe, a horrible strategy for proselytization.

The canonical gospels do not record any extensive comments by Jesus regarding the

---

[1] Einstein, Albert. "Autobiographical Notes." 1949. In *Einstein: His Life and Universe,* Walter Isaacson. New York: Simon & Schuster, 2007. Pg 20.

creation stories of Genesis; He acknowledged God as the creator, but did not address the means or time table of the creative process. It is difficult to understand why acceptance as science of what is clearly a set of collected myths – myth in the sense of being a traditional story involving a deity (or in other cases, heroes) that plays a cultural role in explaining and justifying a belief, without the negative connotation of being false – is so crucial to creationists. Besides asking why a creation myth from the dawn of recorded history must be accepted by modern Christians, one must ask which of the at least three Biblical creation myths should be adopted. And why are the creation myths crucial while other science of the time – the dome cosmology of the ancient Hebrews and ancient concepts of the influence of non-genetic factors on inheritance, to take two examples already developed – is so easily discarded?

Dome cosmology, at least, persisted into New Testament times, as evidenced by Jesus' reference in the twenty-sixth chapter of Matthew to stars falling from the sky to earth. It is clear that the Word Incarnate saw stars as decorative points of light emanating from small objects in the nearby dome over earth that could, under the influence of earth's gravity, fall to the ground, rather than as distant objects with masses and gravitational fields that far exceed that of earth. No credible witness of Christianity demands that fellow Christians adhere to the cosmology of Jesus Himself, yet they insist that the mutually contradictory creation stories recorded by unknown ancient scribes – and their own narrow interpretation of them, at that – be the last word in science.

Creationists, then, attempt to win new converts to Christianity by insisting that the one interpretation of the first three chapters of Genesis among the multitude of interpretations that have been proposed over the centuries that is least consistent with verifiable physical evidence is essential to the faith and, by implication of the vigor of their arguments, more important than the remaining portion of Genesis or any of the other sixty-five books, including those that record the life, death, and resurrection of Jesus. The prospect must deny the evidence of his or her own senses and reason, the wisdom of centuries of biblical scholars and theologians extending into the present day, and the values of integrity, learning, and humility respected and esteemed by the faith's holy writ and tradition, and by human society in general. In the presentation of creationists, the merciful grace of God represented by the sacrificial death of Jesus, and the promise of eternal life realized in His resurrection, is overshadowed by devotion to a creation myth that was selected from among the many stories of the Bible for strict literal interpretation and undue preeminence.

Perhaps the most bizarre and harmful component of the creationist position is that they ally themselves with atheists in declaring that the truth of evolution excludes the existence of God. The proclamation by creationists that biological evolution, and to a lesser extent other scientific theories of development as well, are incompatible with theism in general and the faith and scripture of Christianity in particular is a tactical disaster that plays directly into the hands of the most vocal atheists. The creationist stance, by insisting that only the separate, spontaneous, and miraculous creation of species is consistent with the existence of God, essentially concedes that any evidence of gradual change or natural processes is proof of atheism. By equating creationist dogma with Christian faith, creationists unwittingly concur with atheists that every observation of astronomy, physics, paleontology, taxonomy, biochemistry, and genetics that confirms or expands existing scientific theories – and they occur every day – is an effective and valid argument against their faith. The false concession that a belief in God is incompatible with the scientific theories born of empiric observations is seized upon by those inclined to argue for atheism, for they understand that unconfirmed faith will not overcome the evidence of the senses and rationality in most people, and the evidence in favor of biological, geological, and cosmological evolution is overwhelming.

Kenneth Miller said it well in *Finding Darwin's God*:

> Religion, however, is drawn into dangerous territory by the creationist logic. By arguing, as they have repeatedly, that nature cannot be self-sufficient in the formation of new species, the creationists forge a logical link between the limits of natural processes to accomplish biological change and the existence of a designer (God). In other words, they show the proponents of atheism exactly how to disprove the existence of God – show that evolution works, and it's time to tear down the temple. . . [T]his is an offer that the enemies of religion are all too happy to accept.[1]

Taken another way, the creationist viewpoint sees God only in those things that cannot be explained by natural laws, instead of attributing the laws of nature to God. To the creationist, the laws of nature are impediments to God rather than tools, and boundaries to God's work rather than the result of His intellect and wisdom. The effect is that, as mankind's understanding of natural laws expands and is able to explain more and more of the observable phenomenon of the universe, the God of creationists becomes smaller. In the late twentieth and early twenty-first centuries, He is now so small that He is, in the view of creationists, virtually absent from the physical realm if present-day science is to be understood and accepted. The error of creationists is that instead of rejecting such a narrow view of God and standing in awe of His creation as understood by modern science, they reject the observations and theories of science and strain to see miracles where the laws of nature reign. Why they cannot see the natural as being equal in importance to the miraculous in affirming their faith is a mystery that outsiders have difficulty penetrating.

---

[1] Miller, Kenneth R. *Finding Darwin's God.* New York: HarperCollins, 1999. Page 265-267.

Philosopher Daniel Dennett is one who has seized the concession of creationists that theories of evolutionary change exclude the existence of God. In his popular book *Darwin's Dangerous Idea*,[1] Dennett explores in enlightening ways the implications of that fact that Darwinian evolution is an algorithmic process, but he incorrectly concludes that because of its algorithmic nature it is necessarily an atheistic process. For all his brilliance and insight, Dennett repeats the fatal logical flaw of concluding that because something (in this case God) is not necessary, it is not possible.

Dennett and others recognize that algorithms are branching structures of chance, but they seem to forget two important points. First, chance is not synonymous with randomness. Gamblers recognize this fact by rewarding higher risks with higher payoffs –bookies make odds and spreads based on the relative strengths of sport teams and the payoff is higher for narrower bets at the roulette wheel, for example. Second, algorithms can also be mechanisms for conscious choice and logic - algorithmic diagnostic plans in medicine are an example, as are algorithms for the taxonomic identification of plants and animals. As has been argued in the preceding chapters of this book, there is room within the principles of science, especially in considering the probability-guided mechanisms of quantum mechanics, for the guiding hand of a deity to remain unseen. Dennett pretends to argue for atheism from a premise of Darwinism, but a close reading reveals that atheism is both his premise and his conclusion, a fatal flaw of logic.

Not even all atheists have maintained such a narrow view of the relationship between science and religion. Stephen Jay Gould, who along with Niles Eldredge proposed the punctuated equilibrium modification of evolutionary theory and authored innumerable technical articles for professional journals, was also a popular essayist and speaker, and an atheist. As he neared the end of his life after having been diagnosed with cancer, he proposed in the provocatively titled *Rocks of Ages: Science and Religion in the Fullness of Life* "a blessedly simple and entirely conventional resolution to . . . the supposed conflict between science and religion."

> [The] magisterium of science covers the empirical realm: what the Universe is made of (fact) and why does it work in this way (theory). The magisterium of religion extends over questions of ultimate meaning and moral value. These two magisteria do not overlap, nor do they encompass all inquiry (consider, for example, the magisterium of art and the meaning of beauty). To cite the old clichés, science gets the age of rocks, and religion the rock of ages; science studies how the heavens go, and religion how to go to heaven.[2]

---

[1] Dennett, Daniel C. *Darwin's Dangerous Idea.* New York: Simon & Schuster, 1995.
[2] Gould, Stephen Jay. *Rock of Ages: Science and Religion in the Fullness of Life.* New York: Ballantine, 1999. Pg 6.

It would be reasonable, and justifiable to proselytes, for Christians to embrace the gentle concession of Stephen Jay Gould that there is a place for religion alongside science in human endeavor, and to criticize the faulty logic of Daniel Dennett and like-minded polemicists. The words of Pope John Paul II in a 1981 address to the Pontifical Academy of Sciences are strikingly similar to those of Gould, but spoken from the viewpoint of one convinced of the sanctity of scripture and dedicated to religious thought:

> [T]he Bible does not concern itself with the details of the physical world, the understanding of which is the competence of human experience and reasoning. There exist two realms of knowledge, one which has its source in Revelation and one which reason can discover by its own power. To the latter belong especially the experimental sciences and philosophy. The distinction between the two realms of knowledge ought not to be understood as opposition. The two realms are not altogether foreign to each other, they have points of contact. The methodologies proper to each make it possible to bring out different aspects of reality. . .
>
> The Bible itself speaks to us of the origin of the universe and its make-up, not in order to provide us with a scientific treatise, but in order to state the correct relationships of man with God and with the universe. Sacred Scripture wishes simply to declare that the world was created by God, and in order to teach this truth it expresses itself in the terms of the cosmology in use at the time of the writer. . . Any other teaching about the origin and make-up of the universe is alien to the intentions of the Bible, which does not wish to teach how heaven was made but how one goes to heaven.[1]

Such a perspective is not unique to Catholicism, for as we have seen, the founders of Protestantism taught and demonstrated a respect for learning and reverence for the knowledge of God revealed in His creation that was equal to that expressed by the Catholic Church and, at least at times, more consistently practiced. Creationists have, in the last century and a half, been uniquely eager to endorse the argument of the most vociferous atheists that religion cannot find common truth with science. One would have expected creationists to reject the argument simply because of its origin, but they have instead not only adopted it as their own, but trumpeted it more loudly than its atheist originators.

The backward appearance of Christianity as regarded by modern day prospects for conversion was aptly captured by the inimitable C. S. Lewis:

---

[1] Pope John Paul II. Address to Pontifical Academy of Sciences 31 Oct 1981. Accessed 8 Jan 2008 at <http://www.its.caltech.edu/~nmcenter/sci-cp/sci-9211.html >.

> The ordinary man is not thinking of particular dogmas and particular scientific discoveries. What troubles him is an all-pervading difference of atmosphere between what he believes Christianity to be and that general picture of the universe which he has picked up from living in a scientific age. He gathers from the Creed that God has a 'Son' (just as if God were a god, like Odin or Jupiter): that this Son 'came down' (like a parachutist) from 'Heaven", first to earth and later to some land of the dead situated beneath the earth's surface: that, still later, He ascended into the sky and took His seat in a decorated chair placed a little to the right of His Father's throne. The whole thing seems to imply a local and material heaven – a palace in the stratosphere – a flat earth and all the rest of those archaic misconceptions.[1]

There is no debating the fact that Christian proselytization has success in certain quarters by representing itself as the domain of archaic misconceptions. Polls clearly show that the acceptance of creationism decreases sharply with education, however, so churches that hold creationism to be essential to Christian belief face a dilemma in evangelizing and ministering to people with knowledge of the physical sciences, in particular biological sciences. Is education to be either explicitly or implicitly asserted to stand alone, among the many heinous acts of depravity of which humans have proven themselves capable, as an unforgivable sin, beyond the mercy of God,? If so, those churches must justify to prospects and congregants why and how they take a position opposite to the respect for knowledge expressed in scripture, the Old and New Testament admonition to worship God with the mind, and the long-standing Judeo-Christian tradition that holds the physical realm to be a supplementary revelation of the nature of God and its exploration an act of veneration. If not, they must justify, with equal difficulty, why they refuse to minister to a segment of mankind to whom God has extended His grace. When a person by faith accepts the forgiveness and knowledge of Christ, and concurrently is or seeks to be conversant in physics, astronomy, and biology and well read in the works of Einstein, Bohr, Hawking, Darwin, and other great minds, should the role of the church be to discourage and burden that faith or to ridicule and demean that knowledge?

Evangelical churches for the most part fail to minister to the well educated. Their sermons and teaching frequently lack depth and erudition; their preferred music most often is a body of simple choruses in major keys, with reduction or elimination of hymns that are more complex musically and lyrically; the very word worship has been co-opted and redefined as clapping, raising hands in accepted gestures, and dancing to loud music, while quiet contemplation, hushed reverence, and moments of penitent humility in the presence of the worshiped God are looked down upon as being less spiritual and insufficiently demonstrative of devotion. The evangelical movement is

---

[1] Lewis, C. S. "Horrid Red Things." God In The Dock: Essays on Theology and Ethics. Edited by Walter Hooper. Grand Rapids: Eerdmans Publishing, 1970. Pg 68.

widely viewed, even by the more lettered and cultivated minority within its walls, as being theologically shallow, culturally backward, and dismissive of intellectual pursuits, including the scholarly pursuit of religious understanding. The worship of the mind, to which scripture calls all of humanity and to which the well-read are most attracted, is largely neglected by evangelical churches. Those churches which preach creationism or intelligent design even more forcefully exclude any with a thorough knowledge of biological sciences. Recall that fifty-three percent of college graduates and seventy-four percent of those with graduate degrees reject all forms of creationism in favor of evolution,[1] and over a hundred and ten million Americans, well over one third of the population, believe in theistic evolution,[2] and consider that every church that endorses creationism or intelligent design chooses to exclude those millions of people from its evangelism and its ministries. Professional men and women, if they do not feel rejected by Christianity as a whole, find churches that are more tolerant of their learning and more satisfying and diverse in the opportunities they provide for worship and spiritual growth, and they take their expertise, talents, and financial support with them.

The belief in creationism is unifying to its adherents, but it unifies them against the very world that they profess a desire to evangelize. It promotes a feeling of "us against the world," and is often presented thusly by those who preach and teach it. Creationism is, then, in theory and in practice, inherently exclusive in its nature, contrary to the words and spirit of Christian scripture, teaching, and tradition.

Reconciliation

Evangelism is not terribly unlike the sales of goods or services. According to the faith, the stakes are extraordinarily higher, but as in sales of other products, there is an attempt to persuade a prospect of the benefits of an exchange – of money in exchange for goods or services, or of devotion and a revised set of values in exchange for an old way of living or believing - and like any conscientious business person with goods or services to sell, Christians need to evaluate their product from the perspective of the customer.

A significant portion of Christendom, including the preponderance of evangelicals, fails to acknowledge that Christianity as a religion cannot be proved. Details of the life of Jesus that speak to His divinity, such as Mary's virginity at His birth, the descent of a dove and the voice from heaven at His baptism, His several miracles, and His resurrection, are themselves articles of faith accepted only at the testimony of other devotees. Other religions have claimed virgin births (Perseus of Greek mythology,

---

[1] Newport, Frank. "On Darwin's Birthday, Only 4 in 10 Believe in Evolution." *Gallup*. 11 Feb 2009. Accessed 19 Feb 2009 at <http://www.gallup.com/poll/114544/Darwin>.
[2] "Evolution, Creationism, Intelligent Design." *Gallup*. 2009. Accessed 19 Feb 2009 at <http://www.gallup.com/poll/21814/Evolution>.

Augustus of the Roman cult of the divine emperor, and some of the several versions of Mithra, for example) and nearly all claim miraculous events caused by or acknowledging the deity of their central figures. Accounts of miraculous events associated with Jesus are exclusively reported either directly by His followers or as second-hand anecdotes related by His followers; attempts at objective verification have not proved fruitful. The myths at the heart of the worship of the Egyptian god Osiris, Tummuz of the Babylonians, Adonis of Greek mythology, and the semitic Hadad Ba'al all include resurrection, some of a seasonally cyclical nature. Although the resurrection of Jesus is an orthodox belief of Christianity, all of the people to whom He appeared according to scripture were admirers of His person and adherents to His teachings, and independent verification is lacking. Accounts by neutral contemporaries sometimes mention Jesus as a prophet with a significant following, but often also mention other messianic figures of the same era along with similar reports of claims by their followers of miracles presented as proof of their special status. A prominent rabbi a generation after Jesus, Hanina ben Dosa, is credited with a miraculous healing[1] that bears similarities to the healing of the servant[2] or son[3] of the centurion by Jesus. The divinity of Jesus is accepted by Christians, along with the supporting evidence of scripture, as matters of faith, but they cannot be independently verified to the satisfaction of unbelievers.

Likewise, the emotional sensation of conversion and changes in lifestyle and values are not unique to Christianity and therefore not convincing evidence to unbelievers. Feelings variously described as a perception of forgiveness, peace, satisfaction, and fulfillment, no matter how real to the disciple, can be neither documented nor quantified by an outside observer, and similar feelings are attested to by devotees of other religions. Regardless of one's system of beliefs, reconciliation with the force or deity representing goodness is likely to produce in the human mind a similar sensation of wellness of the soul. There is no doubt that lives are reformed by a commitment to Christianity – frequently, addictions are overcome, personal estrangements are resolved, and hopes and aspirations are renewed in the conversion experience – but as reticent as we may be to admit it, such experiences are not unique to Christianity; it appears that the inward effects of a resolution to make a new start and to follow the good has a significantly similar effect on behaviors and attitudes when exercised within the structure of other religions, as well. And zealotry is not evidence for the truth of a religion: radical Islam produces suicide bombers and others willing to give their lives in jihad, and devout Buddhists are willing to self immolate as a means of protest against perceived wrongs.

---

[1] Wansbrough, Henry. "The Four Gospels in Synopsis." *The Oxford Bible Commentary.* John Barton and John Muddiman, ed. Oxford: Oxford University Press, 2001.

[2] Matthew 8.5-13, Luke 7.1-20.

[3] John 4.46-53.

Essentially, one must possess belief in the scriptures of the faith in order to confirm the faith. The belief of Christians, however strong, remains in the realm of faith rather than fact in the sense that it cannot be objectively verified or proven correct by a logician. But even that statement is consistent with scripture, for faith is defined in the New Testament as "the substance of things hoped for, [and] the evidence of things not seen."[1] Mainstream Christianity has held in recent centuries, thanks largely to Søren Kierkegaard, that definitive proof of God's existence is lacking because of His desire that men and women make their faith and service of Him a choice rather than a compulsion. Kierkegaard maintained, furthermore, that human faith is strengthened by being exercised in uncertainty; as phrased by Kierkegaard, "If I am capable of grasping God objectively, I do not believe, but precisely because I cannot do this I must believe. If I wish to preserve myself in faith I must constantly be intent upon holding fast the objective uncertainty, so as to remain out upon the deep, over seventy fathoms of water still preserving my faith."[2]

It is fundamental that Christians approach the task of evangelization – and their own faith - with the realization that it is the acceptance of religious belief that requires trust in the unseen, while the understanding of the material universe that is at the heart of the scientific endeavor is the product of observation and rational thought. It is natural that there would exist in a believer a longing, more desperate in some than in others, for confirmation of the existence of a deity to which one has entrusted the values by which one chooses to live and the hope of an afterlife of reward. That longing finds expression in formal and informal logical arguments, but all are flawed at some level, usually by falling into a circular argument of assuming the truth of some element of faith or scripture in order to prove the truth of faith or scripture. The yearning for a glimpse of a miracle is part and parcel of that longing for confirmation – if we could see that the laws of nature were purposely violated to our benefit, we would have confirmation that there is a God who is both all-powerful and benevolent.

The emphasis of charismatic groups on such displays as the gift of tongues, faith healing, slaying in the spirit, and prophecy reflects in large part the desire to witness the substantiation of faith through the miraculous. The multitude of miracles inherent to creationism provides just such validation to adherents, but the miracles are illusions dispelled by scientific inquiry. But a faith that depends on the observation of miracles is a tenuous faith indeed, for miracles by their very nature are not repeatable and therefore not verifiable, and it would seem to be a violation of the sovereignty of God to demand a steady stream of miracles to prove and bolster one's faith. Thomas, one

---

[1] Hebrews 11.1. King James Version.

[2] Kierkegaard, Søren (pseudonym Johannes Climacus author, S. K. editor). *Concluding Unscientific Postscript to the Philosophical Fragments.* Trans. Howard V. Hong and Edna H. Hong. Princeton, NJ: Princeton University Press, 1992. First edition 1846. P 207.

of Jesus' disciples who was so devoted that, when he perceived a threat to his master's life, urged his fellows, "Let us also go, that we may die with him,"[1] nevertheless initially discounted reports of Jesus resurrection: "Unless I see the mark of the nails in his hands, and put my finger in the mark of the nails and my hand in his side, I will not believe."[2] Jesus' reply to Thomas was to both provide the proof that he required and to admonish him, "Blessed are those who have not seen and yet have come to believe."[3] In other words, the faith unconfirmed by physical evidence is the stronger and more honored by God.

It appears to be a valid observation of the nature of God that He chooses to remain invisible to the natural and material world in order to make the acceptance of His dominion by humans a matter of choice rather than one made by compelling reasoning. The magesteria elucidated by Gould and the realms described by Pope John Paul II are cogent – the nature of science is that it embraces as truth only that which can be tested and verified, while the essential nature of faith is that it embraces as truth that which cannot be tested or verified but depends upon belief.

There is yet a subtle difference between the views of Stephen Jay Gould and Pope John Paul II that should be considered: according to Gould the magesteria of science and religion "do not overlap,"[4] but the in the view of the late pope "[t]he two realms are not altogether foreign to each other, they have points of contact."[5] The point of contact that was invisible to the atheist but apparent to the man of faith is that, because of his belief, John Paul could see the material universe as revelatory of the nature of God.

The God revealed by the observations of science has characteristics that distinguish Him from the God of creationists in ways that make Him more appealing to prospective converts and believers alike. He is patient to create over millions and billions of years, rather than feeling a need to impulsively create a multitude of separate entities, each without a past or a future; the billions of years of prehistory are testament to the immensity of His vision and His plan. His wisdom is vast enough to encompass the complexity of the natural world, and His foresight is so limitless that the eons of time that the processes of His creation have taken to accomplish their current fulfillment and a future beyond our comprehension are enveloped within His view. He is consistent in the display of His integrity both in unifying the testimonies of His Word

[1] John 11.16, New Revised Standard Version.
[2] John 20.24, New Revised Standard Version.
[3] John 20.20, New Revised Standard Version.
[4] Gould, Stephen Jay. *Rock of Ages: Science and Religion in the Fullness of Life.* New York: Ballantine, 1999. Pg 6.
[5] Pope John Paul II. Address to Pontifical Academy of Sciences 31 Oct 1981. Accessed 8 Jan 2008 at <http://www.its.caltech.edu/~nmcenter/sci-cp/sci-9211.html >.

and His creation to the essence of His nature and, although being both sovereign and omnipotent He was not bound to do so, in honoring the laws of nature that are His decree.

The doctrine of creationism, besides dangerously misrepresenting the truth of the created material world and thereby damaging the credibility of the faith, proposes a God that lacks these very qualities of patience, wisdom, and integrity. It is for this reason that C. S. Lewis wrote, "Science twisted in the interests of apologetics would be sin and folly."[1]

Within the framework of Christian faith, the modern theories of science illuminate a God that created not by spontaneously generating independent entities without precedents, but via a system of properties of matter and energy that caused them to be endlessly interrelated and to progress towards complexity in an algorithmic process defined by probabilities. The algorithmic nature of the process does not exclude the influence of God; rather, the existence of varying probabilities of outcomes allows Him to work unseen. The invisible guidance of God in matters that appear to the human perspective to be governed only by chance is explicitly endorsed by scripture. In the book of Proverbs we read, "The lot is cast into the lap, but the decision is the LORD's alone."[2] Accordingly, Joshua cast lots to identify for execution a man who had illegally kept plunder for himself, with an accuracy that elicited a confession from the accused;[3] Saul was selected as the first king of Israel by lots cast by the prophet Samuel;[4] Saul prayed over a casting of lots that identified his son Jonathan as one who broke an oath to fast;[5] casting lots was endorsed by scripture as a means to settle difficult legal disputes.[6] If God can influence the casting of lots to successfully manage human affairs and administer justice, there is no apparent bar to Him likewise influencing biochemical systems that have a similar appearance of randomness; quantum mechanics gives exactly such opportunity for divine intervention in apparently random physiochemical systems.

Pierre Teilhard de Chardin, in his essay "The Modes of Divine Action in the Universe," recognized both the validity of scientific exploration and the futility of seeking scientific proofs for spiritual concepts:

> The First Cause is not involved in effects; it acts upon individual natures and on the movement of the whole. Properly speaking, God does not make: He

---

[1] Lewis, C. S. "Christian Apologetics." *God In The Dock: Essays on Theology and Ethics.* Walter Hooper, ed. Grand Rapids, MI: William B. Eerdmans, 1994. Pg 103.

[2] Proverbs 16.33, New Revised Standard Version.

[3] Joshua 7.10-21.

[4] First Samuel 10.20-21.

[5] First Samuel 14.24-42.

[6] Proverbs 18.18.

> makes things make themselves. That is why there is no breach or cleavage at the point at which he enters. The network of determinisms remains intact – the harmony of organic developments continues without discord. And yet the master has entered into his own.
>
> But, it will be objected, if the condition of the divine action is that it is always shrouded in chance, in determinism, in immanence, then we are obliged to admit that the divine causality is not directly apprehensible – either as creative in the movement which orders the world, or as revealing in the miracle.
>
> That is perfectly true.
>
> Whether it be ordinary Providence, or miraculous Providence (extraordinary coincidences), or even, again, the prodigy, we shall never be enabled scientifically to see God, because there will never be any discontinuity between the divine operation and the physical and physiological laws which are science's sole concern.[1]

Successful evangelism, particularly to persons educated in the physical sciences, will not proceed from the denial of natural law, but by the engagement of a guiding force working within the understood and documented processes of cosmological, geological, and biological evolution, and such an engagement is eminently plausible under modern scientific theories. The primary effect of such an engagement on evolution is to ascribe teleology to the process, which although anathema to atheism, answers the chief philosophical concern of theists that an unguided fully random algorithmic process is without purpose, leading to the conclusion that its most intellectually advanced product, the human race, is equally without purpose. Instead of denying the rational investigation of natural law, theistic evolution credits natural law to God, recognizes, with scriptural justification, a role for God in guiding events that appear to be otherwise random, and thereby restores teleology to the creative process and the possibility of a purposeful existence to mankind as a species and as individuals. Purposefulness is the only trait that differentiates atheistic evolution from theistic evolution, and it is a trait that, once again, cannot be scientifically tested and therefore remains an article of faith.

Essential to the defense of Christianity is the realization that it is teleology that is assaulted by atheism. It is the sense of purpose in creation, not the method of creation, which must be defended by Christians who find meaning and purpose in their belief. In other words, it is atheism rather than science that must be identified as the opposing viewpoint to Christianity, and countered by arguments that incorporate rather than deny rational observations and conclusions regarding the process and status of the

---

[1] Teilhard de Chardin, Pierre. "Note on the Modes of Divine Action in the Universe." *Christianity and Evolution.* Rene Hague, trans. New York: Harcourt, 1971. Pg 28.

created universe.

The relationship between Christianity, creationism, atheism, and agnosticism can be modeled as a complex competition between these concepts for the minds of men. Such a competitive situation is akin to the theory of memes, for those who are willing to extend evolutionary theory to that extent; the somewhat controversial theory of memes treats theories, beliefs, traditions, and behaviors similarly to genes by considering their survival and those of their hosts to be subject to selection pressures. The number of minds available to creationism – its market as a competitive idea, or its habitat as a meme, if you will – is both small, being limited to those minds that have been neither been correctly educated in the physical sciences (including those that have been misled by those espousing creationism and intelligent design) nor have fruitfully sought resolution of religious beliefs with the material world, and decreasing, by the inevitable progress of scientific understanding and education. Furthermore, the sheer power of the theories of cosmic, geologic, and biological evolution in understanding the world around us and predicting the behavior of inanimate and animate matter has made them indispensable in a variety of scientific fields, and anyone seeking gainful employment in those fields must come to grips with their reality; this adds both intellectual and financial pressure to the rejection of creationism. Those who believe in creationism are a subset not only of those who believe in Christianity, but of other religions as well (both Islam and Hinduism have significant creationist segments, for example) and, to the extent that they erroneously equate creationism with Christianity and count it among the reasons for rejecting a belief in God, atheists as well. Theistic evolution disarms atheists and reduces their arguments to personal beliefs, neither more nor less subject to objective validation than the belief in God. By abandoning creationist rhetoric and either tacitly accepting or, even better, actively proclaiming theistic evolution, Christians and Christian institutions can eliminate a powerful argument of atheism in the competition for the minds of agnostics, increase the power of evangelism, and more effectively maintain the beliefs and devotion of existing Christians. Theistic evolution threatens the survival of the atheistic meme, and does so not by abandoning the Christians' belief in God's role as the Creator, but merely by adapting one's opinion of His means of creation to the observations and theories of modern science.

The progress of scientific understanding is both inexorable and inevitable. It is powered by the intellect of the human mind and motivated by its thirst for knowledge, which are themselves both as much the creation of God as the world which science investigates. There is ample evidence, in scripture, Christian creeds, tradition, and the attitudes and motives of Christian scientists of the past and the present, that scientific investigation can and should be rightly considered a form of worship and an exploration of the revelation of God in His work. Pierre Teilhard de Chardin wrote in his 1934 essay "How I Believe":

> If we Christians wish to retain in Christ the very qualities on which his power and our worship are based, we have no better way – no other way, even – of doing so than fully to accept the most modern concepts of evolution. Under the combined pressures of science and philosophy, we are being forced, experientially and intellectually, to accept the world as a coordinated system of activity which is gradually rising up towards freedom and consciousness. [1]

It is largely up to Christians whether the progress of science is seen as a triumph over faith or a triumph of faith. There is no plausible reason that pastors, authors, and institutions of the greater church cannot lead their faithful in embracing the findings of science. By doing so, they can lead, too, in rejoicing at a higher level of understanding of the revelation of the nature and laws of God that is embodied in scientific research and theorization, in praising God both for His revelation and for the human intellect and curiosity to seek and achieve the understanding of it, and in expressing the profound sense of awe at the wisdom, foresight, and patience of God that each new finding should produce in the faithful. The works of God that are still being discovered and understood by science after thousands of years of diligent effort reveal a deity that is infinitely greater than one that can work only within the bounds of creationism. George V. Coyne, the Director of the Vatican Observatory, is fond of quoting the words of John Henry Newman, a Cardinal of the Roman Catholic Church from Great Britain, uttered in 1868 when the furor over Darwin's theory of evolution was fresh: "The theory of Darwin, true or not, is not necessarily atheistic; on the contrary, it may simply be suggesting a larger idea of Divine Providence and Skill."[2] In a 2006 lecture at Palm Beach Atlantic University, Father Coyne went on to say:

> How are we to interpret the scientific picture of life's origins in terms of religious belief? Do we need God to explain this? Very succinctly my answer is no. In fact, to need God would be a very denial of God. God is not the response to a need. One gets the impression from certain religious believers that they fondly hope for the durability of certain gaps in our scientific knowledge of evolution, so that they can fill them with God. This is the exact opposite of what human intelligence is all about. We should be seeking for the fullness of God in creation. We should not need God; we should accept her/him when he comes to us. . . . Judaic-Christian faith is radically creationist, but in a totally different sense. It is rooted in a belief that everything depends upon God, or better, all is a gift from God. . . The universe as we know it today through science is one way to derive analogical

[1] Teilhard de Chardin, Pierre. "How I Believe." *Christianity and Evolution.* Rene Hague, trans. New York: Harcourt, 1971. Pg 127.

[2] Coyne, George V. "Science Does Not Need God. Or Does It? A Catholic Scientist Looks at Evolution." 1 Feb 2006. *Catholic Online.* Accessed 20 Mar 2009 at <http://www.catholic.org/national/national_story.php?id=18540>.

> knowledge of God. For those who believe modern science does say something to us about God, it provides a challenge, an enriching challenge, to traditional beliefs about God.[1]

Science is inherently skeptical in requiring substantial proof of falsification to discard working theories, but concurrently innately flexible in accepting verifiable new knowledge, regardless of whether it confirms, modifies, expands, or upsets existing theories. Christianity would serve itself well in the modern world by uniformly exhibiting a similar balance, for no other policy can restore and preserve the witness of the created material world to its believers or prospective proselytes.

By reestablishing as a permanent policy the embrace of scientific knowledge and its incorporation in the faith as a means of knowing and understanding the God we worship, Christianity can assure that future progress in science is not a threat to theology or a hindrance to faith. By viewing biological evolution as a tool of God in the process of creation rather than as evidence of atheism, new discoveries in paleontology need no longer be considered a threat to the desperate desire for gaps in the fossil record for God to fill with miracles, to be discredited with equally desperate contortions of fact and rationale, but can be welcomed as further confirmation of the marvelous capacity for change and adaptation of biological systems. Advancements in the understanding of cellular biology can be greeted as evidence of the complexity and richness of God's planning and design instead of being falsely obfuscated out of fear that they constitute evidence for a mechanism of evolution that by conforming to natural laws excludes the workings of God. The Christian religion becomes completely and permanently defensible and beyond falsification by science if it incorporates, with awe and thanksgiving, all that scientific inquiry discovers.

Among the most enthusiastic string theorists are some who predict that the theory of which they are enamored holds the key to understanding the nature of space and time, including even such basic questions as why there are three spatial dimensions and a unidirectional dimension of time. Under relativity, the shape of space-time is determined by the mass of objects and their gravitational effect; in the language of particle physics, the shape of the space-time continuum is established by swarms of the elusive graviton particle. Similarly, the passage of time is inextricably linked to the speed of light; time is shaped by the motion of photons with their inherent constant velocity. Under string theory, both gravitons and photons are strings vibrating in different patterns. Strings without vibrations are, therefore, transcendent of space and time, eerily reminiscent of the nature of God taught by Christian theology; a time

[1] Coyne, George V. "Science Does Not Need God. Or Does It? A Catholic Scientist Looks at Evolution." 1 Feb 2006. *Catholic Online.* Accessed 20 Mar 2009 at <http://www.catholic.org/national/national_story.php?id=18540>.

before strings began to vibrate does not exist, because words like "time" and "before" are meaningless without the vibration of strings that define them as the elementary particles of energy like photons and gravitons and those of matter like electrons and quarks. If string theory is eventually supported by experimental and observational evidence, and such a beginning state of the universe is accepted, a Christian who embraces the exploration of science as the welcome exploration of a revelation of the nature of God is neither alarmed nor disconcerted; he or she merely adapts a new and deeper meaning to the description of "formless and void" in the opening lines of Genesis, and steps closer to understanding God's own transcendence of time and space. The Christian who accepts the findings in science could then, in fact, assert that in knowing the One who provided for the vibration of strings he knows the Composer, Arranger, and Director of the music of the spheres.

A unified gospel

The visionary Pierre Teilhard de Chardin saw in the history of creation the process of "complexification" (his word) of form and thought: atoms joined together to become molecules, molecules became macromolecules, macromolecules became cells, unicellular organisms became multicellular organisms, multicellular organisms became vertebrates, vertebrates progressed to mammals, mammals to primates, primates to mankind, all planned by God to follow His laws towards His goal of reflective thought. Teilhard de Chardin went on to prophesy that mankind, as the inhabitant of the realm of contemplative thought that he termed the noosphere (from the Greek, the prefix no- referring to thought, as in knowledge and gnosticism), would continue in the process of unification by unifying knowledge and thought, that each individual would reach his or her greatest sense of identity and worth within the unity of the noosphere, and that the knowledge of themselves and others would produce and enhance a universal understanding and love, in the sense of a respect for the rights and dignity of each other and a resulting concern for the universal welfare of mankind, that would eventually unite humanity with God at an end that he referred to as the Omega Point.

The truth of Teilhard de Chardin's prophecies, after the nature of prophecies, remains to be seen, but he went farther than perhaps any other Christian philosopher in reconciling the two realms of science and theology in which he was unusually and exceptionally conversant. Without necessarily accepting his predictions as authentic (and he did not, in any published writing, claim them to be inspired in the manner of biblical prophets), we can consider the value of unifying Christian beliefs with the data and conclusions of scientific inquiry.

The testimony to the nature of God contained in His creation is referred to in some creeds as the first revelation, because it was revealed chronologically before the second revelation of holy writ. The abandonment and denial of the truths that are to be gained by the study of the first revelation is a wrong course that demands to be reversed. The God revealed by the deepest contemplation of modern scientific exploration is enormously larger, more complex, and more possessed of the omniscience that is attributed to God in Judeo-Christian theology than the God that is bounded by the understanding of creationists. Attempts at evangelism of the God of creationists are predictably unsuccessful when addressed to those who see in science a greater realism, intellect, intricacy, and rationality than those attributed by creationists to God Himself.

The position of creationists that God created the world as we know it is not only illogical from the standpoint of our observations of a changing earth and cosmos, but theologically irresponsible in that it is essentially a Deist argument. This viewpoint necessarily concludes, in the absence of any stasis of the forces that produce change in the heavens and on earth, that God created everything in a single burst of miraculous creative energy, which has now ceased and been replaced by a process of gradual change of His creation by the various means documented by science to account for the vicissitude that is observed in the current day. Inherent in this position, too, are the difficulties of accounting for the day of rest ascribed to God in the first Genesis account of creation and the problem that God allowed change to a perfect creation.

The reality that God works through natural processes, on the other hand, is not foreign to even the most conservative branches of Christianity. Almost all Christians view each human as a unique creation of God, yet none deny the role of meiosis, fertilization, mitosis, and tissue differentiation in that creative process, and none deny that growth and maturation continue after birth. There is no defensible reason for creationists to deny His capacity to use other natural processes in other acts of creation. From such a viewpoint, God is still the Creator when He employs natural processes, because He is the Creator, too, of those processes of nature, as well as the determinant agent of the innumerable interactions in nature that give the appearance of randomness.

Neither should a changing insight into the nature of God be troubling to Christianity, because even though Christian theology teaches that God is unchanging, mankind's perception of God has undergone demonstrable changes in ways that are visible in scripture. God first appeared to man as a corporeal being that walked and talked with the *'adam* at the beginning of time, later ministered to humans through the appearance of angels, still later addressed His people through human prophets, and in the current age is present in the world as the Holy Spirit, speaking and working through the thoughts and inspiration of ordinary humans. Mankind's understanding of the afterlife underwent similar evolution in scripture. Some scholars believe that an afterlife was not a part of early Jewish belief due to the conspicuous absence of comments about it in places in the commentary that would appear obvious, and the knowledge that the Sadducee sect of Judaism did not believe in resurrection as late as the time of Christ. The bulk of the Old Testament makes reference to the concept of *Sheol*, an abode for the souls of men that entailed neither punishment nor reward. By the last century or two before Christ the *Sheol* of Judaic tradition had become a place of torment for the evil and comfort for the good that could be immediately transformed to the Christian concepts of hell and heaven. Early portions of scripture refer to gods in the plural, and to *YHWH* as chief among them, while later portions assert that He is the only God. Did the nature of God change from physical to spiritual, or was His treatment of the departed souls of men at some point altered, or did His fellow gods die off? Traditional Judeo-Christian theology would answer no, that God is eternally unchanging but that the human perception of God has been subject to development and learning. It would then seem to be a logical conclusion that, since additional contributions to the Word of God have not been forthcoming in nearly two millennia, further gains in the human understanding of God must needs come from the further exploration of His work.

Scientific inquiry is the means of understanding the first revelation of God and must be embraced by all of Christianity as it once was, in principle if not always perfectly in practice, by the fathers of both Catholicism and Protestantism. It may be that each new layer of understanding inevitably uncovers yet another layer of ever more intriguing questions; if so, we should not be surprised, because that would mean only that the quest for understanding of the material world is just as infinite as its Creator, that the comprehension by the finite human intellect of the infinite mind of God is impossible.

Regardless of the ultimate fruit and fruitfulness of scientific inquiry, it is essential to the unity of the two revelations that scripture be continuously interpreted and reinterpreted in light of scientific knowledge. Truth cannot contradict truth, and the truths of the two revelations must be reconciled for the revelation of faith, the scripture, to maintain in the minds of both believers and prospective converts credibility equal to that of the revelation of substance, creation, the latter being validated by the physical senses and reason.

That sort of scriptural interpretation entails a degree of inclusiveness that is both consistent with Christian humility, being diametrically opposed to the pomposity by which some claim an exclusive clarity in the interpretation of holy writ, and strategically wise in proselytization. Saint Augustine could have claimed, with as much justification as any man, complete certitude in his deeply thoughtful and thorough consideration of scriptural truth, yet he humbly said of his own exegeses:

> Whatever appeared to me as certain, I maintained and defended; whatever uncertain, I investigated according to my ability, sometimes venturing opinions, at other times expressing doubts. Still it was not my purpose to determine the judgment each one should form in regard to obscure questions,

> but rather to show the need we have of instruction in doubtful matters and to caution the reader against rash statements where we have been unable to arrive at certain knowledge.[1]

The rational interpretation of scripture with appeal and credibility to the mind of modern man would also be facilitated by a universal acceptance by Christians of some version of the Documentary Hypothesis. By acknowledging that portions of the Bible are redactions of multiple traditions and authors, the unsupportable claims to scientific and historical inerrancy can be gracefully abandoned. Contradictions between different passages of scripture and between scripture and other historical documents, being easily understood as arising from sources with different viewpoints, historical backgrounds, and cultural traditions, are relegated to being pointless details instead of giving cause for the rejection of scripture in its entirety or of necessitating contorted justifications that themselves compromise the credibility of the perorator. The Bible is thereby in many respects more easily understood, and the focus is shifted to its essential character as a document of spiritual and theological significance as its lack of historicity and its antiquated scientific ideas are fairly dismissed.

The inspired nature of scripture need not be compromised by the acceptance of redacted multiple authorship of the Pentateuch. Accepting, against considerable evidence, that the Pentateuch was authored entirely by Moses, the Protestant Bible has a minimum of thirty-two authors, more reasonably forty, and probably many more.[2]

---

[1] St. Augustine. *The Literal Meaning of Genesis.* Translated and annotated by John Hammond Taylor. New York: Newman, 1982. Vol 2 of 2, pg 178 (12.1.1).

[2] The former number makes several assumptions, besides the sole authorship of the Pentateuch by Moses, that are difficult or impossible to support: that King David composed each of the Psalms; that Solomon penned all of the Proverbs, the book of Ecclesiastes, and the Song of Solomon; that the book of Isaiah was written entirely by its namesake; that the prophet Jeremiah wrote Lamentations as well as the book bearing his name; that the book of Daniel was authored by a single person; that the Epistle to the Hebrews was written by Paul, as is presumed in some traditions even though it lacks his characteristic clear statement of authorship and differs substantially in style and substance from his other letters; that the Revelation was penned by John the Apostle rather than a namesake. Other assertions are more plausible: that the books of Joshua, Judges, the two books of Samuel, and the two books of King share a single author; that the two books of Chronicles share a single author; that the Gospel of Luke and the Acts of the Apostles were once a continuous document. The latter number is arrived at by assuming separate authorship of Proverbs, Ecclesiastes, and the Song of Solomon; likewise of Jeremiah and Lamentations; that the anonymous author of Hebrews did not author another New Testament work; that the epistles attributed to Peter and John, as seems likely, were authored by different ones among their followers, and that Revelation was authored by a different John than the Gospel. Since the collected Psalms and Proverbs each likely had many contributors, the book of Isaiah is believed to have been compiled by a school of prophecy founded by Isaiah over a period of several centuries, and the book of Daniel is believed to be a similar compilation, an upper limit is impossible to determine. The authors of the books of the Apocrypha, long considered a part of scripture, are not considered for this purpose.

Acceptance of the classic Documentary Hypothesis of the origins of the Pentateuch increases the number of authors inspired by God to contribute to canonical scripture by just four (from Moses alone to the Elohist, Jehovist, Priestly, and Deuteronistic sources, and the Redactor). There is no apparent reason that these few additional authors could not be considered to be as inspired as the other thirty-two, forty, or multitude of writers who contributed to canonical literature. The act of compiling literature took place in the assembly of the canon without controversy, even though books such as Kings and Chronicles clearly relate the same events twice from two different perspectives and occasionally contradict each other in details. The book of the Psalms is a compilation of hymns by various composers, perhaps including but certainly not limited to King David, and it is just as likely that the Proverbs were the collected sayings of sages and folklore rather than the produce of a single pen. Allowing that similar compilations from different highly valued sources occurred in the composition of Genesis and the other books of the Pentateuch should not be problematic. In the case of the four or more source contributors to the Pentateuch, the fact that their words and the underlying oral traditions were preserved and redacted is clear evidence that the lessons available from them regarding the nature of God and His relationship to mankind were valued, and the belief that they were the subject of compilation and redaction in no way dishonors them, devalues them as spiritual and theological truths, or casts doubt on their inspiration.

The very fact that Christians recognize within our scripture so many different viewpoints as being divinely inspired and therefore worthy of preservation and contemplation implies that diversity of thought is a value to be esteemed by Christianity, a value that needs to be renewed in many evangelical churches of the present day. The call of Christ is not a call to meaningless conformity, whether in worship styles or in non-core beliefs. The Jews were non-conformists from their earliest moments, rejecting the polytheism of surrounding cultures in favor of monotheism; indeed, the temptation of conformity to polytheism was a cause of many of the travails recorded by the Jews in their scripture. Judaism revered its prophets, human beings who were at best eccentric and at times displayed behaviors that would be considered psychotic in modern terms. John the Baptist, the New Testament forerunner of Jesus and, according to Luke, His cousin, carried on a campaign of repentance and baptism while living a nomadic life, dressing himself in camel hair garments and living on a decidedly non-kosher diet of locusts and honey. Jesus largely sought to overturn the established order of Judaism, challenging traditional teachings and authority. Any denomination, congregation, clergyman, or believer who expects to win and retain converts to the faith must take care to interpret scriptures in inclusive and tolerant ways in order to incorporate the non-essential views of parishioners and prospects; a demand for conformity of thought is antithetical to Christian scripture and tradition. In particular, interpreting scriptures in such a way that verifiable facts and rational conclusions drawn therefrom are excluded will not bear fruit among men and women knowledgeable and conversant in the realities of God's creation that have been made apparent by the work of science.

Clearly, a unity of truth by which God can be most fully known and Christ most effectively proclaimed requires the thoughtful, sincere, and candid consideration of all that God has revealed in both His word and His work. Clinging to comfortable but outdated notions of either science or scripture can be expected to hinder both efforts. When we approach either or both revelations with bias, we seek to conform God to our preconceptions rather than seeking true knowledge of Him. Each of the revelations of God has a complexity and elements of mystery that make their continued exploration challenging and rewarding. Discarding the evidence of science isolates churches and their adherents in ignorance of the creation of God, and adopting without consideration of other viewpoints a singularly narrow interpretation of scripture sequesters them from centuries of learned discourse in the study and exegesis of holy writ.

The New Testament makes frequent reference to the fact that human knowledge of God is and will remain incomplete; most often quoted is a passage from Paul's first letter to Corinth: "For now we see in a mirror, dimly, but then we will see face to face. Now I know in part; then I will know fully, even as I have been fully known."[1] It is worth recalling the context of that verse: Paul in the previous two chapters discussed the gifts of tongues, or ecstatic utterance, and that of mystical knowledge, both apparently highly valued by elements of the Corinthian church. Immediately following is perhaps Paul's most famous assertion, that faith, hope, and love, being in the character of God, are to be valued above all other gifts. The context is interesting in two respects. First, that creationism is, in the present day, even though not exclusive to charismatic churches per se, strongly associated with churches that tend towards highly demonstrative and emotive worship experiences. Secondly, there is a certain Gnostic component to creationism, in that adherents in essence claim to have a mystically revealed knowledge of the beginnings of living things and the means of their creation that contradicts the common and rational interpretation of material evidence. Paul's comparison of the limited value of such gifts juxtaposed against the more highly valued gifts of faith, hope, and love would seem to aptly address the relative importance of creationism or intelligent design as doctrine.

In the larger sense, Paul's words reflect the impossibility of a complete knowledge of an infinite God by the finite mind of an earthly man, restrained as mankind is by his material existence and the inherent limits to knowledge thus bestowed. Just as the insights of science into the nature of God is incomplete, so the Bible is an incomplete

---

[1] 1st Corinthians 13.12, New Revised Standard Version.

revelation of God; containing as it does a finite number of words, it cannot adequately express the boundless and incomprehensible knowledge, power, glory, or goodness of the God that it seeks to reveal. Since our scriptures make it clear that our knowledge of God is incomplete, it need not be a hidden secret in worship or teaching; rather, Christianity can confidently proclaim that our God is beyond comprehension, and that the efforts of science to understand His creation, as fruitful and deeply appreciated as they may be, can only reveal a portion of what we will know when, in the unity with God with which we expect to be rewarded, we will enjoy the bliss of complete understanding. It can, and should be, preached that learning of the work of God is not a barrier to knowledge of Him, but a window through which to glimpse His greatness, which itself encompasses the wisdom and foresight to act through the laws and mechanisms of nature that mankind has only begun to understand, to shape a world and a universe of unspeakable beauty, and, in man, a spirit that could seek and find communion with Him. To claim a full knowledge of God while entrapped in an earthly body is arrogant and, in consideration of this and similar scriptures, heretical; to reject the truths placed in His creation by His hand is to reject truth from God, and thereby to reject God Himself. As Augustine said, "The truth is rather in what God reveals than in what groping men surmise."[1]

Every major culture has sought to explain the origins and workings of the heavens, the earth, and living things. Most have done so through myths; only in the relatively recent past has mankind developed sufficient technology to make observations beyond those available to the naked eye and a sufficient accumulation of knowledge to formulate sound and verifiable theories about the natural world. At least two creation myths of the ancient Hebrew culture are recorded in Judeo-Christian scripture. The Hebrews of the period were demonstrably in error in such matters as cosmology and the inheritance of coat colors and patterns, but they developed the theological concepts of monotheism and omniscience that became the basis of Judaism, Christianity, and Islam. It would be equally foolish to hold the ancients to modern scientific standards or to expect knowledge of the material world to be arrested at the level represented in writings over three thousand years in age, but modern man can accept the progress of knowledge of the means of creation and still accept that the God of the Jews was the agent of creation.

The book of Ephesians, an encyclical written either by Paul, or, as is more commonly thought by modern analysts, pseudepigraphically by a close associate, ends with a much loved and oft quoted benediction:

---

[1] St. Augustine. *The Literal Meaning of Genesis.* Translated and annotated by John Hammond Taylor. New York: Newman, 1982. Vol 1 of 2, pg 178 (2.9.21).

> Now to him who by the power at work within us is able to accomplish abundantly far more than all we can ask or imagine, to him be glory in the church and in Christ Jesus to all generations, forever and ever. Amen.[1]

The Christian who accepts that blessing must accept with it the assertion that God is more than the mind of man can imagine. God is not limited by the mind of man, and the man who insists that God is limited to time periods and processes that are easy for the mind of man to comprehend contradicts scripture. That God is the creator is the realm of religion; the means and methods of creation are the domain of science. God is not diminished by the knowledge of mankind, but the knowledge of mankind can enhance and enlarge our perception of the eternally unchanging God.

The greatest miracle of God does not lie in His creation, but in His love for mankind, the creature of His creation, that causes Him to extend to every human soul the offer of forgiveness, achieved by the propitiating act of His own sacrifice.

The message that Christianity has for the world is not a message of exclusion, deceit, or backward thinking, but a message of grace born of God's love.

But that grace must be accepted in order to be realized. If God chooses to work invisibly, inside the laws and processes that we see as those of nature, it is within His sovereignty to do so. He chooses to do so because it is His desire that mankind choose to accept Him rather than to have Him forced upon the mind of man by the rationale of irrefutable proof; He chooses to remain a choice of faith. His existence is no more forced upon us than His forgiveness.

Each man and woman must choose his or her belief, and choose to accept or reject the grace of God. But regardless of choice, God is unchanging, and by all available evidence, the God of the ages chose to create all that is by a process governed by the properties of matter and energy that are themselves His own creation.

> There is grandeur in this view of life, with its several powers, having been originally breathed into a few forms or into one; and that, whilst this planet has gone cycling on according to the fixed law of gravity, from so simple a beginning endless forms most beautiful and most wonderful have been, and are being, evolved.[2]

Thus wrote Darwin to close *The Origin of Species.* Modern Christians would do well to join Darwin in seeing the grandeur of this, the truest known depiction of the development of life, and to attribute that grandeur to God with the awe and

---

[1] Ephesians 3.20-21. New Revised Standard Version.

[2] Darwin, Charles. *The Origin of Species.* New York: Random House, 1979. Originally published 1859 by J. Murray, London. Pg 459-460.

thanksgiving that it and He deserve.

Deo est veritae, et veritae est ex deo. Pro deo et veritae.

INDEX

ABOUT THE AUTHOR

Dr. P. David Moon is a graduate of the University of Florida,
receiving a bachelor's degree in 1977 and
a doctorate in veterinary medicine in 1982.
He currently lives and practices veterinary medicine
near Vero Beach, Florida.
Dr. Moon has been married since 1983
and has two daughters.
His hobbies include piano, kayaking,
photography, and bird watching.
He and his wife worship in the
United Methodist Church.

39298092R00200

Made in the USA
Charleston, SC
04 March 2015